Courage in a White Coat

A Wartime Biographical Novel based on the experience of
Dr. Dorothy Joy Kinney Chambers
and her family

by Mary Schwaner
with Bobbi Joy Chambers Hawk, M.D.

Taken from the childhood experience of
Robert Bruce Chambers
and his sister Carol Chambers Park
and the detailed written record of their mother
Dorothy Kinney Chambers, M.D.

PRAIRIE MUSE PLATINUM

www.prairiemuse.com

"A lovely story of an extraordinary woman! The use of contemporary sources adds authenticity to an ordeal that could be overwhelming in its grimness were it not described so vividly and poetically."
—*Dorey Schmidt, Ph.D.*

COURAGE IN A WHITE COAT

Copyright © 2018 by Mary Anne Potter Schwaner and Robert Bruce Chambers

First print edition

ISBN 9781719542654

Contact info@prairiemuse.com

Cover design by Prairie Muse utilizing selected photos from the archives of Dr. Dorothy Kinney Chambers.

www.prairiemuse.com

Dedication

In loving memory of
Dorothy Kinney Chambers, M.D.
and the women across the globe
who have been led and inspired by
her selfless work

*But strive first for the kingdom of God
and his righteousness, and all these
things will be given to you as well.*

MATTHEW 6:33 (NRSV)

DOROTHY JOY KINNEY
1924

DOROTHY WITH PATIENTS
SATRIBARI COMPOUND - HOSPITAL FOR WOMEN AND CHILDREN
GAUHATI, INDIA
1929

Foreword

We are all influenced by figures both real and literary, historical and contemporary. Many lives have crossed ours, even if only through written words, recorded speeches or letters. We each may have a memorable quote that guides us, be it from Teddy Roosevelt: *"Far better it is to dare mighty things, to win glorious triumphs even though checkered by failure, than to rank with those timid spirits who neither enjoy nor suffer much because they live in the gray twilight that knows neither victory nor defeat;"* Atticus Finch: [Courage is] *"when you know you're licked before you begin but you begin anyway and you see it through no matter what. You rarely win, but sometimes you do;"* or Kent M. Keith's quote made famous by Mother Teresa of Calcutta: *"The good you do today, people will often forget tomorrow; do good anyway."* What if we could get to know these people in the lives they were living that shaped who they became?

I knew my Grandma Chambers as a matriarch of the family. She insisted on wearing oxford shoes with a two-inch heel as it was better for her back. She wore girdles and garters to hold her stockings in place. She could sew anything—men's suits, Easter dresses for the girls, or hand-pieced double wedding ring quilts. She could cook a pretty mean Chinese yum-yum and made the best marmalade and zucchini relish stored in jars topped with paraffin. She could knit a sweater without a pattern—simply pick your yarn color and stand still while a tape measure makes its way around you. Your next birthday or Christmas your completed sweater would arrive and fit—because she would add extra inches when she knew you were still growing.

And, she could tell stories. She told stories of her working days in India about various cases that had made lasting impressions on her. She told stories of Baby Junaki. She told stories of the challenges faced when returning to the U.S. on furlough and the difficulty of being recognized as a woman and a practicing physician. She told stories of great accomplishments, of survival by wit, skill and thrift such as the sweater for Fred that was unraveled and re-knit to a dress for Carol and subsequently a sweater for Bobby. She had made three different garments sequentially out of the same skein of yarn.

Through these pages I am delighted to meet and journey with my grandmother, Dorothy Joy Kinney. I can venture with her around the world, just out of internship to blaze a trail for others to follow—other missionaries, other physicians, other women. I can ponder her frustrations with missionary needs abutting local culture, her delight in her vocation serving others and her wishes for a family of her own. I can worry for sick patients with her, waiting to hear the next installment for news of recovery or news of dying. I can share in her heartbreak of feeling and knowing that sometimes you can't do anything other than wait and let time pass. I can feel the drive of service to others. I can feel the immense power of the love of Christianity as it touches so many lives.

I hope you enjoy getting to know Dorothy. She was a truly remarkable woman with a passion for service to others whether as a physician, a missionary, a daughter, a prisoner of war, a wife, a mother, a member of the Peace Corps, or a mentor to young families of foreign graduate students in an American university. Even when wheelchair-bound her last years in a nursing home, she would announce herself and say, "I'm a doctor, can I help?"

—Bobbi Chambers Hawk, M.D.

Chronology

Dorothy Joy Kinney was born September 16, 1901, in New Mexico. Her father, Reverend Bruce Kinney, was an American Baptist minister.

She received her Bachelor of Science from Denison University in Iowa, and her medical degree from the University of Colorado Medical School in 1926, graduating second in her class.

In 1928, Dorothy traveled to Assam in northeast India as a medical missionary for the American Baptist Foreign Mission Society. She served almost nine years as director, physician, and surgeon at the Satribari Compound in Gauhati, India. With few resources, she learned to rely upon her own ability to devise innovative surgical interventions.

On June 30, 1936, Dorothy married Dr. Fred R. Chambers, who had previously been widowed during his educational missionary posting in Jorhat, Assam.

After enduring a six month separation following their wedding, Dorothy's replacement arrived in Gauhati, and Dorothy took up residence with her new husband in Jorhat. She provided medical services for Fred's students at the Jorhat Christian School for Boys.

Their daughter, Carol Joy, was born in November 1937. The Chambers family traveled on furlough to the U.S. in February 1938. After more than a year of furlough, they were posted to the Philippines and sailed from Vancouver, Canada on September 2, 1939. All their possessions which had been stored in India were sunk when the ship carrying them to the Philippines hit a British land mine in Singapore Bay.

Robert Bruce Chambers was born in February of 1940. At the time, Fred Chambers was Dean of Theology at Central Philippine University in Iloilo City and shortly thereafter became president.

Dorothy served as associate physician at the Iloilo Mission Hospital and as director of the Central Philippine College Dispensary.

When the Japanese invaded the island, Dorothy and Fred removed their family inland to Calinog, and Fred hid the university's important papers in a cave outside Iloilo.

There were thirty missionaries in the region, and nineteen of them fled into the hills to evade the Japanese. Not wishing to put the Filipinos in jeopardy by hiding them, Dorothy and Fred stayed in Calinog and were taken into custody shortly after Easter of 1942. For fourteen months they were interned in a make-shift prison at an Iloilo elementary school.

In June of 1943, the family and other prisoners were transferred to a larger internment camp in Manila, where they were held with 4,000 others on the grounds of Santo Tomás University. Dorothy and the children were housed in a six-foot by four-foot space and Fred was assigned to the balcony of the gym where cots were lined up six inches apart. Dorothy's space was in a room that was shared by seven mothers and twelve children, each group with their own six-foot area. Of the 4,000 internees, about 400 were children and one-third of the population was over the age of 65. Approximately 328 internees died while in camp. One-third of those deaths, mostly attributed to starvation, happened in the last four months of captivity.

Fred served on the camp committee and taught in the camp school. Dorothy was placed in charge of the children's hospital, a twenty-cot shack. The ward had a Japanese director and American doctors and nurses. Not a single child was lost while Dorothy was in charge.

On February 3, 1945, the camp got their first indication that liberation may be coming soon. That evening, General MacArthur's Flying Column broke through the Japanese lines.

On February 11, after even more deaths (including a number of internees) in the skirmish, the Japanese were vanquished and the military began to evacuate the remaining 3,785 internees.

It wasn't until April 19, 1945, that Dorothy, Carol and Bobby left the Philippine Islands for repatriation to the United States. Fred stayed behind to do what he could to reinstate the college, and was reunited with his family in August. They resigned from missionary service the following year.

Fred provided post-collegiate placement services on several campuses before taking the pastorate of the American Baptist Church of Fort Collins, CO, in 1954. He became Professor of Missions at Central Baptist theological Seminary in 1958.

Dorothy continued to serve on the American Baptist Women's Foreign Mission Society Board, on the National Council of the American Baptist Women, and was a Vice President of the American Baptist Convention in the late 1960's, also serving as program chair for the National Council of American Baptist Women.

Fred provided post-collegiate placement services on several campuses before taking the pastorate of the American Baptist Church of Fort Collins, CO, in 1954. He became Professor of Missions at Central Baptist theological Seminary in 1958. Fred died in 1985.

Dorothy continued to exercise her sense of service. She helped a Fort Collins church establish Elderhaus, the first daycare for the elderly in the state of Colorado. Throughout her years following repatriation Dorothy gave untold hours of service and support to foreign students who found their way to Colorado. In 1982 she was honored as Church Women United's VALIANT WOMAN.

Dorothy died on the third of December, 2001, at the age of 100.

Acknowledgements

It's the most humbling thing to immerse oneself in the life of so accomplished a woman with any hope of doing her justice. So I must thank Dorothy Kinney Chambers' son Bob and her granddaughter Bobbi Chambers Hawk, M.D. for walking that tricky line between telling Dorothy's emotional journey and dramatically fictionalizing her story. Dorothy's own accounts sent weekly from India to her family were a vast and nearly overwhelming resource. Those voluminous pages kept me walking the straight and narrow course as I sought to reveal her remarkable work.

Those who dared to tread the many paths of Dorothy's experience with me and helped preserve the integrity and love that spills from these pages have forever earned my gratitude. Mame Chambers was a charming lamp illuminating many of Dorothy's personal traits. Linda Hoegemeyer managed insightful edits in the kindest way possible, and my brilliant Latin teacher, Joan Yentes, nudged me back on course more times than I can count. To my great delight, Marty Magee managed to research questions that might have otherwise gone unanswered. These women will never truly know what it meant that I could place my complete trust in their suggestions and yes, their cautionary words.

Not one of my stellar street team let me down, always providing me with the most necessary notes to complete this work. Vicki Woodburn, Susan Macy, Lovell Moser, Roberta Kroeger, Shirley Tachenko-Accord, Brenda Kranz, Steph Wirth, Pastor Wayne Alloway, and Sharre Jahde suggested edits that could only make this book better. And in the final hours before publication, Dr. Dorey Schmidt was a truly unexpected gift.

And last, I could not hope to have accomplished this task without the help of my husband Bill, whose encouragement and willingness to keep our household running gave me great peace.

—Mary Schwaner

INDIA

Calcutta

ASSAM

Jorhat

Gauhati

Shillong

BAY OF BENGAL

SOUTH
CHINA
SEA

LUZON

★Baguio

Cabanatuan★

PACIFIC OCEAN

Bataan Peninsula
Manila

MINDORO

PANAY

Calinog
Iloilo

SAMAR

LEYTE

NEGROS

CEBU

PALAWAN

THE
PHILIPPINE
ISLANDS

MINDANAO

INDIAN
OCEAN

DOROTHY WITH HER PATIENTS AND NURSES
FIRST CHRISTMAS IN ASSAM
1928

PART ONE
WINGS

Gꜱᴀᴜʜᴀᴛɪ, Iɴᴅɪᴀ — Aᴜɢᴜꜱᴛ 1935
Sɪx ʏᴇᴀʀꜱ ɪɴᴛᴏ Dᴏʀᴏᴛʜʏ'ꜱ ᴀꜱꜱɪɢɴᴍᴇɴᴛ

CHAPTER ONE

ON THE BREATH OF A SONG

Six years, five months and four days into her dream, Dr. Dorothy Kinney tumbled to the realization that she wore it quite easily now, that mantle of womanhood that had slipped and slid across her shoulders in fits and starts through medical school. But tonight, the realization hit her squarely between the eyes. It fit her almost as elegantly now as did the white coat of her trade, the crisp linen jacket that defined her mission as healer to these people. Her people now. The women and children of Gauhati, India.

Tonight the hospital seemed to be holding its breath in this dark hour. Its new walls and windows buffered the sounds of the nighttime jungle, creating a haven of sorts. Quiet. Waiting.

At the fringes of her mind, Dorothy became aware that someone had opened an outer door, letting a gentle breeze trace its fingers across the doomed child who lay before her. It seemed a welcome embrace.

She'd seen hundreds of children in her six years here. Trembling little boys and girls and hysterical toddlers, most of whom left her care with smiles and hugs before bounding back into the arms of their families.

Not so this dear child. Not even in the world's finest facility would this child survive.

And certainly not here in Gauhati.

The hospital Dorothy transformed in those six years boasted running water these days. And electricity. These were luxuries she remembered doing without when she arrived in 1928, fresh from the University of Colorado School of Medicine. She never touched the tap without thinking of it, of the early days when her inventive genius was birthed of necessity.

In those first chaotic months, gleaming new sterilizers sat covered and unused, waiting for her to marshal the locals into an effective workforce, to lay pipes, to plumb the surgery, to string wiring along thin, newly plastered walls. Waiting for her to show by example what progress could mean to their rustic community. How many more lives could be saved. And then waiting yet again until some provincial male authority examined every aspect of the carefully designed blueprints and pronounced that yes, this plan would work. Never your plan. Never her plan. That would have rankled their brains too greatly to identify the plan as one drawn up by a mere woman.

But it had always—in large part—been *her* plan, unfolding in its own time, adding new grains of patience to her oft-challenged core. And she could not help but believe that it has changed the face of survival in Gauhati.

On this January day, dusk has come and gone and night has overtaken the hospital grounds. Dorothy continued to maintain her long vigil at the child's bedside, the thick, damp night hovering beyond the ward windows like a lost soul come to take the child away, the child she has tended for the last ten hours. The delicate eight-year-old girl struggles less now, as she slips from this life to the next.

Dorothy leaned closer, careful not to touch the shredding, blistered skin of the child engulfed in flames just hours earlier. It was an accident. A horrid, tragic accident. When would her people begin to recognize that feeding their cooking fires with kerosene put their entire village at risk?

The stricken villagers had borne horrified witness to the little girl's stuttering progress as she stumbled into the hospital on spindly, singed legs, her family swirling around her, wailing, desperate to help, knowing they dared not touch her lest she shriek in agony once again.

The Satribari nurses experienced the same horror, by nature needing to sweep her into their arms and take away her pain. But they dared not. Their cries had drawn Dorothy to the central hallway, and in a flash she discerned the child's desperate condition and darted back into her office. The beautiful sari she kept there wafted its delicate wings around her as she dashed with it back to the corridor.

Take the other end, she had called to Lahaori, her steady right hand. *Come behind her with me!*

In one delicately maneuvered scoop they swept the child into the soft hammock they'd created. The little girl keened, jarred into new heights of pain. From every mouth came an answering keen.

We did not mean to hurt you, little one! Be brave, little one!

Quite without realizing it Dorothy began to rock the makeshift hammock as she called out instructions to her staff. It was the most natural movement a mother might make to comfort her child.

Make the softest bed you can, Dorothy cried to the student nurses, and together they created an improvised cradle of feather down pillows.

Through the next sobering hours the young nurses stood at their stations on either side of the child's bed, spraying a fine intermittent mist laced with honey into the air above the unconscious child's body. The droplets fell in slow motion, keeping the beautiful fabric of the sari cool and damp.

The breaths were fading now, fragile puffs escaping the child's lips in between long stretches of silence, little whiffs of air still carrying the kerosene fumes up from lungs the lethal gas has viciously decimated.

> *When peace like a river attendeth my way...*
> *When sorrows like sea billows roll...*
> *Whatever my lot thou has taught me to say*
> *It is well, it is well with my soul.*

The song was a mere whisper, spilling from Dorothy's lips that hovered just inches from the child's ear, more prayer than melody.

The bamboo fan whickered softly in the corner.

Go now, little one.

And there it was. The chest stilled, the face quieted. Dorothy waited until the silent prayer roiling within her own heart found its tortured resolution.

She looked up, unable to dispel the grief from her eyes.

Outside the wailing resumed.

CHAPTER TWO

THE STICKING POST

Wispy shreds of a pre-dawn fog still floated beyond her window, like remnants of the shroud that had engulfed her through the sleepless night. Anguish over the loss of the child plagued her still at sunup, yet as always, it had begun to quiet itself, allowing the first glimmer of calm to nudge its way into Dorothy's awareness.

There was nothing more that could have been done for the child. She knew it, even if she could not yet reconcile it. Alice said so as well, the aging Doctoroni who shared the surgical duties of the burgeoning hospital. Still, the agony of it lived in Dorothy's bones this morning, and weariness remained, visible in her plodding steps as she retraced her path from the hall table of her little bungalow back to her private bedroom.

She has a letter from home.

Her finger traced the swoopy, loopy lines of the address, following its free and unbounded scrawl across the entire face of the envelope, which was liberally pitted and poked by something held inside. Something more than a letter.

Oh, Wink, you darling girl.

With typical care she sliced the edge of the envelope, almost giving in to the glee that bubbled up as she chased a host of hair pins that cascaded wildly from the folds of her sister's letter.

Hair pins.

More than a dozen of them.

She caught them up before they fell from her lap and corralled them in a small carved bowl that sat on the dressing table. Who but Wink would even realize what an unexpected bit of joy this would pitch into her day.

Dorothy is the eldest of the four Kinney girls from Colorado. Wink is the baby, the one with the buoyant spirit, who lives every moment on the edge of a whim. In truth, Dorothy suspected that she herself might carry a few of those same whimsical genes. It constantly pestered her with the impulse to dive into the thing that has captured her attention and let the world pass her by as she explores it. But her hard-earned, self-imposed discipline cannot allow it. And so—unlike her baby sister—Dorothy's free spirit exists under careful internal supervision.

Not so Wink, although she is bright as a button. But the young lady has had long experience at indulging the whim. Pretty Wink gets to be the smart dresser of the four girls, now that Dorothy is out of sight halfway around the world in India. But side by side, one would be hard pressed to guess which of them had just stepped most recently from the jungle, and which one had danced demurely from the pages of the latest Vogue.

Pin curls!

Dorothy chortled. There were pincurls in her future again, thanks to Wink who knew that Dorothy was always losing her hairpins and had no corner drugstore where she might replenish her supply. So Wink took it upon herself to regularly send a few, and they were always welcome. The simple pleasure rendered her ridiculously breathless.

She had been shipboard on the Edavana in the South China Sea in the Fall of 1928 the first time the universe conspired to relieve her of her hairpins. A major squall kept the seas rough for hours, and while other passengers kept to the shelter of their cabins, Dorothy stood at the prow, her face alternately stung by salty waves and pelting rain as she strained toward the future on which she had just embarked. She leaned forward into the buffeting wind, rooting herself at the farthest point from home, and the nearest point to her destiny.

In a matter of moments, the elements had ripped off her scarf, undone her hair, and sent her carefully placed hairpins into the void.

It blew my hair in forty-leven different directions, lost three-fourths of my hairpins for me and more than once put my skirts up over my head. ...Then after breakfast I put on my oldest shoes, my bathing cap, and my raincoat, and stood at the end of the deck with the Van Putten's and my, how it did rain.

Oh, how she did love a good storm.

And later, when she sought a bit of privacy on deck, the storm had continued to oblige, wrapping her in a cloak of gusting rain and clashing waves, pelting just hard enough to keep the passengers—and a certain condescending ship's doctor—sequestered below.

Why was it that she was constantly confronted with men who could not quite grasp the idea that she was a physician?

Miss Kinney, indeed. That's Doctor Kinney to you, sir.

To make things even messier, there had been another doctor on board. A tea garden doctor who quite openly declared his infatuation for her. Between the two of them trying to impress her with their medical acumen and her employing every bit of subterfuge she could think of to avoid them, Dorothy had found herself quite entertained.

~~~~~~

> ...then there is a little Scots Doctor—one of the tea garden doctors
> from near Jorhat. He looks and acts like Charlie Chaplin and has
> been a regular clown. I think I could have had a proposal last night
> had I been willing to stay out in the moonlight with him but . . . . I am
> afraid that my time for matrimony has not arrived yet.

She was happy to isolate herself from them rather than to try and erect some aloof barrier against their wheedling charms.

Dorothy fiddled with one of the hairpins until her hair took on a more polished look. She hadn't thought of those early days for some time. Of her innocence and midwestern sophistication.

What had she known then of barriers?

There she had been, on a voyage halfway around the world, embarking on a mission for which she knew she'd been born. Afraid to admit she was afraid.

Screw your courage to the sticking post had become her daily litany.

Truth be told, she'd worked that one to the limit, taken by surprise as she was by the pettifoggery and crises she'd been faced with daily in Assam, and the primitive, makeshift hospital facility that awaited her in Gauhati.

She'd been told it was primitive, that she'd have to make do until things could be modernized. So in her mind she'd pictured a light bulb on a string, or perhaps old lath and plaster walls. But when she arrived she found she needed to seriously revise her definition of primitive.

The hospital actually had no walls. Just a mere roof with open air sides, except for the surgical suite, where operations were performed by the light of a simple Coleman lantern. The beds were little more than pallets, with minimal screening to keep insects at bay. There was no running water, no electricity, no indoor plumbing of any kind and no septic tank. Yet never did she perceive any of these things as barriers. Not one of those deficiencies could put a chink in Dorothy's positivity.

> We arrived in Gauhati on November third [1928] and received a warm welcome. I am much in love with the place (not having spent a hot season here) and also with the people. The hospital is very workable—or will be when we get the present plans for running water, septic tanks, and electricity carried out.
>
> I really think that we will have all of these things, and then some, before the rains set in this year. We have just had a property committee here and they have approved the suggestions, and we have the money in the field to carry out these plans.

How naive she'd been thinking all that could be accomplished in a matter of months instead of the three years it had actually taken.

. . . .

Breeching the cultural walls of rural India had proven to be as much of a challenge as carrying on her work in a building undergoing constant change. Cultural taboos, caste boundaries, traditions stringently observed by Hindu, Buddhist and pagan, and a complicated language to learn—those were the things that challenged her to this very day.

> My language study is coming along pretty well in spite of interruptions, and I do like Rodnadhar as a teacher very, very much. He is a very nice looking young man of about thirty, speaks

beautiful Assamese and very good English. He is much interested in Christianity, and I think really has Christ for his ideal, but has never openly decided to follow him. He would be such a wonderful power for good if he would come out four square, but it would mean a lot of persecution.

I tell you, we at home do not even know the meaning of the word. A boy who has been working on the compound went to Miss Holmes the other day and said that he wanted to become a Christian. His relatives all came and one after the other pled with him and then threatened him, but he was adamant.

Finally, his father came and said, "Have either your mother or I been unkind to you? Haven't we always given you plenty to eat, a place to sleep, and clothes to wear?" etc., and finally said, "Will you come home?" and again the boy said, "No."

The father said "A second time I ask you, will you come home?" and again the boy said, "No." The father was furious and said, "Think well before you answer the third time. Will you come home?" Again the boy said, "No."

The father tried to drag him away by force, but Miss Holmes intervened. The father then turned to the boy and said, "Never tell anyone that you are my son, never say that you are the son of your mother, never say that these are your brothers and sisters. You have made of my name a jest and disgraced me because you have refused to follow the religion of your people and of your race. Someday we will be avenged."

The boy will probably be baptized next Sunday in the river near the church.

Traversing the distance between cultures was a challenge Dorothy had expected, but oh, how she had underestimated the distance. Her nursing staff were the remarkable living testimony to that fact. Some of the girls had become Christian, but some had not yet reached that decision. And brought up as Hindus, all of them had to break caste to be a nurse. They promised to serve *all* patients, not just the ones who were born to the same caste as they were. If they couldn't promise that, then as good Hindus it would be taboo for them to even touch most of the patients who came through the door, patients who were born into a different caste.

What a nursing nightmare that had been! It had become immediately clear to her that it would have to be the first issue of any import into which she must land with both feet. She was repeatedly told that an Indian woman must never directly touch a person born into a caste higher or lower than herself. So, one nurse might touch this patient but not that one, and another might be allowed to touch that one but not the eight others in the ward. This nurse might be able to handle night soil, but another might be breaking caste to do the same task.

At first they had recoiled. But her young nurses carried such a commitment to healing in their hearts that every single one of the nursing students from the village had made the decision to break caste, to defy their heritage, and use their healing gifts indiscriminately. Now *that* took courage.

Oh yes, Dorothy had been presented with more than a few daunting barriers upon her arrival in Gauhati. Some posed ideological conflicts, but the most vexing on a daily basis were the ones that played havoc with practicality, common sense, and expediency. One of the most immediately frustrating issues to Dorothy had been the simple practical task of getting from one place to another without benefit of motorized transportation. The hospital simply had no car.

Of course, there were plenty of other options available to her. Dorothy could hike as easily as any seasoned athlete. She had sensible shoes and excellent posture to thank for that. But if she had much to carry, she could either wait and hitch a ride on the mail truck, or make do with one paniwalla (bearer) to carry her bundles. And when she took the dispensary into the hills once a month, it could take a whole crew of paniwallas to carry all the medicines, wound wraps, minor surgical instruments and more. Half a dozen bearers at least, to carry what one vehicle could have accommodated.

The most disagreeable part of the equation, though, was the fact that while a vehicle might carry her baggage, it might not always be able to navigate the traffic on Assam's over-burdened roads and bridges any faster than she could walk it.

You wouldn't believe that the traffic here is even more nerve-wracking than it is at home. One starts off down the road in a car or cart, and the road is narrow to begin with. On either side of the road and sometimes in it there are tiny babies and youngsters playing in the dirt.

Then as one gets by these, a goat decides to meander across the road and a cow and her calf decide that the middle of the road is the best and safest spot and they have to be dodged. About this time one arrives at a street meeting over which a holy man is presiding. They are ghastly looking beings as they have covered their bodies with dust and ashes and wear nothing but a loin cloth. The dust gives a deathly grayish tinge to the skin, and their hair hangs in long mats to their waist, or is roped (that is the only word that expresses it as it looks more like rope than hair) around their heads. It is well dusted.

Some of them have such hard cruel faces and one wonders how people can believe and worship them.

After getting safely thru this crowd, one usually has to wait at the railroad crossing in order that a train may switch, and when one finally arrives at the bazaar, the street is so filled with people that going is difficult. It certainly is a paradise for cows that are able to fend for themselves as they are allowed to go and come where and when they please. Here in Gauhati there is a cow farm for disabled cows and a great deal of money is given yearly for the upkeep of it. Most of the cows starve to death, however, and the proprietors get most of the money.

Whether or not she might have imagined these strange and challenging circumstances before she left the U.S., she hadn't truly understood their dimension. And every complication that existed was doubled on a Hindu holy day to the point that it took a fair amount of courage just to venture out on those days.

Even now, approaching her seventh year of facing and vanquishing every hurdle, that innate underpinning of courage bolstered her senses and steadied her nerves. If courage flagged, if training forsook her, and if the sticking post broke, her ingenuity nearly always carried her through.

Dorothy tidied the vanity, dropped the hairpins in the carved wooden box, rose to check her underslip, and made a mental note to not fall asleep tonight without setting her hair with Wink's hair pins. She passed the kitchen on her way out of the bungla, sliding the previous night's sadness into the secret corner of her heart that she reserved for the patients she could not save.

Never forget. Don't dwell.

"Monglu, good morning."

"Missahib," he said softly with his usual shy deference. Monglu had cooked for her at the medical bungalow for over six years now, a welcome, stabilizing figure in her household. The deep crinkles that appeared at the corners of his eyes reassured her as they did each morning. All was right with the world. Whether those familiar crinkles were the result of myopia or a self-conscious smile, she was never sure. But to her mind, they would always be clear evidence of Monglu's happy soul.

She had come to rely on the little fellow, more than she would ever let him know.

A man may bring his wife into the mission field to provide all manner of conveniences for him. Not so for a woman. Not that there had not been a suitor or two. Or three.

~~~~~~~~~~~~~~~~~~~~~~~~~~~~

September 16, 1931

Last night I went over to the Longwells for dinner with Lucile, Dr. Savage (a research man who is very unusual in that he is a devout Christian and much interested in Missions and very friendly) and Dr. Abraham, a man from the Malabar Coast who is head of the English Department in Cotton College here. Had a delightful time. Dr. S. brought me home about 11:20. First time I have ridden with an unmarried man since I arrived I guess. (Don't put this in the mimeograph!!!!!!!)

Yes, there had been opportunities lost. Not that she'd have it any other way. She relished her single-blessedness. No wife to cook and clean. No strapping husband to carry the heavy loads.

But praise God, she did have Monglu.

Dorothy accepted the china teacup he held out to her and sipped the warm morning chota he never failed to have ready for her no matter what hour she rose. Near the edge of the table she spied a tin of apple rings that had arrived in a box from home along with Wink's letter.

"Mm," she smiled. "Let's have the apple rings for supper, shall we?"

He nodded and reached for a can of peaches. Dorothy slid the tin of apples toward him as he realized his mistake. His spoken English was quite good, making it easy to forget that he could scarcely read a printed word. And the printed labels made one foreign fruit look much like the other.

"They'll be best if you soak them for several hours, Monglu. Would you see to it for me, please?"

The little cook's straight back and bobbing chin reassured her that she had managed to correct his misunderstanding while leaving his pride intact.

Apple rings for supper.

Marvelous.

CHAPTER THREE

LASTER DAY

Her faraway sister lingered cheerily on Dorothy's mind as she followed the path to the hospital clinic almost without thinking. Its plain rocky borders no longer depressed her as they had in the early years thanks to the abundance of poinsettia and English violets that now whispered along the path's winding perimeter. She must remember to tell Edna how very much the little floral border has cheered her this morning.

Two years previous, Edna Stever, who shared the bungla with her, had spent hours and hours lining the path with rock and planting countless seedlings along its edges. What a gift she had given them all, even though week by week the jungle crept in to try and reclaim it.

Still, this *was* India, and the path *was* perpetually dusty. She could never in her wildest imaginings picture this place without dust.

Over time, Dorothy had half-consciously customized her gait, modifying her step so as not to raise great puffs of dust that would settle on her ankles and stick with her for the remainder of the day. It had taken some doing, perfecting what Edna called her "Greta Garbo" walk.

Wink, she sighed, if she were here, would execute a perfect Lillian Gish skippity-hop and to hell with the dust. Singing along her merry way, tra-la.

It was a ridiculous exaggeration, but it kept Dorothy moving along with a smile and a nod to the dhobies (washermen) she passed along the way. The piles of laundry the men carried seemed staggering in weight, but the launderers were clearly undeterred by it as they managed their own masculine dance along the pretty path.

A man to carry the heavy loads. She had them in spades here. Paniwallas were practically a dime a dozen. Dhobies even less. And the dherzies (tailors) were actually quite good for the pittance they were paid. So why did the words *husband* and *companion* and...*mate*...batter her most private thoughts so relentlessly these days, when she had such ready help?

Dorothy cast off the thought. She knew why. She was thirty-three years old. And home and hearth and a child in the cradle were the stuff of her dreams. They were the epitome of a life fulfilled.

Dorothy shook the dust from the freshly laundered white coat she carried over her arm and slipped it on, smothering the unbidden longing for something greater. She knew full well she was the most fortunate of souls. She was, after all, engaged in the most exhilarating enterprise—building a future not only for herself, but for every patient she discharged well and whole.

Home and hearth and a child in the cradle? Now *that* was the stuff of sacrifice.

She stepped into the hospital's airy vestibule and stopped in surprise, sensing immediately something was wrong. It was far too quiet. Eleven student nurses, even when they were attempting to work quietly, created a certain energy in the wards, a subtle rustling and soft chatter, a busy movement of air redolent with healing.

Dorothy listened. No footsteps, no rustling.

Nothing.

She walked down the wide hall, casting her glance left and right, and there they were. All eleven of them. Clustered on the south verandah, hands folded, heads down.

"She will not have it, do you hear me?"

It was Lahaori, Dorothy's prized student from early days, now her right hand and head nurse, indispensable in her gift for teaching the new girls.

"Do you think you will see *her* cry?" Lahaori looked around at the downcast heads. "Do you think she will hide her smile from you, from the patients? Do you think she will wear her grief on her sleeve as you do and mope around in front of the new mothers all the day? Do you think she will make them suddenly worry that they might lose their beautiful new baby just as their friend lost her little daughter lasterday? Hm?"

Lasterday.

The childish word caught Dorothy off guard, and she stifled a nostalgic gulp.

Lahaori's English had become quite marvelous, and the few mistakes she made from time to time were so endearing that Dorothy had not sought to correct her over the years.

Lasterday. So much more expressive than yesterday.

"No. No. And no," Lahaori said. "Never. And never will you. You will never forget that poor little girl we lost last night. But never will you remind these patients of it. Do you understand me?"

Slow nods.

Dorothy caught her breath. How many times had she schooled Lahaori in this way? How many times had she denied a mother's instinct to put an arm around a wailing nurse, to comfort her, to let her cry her little heart out. Such a thing could never happen. Not here. Such coddling would never make a nurse. Denying such tender gestures didn't make the grief any less painful, but it kept her staff strong and efficient in the face of any trauma.

"Lahaori, there you are," she called quietly. "I'll be in my office when you're ready with your morning report." She turned to the group. "Good morning, ladies. And thank you," she said, sweeping her eye over the small group and making sure she had a moment of contact with each set of young eyes. "Thank you for your excellent work yesterday. You are the jewels of Gauhati, each of you. Truly."

She smiled. They were startled, momentarily unsettled at the unexpected compliment. Their day would go well now—better, anyway—girded as they now were by Lahaori's lesson and bolstered by her own praise.

"Carry on."

HEAD NURSE LAHAORI BUHYAN, L.M.P.

CHAPTER FOUR

DEPOT BRIDES

And carry on, they did. Her student nurses' curiosity was a constant source of amazement to Dorothy, almost as much as their constant misunderstanding of the English language. Reading their notes on a patient's chart was often the most fun she had all week.

"Patient temperature good on arms all over body."

"Patient like food yes stomach like no."

"Take patient head for stitch."

It was clear that even though their chart notes were a bit scrambled, they actually comprehended a great deal, and when Dorothy drew pictures for them, she saw veritable light bulbs of understanding flash in their eyes.

So Dorothy had taken to sketching illustrations for them on a regular basis, and tacking them up on the walls of the nursing students' bungla.

She had been surprised to discover that student nurses at the Satribari Compound had very little in the way of textbooks. And stunned to discover that the widely accepted nurses' training "bible" had never been translated into Assamese.

So Dorothy did what anyone would expect Dorothy Kinney to do. She translated the English nursing guide into Assamese. It had taken a year to accomplish, and had proven to be a huge boon to the student nurses. Where it was woefully lacking in images that, to Dorothy, were so vital to conveying the book's meaning, her own sketches made up the difference.

She'd been working over an hour tonight on sketches for her journal, and had fallen easily into the comforting rhythm of her endeavor. Life was replete with rhythm, and this particular rhythm was one of her favorites, perhaps because it marched to her own internal beat rather than the excruciatingly slow tempo in which the people of Assam seemed to be locked.

Move. Wait. Sigh... Speak. Wait. Smile.

That was the rhythm of life here. It had its own languid melody.

But Dorothy's internal song moved faster. Stronger. More decisively. She could not modulate her melody if she tried. To her, any other pace felt awkward, unproductive. So she kept her own steady beat, moving briskly through her days with the rhythm dictated by her heart. In truth, it had a dance of its own.

Dorothy sipped the last of her tea and spilled the remaining drops onto the saucer. She dipped the nib of her pen into the small Waterman Ink bottle and resumed drawing.

Scratch. Dip. Glide.

Dip. Dot. Glide.

Even the mere sound of her sketching was comforting, the feel of it magically fluid as the nib scratched evenly across the page of her journal. Long curving swoops defined the outline of the image she sketched in today's early morning light. It was better than a photograph as it documented the massive sores that had brought this morning's little patient to her. Kala Azar. *Leishmaniasis.* A parasitic killer nearly as deadly as malaria. And far more brutal.

The leaves of her book bulged with similar drawings, all attentively lined in pen and ink. The images—accurate in both detail and drama—chronicle the medical cases Dorothy has encountered, a lavish tale more vibrant than mere words. The pages illustrate in grisly splendor the plights of her many patients, like this boy decimated with the horrid sores, fever and weakness of Kala-Azar; or the nasal passage and sinus of the toddler from whose high nostril she removed a truly remarkable amount of putrefying wood; or the shocking condition of a cervix decimated by tetanus before she removed it.

Here and there in many of her sketches are brownish areas, intentionally stained with the simplest of watercolors—a mere drop of tea or sometimes chota from an ever-present teacup. The tea splotches have been meticulously dabbed with a fine horsehair brush, and identify places of inflammation or infection. Once she discovered the effectiveness of enhancing her sketches with her "watercolor tea", her journal took on a rather artistic life of its own.

Sketching became more than an instructional or archival endeavor. It became a pastime. A meditation. An escape.

Silence was never mandatory as Dorothy lost herself in her sketching. Always within earshot, monkeys called to one another—a surprisingly normal sound. An expected sound. After all, this was rural Assam. A morning without monkeys, in fact, might even signal alarm to dwellers on the fringes of the reclaimed jungle that covered the hills beyond the near edges of the Satribari compound. So let them screech on. The sound came from a great distance. Muted. Welcome. A morning melody of its own.

Time and space seemed altered, nearly parallel, in hours like these when Dorothy could sit alone sketching the day's cases into her journal that consumed five volumes now. She could never fully explain the sensation of seeming to be led, as if her mind detached and merely watched her hand curve across the page, sketching veins and swollen tissue and lacerated muscle and taut, distended bellies—the ghastly and beautiful things that have made up her day in the hospital, or in the traveling dispensary.

She picked up the horsehair brush and dipped it into the puddle of tea she had spilled into her saucer. With utmost care she dabbed at the areas of her drawing that her memory told her were most inflamed. Minuscule spiders of tea formed their own spontaneous designs on the fringes, soaking the margins.

Dorothy smiled at the irony of it. Tea. How perfect that it should be tea, so abundant in Assam, this land of tea gardens, that brought her illustrations to life. How ironic to be painting these angry, infected sores with tea, the very reason so many of her patients come to her in such dire straits. Their work in the tea gardens kept them in perpetual, abject poverty, and in constant danger of contracting Kala Azar.

Less than a hundred years earlier this part of India had been practically unpopulated. Then the Indian tea managers came looking for areas where their precious tea bushes would take kindly to the soil. Most of these people would not be here today had the tea managers not made just such a discovery in the soil of Assam.

But they had. And they had rejoiced over the untouched land that stretched for miles and miles on both sides of the beautiful Brahmaputra River. No wonder Gauhati and much of Assam caught the eye of the British colonial tea industry. It didn't take them long to make their mark upon it, as well.

By the 1860s, massive immigration of tea plantation workers—low caste from Bengal and central India—brought many of Dorothy's patients' great-grandparents to the area seeking work in the tea gardens—a charming and colloquial name for an industry riddled with dark sides.

She knew just enough about these people's history that unholy images of the meager life they must have found here floated in her consciousness as Dorothy darkened the tea stain around the festering sores she sketched. The boy who bore these sores suffered terribly from Kala Azar, as did many of her patients from the jungle regions. These jungles were infested with monkeys carrying the parasitic disease, the very reason not even tribal hunters could be coerced to go into the jungles and clear them for the tea plantation owners. They had known that entering that disease-ridden den was a near-certain death sentence.

What the tea plantation foremen needed were workers who had no fear of the jungle, and no such human existed in the sparse outlying villages. So the tea plantation owners would say they had little choice but to begin importing labor.

A few workers came of their own accord, drawn to work with the cultured British who had begun populating their land. But when the British needed more and more laborers, more than the native agents could recruit, the agents turned to unscrupulous methods of securing workers. Soon thousands were being kidnapped by "certified" agents and transplanted in Assam.

And some girls, as Lahaori's family told it, became *depot brides*. Lahoari never failed to cry every time she told the story of her grandmother's thirteen-year-old sister, who had been stolen from their beautiful home and whisked away to the train station before anyone even knew she was gone. Someone had spoken a few hurried words and suddenly she was married to a man—also stolen—whom she had never seen in her life, and between sobs her train left the depot and carried the new bride into a dark and soul-scarring life in the tea garden.

Eleven years later, the story went, Lahaori's great aunt stumbled back to her home in Gauhati, emaciated, gray-haired, carrying three small children—the only surviving three of the seven she had borne in the eleven years married to a man she'd never truly come to know. She was only twenty-four.

· · · ·

So it seemed that the very tea that had been a blessing in Dorothy's daily life, an ever-present tool for journaling, had also been the curse behind the poverty and disease that plagued so many of her patients.

Now in the very modern 1930s it was that poverty—the legacy of the tea gardens—that made this valley such fertile ground for strike-organizing activists. Activists like a man named Ghandi who was a quiet firebrand for change.

Dorothy dabbed the page with a scrap of blotting paper and closed her journal. She rose to put the book on its shelf behind her desk just as one of the new student nurses stepped into the doorway and called her respectful greeting.

"Ah, thank you, Achala." Dorothy turned to accept the medical file the girl offered. She glanced at the recent notes and nodded her appreciation of their thoroughness. The girl beamed with pleasure and turned to leave.

"Achala, one moment please."

The girl turned, and the delight on her face turned to apprehension.

"Yes, Doctor Kinney?"

"I see you're not wearing your uniform today."

A half-smile crept onto the girl's face. "No, missahib, I do not wear it today."

Dorothy sighed. "Did something happen to it?"

"Oh no, missahib!"

"Ah. Did it not get laundered?"

"Oh no, missahib! I mean, yes, missahib."

"Well then, would you please explain why you are on duty today but your uniform is not?"

The girl blushed and cleared her throat. Her hands self-consciously brushed at the fabric of her obviously homespun sari. "I do as the Ghandi instructs."

"As the Ghandi instructs?"

"Yes, missahib! We are not to purchase the cloth that is not made in our land."

Dorothy smiled. He was at it again. Or rather, still. His never-ending battle to press for independence from Britain.

"So you made your own?"

The girl nodded. "On the Ghandi's loom." She spoke with such pride that Dorothy was loath to squash her enthusiasm. But really. Women all across the country were weaving their own cloth on the rickety little portable looms the man himself had invented. And not doing it very well, from the looks of Achala's sagging garment. It was sure to make an entire country look like beggars.

"A very noble endeavor," Dorothy smiled, determined not to say what she actually thought about the man's meddling. "But may I ask if we have changed the procedure here? If you were required to purchase the cloth for your nurse's uniform?"

"Oh no, missahib! The most generous hospital has provided our uniforms. I—" Achala's face fell further as her quick mind followed Dorothy's reasoning.

"Very well, then. I see that you understand. Since you did not have to purchase the uniform that was made in Britain, you will not be going against your Ghandi's ultimatum if you simply wear it. Correct?"

"Yes, missahib! Yes, I see!"

At her dismissal the girl fled, though she seemed to show great relief at the prospect of no longer having to wear her homespun garment alongside her classmates in their crisp uniforms.

Dorothy sighed. This girl was a progressive, so typical of young Indian women these days. If it was a new idea, she jumped on it. A new expression? She was the first to employ it in her everyday speech. She was bright. Independent. Aware. Not anything like Lahoari's great-grandmother, Dorothy guessed.

God help the tea plantation that tried to make *this* one a depot bride!

~~~~~~~~~~~~~~~~~~~~~~~~~~~~~~~~~~~~~

> Ghandi is not a Christian and does not lay claim to being one—he is frank to admit that he is a Hindu but has simply borrowed some of Christ's teachings that he considered good. He is spoken of as being Christ-like which to my notion is nothing short of blasphemy. He is too inconsistent, and not only that he is working entirely for an earthly kingdom and not a spiritual one. Your letters have all been full of eulogies about Ghandi from this one and that one. Well, honestly, I did think that my own family wasn't quite so gullible. It is nothing short of propaganda and lack of brains on the part of some folks at home that Ghandi is being talked of as he is. Don't believe anything and everything in the papers. If I did that, I surely wouldn't have a very good opinion of the USA from the things that find their way into our papers out here.

The day fled into night and at last her lamp began to flicker as it did after long use. Though it seemed that the day filled with patients and reports had barely begun, it was over, and Dorothy wandered the path home slowly. The letter she would write while waiting for Monglu to put the supper on was already composing itself in her head.

> The hospital is still full. There are twenty-one just at present—fourteen of them children, and ten of them under four. Isn't that grand. I get so thrilled over the opportunities out here, and then so heart sick over the tragedies. The little boy who came in for hernia is getting ready for the operation very well. Think we can do it this week.

Anywhere else a child might come for surgery one day and be on the operating table the next. But here, in many cases, a restorative regimen was necessary for a time before a malnourished, worm-ridden, vitamin deficient anemic child could be expected to survive the scalpel.

That complication was seen around the hospital as a great blessing. It took a significant toll on the hospital's financial resources, but the longer it took to build up the child, the more time they had to introduce eager little ears to the Christian God. Happy, healthy children would return to their parents and neighbors with the seeds of something beautiful in their hearts.

Often, however, a healthy, restored child was returned to its parents only to be introduced to something horrid and dark.

> Karmoti continues to gain and get fat but the other day we found that her father (her mother died two or three months ago) has bunderbusted (that is good Assamese for making a bargain or arrangement) for her in the prostitute lines and has sold her to the women there. It seems as tho we couldn't let that little bit of sunshine go to such a place, and we are hoping and praying that some way will open so that we may be able to either keep her in the orphanage or put her in a good home.
>
> She is so winsome now and is beginning to talk. When you ask her if she has had her rice she will look as arch and say in a soft little voice "Nai, nai" (no), and when you ask her where Bitee is (Assamese for big sister) her little finger will go toward a certain one

of the nurses of whom she is very fond. She sings and plays with her toys and is so happy and lovable.

Dorothy stood a moment on the bungla's bottom step and looked down the road toward the orphanage. Thinking of Karmoti and the orphanage and saving her from her dreadful fate brought a boatload of emotions tumbling into the space in her heart where another baby lived.

Baby Junaki. Not so much a baby now. All of six years old, and the most precious bundle of sunshine. Junaki only had eyes for Dorothy, as well she should. She would forever and always be Dorothy's first delivery nearly seven years ago now, the young American doctor delivering her first baby to a mother whose family had waited too long to bring her to the hospital. Junaki lost her mother in childbirth and her father that same day—she was a baby girl, after all, and of little use to a widowed man.

Dorothy's heart had opened completely, fully, engulfing the child with every bit of a mother's love. She kept the child at the hospital much longer than anyone thought reasonable. Longer than she knew she should. For two years Baby Junaki toddled around the hospital, reaping hugs and stories and sweets and smiles from Dorothy who was over the moon in love with the child, until the day came at last when Dorothy realized she must part with Junaki, for the child's own good.

And when that day came, it was dear Monbahadur, the compound's general mahorie (handyman) and his lovely wife who adopted Junaki. Their home was a model of joy. That and only that made it possible for Dorothy to let loose of the little Garo girl.

Karmoti and Junaki had—by the grace of God—been spared the life of prostitution for which they were destined. They were two little girls, two precious little souls, who now thrived in a life that promised infinitely more than fate had dealt them.

They had lost their mothers, and Dorothy had taken them into her heart. She could feel their small arms wrapped fiercely around her neck. She could see clearly in her mind's eye the bright intelligence that shown from their beautiful brown eyes. She never lost the tug at her heart that happened without fail when anyone mentioned those two dear names.

Junaki. Karmoti. Their names made her smile as she wearily slipped her shoes off and clapped the dust from them before she entered her quiet bungla. Overhead the first stars of a lovely northern India evening graced the dark sky.

Aha. Her letter home would have to wait, if the enticing aromas indicated as she thought they did that Monglu had dinner ready to set out for her. She stowed her Oxfords and stepped into the kitchen to let him know she was home.

The table was nicely set as always. And in the center was grandly displayed the special dish she had requested of Monglu that very morning.

Apple rings.

In a lovely china bowl.

Still soaking.

Still in the tin.

MOSEE - COOK, MONGLU - COOK AND BEARER,
KOPEEL - WATER CARRIER, PAUL MALI - GARDENER

MON BAHADUR
DOROTHY'S "MAN OF BUSINESS" OR WORK SUPERVISOR
AT GAUHATI HOSPITAL COMPOUND.
HE AND HIS WIFE ADOPTED BABY JUNAKI.

TYPICAL FLOODING ON SATRIBARI HOSPITAL COMPOUND

CHAPTER FIVE

USE WHAT YOU HAVE

As they are wont to do, a hundred golden mornings passed in the blink of an eye. Some heavy with fog, some sodden for weeks after torrential downpours, some still and dry. Yet each and every morning dawned golden in Dorothy's eyes, gilded with opportunity and laced with anticipation of yet another chance to feel God's will at work through her own hands.

This particular golden morning quickly lived up to its promise, delivering a solution to a medical problem in the form of a brilliant idea.

Accomplishment sang in her veins as Dorothy gathered the items with which she hoped to achieve her latest inspiration. Yesterday's cares fell away, allowing her muse to put wings to her feet.

It never failed. A plan waiting to be fulfilled invigorated her in a way no other thing could, sharpening her senses, honing her creative edge, stoking her ingenuity. Better than sugar on cinnamon toast, she always said—and to Dorothy there was very little better than sugar on cinnamon.

With barely repressed eagerness she selected and rejected items from her small storage closet, gathering unlikely objects to achieve an unlikely purpose, but one she was certain would work. She felt it in her bones.

No day here was without its challenges, but for a born problem solver a new dilemma was like Christmas all over again. Another test. Another mystery. Another conundrum.

She welcomed them.

"Edna, where is that length of mosquito netting you were showing me the other day?"

Edna Stever was busy at her bookkeeping just a few paces away. She looked up and dropped her spectacles down the bridge of her nose.

"That? It's not much use, Dorothy. Not much more than a scrap. Dunno what they were thinking. Doesn't even stretch across a baby's bassinet. Bottom shelf, I think. Toward the back."

She poked her glasses back up where they belonged and bent to her work. Dorothy smiled. That was actually quite a long, eloquent oration. For Edna, anyway.

Dorothy shook her head at some of the improbable things stored in her little closet. Silk sheets. Books on star-gazing. And for heavens' sake, how many homemade tea cozies could one hospital possibly use? All were things that had been sent from the States. By well-meaning church ladies bent on being helpful to 'those poor missionaries'.

How simple it will be when people finally learn to just read my lists and fill my requests.

Too simple, she knew. Still, no matter how clearly she stated their need in her letters, the Board of Missionaries could seldom manage to send the things she actually requested, or authorize her to have the work done or items made by local craftsmen.

It frustrated. It maddened.

A care package would arrive from a well-meaning patron back home and the tingle would rush from the nape of her neck to her fingertips. What could it be?

The brown paper would be carefully removed, folded, and set aside, and the string that bound it would be neatly coiled before she opened each package. This could be the one! This could be the surgical instrument she has asked for... repeatedly. Or the sheets made to order for the new hospital bed. Or, praise God, it might even be the crinoline she needed for plaster casts, or...

But no. It would be some frilly furbelow chosen especially to thrill the sensibilities of an isolated missionary female working in the hinterlands. Or a new appliance that drew off so much of her precious electricity that she could never—almost never—use it.

June 15 — The gloves and syringe from Durbins have not come altho I think you said a week or two ago that you had sent them. How we do wish we could get someone to just give an operating table or the money for one. Have asked Miss Tufts if I could ask for it as a specific, but don't imagine that they will be willing. Have heard nothing from the Board so far as to any chances for our septic tanks, pump, etc. If they just had to live and work without a septic tank, they would change their minds in a hurry.

The Bets Catalog came but it doesn't help us much inasmuch as we haven't the money for the table much as we need it. Oh, for more equipment. If we could just have about five hundred dollars we could have a decent table that would fill all our needs for years to come. We stand on our heads, we break our backs, we use bricks, and then we can't do the things we could do if we had better equipment. How I wish somebody would just give us about five hundred for a table and give it to us quick.

Oh yes, about the ether machine that Paul wants to get. We would surely welcome such an instrument with open arms, many blessings on the donor, and with much relief for some of our patients. However, we have an alternating current and a 210 volt current. A couple of our nurses know just how strong it is, because one of our desk lights that we were using as a physiotherapy light short circuited and the nurses had turned it on, and then took hold of it to adjust it, with the result that they couldn't take their hands off and none of them had sense enough to turn off the current. Needless to say, both of them, altho not badly damaged, were scared out of about ten years' growth each. They certainly let out some blood curdling yells.

Still, an ether machine was infinitely more welcome than the stack of men's pajamas that had arrived a few months earlier. Men's pajamas, sent to a women's hospital in rural India.

What got into people? Money was too dear to waste it on trifles nobody out here could use. These things were not only useless to her, they often represented great sacrifice on the part of the sender.

And yet, her natural ingenuity refused to allow anything to languish for long in the closet. Everything found a purpose. Once she had repurposed the gifts, few could even recognize the item's original intent. Men's pajamas became layettes for newborns. Tea cozies were ripped apart, combined, and remade into quilted nursing jackets for the new mothers.

But it took time to sort it all out. And time was not always her friend.

Dorothy crossed the hall, her arms laden with the treasures she had collected from the seemingly bottomless closet. The little boy with tuberculosis of the spine was in need of a plaster cast, and after two failed attempts, she had finally contrived a way to fashion it. She had seen only one instance of this type of cast, and that was in her first year as an intern. Now little Vachan presented her with her first opportunity to actually do one herself and so far—without the proper materials—it had not gone well. But in the pre-dawn hours as she struggled to rest, some corner of her mind remained hard at work refining ways to accomplish the task of making a plaster cast without the proper crinoline bandages that would bind to the plaster and hold it in place—on a fidgety little boy. Around dawn the picture fully matured in her mind's eye.

Lahaori and two of the students prepared five-year-old Vachan, who now lay trembling on the exam table she'd created years ago from an old potting table. It was a far cry better than the collapsible examining table the board had sent out to her. After it lived up to its name one too many times, collapsing under the weight of a critically ill patient, Dorothy consigned it to the closet in favor of the potting table. Cleaned and enameled and with the thin rubber pad she had attached to the surface, it seemed comfortable and less threatening for the children.

~~~~~~

April 30

Mother Dear:

Just how much money is there in my account now, aside from my own personal savings? We have simply got to have some other kind of an operating table. The one that we have is a $39 collapsible one, and it sometimes lives up to its reputation, besides having none of the fixtures necessary for certain important positions. We have to makeshift and then don't have a safe result. If we could get one that would be safe, work with gear and ratchet in changing the position of the head and body (not on cogs where one has to lift the patient, and the table too in order to change a position) and which had some shoulder braces, knee crutches, etc. It would be marvelous. We could get such a one for about $175. All told if we could have it sent out on Alice's unused freight allowance, but would have to get the order in very soon if we did so. That can be used within a year, and that would mean that it would have to be started before September first. Don't order one for us, but let me know as soon as possible.

"Hello, Vachan," she smiled. The little boy looked at her armful of items and his fear only escalated until she placed a calming hand on his chest and began to massage slowly back and forth.

"I can see that you are so very tired of lying down. Am I right?"

Vachan's eyes flitted to his mother who stood opposite Dorothy, then quickly back to her as he nodded tentatively.

"Well, of course you are! Why, you can hardly throw a ball or carve an elephant or do any of the things boys your age like to do when you have to lie down all the time, can you?"

This garnered a far more assertive response from the boy.

"Just as I suspected! So I was thinking, we could make a sort of body brace that would help your back when you need to sit up. Would you like that, Vachan?"

Now the boy smiled as he nodded, and Dorothy set to work. The child had granted permission so she would waste not a moment more. Besides, if she didn't concoct a brace that worked, the boy's muscles would continue to atrophy until simply throwing a ball would become an impossible dream.

~~~~~~~~~~~~~~~~~~~~~~~~~~~~~~~~~~~~~~~

We couldn't get any crinoline for the bandages, and we couldn't get any bandages already made. We could get the plaster and something that would do very well for the felt. We got the plaster and then debated as to what we could use for the bandages as it has to be stiff. Finally Edna brought out some big pieces of mosquito barring that had been sent out to her which were not large enough to use for nets and which she had wondered what on earth she could use it for. By careful work, and making the bandages double we contrived to get ten three-yard bandages, each six inches wide. We wanted some reinforcing for the cast and used some old corset stays that we found. A long undervest took the place of the stockinette.

"Now take a deep breath, please, Vachan." She inhaled slowly to demonstrate. Across from her, the boy's mother inhaled, and then Lahaori—everyone in the room encouraging the child to expand his chest as much as he was able.

"That's right. Now once again, and hold it for me as long as you can without coughing. That's it. Good!"

> By rubbing the plaster in extra well while we were putting the cast
> on, we obtained a very smooth looking one which set rapidly and
> was very firm. Then we trimmed it out with ordinary shears and Shan
> knives (more like paper knives but somewhat sharper).

She ran her fingers one last time across the small boy's plastered torso before the stretcher-bearers carried him to the ward where he would begin his therapy. Smooth. Solid. Not brittle at all, but cool and firm, just as she'd hoped.

"As soon as it's dry we'll play a game," she called after him.

Dorothy took a step to follow him and stopped as her feet crunched across bits of plaster that littered the floor. She raised a hand to fetch a broom, and found one already in the hands of the young nurse attendant, Noori. The quiet girl had seen the need to sweep the floor and was already tending to it.

A thrill of sorts skittered up Dorothy's spine. The whole affair had proceeded with clinical order. Her staff had quite nicely assimilated the methods she had outlined over and over. Clean and prep, then restore, sterilize, then clean and prep. All about her the small staff could be seen engaging in these very activities—of their own volition—carrying out the tasks without being reminded.

The dustbin rattled and sang as Dorothy brushed small bits of plaster from the soles of her Oxfords. She clapped her shoes together to dislodge the most stubborn bits, and brushed away a small dusting of dried plaster that spilled from the cuff of her sleeve.

A drying clump of plastered bandages caught her eye, and Dorothy dropped her shoes to retrieve it. It rolled nicely in her hand, lightweight, shaping easily into a ball. She set it on the bench and quickly slipped into her shoes.

With a pencil from the pocket of her white coat she scratched a quick but very recognizable portrait of Vachan on the ball's drying surface as she crossed the hall. His beaming face when he saw it brought a smile to her own.

The day was progressing well. A bit of ingenuity worked for her today, and would work again tomorrow. The practicality of it remained her mantra.

Use what you have.

~~~~~~

> Someone asked me just how far money will go out here. That depends on whether you are buying food, paying coolies, buying medicine, or buying equipment. We pay 5 Rupees (about $2) for one mond of rice, 80 pounds, and one person eats from one to two pounds of rice a day, so you see that one mond doesn't go very far. This is especially true when we are feeding many of the patients in the hospital. Some of our patients have all their food brought from home. This frequently complicates treatment considerably. Five dollars will go quite a long ways–it will buy a baby basket and standard, it will keep a baby in the hospital for one month, or it will pay for the support of a student nurse for a month.
>
> Seven dollars will buy a hospital bed for an adult, not a Simmons to be sure, but a Simmons as far as they are concerned. The other day we purchased five lovely wool steamer rugs for the equivalent of ten dollars. These we split into two or three parts each, and so, from the five blankets we have twelve—six for the children's ward, and six for the woman's ward. They are fairly good size, too. There are a thousand ways to use every piece, but we have been able so far to grow, and we are trusting that we can continue to do so.

She tossed the lightweight plaster ball to Vachan, who caught it with the clumsy hunger of a child too seldom allowed to play.

Dorothy slowed her racing mind and focused on the boy. She would take a few moments with the little fellow. After all, she had promised him a game.

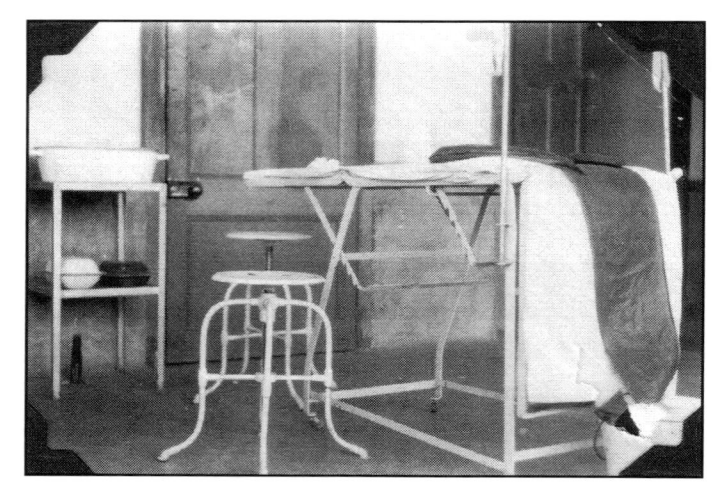

COLLAPSIBLE EXAMINATION TABLE

DOCTORONI ALICE MARK (RIGHT) WITH HOSPITAL NURSES

CHAPTER SIX

TOO LATE. TOO LATE.

The colorful Bohemian mirror Dorothy had just hung on her office wall refused to hang straight. She tapped it lovingly, once on the right, then twice on the left, until it was perfectly plumb. The obliging nail had stood bare since its last occupant had crashed to the floor and shattered to smithereens.

The simple, unadorned but serviceable mirror had gone unreplaced for months, until Dorothy made her long overdue voyage to the States on furlough and rediscovered this charming mirror in her own bedroom in her parents' home. It had taken some doing fitting it into her already overburdened steamer trunk, but on the matter of the mirror Dorothy would spare no effort. If it came to a choice between sailing back to India with her new walking suit from Bloomingdale's basement, or taking along the mirror, she would have had quite a battle of it. But as it happened, the mirror finally settled snugly into the trunk's midsection, padded on all sides by her unmentionables.

Something stirred within her each time she looked at the colorful mirror. It did so much more than simply reflect her image. It seemed to Dorothy that somewhere in the depths of its silvered glass it held a record of her childhood, her youth, her sharply focused medical student determination. Like photographs burned into its invisible depths. And now it would capture and hold the scenes of her life here in Gauhati.

She sat at her desk, still aware of the mirror behind her, cataloguing her every move. It was a nonsensical bit of comfort having it there. It was simply a mirror. Boldly occupying an otherwise bare wall and out of congress with the sparsely furnished, austere office.

But it made her smile.

More often these days Dorothy realized with regular surprise the subtle changes these six-going-on-seven years had wrought. If she stood back far enough from a mirror, there wasn't a penny's worth of difference between 1926-Dorothy, second in her class and fresh out of med school, and 1934-Dorothy, fresh back from a six-month furlough to the States. Same weight, same girlish figure, same wavy hair, same smiling countenance. Same impeccable fashion sense.

But sitting here at her desk, with her fingers tracing the worry lines above the bridge of her nose, the creases knit in her forehead when she concentrated, she felt the full weight of her mission. Decisions made in split seconds to save a life, disappointments shouldered when patients refused life-saving treatment, devastating losses of innocent children. These were the things that had reshaped Dorothy's forehead and robbed her of the easy laughter that she knew now she had taken for granted. The laughter that she sorely missed.

Furlough in Baltimore had brought that crashing home to her. The easy laughter of the young students in the seminar she led at Johns Hopkins seemed so foreign to her, something she had to work at relating to. It was a time she expected to savor, but found that strangely enough, it was Gauhati that felt most like home these days.

Here there were smiles—some easy, some forced, some shy—and the usual light-hearted banter. But laughter? Genuine, from-the-belly laughter? She could no longer summon a mental picture of what that would look like here. What that would feel like. What that would sound like.

The thought had barely formed when a small cry banished it and broke the stillness beyond the window at Dorothy's back. It startled her enough to drop the chart she'd been updating. Saanji's chart. Hers was the same story yet again. The family waits too long to bring their daughter, wife, mother to the hospital, until she nearly dies. But at least this time they did bring her. And with every bit of surgical skill within her, and a long, vigilant night, Dorothy had been able to save the woman. Her family would be thrilled, and she intended to praise them publicly for bringing Saanji to the hospital in a timely fashion.

She turned to peer through the jacaranda bushes beyond the window, just in time to see the tail end of a procession scurry through the hospital gates.

"Missahib! Miss—"

"Kika, whatever is—"

"Doctor Kinney, they have taken her! They have taken Saanji!"

"Wh—?"

Dorothy flew to the door in her stockings. Her feet ached so wickedly after long night hours tending to Saanji that she had shucked off her shoes beneath her desk. Now the pebbled path bruised her arches even as her toes crushed jacaranda petals, sending up a fragrant apology that whipped about her skirt. She ran after the small group of peasants that gabbled and grunted excitedly as they scuttled down the path, carrying the barely conscious Saanji who had nearly died the night before.

"Be careful! She's...oh no! Be careful! You must bring her back! She's going to be fine! Truly!"

Dorothy scrambled along beside them, trying to make them stop, to listen, desperate to convince the woman's family that their daughter-sister-wife was going to survive her illness. But the resignation in their eyes, the conviction that the young woman they carried was going to die, was impossible to miss. And they would not let her die in the Christian hospital. They would not dishonor this dear relative by allowing her to die surrounded by things foreign to Hindu. Surrounded by heathen Christians. It would be a humiliation, a disgrace they could not countenance in Saanji's behalf. They loved her too much.

That is where the heartbreak comes into the work out here—they wait so long to bring them in and expect so much in such a short time, and are not willing to give us a chance. To die in the hospital (non-Christian) means that none of her family can touch the body and that the body will have to be taken care of by a very low caste— the matroni and maters (sweepers and those who care for the night soil, etc.).

It would be a terrible disgrace.

The young woman's father silenced his family and turned to Dorothy. With pain in his eyes he spoke quietly, his words robbing her of breath.

"It is written on her forehead. If she lives or dies, it is already written."

Dorothy held her tongue, her pleas filling her throat like pitiful fireflies swallowed by the sun. The morning heat warmed the light linen of her hand-tailored surgical coat, caressing her shoulders as she consigned the woman to the care of her relatives. It seemed doubtful that Saanji could survive without continued medical treatment. Maybe after two or three days in the hospital, perhaps, but not so soon after her surgery.

Dorothy could only pray that the inevitable pain they caused the poor girl would not be too great.

That was the way of it out here, in this place with its strange attitudes toward death and dying: a young woman is removed from medical care where she might have survived, in order that her family can prepare her for a death she might have avoided.

Even the children of the village were already steeped in the rituals. With her own eyes Dorothy had watched an eight-year-old son forced to break the jaw of his dead father to ensure his perfect journey in the afterlife.

It is surely one of the hardest things she's had to do so far in this foreign place, to lift her hands from Saanji and step away from the mewling crowd.

With one last supplication she turned from them, the plea on her lips becoming a prayer while the crowd moved on and the sun warmed her back and the stockinged toes of her shoeless feet curled and flexed in the powdery dust.

. . . .

Dorothy slumped at her desk. The pain of standing by as they carried the woman to her death still sat like a barrier between her and the work that lay on her desk unfinished. She could not move her hand to pick up her pen.

She prayed. Prayed for Saanji, for Saanji's family, for her staff that surely at this moment felt the same despair she herself struggled against.

It is written on her forehead.

A letter home seemed the only cure to drag her heart and mind back from the dark edge it threatened to occupy. There was never anything quite so effective as "speaking" with her parents to jolt her back onto a productive course.

Saanji's story was too fresh, too sharp-edged to put on paper as yet. But a half hour at her typewriter worked its therapeutic magic, and Dorothy wrote. Her fingers flew, punching harder than necessary, tangling the keys and ribbons more often than usual, sending the carriage clattering brutally back and forth. But slowly, surely, her pulse returned to normal.

~~~~~~~~~~~~~~~~~~~~~~~~~~~~~~

The other day a girl or rather a woman came to the clinic. She had her four-year-old son with her, and during the conversation, she squatted down on the ground and the boy began to hunt for his dinner—still nursing. We made a lot of fun of him for it, and the mother let drop the information that he had been married for a year. A married man and still dependent on his mother's breast for his milk. It struck my funny spot as well as made me heartsick. The little girl is the same age. Of course they will not live together until she reaches puberty, but that will bring them together as man and wife when they are about twelve or thirteen.

Had another eclampsia case this week. The girl was brought in by the relatives. They live in Pandu—about six miles from here. Last summer Edna and Doctoroni had a very bad case of that sort and the woman died. They told the relatives that if she had been brought in sooner that she might have lived. The next case from that region (Ob. case) was an eclampsia that we had the latter part of January. She was very sick when Edna and Doctoroni who went out on the call brought her in to the hospital and the baby was dead, but she recovered.

That particular morning while we were working in the office a man ran up on the hospital verandah and said that they were bringing a patient in. Found out that it was an eclampsia who had been in labor only four hours and had had only two seizures. The people said that the others in the village had said, "Take her to the Memsahib right away". She had one more convulsion in the hospital shortly after arriving but had no more of them and delivered normally this morning about five-thirty of a four or four-and-a-half pound boy (her first baby) and the little fellow seems quite hale and hearty in spite of his diminutive size. The girl is doing beautifully. We have been tickled to pieces over the case and very thankful as well.

It is encouraging to have them bring a case in voluntarily and early, and the results have borne out our statements that they must come early in such cases. Dr. Ahlquist says that we certainly do get the most abnormal cases down here. Said he hadn't had an eclampsia case in all the time he had been out here. He wouldn't—he is a man, and women die here before they will let a man attend them in such times. Magnesium sulphate surely has worked beautifully in the cases that we have had so far, and the Great Physician has been very near.

The last big tumor case that we operated on is going home today. She says there will be some other cases similar to hers come from up there now that she has been helped, and best of all she says that she is going to tell them about Jesus. Her face was so hard and unyielding when she came down, and has softened and brightened so much in the time she has been here.

More and more of the babus who come to the hospital with their wives are accepting Testaments to read, and some of them are buying them. I had rather a long talk with Ratnadhar the other night, (My Pundit), and he is most unhappy. Is trying to be a Hindu outwardly, and Christian inwardly, and realizes he is cheating no one more than himself. His father was a rather prominent Hindu priest, and because of this he is a Brahmin of the Brahmins so to speak. He says that it would be talked about thruout the province if he were to come too openly for Christ, but admits that most of his friends know that he does not follow Hinduism in all of its ritual and customs, but says that as long as they cannot prove it, that he is safe. I think he would find that things would not be quite as bad as he thinks they would be if he were to come out openly. His mother is much opposed to it, and he can't see the possibility that she too might take up Christianity if he did so.

Must go now.
Loads of Love to All, Dor

Dorothy reread the letter as she slowly pulled the paper from the typewriter's platen, then signed it. It highlighted only a few of this weeks' cases, gravely skirting the tragedies whose stories were too fresh yet to tell. It was no wonder she felt weary. It was no wonder her bones cried out for a bit of relief.

Thank you, Lord, she whispered, *for every opportunity you have set before me today. And for those to come. And Lord? If you can? Keep sending them sooner. And let them stay longer. Open their minds and hearts. But if you can't? Just send them. I'll be here. I'll take them any way they come.*

And they did come. Wrapped in rags and dragged to the hospital steps on primitive, rickety travois-style rigs, or less often, swathed in rich, colorfully splendid fabrics and carried in a motor car. Hindu and Buddhist, heathen and Christian, they came. Growing the hospital, growing her skill, growing God's kingdom.

CHAPTER SEVEN

WRITTEN IN THE STARS

~~~~~~~~~~~~~~~~~~~~~~~~~~~~~~~~~~~~~~

August 28

People, my table cloth is finished and washed and ironed and ready for the first dinner party, and is it good looking. Wink, if I was at home I would let you use it for your wedding tea or whatever you are having.

~~~~~~~~~~~~~~~~~~~~~~~~~~~~~~~~~~~~~~

September 4

I thought about you all a lot, particularly Sunday night as that would be the wedding day at home. I tried to picture each one of you, what you would wear, where you would stand, the guests, etc. Shall be so anxious to get the first reports.

I sent the cable from here Sunday about noon. Your cable arrived here Monday about two P.M. According to the blank it was sent about 7:25 P.M. which would mean that it came thru in about seven hours. The cable was well worded for it told me that the wedding had taken place according to plans, and that Marian and her family were there. That meant so much. It was a thrill to get the cable, all right.

There were days when thoughts of home were nearly overpowering. Today was one of them. Her youngest sister had just been married, and she couldn't be there to support her, to hug her close, to send her off joyfully into her new life.

Dorothy had spent half the day imagining what her beautiful Wink looked like in her bridal clothes, how romantic the setting might have been with her pretty sister standing in the family drawing room pledging her future to the man with whom she had fallen in love.

There would be stars in her eyes, that was for certain. After all, Wink was an incurable romantic.

A small brown hand tugging at her sleeve broke her reverie. They'd caught her daydreaming. Again.

Five little sets of beautiful dark eyes peered in wonder at the storybook picture Dorothy held, all but forgotten. Each child clung tightly to the hand of the child next to them. They loved it when she read them a bedtime story. She loved it, too, their eager, breathless anticipation, their delight in heroes and the way they always yelled loudly at the villains.

"Foo! Foo!"

Who could ever tire of sharing a moment with these precious angels? She took a long breath, prolonging the suspense to a nearly wicked degree.

"The great tall warrior stood slowly, raising himself to his majestic height." Dorothy drew out the words with as much theatrics as she dared. *"And then,"* she paused dramatically, *"then, when every person from the village had stopped crying and looked solemnly up at him, he lifted high his ceremonial torch and said, 'Fear not, my people, for it is I who will save you. It is I who will set you free.'"*

The children clapped wildly, as wildly as their various illnesses allowed, then gasped as Dorothy's voice dropped in volume and rose in pitch to one of child-like innocence. *"But how, O Great One, how do you know that you shall win?'"*

The children nodded soberly. It was an entirely logical question.

"'This I know, my child,'" Dorothy finished in a solemn tone, *"'this I know."* She held another dramatic pause as she captured the eye of each child. *"For it is written...in the stars.'"*

There was silence all around as the children soaked in the final ringing words of her story. Each little head turned to follow with their eyes the finger she pointed out the window at the night sky. She let them sit for a moment, enthralled.

Oh, how she loved these impromptu storytimes. These little ones were so fresh, so eager, so malleable.

"And now," she smiled, snapping the book closed, "I shall tell you something else that is written in the stars."

"Yes! Yes!" they cried. "Tell us!"

She laughed. "It is written in the stars, my little angels, that if you all take your medicine like good little warriors tonight, there will be sweets from the Khetri ghat under your pillows in the morning."

"Yes! Yes!" they cried, and scrambled into their beds, ready for the student nurse to come around with their bedtime medicine. Some could not resist looking beneath their pillows, on the chance that the goodies had already been delivered.

There were often sweets under their pillows in the morning. Dry honeyed figs stuffed with almonds, segments of oranges wrapped in waxed paper, or some other such tasty treat. As welcome as candy, yes, but desperately necessary for these poorly nourished little ones. Not every bit of nourishment needed to come on the breakfast tray. Some could come in the form of a magical treat. Dorothy made sure of that. The children loved it, and a treat guaranteed that most days around here would begin with smiles. At least in the children's ward.

Each month when she made her sojourn to the village ghats, or markets, she kept an eye out for something special for the children as she shopped for the various and sundry things on her list. They were marketing trips, to be sure, but Dorothy had learned never to expect one trip to be exactly like another.

And she was never disappointed.

Last Wednesday we left here about eight and went to Sonapur and then on to Khetri. I was congratulating myself that we had picked a good day to go (it was the regular day) as the next day was a big festival day, consequently there would be more at the 'ghat' or market. However, altho there were crowds at the market, we were for the most part shunned and then some. I couldn't quite understand it.

We went on to another village where we had several people who had been in our hospital. They were very glad to see us but wouldn't touch us or allow us to touch them in any way. Reason? The next day was the final day of the big festival and they would have to stop and get purified again if we were to touch them, and they didn't have the time to stop and do it.

This festival comes just two months after the light puja that I wrote about and is sort of a harvest festival as all the rice has been garnered.

They gave us some eggs, but I had to hold a towel in my hands and she dropped the eggs into it one at a time—I was scared that they would break but they didn't. When she gave us some rice it was wrapped up in cloth, and as she wanted the cloth back we put it into something else. Lahaori then had to throw the cloth over to the side of the road and then she (the egg lady) went and picked it up.

We decided that we wouldn't go to the 'ghats' again on a puja day or thereabouts. This particular puja is celebrated by building bamboo structures and after much noise making, very early in the morning, these are all burned and anything else they can lay their hands on (a la Hallowe'en). The bamboo makes a terrific noise when it burns as the stocks are hollow between joints and these explode. Some fireworks, I can assure you.

Dorothy tucked each child into bed with a smile. She didn't always have the time, but when she did, she savored the ritual.

"Doctor Kinney?"

Dorothy turned back toward the small girl she had just bade goodnight. "Yes, sweetie-kin, what is it?"

The small child fingered the bandages that covered her left eye. This little one had the worst case of ingrown eyelashes Dorothy had ever seen. They perniciously disfigured her left eyelid and threatened to damage her sight if they were not managed.

"I want my bofe eyes," she said, expressing eloquently as children do her deepest wish.

"You shall have your both eyes soon, sweetie-kin. Very soon, indeed."

In fact, the bandages may very well come off later tomorrow, she thought, if all went well. And Dorothy had been completely satisfied before bandaging the child that there had been no serious damage to the child's vision.

"How can you know?" the child asked, then cried, "Oh! Is it written in the stars?"

Dorothy smiled as she bent toward the child and tipped her head toward the nearest window. "Oh my yes, little one. It's written in the stars. And it's written on your nose," which she tapped with her forefinger, "and it's written on your toes," which she wiggled with her hand, making the child giggle, "and it's written in my heart," she said.

With her finger she drew a cross on her heart and then touched the tip of the same finger to the little girl's heart. "Tomorrow you shall have your both eyes."

"Tomollow is long time?" The child's voice broke with anxiety. She was too little still to completely understand the passing of days from yesterday to today to tomorrow.

"Oh not at all! Tomorrow is one sleep away, see? You close your eyes, get a good night's sleep, and when you wake up in the morning it will be tomorrow."

The child sighed a huge, satisfied sound of total contentment. Then she slipped her own hand from beneath the covers and drew the same cross over her own heart before reaching out to touch the tip of her small finger to Dorothy's own heart.

"Tomollow," the little girl whispered as her unbandaged eye fluttered shut.

Dorothy sat utterly still watching slumber overtake the sweet little one. The child's small gesture moved her so profoundly that it drew tears to her eyes. They spilled over her lids and rolled relentlessly down her cheeks.

She found she was helpless to stop them.

Ever so silently she wept for the trust in her the little girl had shown. She wept for the miracles that had happened here in their burgeoning hospital at the edge of the jungle. And she wept for those for whom a miracle had not taken shape. She wept for the wedding she had missed, and she wept for the grace of a loving God who had brought her to this place, to be here with these children.

And she wept for a child of her own.

HOSPITAL STAFF BUNGLA [BUNGALOW]

CHAPTER EIGHT

NO NIGHT HERE

Warm days turned to velvet nights, which dawned on rainy mornings and weeks of monsoon. In good weather the temporary boardwalks were removed and the dusty, flower-bordered paths around the compound were easy to traverse. And then the rains would come again and the boardwalks would once again appear as if by magic.

Dorothy kept a spare pair of shoes at the hospital, so that even if she popped into the surgery looking like a drowned rat, her feet would be dry.

It would be one thing to simply give in and live an unsophisticated, even rather rustic life in this remote compound. Wet feet and all. But it was quite another to attempt civilized living in the middle of a mostly primitive population. She had not seen a pair of nylon stockings for more years than she could remember, but in every way available to her, Dorothy maintained a look that she was certain could be seen on most streets back home.

No matter what it took, Dorothy required of herself to always look the lady. No sagging hems, no uniform without the proper-length slip beneath it, no unruly locks. And always the pristine white coat. And she was in good company. She had set the standard on the compound and everyone made a conscientious effort to meet it.

The European women with whom she occasionally shared tea did the same. As wives of British attachés and other government, medical and missionary men, they clearly held themselves to that standard, too.

It would be a mistake to think that western women cornered the market on ladylike demeanor, though. In truth, she was surrounded daily by the kind, thoughtful, graceful, tactful, gentle Indian women who could be called nothing other than "lady", as well.

On Dorothy's first free evening in ten days, it was a British lady, a Mrs. Lancaster, who was the reason Dorothy had set about the task that had occupied most of her evening on this particular date in late spring. For several hours tonight her prized treadle sewing machine filled the back of the bungalow with its steady *ratcha-ta-ratcha-ta* sound—always as welcome as music to her ears. The lush feel of the elegant fabric she'd chosen made her smile as her fingers expertly guided it beneath the presser foot that held the needle in its track.

Mrs. Lancaster had invited her to tea, and Dorothy would arrive appropriately dressed or not arrive at all.

Her own slippered toes hugged the treadle.

Toe, heel, toe heel.

It was a sublime dance that had been part of her makeup since...well, since before time. One sure foot on the treadle kept the needle singing smoothly through the sheer fabric, then two feet on the treadle where the filmy material joined the heavier fabric of the bodice. She could gauge the need for one foot or two as easily as she could sense the need for one lump or two in her morning chota.

What would she do without her Singer?

It was hard on the ankles, to be sure, but the very thought of using a new electric machine was impossible for Dorothy to contemplate. It would be akin to Samson losing his strength when Delilah cut off his hair. Not using her feet in the delicious rhythm of the treadle would be like cutting half of her being out of the creative process.

Dorothy pressed her heel on the back of the treadle to bring it to a halt just long enough that she could smooth the chiffon sleeves that were shaping up nicely. They were such a radical departure from the pattern that she had breathed a sigh of relief when she saw them take shape just the way she had envisioned. She'd had the fabric for a month now, but it wasn't until this morning that she'd conceived the idea of changing the sleeveless pattern. It was the clever idea of incorporating chiffon sleeves that allowed her to finally begin working on her new creation. And already she knew it would be brilliant. The *bee's knees*, to be sure.

A tap of her toe had the treadle humming once again.

She eased the back of the fabric with her forefinger as she gently helped the sleeve pass smoothly under the needle. There were a couple of minutes of good light left, and then she'd have to light the gas lamps. The supply was low, and she would not be lavish in her use of it. But they were all to have dinner with the Lancasters tomorrow evening, and she was determined to have the new dress finished by then.

"Missahib!"

Dorothy lifted the presser foot and stopped the flywheel that engaged the needle. It was an instantaneous reaction the moment she heard the pounding feet that accompanied the musical voice that called out to her. She was up from the stool and hurrying to the door before the treadle finished its last revolution.

It wasn't a panicked cry, no frantic alarm. It was merely the excited voice of one of the paniwallas who often served as runners between the hospital and bungalows on the Satribari Compound.

It could mean anything. *Come see the elephant!* Or, a cobra was seen on the path and to keep a sharp lookout for it. Naturally, that particular bit of news would never go into a letter home. No use conjuring that kind of vision in the imagination of her loved ones.

But tonight the bearer brought news that Pura's father had finally shown up. It was good news, news worthy of sending the paniwalla pounding up to her front door.

Ten days earlier, Pura's father had brought his son to the hospital, dumped him in the arms of the first available nurse, and promptly fled. Nobody knew who he was, and the only information he had given was that the toddler writhing in the nurse's arms was named Pura.

The child had severe burns across his head and neck, and they had acted swiftly to relieve his excruciating pain. The entire staff sprang into action, even as the father slinked away.

Pura was doing well now, a favorite patient in the ward for children and babies that was somehow nearly always full. The fact that most of the beds were almost always filled was a conundrum Dorothy could not explain. Everything about the culture here worked against the idea of villagers or hill people taking themselves or their children to some distant hospital when they were ill or thought to be dying.

Yet for every woman or child who refused treatment, another woman or child came. Children were brought in by mothers pleading for someone to help them. Or a woman with a sick child would be found on the side of the road on one of their dispensary sojourns into the hills. And all too often a lone child might be found in a ditch succumbing to dysentery, leprosy, or worse. After a frustrating search to gain permission, Dorothy would often manage to secure consent from a village headman to bring the child to the hospital.

One day a very poor villager came to the Medical bungalow in Gauhati and asked that the Missionary Doctor go out to his village, some twenty miles distant, and see his wife who was too ill to be moved. The doctor and a nurse went. They found a young woman desperately in need of hospital care. She was lying on the floor of a tiny mud hut.

As usually happens when a white person arrives, a crowd soon gathered. The doctor tried to persuade the relatives to let the little patient be taken to the Hospital. "What! Take this woman away from her home to a strange place—perhaps to die!" This was not according to the custom. It was written on her forehead and if she were to die, she would die in the hospital, and if she were to get well, she would get well at home as well as in the hospital. Therefore, why take her to the hospital.

Such was the talk, and time was slipping away. Then a little woman slipped away from the crowd and coming toward the patient, knelt down beside her. She began to talk to her, She told her that she had been a patient in this Hospital, of what it had meant to her, of the love and care which she had received, of the Message she had heard, and ended up "You must go to the Hospital. It is a good place and there is no night there."

To this little woman, as to hundreds of others, the Hospital had been a haven, a bit of heaven, a place where there was always some-one ready to serve, always a light. May it always be so—no night there.

Some patients arrived at the hospital too soon, some came on time, some came too late. And some—particularly the children—might have died if Dorothy hadn't learned to seize the opportunity and talk turkey to their parents. Doctoroni Alice Mark had explained that to her early on, and introduced her to the stern way one must speak to some of the locals in order to get them to comply with even the simplest medical procedure.

It was God's perfect timing that little Pura's father chose tonight to reappear. Pura's wounds were at the ideal stage to tolerate the procedure Dorothy wanted to perform. She might have to have a very pointed word or two about what needed to be done to guarantee a good outcome for the little fellow, but that had never been a problem before.

～～～～～～～～～～～～～～～～～～～～～～～～～～～

> Little Pura never moves while we are dressing his head, and is frequently asleep when we finish. He can yell loud enough when there is no one paying any attention to him, however. He is getting along fine now, and I am going to try and persuade his father to give him a bit of his own skin so that things will heal in faster. If he won't, I think one of the nurses will.

Dorothy hurried along the path that was nicely lit by the paniwalla's lantern, though dark curtains descended just beyond its field of light. Jungle noises melded with the sound of leaves rustling in the evening's gentle zephyr, and she found that this little late evening excursion was actually quite a pleasant diversion. It was good to stretch her bones after two hours hunched over the Singer.

As they stepped into the open foyer, Dorothy caught pieces of Lahaori's explanation of the procedure they hoped to do to hasten healing for little Pura. The father's head nodded and bobbed like a windmill as he listened.

"Ah yes! No, no!" the father cried, once he understood what the skin graft procedure entailed. He was shocked, horrified, elated all in one huge emotional response. In his experience, children rarely survived burns or the infections that nearly always lurked within the decimated tissue.

"Yes, we may do the skin graft?" Dorothy asked.

"Yes, yes! This you will do for my Pura!"

"Well, then," Lahaori smiled. "Come with me and I shall prepare you." She held her arm to the side, indicating he should go with her. "We can take the skin for the graft in the examination room."

"Take the...no, no. No taking of skin." Pura's father planted his feet and held both hands, palm outward, in front of his chest. "No taking of the skin."

"But that's how it's done, Sahib," Dorothy said with what she hoped was a reassuring smile.

"Yes, yes!" he nodded. "It is done as you say in this way."

Dorothy let out an impatient sigh. "Then you must go with the nurse—"

"No, no. It is done with the skin, in this way, just as you say. But no never Hindi skin."

Dorothy felt her exasperation escalate and she tamped it down by broadening her smile. "But you say you love your son, Sahib."

His eyes grew wide as he glared at her. "Yes, Memsahib. I love my son. As you say. But I am not Brahmana. I am not Kshatrya. I am not even Vaishya." He worked his jaw as if it caused him pain just to speak the names of castes to which he did not belong. Castes that were far above the poor caste into which he was born.

"I am poorest of poor. Shudra. None are so near to the Dalit...the untouchable...as me. My son...my son...he is Shudra. He must not have unclean father."

With immense sadness he began to bow and walk away, but Dorothy's stern voice stopped his retreat.

"There is none so unclean as the man who can help his son but refuses. There is none so unclean as the man who cares more for his place in society that he abandons the needs of his own child." She walked as she spoke and met him eye to eye. "But there is none more loved in the eyes of God than the man who gives no thought to his own need and would give his very life to save his son."

A millennia of caste indoctrination whirled in the man's eyes. It seemed apparent that this was not the first time he'd faced this kind of perplexity. Their unclean tools would cleave his skin, removing a part of him and leaving an unclean mark. He had heard her words and wrestled with the contradiction they made to everything he had known as Shudra, the class of unskilled laborers into which he had been born and would never have an opportunity to climb out of.

Dorothy saw his dilemma and closed the small circle they made in the central hall of the modest hospital. She took the child from Lahaori, and held little Pura out to him. "It's not your *life* Pura needs. It's just a little patch of your skin." She lifted the toddler until he was looking directly into his father's eyes. "Show your son that among the Shudra there is no more honorable and loving man than his father."

The child cooed and smiled. His small legs jiggled and gyrated as his little hands grabbed and fumbled for the primitively braided frog clasp that held his father's tunic closed at the neck. The baby boy's large brown eyes danced with joy.

But the man didn't reach for his son.

They watched as he battled the demons he had inherited, and Dorothy's arms began to ache with the effort of holding the hefty child aloft. If the expressions that crawled across the father's face were any indication, he waged an epic battle. But at last his expression settled.

He looked at his son, then at Lahaori and Dorothy.

"It will be as you say," he whispered. And without a further word, he took his son into his arms and walked past them into the examining room.

The man had done what they constantly begged the locals to do—he had brought his injured child to the hospital immediately. Now with her challenging words she had risked sending him away. Doctoroni's example from years ago had opened the door to changing the man's thinking, and Dorothy had walked through it without a backward glance. To help her patient.

Yes, she had spoken firmly. Yes, she had used more pointed words and more forceful expressions than her ladylike sensibilities preferred. Yes, she had risked shaming the man with her less than gentle scold.

But it had worked.

True, he would most likely remove the hospital bandaging later tonight and replace it with a dirty rag. He'd most likely tell his village he'd sustained his wound while fighting off a ferocious leopard. But always there was a chance that he would feel the weight of her words, that he would sense some god-given courage, and tell the truth.

Time would tell.

Dorothy wasn't at all surprised how often she repeated the scenario over the years, casting doubt in the minds of those who had never sought to question how things worked in their small world. Sometimes talking turkey worked, sometimes it didn't. But speaking her Christian heart had to be making a difference. Because the people came. More each year. And each year, more and more left the hospital healed and whole.

Yes, there were always some who could not come. There were some who would die if she couldn't respond to the desperate emergency call to see a patient in a remote village. Some who would die when she couldn't run fast enough, borrow a vehicle, or find a mule to ride or a boat or bullock cart that would get her quickly enough to the patient's side.

And there were still some who found it impossible to summon the courage Pura's father had found. There were still some who could not step beyond the confines of their religious protocols, even if it meant death for themselves or their children.

But there were others like the small woman who shared her story of healing and hope in order to encourage a hesitant patient to go to the hospital. There were others who chose life and the promises of a Christian god. There were others like little Pura's father who heard Dorothy's words, and the words of the nurses, and who accepted with trusting wonder the healing ministrations of the hospital staff.

Dorothy heard with reverence each new voice, and thanked her God for the way in which He was opening their lives.

And she thanked her God that here at Satribari Compound there was no child left untended, no word of comfort left unspoken. No catastrophic event left to seek its own end.

Because the little woman had been right.

Here, truly, there was no night.

CHAPTER NINE

CHEEKY DEVIL

Week by week Dorothy became more anxious to remove the impediments of mindset, of poverty, and especially the dilemma of distance. And day by day she saw ever more clearly that as in everything, God expected that if she saw a problem, she would tackle the problem.

She might not be able to vanquish the choking bonds of caste identity, of poverty, of religious superstition, but she had learned to dish out a rollicking verbal rap when it was needed, hadn't she? She'd learned how to stand her ground. So when it came to solving the mere matter of transportation, of distance, well, that was a problem she could tackle with gusto. And Dorothy knew just how she would tackle this one.

She'd had enough of scavenging a ride. She'd had enough of begging and borrowing. It was time to take the board to task on the matter.

The hospital should have a motorcar of its own.

In a series of letters, Dorothy pressed her case. First tentatively, then with greater and greater urgency. But as strident as her thoughts on the matter were, Dorothy always modulated them into gentle yet firm, compelling arguments when she wrote to the Board. She couched every justification for an automobile in diplomatic phrases, laudatory words, and subtle reminders of the noble goals the missionary board had in mind when they conceived the very idea of a hospital for women and children in this remote locale.

In truth, she was quite astonished when the words had barely formed in her mind before the idea began to take shape in reality.

Somehow she'd chosen convincing words and the Board had quite readily agreed. In fact, they were surprised she had not pressed the matter earlier. Why of course she should have a motorcar. And she must certainly acquire one. As soon as she could come up with the funds.

Their response both elated and deflated her. Of course she could have a car. Of course she *should* have a car. They'd agreed!

And dropped the matter right back in her lap.

The hospital was barely scraping along with the few rupees they collected from patients here and there. There were no funds that could be diverted to the purchase of a vehicle.

But Dorothy said *thank you, Lord. I think.*

And before Dorothy even had a chance to stew over the Board's conditional answer, things began to happen.

First, a wealthy patient paid over and above his wife's hospital fee. Then an unexpected check came from a stateside patron. Together with a few dollars she was prepared to donate from her own personal funds she had enough to purchase the automobile.

With less cajoling than she had expected, the missionary board agreed to cover shipping and made the actual purchase—with her funds, of course—a Chevrolet, she had insisted, since there were no machinists who could service a Ford in all of Assam.

~~~~~~

The other day I received a letter from the Fed agency in Calcutta stating that they had been ordered by the Bombay agency to deliver to us a new Ford Touring car. The letter was addressed to Dr. Kenny Kin, Hospital, Gauhati.

Edna thought that it might be the gift of a man at home who was much interested in the hospital when Dr. Clossen was out here. I wrote telling them that I would take delivery as soon as I could travel to Calcutta.

They wrote back that inasmuch as I had not signed my name as Dr. Kenny Kin they would have to insist on a letter of introduction. Charlie wrote one, but I have had a hunch that it may be the car that the Board has purchased although I have never had a word from them about any.

I am wiring them this morning to hold it until I know who is sending it. If it is a private gift, all well and good—one can't look a gift horse in the mouth.

If the Board has purchased it with my money, there will be fireworks, because we don't want a Ford when the Chevrolets are almost the same price and when the only service station is for Chevy cars.

I am leaving tomorrow night for Calcutta but hope to be back in about five or six days. Hope to make final arrangements and pick up the car while there and investigate several other things and also visit some of the hospitals. I have a list a yard long of errands for various people.

Among other things I am looking forward to having a bath in a real tub (the first in six months) and perhaps a steak if such can be found. I may take in a movie also. (Frivolous person.)

Before dawn that morning Dorothy rose to write a letter home and then took a few moments to pack for her trip. She washed quickly in the only tub available to her out here, shivering as she stood in the four-foot-square cement depression, whose four-inch depth drained through a pipe that led to the area in back of the bungla. A large terracotta cauldron held water that she dipped into a shallow basin to rinse herself off when she was ready.

The cold water raised gooseflesh in the brisk pre-dawn as it splashed downward, taking the soapy residue with it, and she burrowed into the towel she'd left warming on the brazier. She was clean, invigorated. And quite chilled. She should have waited until sunup.

But the unwelcome blessing of a bath taken in this manner guaranteed one thing. She was most assuredly wide awake.

Her day would no doubt become hectic, but the tranquility of this morning soon had her traipsing quite sassily from closet to bed. Now she carefully folded the new afternoon tea dress she had finally finished making for the excursion to Calcutta. Just in time.

A motorcar! Oh, the freedom of it! To speed out to a village on a medical call, no waiting for a cart. To take a Sunday jaunt and leave mile after mile separating her from the hospital compound. It seemed too much to hope for. And yet her personal funds together with those of a generous donor have made it happen.

In a scant few precious hours she would take the night train to Calcutta, collect the car, see to its proper registration, fill the backseat with the shopping she would do for herself and for her staff, enjoy a steak and a *real* bath—maybe even two of each—and a couple of days later make her merry way home.

A guilty twinge crimped her smile when she considered for a moment the scandalous idea of driving the car back from Calcutta herself. Three hundred miles. Unaccompanied. Horrors!

But no. She would be a good girl and arrange for it to be shuttled out here by some very appropriate and not at all scandalous lackey. And he'd better not put a dent in it, either.

Just getting to wear her new tea dress at the Great Eastern was treat enough for Dorothy. *The cat's pajamas, if I do say so myself,* she thought as she fingered the tucks and darts of the fresh new tea dress she had designed after scouring the months-old copy of Vogue her sister had sent. Stolen moments here and there at her intrepid sewing machine had paid off. But to give credit where credit was due, it had not hurt that her sewing project fell right at the celebration of the Red Powder Pujah.

Yesterday, true to our established custom, we had a sewing bee (it's the time of the Red Powder Pujah when no one can go outside the compound without risk of having one's clothes and person covered with this nasty red stain which doesn't come out easily).

Spent the day at the other bungalow, and I helped Lola cut and fit a dress for herself, made a pair of felt slippers or rather shoes for Leila Forbes' baby, and did a bit of finish work on my new tea dress. We really had a lovely day.

The dress had turned out handsomely. The dress *and* the walking suit *and* the new lingerie she'd brought from Bloomingdales on her fifth-year furlough would make her feel she was showing Calcutta a bit of Fifth Avenue.

Truth be told, perhaps the greatest joy would be in not having to wear the clunky old Oxfords. She dropped her sensibly-heeled but oh-so-lovely strapped leather pumps into the suitcase, wondering idly when she might have last worn them.

In short order her weekender was packed to the gills with everything she would need to get through a week on the coast. She could carry her light linen duster over one arm. No need to risk wrinkling it in the suitcase.

> Wish there was somebody to go with me, but Ruth Paul isn't going until the 6th and that would hold things up here too much. However, I think that by tipping the station agent (that is common custom out here) I can have first class accommodations on a second class ticket. That is frequently done for women traveling alone.

Traveling alone.

She didn't mind it so terribly much, even though the overwhelming wish for a companion sat at the back of her mind and heart most days of late. Someone to share her life. Someone to lighten the burden. Was that too much to ask?

> I wish that we could have a husband or two—we wouldn't want more than one a piece, but it would help out on the work so much if we could just have some men around to look after some of the details that take our time. The General Board lets its missionaries have wives to do this, and I don't think it would be amiss for us to have husbands.

If wishes were horses, then beggars would ride. Still, a girl could dream, could she not?

She whistled her way along the path as she headed to the hospital and nearly missed the warning shouts coming to her from the window next to the pharmaceutical dispensary.

"Please, Dr. Kinney, wait! Do not be coming in!"

What in the world? Dorothy gaped for a moment, then chuckled. It was sweet of them, but really, she didn't need a send-off. She would only be gone a few days.

Dorothy waited with one foot on the cool paved step to the hospital's front entrance. A gentle breeze had kept a spring in her Garbo gait this morning, and now the cool air wafted about her knees, nudging the rayon pleats of her skirt and sending a welcome coolness beneath her slip. The rayon was clearly the wrong choice for today. Better she had chosen cotton that breathed, cotton that might do justice to this rogue little zephyr. Not cloying rayon that blocked the air, but cotton that welcomed the breeze to cool her to the bone on this warm summer day.

That was the way of it here in early summer. Get chilled through trying to bathe before dawn, and roast ten minutes after the sun comes up. She should have worn something different today. But it was too late now. Everything cooler, except for her travel suit, was already packed.

One hand captured her fluttering skirt and the other captured the small curls at her temple that had turned out rather nicely this morning. She stepped onto the porch slab and stopped again as the little nurse popped her head out of the window and took up waving her arms madly.

A whiff of what the breeze had just carried to her nostrils suddenly triggered understanding. Dorothy no longer needed the flurry of warning. Her own nose had sounded an alarm.

The little zephyr wafting merrily about her brought with it the strong odor of Perigoric.

And vinegar.

And nitric acid.

"Bhuba! Are you all right?" She rushed to the young nursing attendant and grabbed up her hands, flipping them front to back to see if she had burned herself with the acid. At the same moment that she realized the little nurse was not injured, she heard it.

Screeching.

Crashing.

Frantic scolding voices.

And something not quite—

"Bhuba? Oh dear heavens! Tell me that's not a—?"

Bhuba's head bobbed up down and sideways. "Yes, Dr. Kinney. A monkey! He has broken everything!"

Dorothy stepped into the vestibule and ducked just as a beaker sailed past her and broke against the far wall. The stench of unhealthy urine flared about her.

Evidently the monkey had quite an arm.

From her vantage point she saw two fellows running around the dispensary, chasing a monkey who easily evaded capture as he sent missile after missile in their direction.

Expensive ammo.

Better he had burned his rascally little hands with the nitric, she thought as she grabbed up a sheet from the linen basket.

"Bhuba! Take the other end of the sheet and hold it like this, high as you can without leaving a gap at the floor."

Bhuba understood, and together they unfurled the sheet like a sail between them. With a nod to one another, they stepped into the pharmacy and tightened the sail into a rippling white wall that advanced slowly toward the monkey, successfully dividing the small room in half. The daft animal looked them over, as if considering what kind of playground this might be.

Monbahadur, the hospital's indispensable man of business, and his groundsman, Pavi, crouched motionless, more in a defensive mode than one indicating they thought they could actually capture the diminutive rogue.

"Don't go near him, gentlemen. We'll go slowly and work our way across and herd the cheeky devil toward the window. Monbahadur, go outside on the verandah and open the window as wide as you can, please." She dropped her chin and turned her most non-threatening gaze upon the little marauder.

"Slowly, Bhuba. Very slowly." She spoke in the lazy speech of one half asleep so as not to spook the monkey. "Then when the window is open we'll make a sudden move. On my count."

Without a sound the window swung open.

"All right," she said. "I will count to three and on three—not *after* three, but *on* three—we'll jump and send the monkey out the window. Ready?"

Bhuba nodded, never for a second taking her wild eyes off the intruding imp.

"One."

The monkey crouched.

"Two."

Bhuba stifled a squeal.

"Three."

The monkey sprang.

At the same instant Dorothy jumped forward, but Bhuba jumped backward, pulling the sheet from their hands. The monkey leaped from the counter and ran between them, catching the sheet in his curling tail.

He fled out the door and made straight for the jungle, trailing the sheet like a ghost on a mission.

Precious sulfa tablets skittered across the floor in the monkey's wake, drawing the gaping eyes of all four humans back into the room. The tablets stopped rolling when they hit expanding pools of vinegar and began to dissolve. It was mayhem's finest hour.

Her first instinct was to rush in and gather up the spilled medicines. But sanity took the upper hand and she reached for a broom.

"It is all sacrificed, Bhuba. Nothing can be used."

"But, Dr. Kinney, look! Some are dry!" She swept a few up in her tiny brown hand and held them out to Dorothy who swatted them out of the girl's palm as gently as she could. In the same fluid motion she reached for a bottle of disinfectant that had escaped the monkey's notice and set to cleaning her own hands and then Bhuba's.

"Dry yes," she smiled, "but compromised nevertheless." Dorothy sighed as she looked about. Was the monkey just an innocent rascal? Or did he carry the horrid disease Kala Azar? It was impossible to know.

"That rascal broke the jars these were in, and may have picked them up and tossed them around, spit on them, sat on them. We can't take a chance. We can't risk introducing E. coli or something even worse by administering medicines that have been handled by a possibly disease-ridden monkey. They must go. All of them. Every last pill and tongue depressor and—"

The break in her voice sounded strange to her own ears, so rarely did she give voice to emotion in front of her staff. But this struck wickedly at her confidence, this massive loss. A loss they could ill afford and from which they might take months to recover. Yet in another instant her mind cleared. She knew what she would do.

She'd take the night train to Calcutta, as planned. Then she'd go first to the telegraph desk at the Great Eastern Hotel and get the list of medicines that needed replacing. Doctoroni and Lahaori would have plenty of time to make the list and wire it to her—as soon as the pharmacy was sterilized, fumigated, and restored to order. Somehow she'd get the suppliers to accept credit with a small down payment. And she would not dillydally in the city. No luxurious baths. No movies. No dinners on the hotel terrace.

She'd get there, get the car, get the medicines.

And get home.

DOCTORONI ALICE MARK CONDUCTS A VILLAGE DISPENSARY

STUDENT NURSE, KATHUNUA, BESSIE, AND BHUBA

CHAPTER TEN

MEN!

The first class compartment to which the porter escorted her had provided a brief haven for Dorothy after the morning's altercation with the raiding monkey. Minute by minute she felt herself decompress, felt her fingers relax from the clenching fists they'd formed much of the day.

A whole day in Calcutta. That's what she would allow herself. A whole day free of the demands of the hospital. It wasn't the week she'd planned on, but a gift, nevertheless. Nothing could sully it. Unless, of course, it kept raining.

She settled into her berth for the night and surprised herself by dropping right off to sleep. By the time she rose, dressed, and breakfasted, the sky was clear, and the day fresh and promising. At least that was the case until just before noon when she stepped off the train at the end of the Assam-Bengal line in Calcutta.

For all the efficient planning she'd done as she rocked her way to the coast, Dorothy's day soon disintegrated into a bevy of failed missions. First, she'd gone to the Great Eastern Hotel and collected the wire from Gauhati. The list wasn't actually quite as dreadful as she'd expected.

Then she checked into the hotel. Or rather, she tried. But there was not a single room to be had. The next three hotels down the row gave her the same answer, delivered by scowling clerks who wondered how a single female might dare to come looking for a room without a reservation.

The fourth, for obvious reasons, did have a vacancy. But she'd have to scour the tub five or six times before she dared climb into it. And the bed—well, it appeared a bit cleaner than the tub. A bit.

Not to be deterred by this minor setback, she located the medical supply house and ordered the medicines. It went like a dream at the outset. She was only too happy to discover that Doctoroni's entire list was available. It would have been a small victory had she been allowed to gather her purchases and head home. But as luck would have it, the actual goods had to be collected from various storehouses throughout the city, and the packages could not be delivered to her hotel until the morning after next.

There went her hopes for a speedy return.

Her next stop was the customs office where the Ford touring car waited for her to claim it.

And that's when things went sideways.

. . . .

"Yes, yes. It is all understood, Memsahib. And where is Mr. Kenny Kin?"

Horsefeathers! She'd stood here for twenty minutes trying to cajole the man, and his obtuse refusal to understand was making her quite cross.

"For the forty-leventh time, sir, there is no Mister Kenny Kin. Or rather, Mister Kenny Kin is me. I am Dr. Dorothy Kinney. Whoever took this information by telephone put down the Assamese reference 'Kennykin'. But there is no actual Kennykin, just me. Kinney. Dorothy Joy Kinney. Doctor. And I'm here to collect my car."

Dorothy cringed. Had she just stamped her foot? Impossible. She wouldn't do such a thing. Would she?

The man just stood there gaping at her. *Oh for pity's sake.* Now she'd gone and frightened him. A quick assessment of her pursed lips, rigid spine, raised eyebrows and driven tone told the tale. Such behavior could only instill a fear that the woman who stood before him was about to attack.

Lord help me, she thought as she drew a slow, measured breath. *I'd be afraid of me, too.*

Dorothy relaxed her lips and coaxed a smile, lowered her voice and slowed her speech. "You're so very patient with me, sir. Let me see if I might explain this a bit better. You see," she hesitated and modestly dropped her eyes. "The Assam provincial officer sent the letter of introduction your people requested.

I am here to pick up my Ford touring car which has been bought and paid for. This letter announcing its arrival came to me at the women's hospital in Gauhati where I am director and chief surgeon."

She held the letter in front of his eyes.

"But this letter is to Mr. Kenny Kin."

Dorothy groaned. "Yes. But I am Mr. Kenny Kin. It—"

"No, this cannot be."

"The letter was incorrectly addressed, Sahib. It says 'Mr.' instead of 'Dr.' A simple typing error. Now if you will just hand me the form I will sign and pay your customs fee and be on my way."

"Yes, yes. But this cannot be done without the letter of introduction. You get the letter and all will be well!"

"All will be well. Won't that be nice?" She smiled to cover her impatience. "But you see, the letter of introduction went to the Federal office."

And, as it turned out, so did she.

By the time all was said and done, Dorothy made three trips between the customs office and the federal office before the keys to the touring car were finally in her possession. It seemed the federal office couldn't release the letter of introduction without the title, and the customs office wouldn't release the car and title without the letter of introduction.

In the end, a congenial British fellow came on duty while the first fellow she'd been dealing with went for afternoon tea and voila! She had the letter in hand and a title to boot, no thanks to the men who had made it a supremely trying experience.

She had been on the verge of embarrassing herself multiple times, but by sheer force of will she maintained her poise, and now that she was the owner of a beautiful motorcar, she wasn't sure which might be harder to tame—a four-cylinder beast or her own temper.

Yes, it was a Ford. But it was *her* Ford. She'd figure out the servicing of it somehow. It wasn't brain surgery, after all. Some clever fellow would surely sort it all out.

Her victory at the customs office seemed to turn the tide. She stopped back in at the Great Eastern to send a cable to the compound to let them know she'd be home on Thursday. Once it was on its way across the wires, she headed to the door where the hotel's concierge caught up with her and handed her a note from the nice young man at the government office who had been so very helpful.

He had collected her bag at the rundown hotel, paid for the use of the room there for the part of the day it had been occupied by her weekender and dress bag, and somehow cajoled the imperious clerk at the Great Eastern to find a room for her—at the government rate, no less.

~~~~~~

I had two tub baths a day while in Calcutta and Oh Boy but they felt good. I lost about two pounds while there and guess it was the extra dirt that came off as a result of real baths. I also had some delicious lamb chops (steaks don't seem to grow in this part of the country due to the sacredness of the cow. But, never mind, I'll be coming home one of these years and then—well, you may as well begin to save money for the steaks that I shall ask for.)

The greatest problem solved by her knight in shining armor whose name she couldn't actually remember truly humbled her. It seemed, he said, that there was a partially filled freight car heading back to Gauhati, and he had taken the liberty of reserving it for her Ford. If, that is, she could deliver it to the loading dock at the train station by five o'clock on Wednesday.

Dorothy hadn't even realized she'd related her multiple dilemmas to the young man. But apparently she had. And apparently he had some admirable connections in Calcutta.

He had singlehandedly solved her problems and completely redeemed the entire male species and hadn't even stayed around for so much as a thank you. She'd slept like a dream on the overnight ride, safe in the knowledge that her Ford was carefully strapped onto a flatcar a dozen railcars back.

When she woke and discovered that her walking suit had fallen off the hanger and lay badly wrinkled in the bottom of the dress bag, she didn't even scowl. Her tea dress had come through without a crease. It was the perfect dress—in fact the only dress—she could imagine wearing for this triumphant homecoming. After all, she was bringing the hospital's very first motor car back to the Satribari Compound this afternoon. And she would be behind the wheel.

She had shamelessly bribed the fellow who off-loaded her Ford from the railcar into driving it—and her—to an abandoned area in the railyard. After a brief lesson, she spent the next hour driving circles and figure 8's about the lot, stopping and starting, and signaling turns. It hadn't occurred to her until she got on the road that she'd forgotten one major element. Backing up. But she would tackle that particular skill at a later date.

Dorothy down-shifted with less grace than she intended and pulled into the long lane that led to the entrance of the Gauhati Hospital for Women and Children.

She smiled at the sign that greeted her. She smiled at the villagers who waved to her. She slowed to five miles per hour and with one hand retrieved her garden hat from the passenger seat. It most definitely was not the right hat for motoring, the way it flapped madly in the wind and threatened to take sail if her foot became the tiniest bit heavy on the accelerator. So it had ridden from the station in the seat of honor.

But now it just felt right to put it on and arrive in full festive array.

She beeped the horn cheerfully as she slowed to a stop and laughed outright at the staff who poured out onto the verandah to see what in the world all the fuss was about.

"Doctor Kinney!" Lahaori cried. "It is a thing of beauty!" She walked all the way around the car fingering it with graceful awe, then grabbed Dorothy in a crushing hug. "It is yours?"

Dorothy laughed. "It is ours!"

The staff and ambulatory patients crowded around now, caressing the black leather upholstery, rolling the windows up and down, tooting the horn, and remarking in awe over every small feature. The air seemed charged, the very day electric, as Dorothy stood back to watch.

This was indeed a great moment. A very, very great day. She would remember this moment in its smallest detail.

"Doctor Kinney, there is a—"

"Oh, Lahaori, give us a moment, just a moment to watch. Isn't it marvelous?" She somehow couldn't let Lahaori end the moment for her. Not just yet.

"But Doc—"

"Lahaori, really, is it something so important? I just brought home our new motorcar. We should celebrate!"

Lahaori lifted her chin and raised a brow in the stern look Dorothy recognized. It was the look that told her with all due respect she had better be quiet and listen. It was rare enough, to be sure, but when she saw that look on Lahaori's face, she paid immediate attention.

In a flash the car was forgotten.

"What is it, Lahaori?"

The young woman's face softened. "The headmaster from Jorhat has come."

"Oh my, all the way from Jorhat? Is it serious?"

Now Lahaori glanced away, an odd look in her eye. "We think perhaps it is. You must see him straight away."

The last time she'd seen the Jorhat headmaster was at his wife's funeral. It had been a heartbreaking scene, so devoted had he been to the woman who had accepted with hesitant heart her husband's missionary appointment to Jorhat. Her illness had claimed her here, in Dorothy's hospital, half a world away from her own home. It must be very serious indeed for the fellow to have returned to the scene of such misery.

Dorothy took a step toward the door and was jarred back into the moment by the light feminine swish of her tea dress. She stopped and turned. "Oh my! Lahaori, dear, get my bag. I'll change in my office. Where is he waiting?"

Lahaori stifled the smallest smile that threatened to overtake the corner of her mouth.

"No, Doctor Kinney. No time to change your clothes."

"Don't be silly, I—"

"No time, Doctor Kinney. He is waiting."

Lahaori stood stock still, her hands clasped at her waist, her eyes fixed upon something beyond Dorothy's left shoulder. Dorothy straightened her skirt and smoothed the bodice of her tea dress. It was entirely discreet, but not at all the appropriate décolletage for examining patients. And in particular not appropriate for a medical consultation with the handsome widower from Jorhat.

Her memory flashed images of the bookish gentleman she'd met the year before at his ailing wife's bedside. He was kind, compassionate, clever, and completely clueless as to his masculine appeal.

She cleared her throat and lifted her chin, understanding in that instant why there was the trace of a smile on Lahaori's face.

"He's behind me, isn't he."

CHAPTER ELEVEN

THE EARTH MOVED

One never really expects the truly earth-shaking events that insinuate themselves into an otherwise ordinary life. They always seem to take a person unawares. While Dorothy's life was far from ordinary compared to the lives of her stateside friends and family, it had nevertheless become quite comfortably ordinary to her over the years.

Women came to the hospital. She treated them and sent them on their way. She dealt with men only as they appeared as husbands and fathers of women and children in her care. She'd treated one male patient in the years she'd been there, and only agreed to that because of his status and the fact that a government official practically begged her to do so.

But to do that, incredibly strict arrangements had to be made. A private room had been quickly prepared for him, far removed from the female patients in the hospital. She had made certain that he was dealt with in the most cautious manner that would ensure that both his dignity and the female nurses' modesty remained intact. And to ensure that they did not lose their license.

The government allowed them to serve women and children. Period.

So when her heart lurched each time she touched the headmaster from Jorhat, she put it up to the simple fact that she rarely examined an English male and had never before, in her tenure at Gauhati, examined a male of the American variety.

But he had a prescription. An official dispensation, of sorts, approving his treatment here. The headmaster required treatments twice weekly for an extended period, and the treatment could only be performed at a hospital. If it couldn't be done in Gauhati, his only other option was to leave his work for an extended stay in Calcutta.

So here he was, a hair's breadth away. In her office. Smiling.

Perhaps it was the fellow's malady that created the unsettled feeling, the fact that in order to investigate his claim of impacted sinuses she was forced to lean close, hold his head at the proper angle, and rest a steadying hand on his square jaw.

A tangent of her thoughts whirled through other maladies that might have been less compromising to examine. A broken leg, perhaps.

No, that would mean she'd have to lay bare his knee and calf that, from what little she had seen, were sturdy and lithe, and laced with the sinewy bands of an inveterate athlete.

No, no broken legs, please.

But perhaps...Dorothy shut down that line of thinking. There was clearly no part of the man's anatomy that was going to make this any easier for her.

To her surprise, she had managed to maintain a professional demeanor through the initial exam in spite of the fact that she was conducting it in a dress suitable only for a garden party. The swishing tea-length chiffon constantly set her off guard as she moved around her patient, and she had become completely annoyed at the havoc it had wreaked with her medical demeanor.

At the first available moment she fled to the bungalow and changed into her usual attire. By the time she delivered a supper tray to the good headmaster, she had herself completely back in control, safely armored in her clinical white coat.

By the next day, just as she had expected, she had herself well in hand.

"Well, Mr. Chambers, it looks—"

"Fled."

"Pardon?"

"Fned."

She laughed. The cotton she'd packed into the poor fellow's nostrils had rendered him unable to speak clearly.

"Oh! Um, well, yes, Fred, I, er, um..." Dorothy cleared her throat and probably would have stamped her foot had it not been so close to her patient's own toes.

She'd sat with her patient as he ate his dinner the previous evening, and they'd become so immediately companionable that they had quite naturally agreed to a first-name basis. But now, in the light of day, with her in her white coat and him with his head in her hands, first names seemed awkward.

But she had agreed.

"It's looking good, Fred. You're responding nicely to the overnight treatment, I'm happy to see."

"Gnuk."

"Yes, good. I agree!"

Her hand involuntarily patted Mr. Chambers' cheek and she stifled her horror at the familiar gesture, hoping he had not noticed.

His head was turned slightly away, making it impossible for her to read his reaction, but as she raised her head, she saw what he saw.

Her lovely Bohemian mirror hung on the wall opposite them, and could not have more perfectly framed their two faces if she had carefully and purposefully arranged it to do so.

He'd been watching her.

And now their eyes met, in the colorful mirror, framed for only an instant, but capturing a moment that would shape their lives.

He was the first to break their mirrored eye contact. And as she watched, mesmerized, Fred turned his head away from the mirror, raised himself from his half-reclining position, and kissed her cheek.

He had noticed.

· · · ·

In the hours that followed, Dorothy found her step lighter, her disposition sunnier, and her brain operating in completely unfamiliar fashion. Mr. Chambers had only been in her hospital for three days, but by the time he left to return to Jorhat, she knew her world would never be the same.

He had noticed, alright. And so had she. And every moment since that brief kiss on her cheek had spun itself out in glittery newness. Nothing felt the same, looked the same, tasted the same. And nothing could ever again capture her entire attention—because the dearest corner of her mind was now preoccupied with one Fred Chambers.

How swiftly it had happened. How stunningly simple it had been to open her heart to him. And how thoroughly shattering it had been to wave him goodbye when they came from the Jorhat School for Boys to collect him.

Dorothy reseated the hair pin that had failed to keep her curls out of her eyes. The curls were damp now, after tumbling for too long across her perspiring forehead in the insufferable heat.

Thank heaven Fred had come last week, when they'd had an unseasonably cool spell. Her sweating chin would certainly not have attracted such a thing as the dear kiss he had so briefly planted on her cheek.

She'd tried desperately not to read too much into that kiss, but every glance from him throughout that day and evening had assured her it had not been forgotten by him. And then, when it came time to leave, he held her hand a few breaths too long, and captured her eyes with his, and she had known.

Oh, yes, he had noticed, alright.

And it had shaken her to her core.

So it was not at all surprising to her when the very ground beneath her feet began to quake. Indeed, at first she hadn't even recognized that this time the ground was truly shaking. And it had nothing whatsoever to do with Fred Chambers.

~~~~~~

Wednesday night, July 2nd, Alice, Marian, Grace and Ruth left Gauhati for Missourie (or however you spell it—it isn't Missouri at any rate). We went to the train to see them off. We came home and retired early as we were tired and it was pretty hot.

At three fifteen I woke suddenly to find myself sitting on the edge of my bed and the house swaying like everything—all the doors and windows rattling, and heard Edna call for me. Got on a kimono and slippers altho I bumped my head on the key in my bathroom door while stooping for a pair of heavier slippers. The house continued to sway and rock, but by the time I had gotten out to the verandah it was subsiding a bit. That earthquake, according to the telegraph office here where it was timed, lasted four minutes.

We all gathered on the verandah, and during the next hour there were four more of much lesser intensity. We then went back to bed, but not to sleep. There were four more before seven, and they kept on recurring every hour or so for the next two days. I lost count of them after twenty.

One of the telegraph sahibs said that there were sixty and over altogether. Here in Gauhati one of the merchants' houses was badly damaged and two men were seriously hurt. Otherwise there were no injuries. Here on the compound there was quite a bit of plaster knocked off in one place in the hall and in one place on the front verandah. But in the dispensary—Boy Howdy—it looked as though seventeen monkeys had been turned lose with malice aforethought. Bottles of medicine were strewn over the floors, many of them broken, and pills, powders, stains, etc. in one grand mess. Our big bottle that we use for distilled water for washing the slides (16 rupees) was broken into fifty pieces. We got Monbahadur and some of the coolies to work clearing up and cleaning up, and things began to look better.

The patients were not as frightened as the night nurses were. Doctoroni went over and found the two night nurses outside. She lectured them properly about staying with the ship, etc. Early in the morning when the husband of a private room case came to see if all was well with his wife, one of these nurses assured him that if the patient died, they would die with her.

Kika, one of the nurses, thought that the end of the world had come, and stayed in her bed praying until the others called to her to come outside. It was not until today that the papers came and the telegraph lines have been down so that practically no news was obtained until the first train came thru yesterday.

At one point about 160 miles from here about twenty miles of track were broken by the bed sinking down. From a letter from Marian we found out that the girls arrived in Calcutta safely and not too late, but that in spite of their being almost in the heart of it, they didn't know that there had been an earthquake until they saw the papers in Calcutta. They evidently attributed the jolts, etc., to a rough road bed. It is notoriously rough over that particular stretch.

It seemed remarkable to Dorothy that the whole episode of caring for a hospital full of patients through a month-long spate of over sixty earthquakes and hundreds of tremors could come to feel so commonplace. For a while it had simply become the new normal.

But whether in matters geological, or in matters of the heart, Dorothy knew that there was nothing whatsoever normal about the manner in which her world had just been shaken.

FRED CHAMBERS
MISSIONARY TO JORHAT

CHAPTER TWELVE

AND TIME STOOD STILL

If Fred Chambers' presence in her life upended Dorothy and set her racing pellmell toward her future, nothing could have stopped time in its tracks more swiftly for her than another emergency foray into the Garo hills.

In so many ways these emergencies were much the same, and yet again each case had its own unique aspect. Each time she came up against a new challenge as she knelt on the floor of a Garo hut, she remembered that first time.

How could she not? Even though there had been hundreds like that first unspeakably jolting experience in her first year in Gauhati, none had truly been more eye-opening than her first case. That night was stamped like a firebrand in her memory, the shocking encounter with a rampaging case of tetanus and the havoc it had wreaked on a simple matter of childbirth.

It happened on February 5th of 1929, little more than six weeks into her mission. She had attended less than a dozen emergencies away from the hospital when this late night cry for help brought Dorothy and the assisting nurse to the hut of a woman who'd suffered horribly for three days before anyone thought to send to the hospital for help.

I love the work here more and more all the time and wouldn't trade places with anyone that I know of. ... About five o'clock there came a call to go out into the jungle on an OB call. It was dark when we got there and the house was dark. It was one of the "better class" huts according to S (the midwife), but looked rather dubious to me. Thatched roof, matting walls etc. There were four lamps which were about the size of my little alcohol lamp and smoked like the dickens.

The woman was lying on a mat on the floor and grouped around her in this room were sixteen women, most of them with a small baby in their arms. In the front room was a circle of men, most of them relatives. S got her things out and put them on a mat on the floor. One of the women brought me a mat to sit on. I finally decided that I might as well. I guess I sat rather gingerly (not being able to see where I was sitting, and knowing that S had just kicked a dead rat off the mat where the woman was lying).

A lecture on cleanliness had threatened to spew from her novice lips as Dorothy had focused on the deathly pallor of the young woman who lay moaning on the mat. Death then as now was the last thing Dorothy would countenance. She had not come to India to allow death an easy inroad. And yet the gray-tinged face that lay beneath her mostly steady hand said death may have already found an open door.

No matter how many years had passed, images from that night were forever burned in her mind's eye.

The woman was barely twenty, her small body terribly brutalized by the labor of the previous thirty hours. The mat was filthy with fluids both new and crusted, the rags that covered her clearly heavy with grime. A few of the women who hovered at the outer fringes seemed freshly bathed and their colorful tunics danced prettily in the light of Dorothy's Coleman lantern. How they managed to look fresh and unsoiled in these impoverished circumstances was nothing short of miraculous.

The women closer by, who tended to the needs of the young patient, had been dressed in rags that could be cast away when the ordeal was over. Their tatters twirled and floated as they tried to conceal their movements, but Dorothy had seen what it was that they had just pitched out of the hut.

The dead rat.

To any seasoned eye, this poor young woman had to die. How could she not, after thirty hours struggling on the dung-glazed floor of her home, as its bacteria-laced varnish mingled with the blood on her soaked limbs and invaded her weakened system.

Centuries-old birthing practices in this ancient Indian community dictated that any articles coming in contact with birth fluids must be burned. So risking contamination of bedding and bed clothes that would have to be destroyed would have been irresponsible, would have been simply too great a sacrifice for these frugal people, to say nothing of the fact that it would have gone against their closely held religious tenets.

Women had no other choice. They birthed their babes on rush mats laid on the maliciously gleaming floor, the floor that could be easily swept, the dirt floor made shiny and smooth by multiple coats of varnish concocted from water and cow manure. The floor that guaranteed a fifty-fifty chance that either mother or child—or both—would contract deadly infections.

These were the women for whom Dorothy had come to do battle. These were the women she'd found in this remote outpost, this place that had no hospital beds, no instrument sterilizers, no bassinets or x-ray equipment in those early years.

And for that matter, no electricity or running water at the time.

She'd labored here for a mere month by then, with none of the tools of the trade her American associates enjoyed. No sterile operating room, no well-trained nurses to tend the patients on whom she performed surgery.

She had her skill. Her intellect. Her ingenuity. And a small staff with a tenacious will to support her.

The rest she had figured out on the fly.

Within seconds of encountering the young woman, a sour gorge had risen in Dorothy's throat and left its bitter sting on her tongue. In order to examine the woman, she had to kneel—or squat—in the middle of the mess that had so recently been vacated by a rat. But Dorothy had abandoned all thought of the filth through which her shoes were sliding and tucked her dress beneath her knees as she knelt beside the woman to confirm the midwife's assessment. The rigid cervix and hardened tissue surrounding it validated her fears.

"Tetanus," she whispered, and her aging associate nodded.

In no time at all it had become clear to both women that neither the mother nor the child would survive without radical measures. The woman's cervix, completely paralyzed from the tetanus she had already contracted, could never accomplish its work of expanding to allow the delivery of the child. And yet the child had begun its journey. It had descended into the birth canal, its head pressing on the frozen cervix harder and harder with each contraction.

"What would you do?" Dorothy had asked, searching the midwife's eyes for evidence of a solution.

The woman sighed and rocked back on her heels. "Nothing to be done. She's too far into labor and no way to open the gate."

Dorothy bit back an astonished reply and swallowed to restore her clinical control. "But we must. It could be days before they both succumb. You know the agony that would entail." She waited until her weary associate raised her head to look at her. "For both of them."

The midwife turned away. "I'm well aware, Dr. Kinney. I wager I've seen it more times than you, and it will never be something I can stomach. But I say again, there is nothing to be done." She wiped her instruments and sighed. "I'll speak to the headwoman."

Dorothy lifted the young mother's limp wrist to take her pulse, and started as the woman wiggled her hand free and clutched Dorothy's. She looked at Dorothy, her eyes pleading as her other hand fluttered spastically to her abdomen. Lying in squalor as she was, it seemed the most eloquent supplication Dorothy had ever witnessed. There was no doubt what she meant to communicate.

Save my child.

The sound of mourning began quietly in a corner of the hut. The midwife was telling them—this woman's friends—what to expect. It would be horrific. It would be so hellish that they would all abandon her and she would die here. Alone. Cradling her dying child within her womb.

Dorothy studied the looks that passed from woman to woman. Disappointment turned to resignation in an instant. One gave a small nod to another. It seemed to be an instruction, or perhaps a granting of permission. Permission to begin mourning?

Understanding crawled to the pit of Dorothy's stomach. It was not permission to begin mourning. It was permission of a far more terminal sort.

They knew how to end the suffering. They would administer some kind of merciful end as soon as she and the midwife left.

That's how it was done. That's what was expected.

"Wait."

Dorothy smiled at the women.

The murmuring stopped.

"What?" The midwife frowned.

"I said wait. We'll take her to the hospital."

"Dorothy, no, you can't. She'll die. It's too far. They'll die anyway. The babe's too far into the canal for a Caeserean."

Dorothy turned to her friend, the old woman who had performed her share of medical wonders. "But I'm not going to deliver the babe by Caeserean," she smiled.

"Then...how..."

Dorothy inhaled, the long, steady breath affirming her belief that she had made the right decision.

"I'm going to remove her cervix."

· · · ·

It had been bold. It had been daring. It had been rife with risk.

And it had been enough. A young American doctor's skill, her courage, and God's good grace had won the night, and twenty-four hours later the new mother lay recovering in the Gauhati hospital in the most sterile environment Dorothy's primitive circumstances could muster in those early days.

Death had been near, and the Great Physician nearer. It felt good. It felt... powerful. And it frightened her more than any other thing in her life. The woman should have died, and Dorothy could have let her. Because it was what they expected.

The fledgling doctor had sat at the end of her own bed at dusk the next day, weary to the bone, shaking like a leaf, and praying like she'd never prayed before.

It was You, Father, I know that it was, who guided my thoughts and willed my hands to save those two dear lives. Forgive my hesitation. Please! Forgive me that I very nearly did not take the risk!

A tear slipped down her cheek. She was in this remote outpost because she'd known better than the medical school staff what work she was best meant to do. She was here because she'd known better than every mentor in her life who tried to steer her away from her chosen medical specialty.

Strong-willed as she was, she'd always believed she knew best what course her life was meant to take. But they had sown a seed of doubt, and it had nearly made her ignore God's quiet prompt to save a mother and her child.

It would never happen again, she'd promised. And with God as her witness, she knew now—a full seven years later—that she'd been keeping her promise.

In Dorothy's Own Words

I taught myself surgery skills by correspondence study, and performed surgery under those primitive conditions. I allowed God to perform miracles through my surgeries. I often felt a divine power just beyond my fingertips as I performed some of the most difficult surgeries under many hardships. I also learned to do cataract surgery which was a big help to the people.

One day I was awakened at 2:00 A.M. A native midwife had been unable to deliver a baby at home although she had followed her usual procedure of having the woman lie on the dirt floor—because a bed or anything else touched during childbirth would have to be burned. The hard mixture of mud and dung which coated the floor was filled with tetanus and other bacteria which often caused illness in both mother and baby. This woman's cervix, covered with mud and dung, was inflexible, and both mother and baby would have died without something being done immediately. So, I removed the cervix so the baby could be born. Six months later the mother came back to the hospital, healed and happy, to express her thanks!

Let me follow up with an interesting little story! Later when I returned home on furlough and wished to pursue some special obstetrics training (which was still NOT a profession for women), one of my medical school professors asked, in a very condescending tone, what kind of cases I'd had out there. I related that case to him. His reply was, "What a radical thing to do!" I calmly asked what he would have done in such a case; he had to admit he'd never had such a case! I could honestly tell him that my cases had included every possible health problem, multiplied by cultural traditions, lack of sanitation, and the social situation.

WOMEN OF THE GARO HILLS, ASSAM

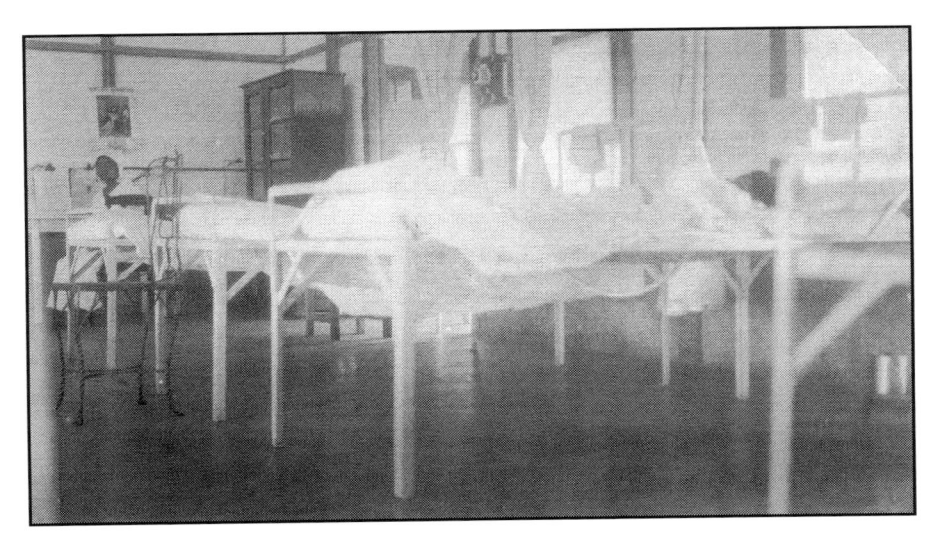

SATRIBARI COMPOUND WOMEN'S WARD

DOROTHY KINNEY 1935

CHAPTER THIRTEEN

SINGLE-BLESSEDNESS

Seven years. When she let herself think about it, the whole of it quite overwhelmed her. And now that she had met Fred, it overwhelmed her nearly every day. Finding Fred cast a lovely glow over every facet of her life. It lightened her heart in a way that made everything seem new and perfect.

It promised that she might come to know a joy that she had never thought possible for herself. And yet all the while she knew that opening her heart to that joy could also mean monumental loss. No matter how much the missionary board might value her service, would they ever entertain the idea of keeping a married woman working in the field?

Fred's letters came almost daily, and each one inched closer and closer to suggesting that somehow their individual futures were becoming entangled, though neither dared to voice just how that might come to pass, or even what it might look like. Would he come to Gauhati? Would she become a housewife or could she break the mold of her ilk and continue to work in medicine? Would she move to Jorhat, find herself forced to leave her practice and abandon her career, to assume the role of contented lady of the house? Sometimes trying to work it all out simply tied her heart in knots.

She chased that idea hastily from her mind.

She wanted to write giddy letters home, to tell her parents she'd met the most wonderful man, a man her father had actually met ten years earlier and didn't even know it, a man who had graduated on the same Colorado stage with her and they'd never known the other existed. If she had read it in a storybook she wouldn't have believed it. Yet it was true. She was living it herself.

And so was he.

He'd somehow turned the page and found her, this man who made her heart sing and her face light with joy at the prospect of another letter from him.

But nothing about Fred fit into the future that her parents understood she had carved out for herself. In fact, her father had often declared that his first-born daughter was destined for single-blessedness, so sure was he that she would live out her days as a spinster missionary.

Each time she sat down at her typewriter, the ruthless chains of single-blessedness twined so heavily about her fingers that she wrote only of the most mundane things and never dared breathe a word to them that she might be, may be, very possibly could be falling in love.

~~~~~~~~~~~~~~~~~~~~~~~~~~~~~

November 11

The Dawali Puja was celebrated on Monday night. It is sort of a puja done in order that the harvest may be plenteous. It is just about the time to harvest the rice. It is really a pretty festival and it is characterized by thousands and thousands of little lights. They make tiny shallow clay saucers, put some oil in them and a wick and light them. These are set around everywhere—lines and lines of them. It made me think a bit of the lights at Christmastime.

You should have been here the other day when the husband of a patient came to see his wife. He arrived on a huge elephant, and left the elephant parked under the portico of the hospital. It is the first time that we have ever had an elephant parked in such close proximity to the hospital. Later, Marian took some snaps—I didn't have any on hand, and then got up on its back and rode over to the bungalow where she was joined by Ethel, and then they rode back to the hospital again. Ethel said she had to hang on for dear life to keep her seat.

In the afternoon I had a queer case. A child of three came in just about wild. They said she had not slept for three days, and had eaten scarcely anything, and had been going about in circles. She was bleeding from one ear. Got one look in her ear, and then Alice gave her some Chloroform. In the next two or three minutes we removed eight nice big fat maggots, each very, very much alive, and each about ½ inch in length. One never knows what will come in next.

~~~~~~

February 2, 1936

It would be hard to convince anyone that the British Raj (rule) was not held in admiration had they been here on Tuesday. King George had requested that the mourning for him should not interfere with the regular work as he knew the hardship that it might put upon wage earners. However, there was scarcely a shop open in Gauhati all day Tuesday, and the ones that were open refused to sell even a penny's worth. The papers have been full of the details of the Lying-in-State, the funeral, etc. The Queen Mother's letter of appreciation to the Empire was published the other day and was beautiful.

~~~~~~

We are going to have to get some more babies' beds soon as yesterday we had one more baby than we had tiny beds for, and at that, both of the twins were in one basket. The hospital continues to run pretty full. We have simply got to have more money for running expenses somehow as we get only about $91 a month for all the running expenses, drugs, helpers, repairs on the compound, bungalow and hospital, and it just will not jury (cover it all). We are getting more and more cases, but we can't count on what we get from the pay cases (have had many more of them lately, and we are at a place where we can't refuse cases if we want the hospital to grow and the people who can pay to come in). With the increase in patients we have increased our income, but not in the same proportion that the overhead has been necessarily increased. If only we didn't have to think about money in connection with a hospital of this sort.

The words flowed like gibberish, all intending to sound like life as usual, but they were mere camouflage for her true feelings. She wanted desperately to tell Wink about Fred, but that would be absolutely disastrous, unless she wanted the whole world to know about him.

But that didn't keep thoughts of Fred and what he meant in her life from joining a maelstrom of thoughts that cluttered her mind one late afternoon as Dorothy walked back to the Satribari Compound from the village ghat (market) with her canvas bag smacking rhythmically against her knee.

Klunk.

How could she manage the rising hospital costs?

Ka-klunk.

Would there be a letter from Fred?

Klunk.

Where could she get more beds for the overflow of patients?

Ka-klunk.

Would Fred really be able to come down for a visit in two weeks?

Klunk.

Where in the world would they put all the newborn babies?

Ka-Klunk.

If she only had a husband, he'd build her some new bassinets.

Klunk.

How soon might she manage a trip to Jorhat?

Ka-Klunk.

What would—

"Memsahib! Memsahib!"

A male voice broke her concentration, shouting with alarm from just inches away. His urgent tone cut through her distraction, banishing thoughts of patients and babies and a certain handsome headmaster.

Dorothy stopped abruptly, startled. Her eyes fell immediately upon the reason for the man's urgent warning. Just inches from her toes sat a small pile of brick atop which sat a crude box of carpenter's tools. One more step and she would have taken a nasty fall across the jagged bricks.

And she would have ruined his tidy pile in the process.

"Oh! I...Thank you, sir!"

Her heart thudded once in relief as she looked toward the craftsman who had stopped her in her tracks. His gaunt face showed his own relief as he rubbed his hands across his makeshift apron. Tattered pants hung below, falling far too short of his muddy brown ankles and crusted feet.

She recognized the tatters immediately.

He was wearing a pair of the men's pajamas that had been gifted to the hospital! She remembered having given several pair to Monglu before tearing the rest into bandages. And in the way these things happen, they must have found their way onto the muddied legs of the man who stood before her wringing his hands.

～～～～～～～～～～

Gauhati, India

Our panniwalla or water carrier is a busy hard-working little fellow. The other day we were surprised to see him come to work in a new suit of clothes. The funny part was that it was a suit of blue and white pajamas which had come out with the White Cross charity things, and as we do not take boys over 12 at the hospital and the women don't wear them, we were unable to use them.

We finally gave them to our derzie which is the tailor and told him to sell them for us. One pair had gone to the paniwalla and he was wearing them as though they were the latest style from Paris. The legs were rolled up above the knees.

We have the matroni sweep the floors and do the bathroom work. We could get along with fewer servants if it were not for the fact that Cook will not as a rule do bearer's work and bearers will not do paniwalla's work and none of them will do the matroni's work and so it goes.

"Missahib, you must please to be careful," he chattered as he motioned for her to walk around the obstruction. The man might easily have reached for her elbow to stop her, rather than screaming in her ear, but that would have required him to touch her. And that was something he would never do.

He was low caste. Touching a high born Indian woman was a sin that could easily get him hanged, and from the habit of a lifetime, he ascribed to Dorothy that same deference.

"Thank you, kind sir, thank you!" She smiled as she daintily stepped around the man's building materials.

Once she had skirted the obstacle, Dorothy could see that the man's project was nearly finished. And it was indeed marvelous.

Three newly constructed half-walls formed an open-air verandah to one of the bunglas on the hospital compound. Unlike other similar structures, this bungalow had decorative teakwood lintels which—judging from the tools in his hands—the man had carved. The artful additions gave an unexpected grace to the little home.

Its lines were clean and plumb, its construction carefully planned and executed, unlike much of the rustic work she regularly saw about the community.

The man was a carpenter! With that realization, Dorothy whirled and nearly bumped into the poor man who seemed to be following to ensure she successfully navigated his workspace.

His distress instantly elevated as he gasped and jumped aside, so as not to touch her with his unclean, low caste hand—and promptly fell over the malicious little pile of brick.

"Oh! Oh, dear!"

Dorothy darted back around and knelt next to the writhing man. He grappled in the air to keep her hands away as she reached to stop the bleeding on his shin and there was nothing for it but to rise and back away.

"Now hold still, sir, and I shall have a bandage for you in a moment." She chatted in a soothing voice while she searched for a clean strip of linen in the bottom of her canvas market bag. There was always a bundle of bandages and a lone bottle of Tincture of Merthiolate in the bottom, along with a small bundle that held scissors, tweezers, and a few odd small instruments. This time, however, she had to dive deep into the bag to find a bandage strip that didn't match the poor fellow's pants.

"Panji humble self cannot pay, Memsahib," he wailed, and the intense agony his tone communicated told her that fact pained him far worse than his bleeding shin.

"Panji? This is your name?" she asked, and his head wobbled up and down.

"Panji, it's my fault you fell, you see, so nothing is owed me for tending to your wound."

He gulped awkwardly enough that she feared he would swallow his tongue.

"Not a thing. In fact, since I caused you to fall, it is my duty to help you."

"No, no, Memsahib!"

"Yes, Panji, it is my duty and I must do the right thing."

The air was stifling, still, practically oppressive as they hunkered there in the dirt. No monkeys chattered in the distant trees at midday. Only a single jungle bush quail cooed in the wild almond that grew crookedly behind the pretty bungla. Everyone had gone home for their post-luncheon nap. She set her bag on the ground, at the same time draping two bandages across it. Now he would not have to take anything directly from her hand. There would be no risk to him of touching her.

Moving swiftly but with great calm she retrieved the Tincture of Merthiolate and set it on the closest brick just as he reached for one of the bandages.

"Now Panji, you must use one bandage to clean your leg, then dab on the Merthiolate," she pointed to the small brown bottle and made a dabbing motion, "and then bandage the wound with this other strip. Understand?"

He grimaced, his eyes straying to the small bottle. Clearly he would avoid the stinging tincture if she were not here.

She raised her brows, cocked her head toward the little bottle, and nodded briskly. There was no doubt he understood her instruction, and he muttered as he moved to follow through with his self-inflicted torture.

"It appears to me, Panji, that you are a fine builder of...things," she said, indicating the nearly completed verandah. "A mistri?"

Panji's eyes darted toward the bungalow then back to her.

"As it happens," she continued, "I myself am in need of a carpenter...a...a mistri, such as yourself. If I were to hire you..."

"No, Memsahib. Panji cannot. It is not allowed."

"And why not?"

"Panji is not free, owe much rupees."

"Ah." Dorothy eyed the patch on the man's tunic, finally realizing its significance.

He was a marked man, a criminal.

"I see," she sighed. It would be just her luck to find that the most gifted artisan in the village was an ax murderer. "May I ask your crime?"

The man shook his head, clearly not understanding her question.

"Much rupees. Why?"

"Ah," he groaned. In a jumble of words and hand gestures, he slowly made it known to Dorothy that he owed four rupees to one of the market stall owners because his pig had eaten half a day's produce early one morning. When he couldn't pay to replace the produce, the stall owner said he would take the pig as payment. But the pig was worth ten rupees. Evidently it was a very fine pig.

The pig would feed Panji's extended family for the winter and into the spring, but if he gave it to the stall owner, his family would starve. So he did the only thing he could do. He hid the pig.

And now he was in jail.

At least his family would not starve.

Dorothy laughed. The poor man blanched, confused by her reaction.

"Well, then," she smiled. "It seems that you may be the answer to my prayers, and I to yours."

Again the man looked askance.

"You need four rupees."

He nodded.

"I have four rupees."

His eyes went wide.

"And I need a carpenter. A mistri."

The two stood, and a slow smile spread across Panji's face.

"You getta mistri. I getta rupees."

She nodded, brushing the dust from her skirt and sliding her face into the somber expression that such an important bunderbusting business arrangement required.

"Come, you follow me," he says. "We go to jail."

To jail.

Of course.

At last God had blessed her "single-blessedness" and provided a man to get the job done.

See there, little daughter? You have no need of a husband. God will always provide a man to accomplish your tasks.

But really. Jail?

The new bassinet that we had made at the jail works beautifully and is rather nice looking. It has a white standard frame and the basket is wicker and the entire thing has been white enameled. They made it a bit too high but that will be easy to remedy and it will certainly help us out. We have put in an order for a chain of four baskets that will fit into our rack side-by-side and will have that white enameled. Won't that be fun! Our baby room will begin to look more like home then and goodness knows it is 1000% better now than it was when we first started to use it for nursery.

CHAPTER FOURTEEN

FICKLE FATE

Even the wood ducks outside her window seemed to understand her excitement this morning as Dorothy readied herself for a full day in the surgery. Their chatter easily overpowered the little tune she hummed. It was a beautiful day.

She would pop into the hospital nursery and give the staff the sheer blue bassinette drapes she'd stayed up half the night sewing, and then she'd start Panji on the youth beds she envisioned. If he was half as successful in crafting them according to her design, they'd be sensational. Falling over the poor fellow's pile of bricks had been the best thing she'd done all week.

But her anticipation this morning had nothing to do with the new baby beds. It was something far more personal that had the butterflies roiling about in her stomach. They flitted and skittered, reminding her that this evening she would embark on her big adventure, an adventure whose outcome she could not yet fathom.

She was entertaining Fred.

A wry chuckle slipped from her throat as she took one last look at the clothes she'd laid out for the evening. The drop-waisted linen with one pleat down the left side was perfectly suited for the evening she had planned. The skirt would give just the right touch of feminine movement if they decided to dance.

Oh dear. Did Fred dance? She'd forgotten to ask!

Monglu had the lamb loin cooling in the Frigidaire that by the grace of God had decided to work this week. Dorothy's favorite music was strategically placed beside the Victrola, and Edna and Millie had already been prompted to be prepared to join in the dancing. After all, she was plying them with a five course dinner. They'd probably agree to do just about anything in return!

She'd planned it all so carefully that she'd been ready for nearly a week now. Ready for more than a highbrow dinner. Ready for so much more than that. Male companionship is what she was ready for. An almost date. The very pitch of it, the colors of it, the brilliant essence of it was already singing in her veins.

It was trilling so clearly now that Dorothy nearly missed the drama that began to play out just beyond her window. But instinct stilled the humming of her heart when the escalating noise drew her across the room to pull aside the lace curtain which had held up beautifully in the five years since she'd made it. Three pygmy goose chicks raced about in the yard below the branches of the tree that almost but not quite gave shade to the sleeping porch of her bungla. They raised almost as much of a ruckus as the fellow who had come to the medical bungalow begging for help.

The recognition of an emergency materialized fully in her brain even as she was already halfway out the door.

Edna hurried from her side of the bungalow and tried to intercept her. Everyone had been holding their breath for a week, worried that something might come to interfere with Dorothy's "big event". They knew what it meant to get a breath of normal life now and then. And they knew it had been far too long since Dorothy had that opportunity.

"Dorothy, really, you needn't go. I'll get Millie, or Lahaori, and—"

One look at Edna's ankles made Dorothy's decision for her. Edna's phlebitis was nearly under control, but she was in no shape yet to run and find Lahaori. And it would have to be a run, since Monbahadur and the car were away in the next valley returning a patient to her home. In a fluid move, Dorothy shrugged on her white coat, checked the stethoscope in her pocket, and sprinted back up the steps.

"No, no. It's alright, Edna. I'll collect Millie and Lahaori on my way past the hospital."

"But you have surgery, and Mr. Chambers—"

"—will be there when I get back. Do get my bag while I change my shoes. And tell Doctoroni to wait until after lunch to prep the patient scheduled for surgery."

Dorothy was already on the run. The man who fell into step beside her had been her most accomplished teacher of the Assamese language and culture when she'd first come out. She owed him everything for not only the language skill he'd raised in her, but the insight he'd given her that had so effectively ingratiated her to this new people in this ancient land.

~~~~~~~~~~~~~~~~~~~~~~~~~~~~~~~~~

Early this morning the pundit that I had when I first came out came running up to the house and wanted us to see his wife right away. He lived in back of the Compound and there is no road there. Millie and I and one of the nurses started out to see what the trouble was.

We arrived and found his wife (really not his wife) in a dying condition. She had been sick for a week and when we saw her had a peritonitis probably the result of a ruptured tubal pregnancy or an incomplete trauma-induced abortion which had become infected. She had been accidentally hit on the back just before the illness started while grinding rice. He had waited to call us until she really "looked bad" and then when she began to gasp for breath he came running for us.

We asked him if there was someone there who could help bring her into the hospital. He said "no-o". When we asked if he did not have friends there he said "no-o". Millie went out and got a man to help. The Hindu (that is, certain of them) believe that they should not put their shoulder to a burden except with one of their own caste is responsible for this.

We took two poles and with a big piece of cloth we found, rigged up a hammock stretcher and brought her in, but it was too late and she died two hours later.

"How oft would I—and ye would not".

He knew us all, had worked for us for years, lived just back of us, and then let his wife die for lack of medical help.

· · · ·

Dorothy concentrated harder than she could ever remember having to do. One foot in front of the other, don't sway too much or you'll topple to the path. *Left. Right.* Just a little farther.

The day had run amok. Almost from the first moment. There had been no hope of saving the wife of her favorite teacher, her first pundit when she had come out to Gauhati all those years ago. He'd waited too long. And it had been too late.

Why? Why hadn't he come for help sooner? She was his wife, for God's sake. Sort of his wife, anyway. But still.

Left foot. Right foot. Just a little further.

Now she could see the lights of the bungla. Just one left on to light the steps. The party she'd prepared so carefully had never happened. No lively dinner. No relaxing glass of bala fruit "wine" beneath a full moon. No dancing. Everyone would have gone to bed by now.

If only for the pundit's wife, Dorothy would have been home in plenty of time for the festivities. But the child they'd stumbled upon on the way back, the small boy left to die by the track, had kept her at the surgical table for the next six hours straight.

He'd been brutally beaten, then cast out of the village. A whipping boy, of sorts, most likely an orphan. Some misfortune—real or imagined—must have befallen the village, and the headman had identified the little boy as the bearer of the demons which had caused bad luck to fall on his community. Whether or not he had called for the child to be beaten, he had at the very least cast the boy out, and the villagers had done the rest.

And then, just as she had the boy stabilized, another patient was carried in, bruised, bleeding, and very, very broken. Dorothy never even left the surgery, but shifted the boy to the care of the nurses and began to work on the girl.

Every hour or so someone had called to her from the door of the surgery, to see if she might be ready soon and they could begin to cook the lamb loin. She had answered the only thing she could.

"Soon, I think! Soon!"

And then another vessel would rupture and she'd set about containing the damage it threatened.

The young girl had been horribly crushed at a bridge-building site. She'd merely wanted to bring dinner to her sweetheart.

The irony of it was too much. Dinner for sweethearts had been the order of the day. It must have been as joyous a morning for this young girl as Dorothy herself had experienced, planning a special treat for her beau. But now two sweethearts had been left waiting, while Dorothy raced to repair fractured bone and torn muscle.

She had even heard Fred's cultured tone as he spoke quietly out in the hall at some point in the early evening. The very sound of his voice drove Dorothy to a startling revelation. Nothing had ever before torn her concentration from surgery, from the fragile life struggling beneath her hands. But his voice had. His voice had caused her heart to roll in her chest, had set her toes twitching to head for the door.

She couldn't hear what he said, or perhaps she might if she stopped working on her patient, but that was not an option. He was most likely telling them to give Dorothy his apologies, that he was leaving, that he'd come again.

That had been hours ago. And now she faced the simplest yet most exhausting task of the day—carrying her weary body home.

Left foot. Right foot. She was at the bottom step. Now she'd have to lift her whole body up one whole step, and then another. It was too much.

Dorothy stood swaying by the bottom step. Perhaps the step was wide enough. She could sleep right there.

Being ridiculous, Dor.

She managed to raise a hand to brush her damp hair back behind one ear, just enough so she could see the step more clearly. It had looked so grand this morning, her hair had. So pert and just the way she liked it. Now it just fell in haphazard clumps.

But no matter. He'd gone home. Who cared what she looked like. Two steps were all she had to navigate and then she could collapse on her bed. Oh, but there was the long hallway. And then she'd have to get out of her clothes, and—

Too much. Too much. Just focus on the two steps first.

Dorothy took a deep breath and checked her balance, preparing to put her entire being into hoisting herself up the two steps.

Imagine that Fred is there. Waiting.

Her imaginary enticement did the trick, and she was suddenly on the first step.

Ah, that helped. Now do it again.

She gathered her strength and focused on the fanciful allure of a handsome headmaster waiting just steps ahead.

"Dorothy?"

Ha! Focusing just a bit too hard, she realized. So hard that she'd actually heard his voice.

"Dorothy?"

It was cruelly real. It was his voice—a sound she had taken into her heart of hearts. But it came from behind her, and not ahead, where she'd put him in her imagination.

Dorothy laughed, a feeble, weary sound of disillusionment even to her own ears.

"Dorothy?"

The voice was still there, closer now, and she turned to cast an eye over her shoulder, mostly to convince herself he wasn't really there. But the movement threw her off balance, and it was only as she began to realize she was going to fall that she saw him.

The moon and the dim verandah light conspired to cast him in layers of shadow worthy of the cinema. But all she saw was the light coming from his eyes, and his open arms.

As she fell into them.

· · · ·

"You stayed."

Fred chuckled. "You've said that umpteen times now." He tapped her chin with his finger. "Why can't you believe that it wasn't possible for me to leave without seeing you?"

They'd brought the Victrola out onto the verandah and now stood swaying to the muted music, he holding her up and she taking a much needed rest dancing in place in his arms.

"If I say it forty-leven times, I'll mean it more each time. You stayed. You have no idea what that means to me."

He chuckled again.

"And you have no idea what it means to me that you are here, dead tired, completely knackered from your brutal day, and yet here you are. So don't you see? It's the same thing for me. You stayed." He sighed.

"Yes," she sighed in answer. "We stayed."

The very idea of it crept through her veins like some invigorating, mystical element that pumped her full of energy.

She lifted her head from his shoulder and stepped back a half step, not so far as to lose the feel of him, but far enough to look up into his face.

"We stayed," she said again.

Fred looked down into her eyes and slowly brought his forehead to rest against hers. "We stayed," he agreed. "And I—"

He stopped and closed his eyes. The record ended and the needle scratched its rhythmic sketch on the ribbed vinyl. Untended. Ignored.

"I—"

"Fred?"

Now Dorothy stopped swaying and took his face in her hands. She couldn't tell from the look of him whether or not she wanted to hear what he struggled to say.

"What Fred? What is it?"

He took a long breath, and with it the most serene smile spread across his face. In that moment, in the cool dark night, with a breeze ruffling the strands of hair that fell across his brow, she knew the next words he spoke would seal her future.

And they did.

"Darling girl," he sighed, slipping his head sideways to kiss her palm that still cradled his cheek. "I don't think there's any place in this entire world I will ever want to be except here. With you. Wherever you are. Whatever you're doing.

That's where I want to be."

Somehow, in that moment, everything around her kept doing what they'd always done. The trees kept swaying, the moon kept shining, the night insects kept up their song, the Victrola needle kept skritchety-scratching. But Dorothy knew that from that moment nothing would ever be the same. Everything in her was newly born. Tonight for the first time in her life she knew that her heart was whole. Because he stayed.

FRED CHAMBERS AND DR. DOROTHY KINNEY

CHAPTER FIFTEEN

IF I HAD BEEN HOME

~~~~~~~~~~

March 1936

Letter to Dorothy's sister

Dearest Marian:

Altho I will be writing to Mother and Dad, I wish you'd treat the following with strictest confidence. If I could have been home, this wouldn't have to be written, but if I had been home it would never have happened—so I'm glad I'm here. I have debated whether to write now or later but decided that it might be too much of a bombshell if things go as they may.

I'm in love—I am afraid—really, deeply and overwhelmingly so. It is an entirely new experience and there is no other diagnosis I can pin on it. You may have read of the death about one and a half years ago of Irene Chambers, the wife of one of our missionaries out here— Fred Chambers. He is in the High School work in our mission at Jorhat. He is splendid, Marian, about my age, and one of the—if not <u>the</u> grandest man I've ever known. Marian, you know my longing for home and family. Do you think I'd be a shirker if I were to marry? There are so many, many problems in it with one who has been trained as I've been, and yet I'm still human and still a woman. Tell me honestly what you think.

We are spending our vacation this year in Shillong and shall see a good deal of each other, and I don't dare to say anything about it

> at home until I know definitely how things are going to turn out. I
> think Fred feels toward me about as I feel toward him. Pray for me,
> Marian, that whatever I or we do may be the right thing and do let
> me hear from you.

She felt so wicked now. Unconscionably deceitful. Writing secret letters to her sister. Lying to her parents.

Dorothy forced herself to put aside conscience and look at her situation logically. It was only March of 1936. It wasn't really lying. More like shielding the truth until it could be shared in a more congenial light.

Yes, that was it. A more congenial light.

She would drop a few very oblique hints in her letters home this spring, then escalate a bit in the summer so her parents had time to adjust slowly to the fact that she was truly going to marry.

Then in the fall of the year she'd outline a plan to be married by the end of the year. The very thought of it lit her face as she rolled a fresh page into her typewriter. Continuing her record of life and medical cases was paramount. She would—as she always had—write letters recounting her days in the hospital.

Just like normal.

~~~~~~

> You will remember that I told you about a little four or five-year-
> old girl we have had in the ward for a long time. Finally despaired of
> her relatives calling for her so sent her over to the orphanage. About
> two weeks later the father came. Took her home and now about two
> weeks afterwards, he and a friend have come back.

The little girl's father had left her here for weeks, and not once had a family member come to check on her. Dorothy stopped typing. It had gone well for this child, but for so many it had not. The casual way so many of these parents regarded their children no longer shocked her. But it would be very different one day, perhaps sooner than she thought, when she herself might be a parent. There could never be anything so casual in her own commitment to a child. But how did Fred feel about children? Could he disregard them so?

She needed to know, even as she already knew. He could never be so callous. She'd seen the way he stopped to chat in the children's ward when she gave him a tour of the hospital. She'd seen in his eyes his genuine kindness and his respect for the little ones, and their immediate liking of him.

Dorothy slid the typewriter's carriage slowly back to begin a new line of text and continued the child's story. How blessed she was, how very fortunate, to know already that the man she was prepared to take as a partner for life shared her love for children.

And how blessed was this child that her father recognized the spark of something new and wonderful in his daughter and did not seek to stamp it out.

> They say that she has been singing and singing the four songs she learned while here, one of which is Jesus Loves Me, and has taught them to a number of the other children. The father said that he heard about the Christian religion when some of the folks from the hospital were out at a market day last year. He has not been happy since and wants to do differently. Wants to know more about Christ, and His teachings, and wants to bring little Habitri here and put her in school. He says that she has insisted on going to school with her brother, and in two weeks has learned to read three pages.
>
> She has a good mind, and is a sweet youngster. I hope that things work out. There are no Christians in that village. "A Little Child Shall Lead Them".

A sudden tear surprised Dorothy. There was so much happening here. So many changes in the hearts and souls of these simple, beautiful people. They were coming to know the God she had prayed to since she was large enough to sit on her mother's lap with folded hands. They were learning about Jesus, His son. And time and again they would quietly give their hearts to Him.

> Saturday I took half of the nurses (Edna took the other half the day before) on a picnic down by the river. We found a place (rather Edna did the day before) where it was much like a beach at the side of a lake—clean white river sand, shady, and yet sunny. The girls roamed around, climbed up to inspect the water reservoir, etc. Then we had rice and curry. It was so good. They had big leaves that they had

gathered at the compound before coming, washed them, and heated them—makes them soft and pliable. They used these for plates. We finished off with oranges. The sunset on the river was gorgeous—all cerise, gold and orange.

Monday morning I worked with the laundry almost all day, and we did about 200 lbs of washing–that is dry weight. We had all the clothes ready to hang up by eleven and most of them out on the lines. Would have had the others but ran out of line space.

We have a really big drying field to use during the nice weather. By one when the folks came back to work, the clothes were dry and ready to come in, and the other things were put out. I then showed them how to use the mangle (our version of an ironing machine with heated rollers), and it works quite well.

By five, everything that was to be mangled had been done, and all the other things had been folded and put away. We're smart! Of course there are lots of things that we will have to learn by experience, and many tricks of the trade that are unknown to us as yet. However, our clothes are getting whiter and whiter.

Whiter and whiter. Even as their souls were discovering the purity of devotion to a Christian God.

But even as the locals came slowly to know about a Christian God, they came even more quickly to know about the doctors in Gauhati who could save people from dying, who could repair a broken leg without leaving the victim crippled, who could bring both a mother and babe through a perilous childbirth.

Over the years the hospital's reputation had grown, and grateful survivors had spread the word far and wide. Farther than even Dorothy dared to suspect.

~~~~~~

April 15, 1936

Last Saturday I went out on the village clinic trip, and got quite a thrill out of it. We saw over sixty patients and some very interesting cases. The little house at Rampur (where we had set up a small dispensary) seems to be doing a lot to stir up interest, and a former patient—a middle aged woman who came into the hospital with what we finally decided was hysteria several years ago, and who is now okay—is the chief assistant.

She is grand at chillowing (managing the people) and enjoys it.

We brought a little seven-year-old boy and a young woman back with us. A little girl of about four came in—tiny, chubby and pretty as a picture. Wasn't at all afraid of us. Came (to the dispensary) because of a staphyloma of the right eye following small pox a year ago. Nothing to do for it just now, and no hope of the sight there.

She came expecting to be cured, and had her mother open up the car door and got in and sat by the little boy. Said she was going to Gauhati where they would make her eye well. It was rather heartbreaking all the way around.

Dorothy addressed and sealed the letter, reviving the pang of guilt over once again not having informed her parents of her plan to marry Fred Chambers, over lacking the courage to bring her love for him into the light of day. But how could she tell her father and still reassure him that she would not be abandoning her medical work? He was a missionary, too. He knew how things worked. He'd be shattered to think his daughter might make a choice that would so radically alter her life's path.

The little girl she'd just written about had been more courageous than she. The child was so trusting, so confident that Dorothy could restore her eye that she had not a doubt in the world that she would get into that car with Dorothy and ride away half-blind and return whole. At four years old her courage and conviction were stunning. But more stunning was the way she handled her disappointment.

Some things were too poignant to write about, and so Dorothy just held them in her heart. No matter what words formed in her mind to tell the rest of the little girl's story, her fingers could not manage to move on the typewriter.

It had nearly brought her to her knees having to explain to the child, then lift her out of the car to stand beside her mother, and then just drive away—after the little girl had simply smiled, bowed her head slightly, and whispered softly, *thank you.*

MARIE HOLMES, ETHEL NICHOLS, DOROTHY, AND EDNA STEVER

CHAPTER SIXTEEN

BEST LAID PLANS

May 25, 1936

This is strictly within the family and no mention must be made of it until I give consent—not even confidentially.

I hesitate to write in a way, until things are definite, and yet if I could be at home I would talk things over freely with you.

What would you say if I were to marry one of our missionaries out here? There is no engagement at present, but there may be. I am giving you a bit of warning so if it happens, you won't have too much of a bomb shell. Also, I'm telling you, as I want your prayers that whatever comes may be the right thing in His sight.

Dad has met the man—Fred Chambers. Fred told me a while ago that he had a long chat with Dad at one of the summer assemblies in California several years ago—said Dad invited him to come down to his cabin.

I am learning to care very, very deeply for him. His first wife died about 1 ½ years ago. I am afraid that if he asks me to marry him I shall. Don't think that either of us will go into it lightly. He feels very strongly about my work and feels that it must not be lost to the Mission. Fred is stationed at Jorhat at the High School there. They very much need a second doctor there and my going might solve more than one difficulty and would perhaps help Jorhat.

However, these factors have not entered into my thoughts and plans. I mean they are not influencing my thinking. I realize there are lots of problems to be settled and I don't want anyone to think I am a piker. I'm a very human person and a woman and know my longing for a home and children. I told Dad of it but rather felt that he thought that single-blessedness was a price I must pay. I can't think that way and I've never been able to think that way.

Of course, even if we decide to marry, it will be several months before it would be possible as I would have to give at least six months' notice, etc. I know Mrs. McCarthy would understand as she told me very frankly once that if I ever wanted to do so, to be sure that she would give me her blessing and would not hold it against me in any way whatsoever.

It would be so much nicer if we could talk as I do want your reaction. When I came back to Assam this time, it was because I had a lot of faith that God knew and understood my desire for a home and family and that it was only "by seeking the Kingdom of God first" etc., that "these shall be added unto you". I can't help but feel that it is part of a plan.

I wish you both knew Fred. He is the most radiant person I know. I hope this may fill you with a joy like mine and not make you feel that perhaps I'm a quitter. Loads of love to the finest Father and Mother a girl ever had.

~~~~~~~~~~~~~~~~~~~~~~~~~~~~~~~~~

June 10, 1936

I seem to be walking on air most of the time these days, and it is hard to keep my feet on the ground long enough to get much of anything accomplished. The high spot of the day is the morning mail (Wink, I see where I have to apologize about what I said about not seeing how it was ever possible to write to the same person every day and find enough to say—I really never thought it would be possible but it is, and I am finding out that so many things that I always thought were impossible aren't).

It seems queer that we have so many things in common with each other and yet never met until we came to Assam. He has taught in Denison, was student pastor at Boulder after Charles Thomas left for two years, then we got our degrees the same day at Mackey (His M.A. and I my M.D.). If you are interested you can find out something about him from the Sutherlands as he was a very good friend of theirs. Dad has met him, but may not remember him.

For the benefit of those of you who haven't seen him, will simply say that he is taller than I by about two inches, maybe more, has light brown curly hair, very blue eyes, medium weight, rather on the slender side. There is only a few months difference in our ages.

He has one of the most radiant personalities that I have ever met— the most radiant. His Christianity is positively contagious. I know you think I am raving, but it is all true and you will find it out for yourself one of these days.

You will be wondering when the wedding is going to take place but I can't tell you that yet. It probably will not be before the last of the year at the earliest altho I could wish it much, much sooner. As to whether we will be located in Jorhat or in Gauhati remains to be seen.

There is some talk of his taking over the student work here in Gauhati, but that is not to be mentioned. It will not be settled until after Dr. Howards' visit out here this winter in all probability. His furlough (and therefore mine) will be due, I think, in the spring of '38.

I know that Mother and Dad will be wondering about my work. That remains to be settled, but I am so convinced that this is the right thing to do that even if it meant giving it up completely, I would do it. It is all a part of a big Plan and of that I am absolutely sure.

Before I left home, before mother was taken sick, I was quite upset along several lines. One of them was that I felt that I couldn't really live, even in my work, unless I could have a home, and that unless I could reach some sort of a solution to my problem, I couldn't come back to Assam. In trying to solve that problem I came upon a verse in my reading one day that just sort of leaped out of the page at me. It produced a very decided effect on me, and I was convinced that the next step in accordance with God's plan was to come back to Assam, and be patient.

I had absolutely not the faintest idea how or where or what was going to happen, but I was sure that it was part of the Plan. Things have fitted in like pieces of a puzzle, and I know that this is the right step and the next step. Fred feels the same way, but he has been very insistent that I face up to all the angles involved. He has been wonderful.

I am so gloriously happy that I couldn't bear to have anyone be unhappy because of me. Fred will write after he has been down this month—when everything has been definitely settled. We know where we stand, but there are some things that neither of us want to write until we can say them first.

~~~~~~~~~~~~~~~~~~~~~~~~~~~~~~~~~~

June 17, 1936

Just nine more days until Fred gets here. The days drag and fly at the same time. Do wish that you could all know him, but you will some one of these days. I can scarcely wait until he gets down here so that we can begin to get some plans made.

I am so happy these days that I sort of walk on air, and wish that you could all be here to share in the joy. Things have happened rather fast, as six weeks ago I was just beginning to think that perhaps something like this might happen. Margie and Mary are going to get a grand uncle as Fred is crazy about children. Don't think I've ever seen a man, particularly one that had none of his own, get along with tiny children or handle them any more beautifully than he does.

Dorothy posted her letters and hurried home. She knew she'd found the right words to prepare her mother and father. Now if only someone would spell out a plan for her, take the whole situation that could easily spin out of control and make sense of it. Not knowing exactly how her future was going to play out kept her on tenterhooks.

But today was no day for fretting. Fred had just arrived, and for the moment, nothing else in the world mattered one whit.

Dorothy reached the steps of the bungla just as Fred swung around the corner and jumped from his car. There was no holding back the fierce hug she gave him. Almost as fierce as the one Fred returned.

Her pulse raced as she breathed in the virile fragrance of the man she had so swiftly taken into her heart. The man she had finally revealed in letters to her parents. Everything about him soothed her being, so much so that even his first words didn't manage to raise any red flags.

"Shillong? Six weeks...just the two of us...in Shillong?" Dorothy grew breathless at the prospect. A vacation was always welcome, but this! This sounded more grand than even a honeymoon.

"Shillong?"

Fred laughed. He still held her close, and in truth had allowed little daylight between them. Now he was proposing they take advantage of a free holiday in one of the most loved resort hotels in the district.

"Tell me how!" she begged, pummeling his chest when he teased her by not answering.

He chuckled.

"The Tuttles do live there, you know, silly goose, or have you forgotten? Their friend owns the hotel, and the hotel has a guest house, and the guest house usually has a resident. But now they find that their tenant will be in Europe for two months and they've offered it to us. Or rather, the Tuttles asked them to offer it to us. So don't you see? They've given it to us for six of the eight weeks. Free and clear. If we want it."

"If we want it? You foolish boy! Of course we want it! When?"

"Well, that's just the thing."

Fred became tongue-tied, a condition that set Dorothy tingling with apprehension.

"Tell me now or off you go, Mr. Chambers. You may not have noticed but I'm dying of curiosity here. So when is it? Hm? When!"

"That's just the thing, darling girl," he said, practically shuffling like a schoolboy.

"Out with it, Buster Brown."

"Well. It's, um, that is, we're to have it from July first through August twelfth."

Dorothy's heart sank. It had seemed such a wonderfully honeymoon-like prospect.

"Oh." She tried to brighten her tone, but knew he'd not missed her deflating emotion. July of next year was such a terribly long time to wait.

"I know, darling," he said, "it's rushing things a bit."

She raised her eyes. "Wait. What did you say? I mean why? Why would that be rushing things?"

Was he having second thoughts? Did he want to put off their wedding?

Fred looked taken aback. "Well," he stammered, "it's already mid-June and July will be upon us before we know it."

Now Dorothy sprang away from his arms. "You mean *this* July? *Now*? Two weeks from *now*? That would be terrible!"

"Why? I...I don't understand."

"Oh, Fred, there we would be in paradise for six whole weeks! In separate rooms! With a chaperone every time we wanted to go somewhere. It would be absolutely horrid!"

Fred stepped close and gathered her once again into his arms. He tucked a loose curl behind her ear and tweaked her nose.

"It wouldn't be *that* horrible, darling girl. And we wouldn't really need a chaperone."

He drew her closer and locked eyes with her.

"Not if we were married."

CHAPTER SEVENTEEN

TUESDAY JUNE 30, 1936
THE WEDDING

June 21, 1936

I know that I have probably knocked the breath out of you several times already, and may do it again this time.

There is a possibility—quite a possibility in fact, that we will be married—don't faint—about July 1st before going to Shillong, and then have the four or five weeks in Shillong as a honeymoon.

I know that it sounds awfully speedy, (but think that Wink at any rate will understand) but there are lots of things to be said for it. If we don't do it then, we can't do it until November, and then Fred would have a hard time to get away for very much, as October and November are going to be full because of Dr. Howard's (N.Y. board) being here in Assam, the Conference (of which Fred is president), school work, etc.

It will mean of course that I will have to stay on down here until about the first of November or until after conference as the hospital can't be left without someone here, and Alice is not due back normally until then.

Have talked it over with the Tuttles, and they think that perhaps it is the best thing to do. They are for it. If we do it, it will be a very simple wedding, probably here at the bungalow, although the details are not settled yet. The Tuttles are the nearest thing to family that I have out here, and I think so much of them.

How I would love to have you all here, but have a scheme up my sleeve that might work so that it would let you in on a bit of it. I wish so much that you knew Fred, but you will one of these days.

It was breathtaking how it happened, how five fateful words changed the course of Dorothy's days like nothing either she or Fred could have anticipated. *Not if we were married.*

Dorothy's letters flew home as quickly as they could, but at best it would be several weeks before she received replies from her family. By then she'd be a married woman. How dearly she wanted their blessing.

The days seemed interminable, and yet they passed in the blink of an eye, packed with wedding preparations, good wishes, but no letters from home. At least none that came in reply to her bombshell announcement.

Still, with all the magic which these occasions of the heart can engender, the ten days melted away and Dorothy found herself on the brink of the most important day of her life.

· · · ·

It was like no other day Dorothy had ever lived and breathed through. Even her lungs seemed confused, sending up long, happy sighs followed by quick, short, panicked puffs.

She was getting married today. It was the most deliriously scary proposition to which she'd ever set her mind. The scattered heaps of Cecile Bruner roses had taken shape exactly as she'd imagined them, transformed from random blossoms on an over-burdened bush into her beautifully delicate bridal bouquet. Her newly fashioned white satin gown sat perfectly on her shoulders, weighted there by the glittering clasps she'd repurposed at the last moment. Her Renaissance-style silver girdle dropped like a low belt to gather in the dress just below her waist. It seemed an anchor, tethering her to this place lest she float into the sky which undoubtedly was populated today by clouds of pink.

In moments she would walk out into the gathering room, stand among her dearest friends, and pledge her heart to—

"Dorothy! *Psst!* Dorothy!"

Dorothy turned half around, just in time to see Millie's hand slip through the cracked open door, waving to beckon her closer.

"Come!"

"But it's not—"

"Shh!" Millie pressed a finger to her lips and caught Dorothy's hand in her own. "I know it's bad luck but we're going to do it anyway!"

By the time her cryptic words were uttered, Millie had whisked Dorothy to the back verandah. They stepped soundlessly through the screened door and Dorothy felt Millie's hand urge her forward. As her foot touched the planked step she sensed his presence and looked up.

Fred stepped away from the overgrown shrubbery and faced her. His eyes caught and held her own, and the love and confidence she saw there calmed her heart in a way nothing else could. He stood there in his dashing tuxedo with his hand extended toward her, good and solid and everything upon which she could trust her future.

Her lips moved, and his replied, but their meaning was conveyed more fully on their faces. So fully, that it seemed eons of understanding were exchanged in that fleeting moment before Millie whisked her back into the bungla.

With each retreating step, Dorothy's heart calmed and her shoulders lifted. Everything she'd accomplished in her life had led her to this moment, to this place where she could finally embrace the precious things God had in store for her. And it was His words that carried her forward into the ceremony.

All these things shall be added unto you. These were the words that sang in her heart as she took her place beside Fred. Before God.

Seek ye first the Kingdom of God and His righteousness, and all these things shall be added unto you. Matthew 6:33

All these things for which she had prayed so fervently. A good husband, a kind and gentle companion, a helpmate, someone to share her innermost private thoughts and needs, to champion her causes, to give her children and to father them in the most charitable, uplifting manner.

For these, God had given her Fred.

DOROTHY AND FRED CHAMBERS
MARRIED JUNE 30, 1936
SATRIBARI COMPOUND - GAUHATI, ASSAM

CHAPTER EIGHTEEN

BE STILL MY HEART

July 6, 1936 Shillong, Assam.
Fred's letter home

Have not come down to earth yet but trust I am sufficiently rational to share something of the experiences of the last few days with you.

Life has held some rich experiences but there has been nothing to compare with the sheer joy of these last few days. If Heaven can be any sweeter, then it will be almost unbearable.

My very soul feels as if it would burst at times for the thrill and deep joy of it all and even prayer seems inadequate to give expression to my gratitude.

It is some satisfaction to know that the Lord does understand my heart and can know the thanksgiving that is there for it all.

Dorothy's letter home — July 7, 1936

Dearest Mother and Dad:

There is so much that I want to tell you both, and it would be so nice if we could just have a grand visit instead of trying to put everything down on paper. Somehow, when it is down on paper, things sound so rather flat, when in reality they are anything but that. I wish so much that I could have let you know earlier so that you could have shared more of the joy and anticipation with us, but things happened in such a rush at the last. I really hadn't dreamed of being married until after Alice [Dr. Alice Randall] returned, until just about ten days before the wedding took place. Everything seemed to work together, and in such a marvelous way, that I haven't a doubt in the world that what we did was the absolutely right thing to have done.

When Fred first suggested it, that we be married before coming to Shillong, I found myself in such a whirl that I scarcely knew which way I was going. The more I thought about it, the more logical and reasonable it sounded, and when he arrived on the afternoon of the 26th (18 hours ahead of the time that I had expected him) and we had a chance to see each other for a little while, we both knew that it was the right thing to do.

The Tuttles have been so lovely to both of us—it has been more as though we belonged to the family. Certainly, they couldn't have been any lovelier had we been their own son and daughter.

Fred and I haven't known each other for a long time, and it is absolutely miraculous the way things have worked out. Last August I spent two weekends in Shillong with the Forbes and Wickstrands, and Fred was staying with them. They were delightful weekends, full of delightful fellowship with the whole group.

We discovered then that we had several things in common, particularly as regarded friends. The fact that he had taught at Denison, had been in student pastoral work in Boulder for two years (the succeeding two years after I left Boulder), that we had received our degrees at the same time from the same platform, all gave us a basis for discovering mutual friends. He knew the Sutherlands well there in Boulder among others.

At that time he was having some nose and throat trouble and had been to Calcutta for some help. The doctor there recommended certain treatments twice weekly, and unless they could be had in Assam, he would have had to spend his vacation in Calcutta. The result was that he decided to risk having me do them.

I saw him only once between then and the Centennial, and that was for just a moment. The only letters that we wrote were more or less business letters. It wasn't until he came down for some x-rays early this spring that we began to write occasionally, and not until about the middle of May after he had been down in the hospital, that we really began to write letters and began to discover each other.

I wish that it were possible to convey in a mere letter all that has gone into and come out of the happenings of the past few weeks. I told you in a previous letter that before I left home to return to Assam this time, that I had a very real conviction that there was something besides the hospital work awaiting me, and knew that it was part of a Plan about which I knew little at the time.

All I was sure of was that the next step was to return to Assam. I was so sure of it that I didn't even feel the desire to question it, altho at the time just what was involved, where it might lead, etc., was absolutely unknown. This conviction grew out of an experience that I had while reading one night near the end of my stay in New York City—I was reading the sixth Chapter of Matthew and the 32nd and 33rd verses seemed to stand out in a way that I couldn't misinterpret. [32 For after all these things the Gentiles seek. For your heavenly Father knows that you need all these things. 33 But seek first the kingdom of God and His righteousness, and all these things shall be added to you.]

A short time ago, when I found that this passage meant a very great deal to Fred, it seemed that the things that had been working together, couldn't have just happened.

I used to think that I was rather a self sufficient person, and rather more than ordinarily reserved—largely due to the work that I was in, I guess—but all that seems to have dissolved into a thin mist, and I find that I am no longer able to run on my own, but am very dependent on another.

I used to wonder that some people seemed to lose themselves so completely when they fell in love, but I don't wonder any more. I am so absolutely head over heels in love with Fred, and it is such an overwhelming love that I am absolutely powerless against it. (Even if I wanted to be, I couldn't help it). I have never known anything like it, and never even dreamed that such a thing could happen or be.

I had been pretty sure in my own heart and mind as to how I felt before I saw Fred last Friday, a week ago, but after seeing him, there wasn't the slightest chance for a doubt, and there hasn't been since.

Surely if marriages are made in Heaven, ours was. It is as though each of us had always known the other, and had a complete understanding of that one. I can't get over the wonder of it all and in the week that we have been married, it has been increasingly wonderful—the naturalness of our feeling toward each other, the completeness of our understanding, and the sense that it's all a part of a Plan have all grown daily, and our love for each other gets deeper and more wonderful every hour.

How I wish that you could know Fred now—you will before so very long, but I so covet your knowing and loving him now. You won't be able to help loving him, I know, and I know that Dad will revel in his fellowship, and Fred in Dad's. He is so fine, so clean, and so altogether lovable—and to think he is mine leaves me absolutely breathless. We should love to have had Dad perform the marriage ceremony for us, and did so long for you all at the time. I am so glad that Dad and Dr. Tuttle know each other so well.

The marriage service was exquisitely lovely and both Fred and I felt it very very keenly, and neither of us has been able to get away from the beauty and solemnity of it.

The weather in Gauhati had been desperately hot for days before, and the wedding day was no exception. Both Fred and I had to stand before electric fans to try and keep dry before the ceremony, and we were almost panicky when the fans all over the bungalow suddenly went off and stayed off for about five minutes.

Have been grateful to Marie for her suggestion regarding the ring for Fred. Had wondered just how I could get a ring, as there wasn't time to send to Calcutta for one, and the one that we had made by the Assamese goldsmith is lovely, and is unique in that it was made especially for him by an Indian workman in the country where our work lies. Fred's ring to me is an exquisite diamond circlet, and I find myself continually trying to fathom the tremendous waves of emotion that it sets up in my heart and soul.

The past few weeks have been very, very rich in their spiritual effect upon me. Never before have I been as conscious of the unquestionable rightness of anything as I am of the knowledge that our marriage is part of a Plan that God has for us, and the conviction that together we can work for the Kingdom as we never could have worked alone.

I know that this letter doesn't begin to tell you all that I want you to know, but I just can't seem to get down to earth to put things on paper as they should be. We are longing to get mail from you all after you received the cable, and are looking forward to the last of the month for that reason especially.

I think of you both so often, long to see and talk with you, and love you so much.

Dor

CHAPTER NINETEEN

TO LOVE AND TO CHERISH

Shillong, July 7, 1936
Letter from Mr. and Mrs. Tuttle to Dorothy's parents

I must say at the beginning that we heartily approve of this union, that we are very happy over it and that it is a great joy to have the children with us during these weeks in Shillong. And they—well, they are absolutely satisfied that they have been divinely led, they are thoroughly in love, completely happy.

We are going to miss Dorothy most dreadfully in Gauhati. She has done such a great piece of work there and made such a fine name for herself. And won the love of everybody.

But because of this we feel that she has earned the right—if a lovely girl <u>needs</u> to earn the right—to give up her profession and take over the happy task of being a home-maker, a wife, and we hope the mother of children. I am sure that her Indian friends will feel that she is merely adding the cap-sheaf to all of the other fine things that she has done by taking this step.

So we give her up gladly to the new life. And you'd almost be surprised to see how completely she has lost herself in this new love. Fred is a fortunate man and he knows it and he is quite humble over it.

Still and all, he is mighty nice too, is Fred! So Dorothy has some reason to be happy. Yes, quite considerable reason!!

July 8, 1936
Letter from Marie Holmes to Dorothy's parents

Dear Mrs. Kinney,

...You will have guessed that the enclosed Cecil Bruner rose buds are from the bridal bouquet. It was a lovely wedding, beautiful in its dignity and simplicity. Several have remarked that it was one of the most impressive weddings they ever saw.

For the previous fortnight Dorothy had looked like a lighted candle, but the day of the wedding her eyes were like jewels glinting from an inner light.

Her corsage was of exquisite Carl Bruner buds and maiden-hair fern. How I did wish that you might see her in her radiant joy and loveliness. A Parisian dressmaker couldn't have designed a gown to suit her more perfectly, yet Dorothy cut and made her gown herself in less than a week!

Of course the staff and some of the patrons of the hospital are rather cut up about Dorothy's marriage. They just never thought she would get married and they recognize the great skill she has professionally and are aware of the blessing of healing which she has brought to many so it will take them a little while to adjust their thinking to the new situation. It was all so unexpected. They hadn't even expected the engagement, although I believe some of the missionaries expected or even suspected an engagement.

Because Dorothy's own home has been such a happy one, it isn't at all strange that she should want to make another such happy one. Part of her professional efficiency is due to her innate womanliness and understanding of home relations. If you could see her great joy you would know that the love of which it is born is a gift of God, even as her medical skill is a gift of God. She has used the one to His glory and I think she will use this new gift also to His glory.

Then there is Fred's side, too. His love for Dorothy and need of her are counterparts of her love for and need of him. He is a man of God and worthy of her love.

Seeing Dorothy's great happiness some of the staff are more reconciled to her decision to change her career. If you could but witness this you would lose any lingering regret that you may have had because Dorothy has given up the profession in which she has been so signally successful, for that calling upon which God first bestowed His blessing and upon which our Saviour too set His seal.

Affectionately yours,
Marie Holmes

Dorothy tucked away her copy of the letter Marie had written to her parents. The hard knot it left in her stomach would not settle. Yes, she knew that the missionary board did not allow missionary wives to work in the field. They were to be the husband's helpmate, but to pursue work of their own simply wasn't done.

Reading Marie's words had brought that stunning reality home, even though she'd been worrying over it for weeks. Perhaps that's the way things had always been done, but surely she could find a new path, a new way to exercise her healing art without breaking trust with the missionary board.

Dorothy Kinney, M.D. had become Dorothy Chambers, M.D. That's all. Marriage did not erase those letters from behind her name. She was a physician. Fred didn't love her less because of her medical skills, and he wouldn't love her more if she left them behind. He embraced them as a most essential part of her.

And that was the most essential hurdle, knowing how Fred would feel if she kept working. The world would come to accept it if she just quietly kept working about the compound. She'd dealt with stubborn attitudes before. She could do it again.

Not even marriage was going to make her hang up her white coat.

CHAPTER TWENTY

WEDDED BLISS

Shillong, India
From Fred Chambers
July 7, 1936

Dear Mr. and Mrs. Kinney,

I am tempted to address you as "Mother and Dad Kinneykin" as we do here in Assam, but until I know whether I am to be accepted "within the gate", it seems proper to forego that pleasure. I told Dorothy I considered you, Dr. Bruce, as my friend but after "stealing" your daughter I am not sure of my status. However, I am sure since you know Dorothy as you do, that even you cannot blame me for falling hopelessly in love with her. I never even dreamed that such a lovable lady existed.

How can I express my boundless gratitude to you for the great blessing you have given me? In the copy of the letter I wrote to my Mother you will get some idea of how deeply I recognize Dorothy's love as a gift of God. When I realize more and more the sweetness and purity of the love she gives me it makes me search my very soul and cry to God for Grace to be even in a measure worthy of it. It is the highest honor to have her love and next to that I count it a high privilege to be so related to your family. I shall never cease to be mindful of the great responsibility entailed by the high privilege and will always strive to be worthy so far as I am able.

I recognize that it is no light matter for one of Dorothy's professional success to lay aside her career for the love of a man and home. I must confess that it creates a certain sense of fear about my heart as I realize the great responsibility that is mine to see to it that her trust is not misplaced; that her hopes are never disappointed; that her freedom and opportunity for self expression and development are never impinged; and that her usefulness to the Kingdom of God is never limited but rather increased. Only the Grace of God can make possible the measuring up to that responsibility.

I am sorry I have not had the pleasure of meeting you, Mrs. Kinney, but . . . after all, you are Dorothy's Mother and that tells so much. Trust you both will forgive me for marrying your daughter before obtaining your consent, but when one is driven by a great love, he may forget some of the conventional things of life. Already I have come to know something of the wonderful home Dorothy had and of the great love you bear toward her. I give you my word that the best I can give her I shall consider not equal to what she deserves, and surely you cannot possibly love her more than I do – just in another way.

This is such a feeble effort to express what I feel so deeply but I trust to your understanding and the future to make it plainer.

With deepest gratitude for your unspeakable gift,
R. Fred Chambers

"Wowzers!"

Fred's eyes popped as Dorothy took a twirl in her evening clothes. They'd been honeymooning in Shillong for four weeks now, and were finally ready to take their twosome public. They might have waited even longer, but an invitation to Government House was too intriguing to ignore.

Dorothy tacked an elegant pose onto the end of her final twirl. Her wedding dress adapted perfectly to the evening's need, ornamented by a sparkling brooch in her hair and a brilliantly black evening wrap.

"Ready, Mr. Chambers?"

"Yes, I believe so, Mrs. Chambers. But...on second thought, I'm suddenly feeling very...very...exceedingly woozy."

"Oh dear! What is it? Are you ill?" Dorothy rushed to him and pressed a hand against his forehead. Fred seized the opportunity to capture her at the waist and draw her close.

"So woozy, in fact, that there is nothing for me but to stay home and allow the famous Doctor Chambers to attend to me."

Dorothy laughed, delighted with her new husband's clever wiles.

"Now don't you just wish," she smiled slyly, then marched to the door and waited for him to escort her to their evening's destination. "What will it be, Mr. Chambers? Dinner at Government House? Or Castor oil?"

Fred blanched and Dorothy grinned. And both gave up the idea of locking themselves away forever and accepted the fact that it was high time they got out into the world again.

The drive was mystical under a star-blessed sky. Every grove and bough was alight with fireflies—more than either of them had seen in a lifetime, and the drive up to the front entrance of Government House was stunning. A valet took the keys to park the Tuttles' car, borrowed for this auspicious occasion, and the Chambers were invited into the grand hallway by a butler or footman or whatever the liveried servant might have been called. Whatever he was, he clearly had just stepped out of a storybook.

"Footman, dear," Dorothy whispered, "I think that one is a footman." She shifted her gaze across the foyer. "That one over there, in the grand tails and, well, rather haughty look...I think that must be His Excellency."

"You're sure that's not the butler?"

Dorothy clucked her tongue and cast Fred a sideways glance. "Hardly," she whispered.

And just as she turned back, the fellow crossed the hall, back ramrod straight, white gloves more pristine than any glove had a right to be, and bowed slightly. "If you'll follow me, Mr. and Mrs. Chambers?"

Dorothy swallowed her chuckle and allowed Fred to preen as they followed the butler into the receiving room.

Ten or eleven couples were already gathered there, and Dorothy soon realized she and Fred were to stay where they were as each of the guests randomly revolved about the room, taking their turns to greet the newlyweds.

The British Aide-de-Camp, stunningly outfitted in his most formal uniform, was the first to greet them. He chatted for a moment, then took up a position next to Dorothy and proceeded to introduce each couple as they came to extend their welcomes and best wishes, each greeting seemingly more eloquent than the last.

Richly woven carpets cushioned her feet as she stood in the most elegant room she'd ever seen and watched Fred chat with British dignitaries as if he'd known them all his life. He was witty. Charming. Intelligent. Insightful. Brilliant. Her husband was indeed the most engaging fellow in the room.

~~~~~~

August 5, 1936 - Shillong

The dinner was at 8:15. After being received by the Aide-de-Camp we were introduced to some of the guests who had arrived, and then taken into the drawing room to wait for His Excellency and Lady Keane. The men were shown the plan of the table (there were eighteen present) and were told where to sit, and whom to take in to dinner. I was asked to stand in a certain place and was told that His Excellency would take me in to dinner. (I was somewhat surprised). His Excellency and Lady Keane came in shortly, were introduced and greeted the guests, and then he and I went in to dinner—heading the procession, and the others followed. I found out afterwards that it is apparently an English custom that a bride takes precedence over other guests, and therefore I was "it".

Had a lovely dinner, and the table was elegant to say the least. His Excellency was most charming, and I had the English Padre on the other side of me and he is a very entertaining person and most likeable.

After dinner we retired to the drawing room (or the women did) and had coffee. Then the men joined us, and we talked, sang, etc. Then His Excellency and Lady Keane left about 10:30, and later, Mrs. Higgins (the Valley Commissioner's wife in Gauhati who was a guest at Government House) whispered to me that as the bride and guest of honor, we could leave anytime, and that it was more or less up to me to start the procession, so being rather weary from the day, we took our leave then.

We are still glad that we are missionaries and do not belong to the official class.

Fred stood aside and watched His Excellency escort Dorothy in to dinner. She'd been quiet. Restrained. Naturally elegant. The most radiant woman in the room. He couldn't take his eyes off her, and he was not unaware that others had kept looking her way throughout the evening, as well.

~~~~~~

Dear Motherkin— (Fred used the endearment so common in India when addressing his mother-in-law)

Must write this to you for Dorothy could not. Last night at the dinner, she and I were seated at opposite ends of the long table. The dessert was served and I took one taste of mine and then laid my spoon on the plate and just sat and enjoyed looking at my wife. She was absolutely the loveliest person I have ever seen, framed by the two pink (burning) candles. Her hair was so nicely arranged, her wedding gown is such a lovely silver and made her throat and neck so white. Then her black evening wrap over that just added another touch to the beauty of it all. And above all, there is a beauty in Dorothy's eyes that just shines out and gives me a thrill that nothing can compare with.

Well, I was just sitting there enjoying Dorothy and forgot all about everything else and was called back to my surroundings by discovering that Dorothy was concerned about my not eating my dessert and had decided that I had not been given a spoon and was ordering a bearer to bring me a spoon. After the guests had gone and I confessed to what had been going on, we had a good laugh about it.

"Tell me, Wife, what made you think I'd lost my spoon?"

"Well, you weren't eating your ice cream. I may not know everything about you, Husband, but I do know you love ice cream more than anything in the world."

"*Used* to love ice cream more than anything in the world."

"Oh? Oh. Oh my." Dorothy blushed. "You do say the sweetest things."

JORHAT BUNGLA

CHAPTER TWENTY-ONE

GET YOUR GLAD RAGS ON

August, 1936

Neither Fred nor I can get over Dad's saying what he did about having told Mother months ago that he wished something like this would happen. Well, it all goes to prove what we believe—that it is all part of a Plan. If only we didn't have to be separated for the next few months, it would be perfect, but even then I think that it is worth it to have had this perfect month here together.

I am finding that married life is even better—lovelier, more satisfying, and more beautiful than I had any idea it could be. Fred is such a dear, and we seem to be well suited to each other.

Fred is such a dear.

How impossible it was to distill her remarkable new husband into one mere word. Yes, he was dear. And winsome and thoughtful and inspiring and devoted and wise and stalwart and spiritual and...

Dorothy sucked in a breath and sought the discipline to focus on the day's cases. She was in Gauhati again. And Fred was six hours away. In Jorhat. And that's the way it had to be until Alice Randall finally wrapped up her furlough and got herself back to Gauhati. Dorothy refused to leave the hospital without a surgeon, and Dr. Randall seemed to be dragging her feet in returning. And the board was doing little to encourage her to make haste.

It was easy to let her fears magnify each small setback, but Dorothy refused to believe that Alice wouldn't return to her post. Because if she didn't, if the worst happened, Dorothy knew it would be up to her to continue to fill the Satribari post until a replacement could be found. And that could take a year. Or more. Living separately with only fleeting weekends here and there with her exceedingly dear husband seemed an impossible thing to survive.

Her heart roiled with apologies to Alice for every bit of head-butting they'd engaged in over the past few years. Compatibility was not something they could claim, though Dorothy was at a loss to know why. But they were both professionals. She prayed that Alice saw it that way and would not knowingly make Dorothy and Fred's separation last any longer than absolutely necessary.

Try as she might, a clear picture of what life with her Fred would be like refused to materialize for Dorothy. No amount of imagination could clarify it for her. Waking up to his smile every morning. Making curtains for the windows of his...of *their*...bungla. Listening to his message when he preached on Sunday mornings. Watching him mentor the boys. Those things she could imagine. But what would normal married life feel like? That was something she could scarcely fathom.

Imagination was something Dorothy had always employed in most inventive ways throughout her life. When it came to designing better arrangements for the hospital wards, or ways to make the most of the scant time she had to see patients in the hill country, her imagination flourished. Everything and everyone benefited when Dorothy unleashed her imagination.

Until now.

Now imagination merely conjured childish pictures. They might once have seemed very realistic, but now that she'd had those blissful weeks in Shillong with the love of her life, she knew her imagination had failed her. Life with Fred was going to be beyond wonderful. Beyond fulfilling. Beyond imagining.

Dorothy's letter home — August 19, 1936

Have good letters from Fred every day, but would give anything if
we could be together and not have to write. He plans to come down
next week end—a week from now, and I am so anxious for the time to
come. Hope to go to Jorhat the middle of September for a few days,
but the way the European cases are stacking up, it looks a bit doubtful.
Still hoping. We are just as much in love as ever, and even more so.

August 26, 1936

> Fred comes Friday morning, and I am more excited about it than
> I was when he came down before the wedding. I guess our case is
> fatal for we seem to be falling more and more in love all the time,
> and I have never spent such a long two and a half weeks in my life
> as I have in the past two and one half since he went to Jorhat. Guess
> I wouldn't make a good wife for a traveling man. Mother, how did
> you ever stand it, (and I think Fred would say, "Dadkin, how did
> you manage to stick it out.")

Stick it out was such an understatement. How did one *survive* it is what Dorothy wanted to know.

But no one had a ready answer for her.

The English and American female medical missionaries with whom she shared her work were not married. And missionary wives were not allowed to engage in professional endeavors. The English and American wives of government emissaries were no help in providing answers, since they enjoyed a unique and somewhat cosseted life. There was not one married professional woman in her sphere, and it was the married professional to whom Dorothy wanted to pose her questions.

She wanted to be prepared. She wanted to make Fred proud of his new wife. But with her imagination deserting her, Dorothy was forced to tread unarmed into the unknown.

It made her anxious, and to quell the anxiety Dorothy did the only thing she knew how to do. She threw herself into her work.

There was no stopping Dorothy now. She knew that even though it was weeks—even months—before she could set up housekeeping in Jorhat, the time would be up before she knew it. So she filled each moment with all the things she felt would leave the women's hospital on the best possible footing.

Student nurses flew from chore to chore as she updated inventories. Paniwallas carried supplies, filled the larder, and cut back another ten yards of encroaching jungle. She organized a task force to dredge the sand out of buried water pipes, a task which they could never manage to keep ahead of.

And she read Fred's letters.

Even the ugly kapok trees seemed enchanting when she lingered beneath one long enough to read, for perhaps the tenth time, his most recent letter that she'd carried in the pocket of her white coat for two days.

> *My darling wife,*
>
> *You shall just have to get used to my impetuosity. I've changed our visitation schedule and shall not take no for an answer. I'm coming this Thursday evening, not Friday. I simply cannot wait. So...*
>
>> *I'll be down to get you in a taxi, honey,*
>> *better be ready 'bout a half past eight.*
>> *Now honey, don't be late, I wanna be there when*
>> *the band starts playin'!*
>
> *So get your glad rags on, lovely wife. And be ready, because I'll be down to get you, darling. Thursday night. Half past eight.*
>> *Your ever-loving Fred*

Dorothy beamed as she tucked the letter back into her pocket. She had almost heard him singing as she'd read the lyrics he'd quoted. They'd sung *Darktown Strutter's Ball* halfway to Jorhat the first time he'd taken her up there.

> *I'm gonna dance out both my shoes*
> *When they play those Jelly Roll Blues*
> *Tomorrow night at the Darktown Strutter's Ball*

She could still see Fred's hands tapping out the percussion on the Ford's steering wheel. When Dorothy reached over to add a toot of the horn here and there Fred knew he'd married a real corker. And she knew she had, too.

Her trip-hammer heart was in full swing today. Anticipation was at its very highest. Because today was Thursday.

At her earliest opportunity, Dorothy hurried back to the bungla to prepare for Fred's visit, swinging along the path to the rhythm of her heartbeat. She'd stayed up late the night before making the frozen dessert he liked so much, all the while sweet-talking the Frigidaire in hopes she could cajole it into working through the day. And it had.

She polished the dusty scuffs off her shoes, pressed the lace on the headscarf she'd need if they went for a drive, knitted a new rosette and pinned it to the bodice of the dress she'd wear. It was remarkable how a dress could take on a whole new look and feel just by adding something as simple as that. Just like a life could.

Around six o'clock she turned off the Victrola, just to make sure she'd hear his car the moment he arrived. She straightened the doily beneath the fruit bowl and let her eyes sweep the corners of the room for any unwelcome guests, then swung into the kitchen for one last check on the dessert.

The Frigidaire hummed steady and strong, and the dessert had the look of perfection. Even in the little china dishes with the chipped rims. They were all she had at the moment, since she'd sent all her good china up to Jorhat.

Dorothy dipped a finger into the corner of the dish nearest her, just to check the consistency. It was firm, not mushy at all. Perfect.

"Thank you, my sturdy little Frigidaire."

She smiled as she patted the fridge with one hand and licked the frozen delight from the finger of her other hand. She danced away from the appliance and made a small twirl in the kitchen doorway.

And then she heard it.

The sound was low and easy, mellow with a bit of a wail. It lifted and dove, lingered and danced, and released a flood of emotion she thought she'd held within so very well.

It said *I'm here.*

It said *You're not alone anymore.*

It said *I love you I missed you I can't wait to hold you.*

Fred had brought his saxophone.

AMU—FRED'S COOK AND BEARER IN JORHAT

CHAPTER TWENTY-TWO

MONOTONY IS NOT IN HER VOCABULARY

Letter from Fred
September 20, 1936

Well, I'm alone and mighty lonesome. Dorothy was here last weekend and this place was a perfect Heaven. She telegraphed on Wednesday a week ago and stated that she would arrive at noon the next day. Well, I simply came right up off the ground and it is only lately that my feet have been touching the soil again. She stayed until the following Wednesday afternoon and since her going this place has continued to hold a kind of fragrance of her that has transformed it into a real home for me.

Dorothy put up some curtains and arranged the vases for flowers, and Amu and I have been seeing to it that things remained just as near like her arrangement as we can keep it. Even he was mighty happy for her being here (she makes everyone love her wherever she goes) and the first morning after she had returned to Gauhati, Amu served my breakfast and then remained standing in the door looking as if something radically were wrong with him, then he came out with this, "I don't feel good. The Memsahib is gone and this place is empty. You and I don't know how to arrange this house but she does. And without her, I don't work hard."

So it would seem that Amu has fallen for Dorothy.

Fred paused midway through writing his letter. Amu had indeed fallen for Dorothy. But how could he not? She didn't treat him as a servant, she welcomed him as a partner in helping to keep the household running smoothly.

Letter home from Dorothy

We will try and get some pictures of the place. It is such a big one that there would be plenty of room for four or five more of you if you could only manage to get here. We are hoping to begin to get some tennis in regularly, and Fred hopes to get in some golf.

...He brought his saxophone...and also his baby organ, and I am having some fun trying to remember a bit of what I used to know so that we can play at least some of the hymns together. Mother, you score again. You said that I would rue the day some day that I hadn't made more of my music, and I guess that day has come, but maybe it isn't too late even now.

Yesterday a box walla came around and I enjoyed getting some of the things that I had planned to get but hadn't had time before we were married.

Fred has a fine bearer-cook by the name of Amu. He speaks and understands English quite well. He was much interested in the purchases yesterday and helped me quite a bit by telling me what linen Fred had, etc. He is a Christian, and is more than just a servant—a real friend. When someone said to him the other day, "Well, you'll have a memsahib to work for now" he said, "No, another helper." We have laughed a good deal over it.

I wish that we could tell you more of our plans for the future, but a good deal depends on what is decided regarding certain phases of the work out here. I expect to go to Jorhat just as soon as Alice gets back to Gauhati, and hope that it won't be more than until November 1st that I will have to stay in Gauhati. Fred's furlough is due in the spring of '38. Of course furlough plans are still in the making, but he is hoping to get his doctorate at Columbia while at home. Later we can let you know more about our plans.

Letter home from Fred

I believe I have the best wife in the whole flat world. I was crazy about her...but that's nothing to the way I feel now and I get worse daily. She can think up the nicest things to do and say for my happiness and then goes on to do them in about the finest way you can imagine. Some folk thought because she was so good professionally that she wouldn't be so good domestically. The fact is, she is showing them all where to get off.

Can she cook! Each time I think she has made about the best there is and then she springs a new one on me and it puts the former one in the shade. She makes such good cookies that they simply won't last any time at all. Then she countered with some doughnuts and they went just as fast. Her green tomato pickles get better all the time and she has turned out a real supply of orange marmalade that beats the market all to pieces and has a much better flavour.

She seems to never lack for originality, and monotony simply isn't in her vocabulary. And on top of all the good food she is giving me, she fixes the house up so tastefully that I am proud as punch every time someone comes to call.

As impossible as it seemed, Fred found ways to manage his angst over the separation. He tried desperately not to take his frustration out on Amu, who had delighted Fred with his instant loyalty to Dorothy. He bit his tongue bloody trying to soften his tone with the Swedish Baptists who had nothing but disdain for his teaching methods. No matter how they disparaged his work, he knew they would come to appreciate Dorothy, if he just gave them a chance.

And he worked equally as hard to maintain some level of patience with the schoolboys who managed to find any number of ways to thwart his plans for an orderly classroom. But to Fred's surprise, one simple phrase wrought magical results. When things began to get out of hand, all he had to do now was shush them and ask, "Gentlemen, please. What would Mrs. Dorothy say about that?"

There was no other word for it but magical. They had only met the new Mrs. Chambers once, and she had utterly charmed them. Who but Dorothy could influence such modifications of behavior while not even being present?

Yet when an insidious viper threatened their small community, it was Fred for whom the boys came running.

From what I have experienced this last week, there is ample evidence that this is India. In the first place, the cobras have kept us going. I think I wrote you about the other one, and this one happened just before Dorothy arrived. One of the boys came to me and asked for a "dhow" (small axe-like knife) and I told him where he would find it. Then he casually remarked that they had found a snake. I went to the killing with them.

When I arrived on the scene, I saw a five foot cobra lying under a wheelbarrow one of the boys had been pushing. We attacked and the snake put up a good fight. It would rise about two feet off the ground and strike ferociously. That swelled neck is an interesting sight and this one had beautiful silver diamonds about a foot along his neck. It was a beautiful sight in spite of all the deadly poison involved.

I feared for the boys, for one lad was going into it with a four foot stick. We finally chopped it into pieces with a hoe. Then I discovered something that nearly made my heart stop. I found that the wheel of the wheelbarrow was holding the snake pinned to the ground and this is what happened. The boys had seen the snake crawling from a small patch of jungle across toward the church building and this one lad had run his wheelbarrow on it to stop it and hold it. It could reach at least two feet and I don't know yet what kept the boy from being bitten.

My knees actually shook when I turned to walk away. This is the first live cobra I have seen and the fewer the better.

CHAPTER TWENTY-THREE

ABSENCE MAKES THE HEART HURT

Fred tapped his knuckles against the screening he'd just stretched tightly across its frame. It would do the job in superb fashion. Taut, very small mesh, just the ticket. No cobra was going to get through that screen.

It was the last of a dozen frames he'd re-screened, and he'd added a dozen more to completely screen the verandah to his satisfaction. He intended for Dorothy to feel safe in their home. Completely safe.

But who was he kidding. He was the one who needed to know Dorothy would be safe here. The project had taken up most of his week, and now he dared any snake, scorpion, or insect for that matter, to breach his defense.

Dorothy had spent hours making curtains, acquiring drawn-work table linens, arranging furniture and more, all to make sure that every evening Fred could come home to the loveliest place this side of heaven. It had taken his breath away, just watching her hum about the house on their few precious days together. The very least he could do was to secure the nest she'd made for them.

Once the last screen was hammered into place, Fred carried a plat of starter plants out into the yard and began digging nicely spaced holes along the edge of the walk. Defensive barriers were great, but he wanted the entrance to her home to look like an English garden. He wanted it to be a lovely, welcoming path to her front door, and the starters he'd collected in order to accomplish that had taken all his resources to gather. But she was so very worth it.

He smiled to himself when Amu stopped what he was doing and came to observe.

"Too close," Amu said.

"What? Too close together? I don't think so, Amu. I want a nice solid row of flowers to line the path. Won't that be nice?"

"Too close to the path, sahib."

Fred's laughter died on his lips. Amu never criticized. Everything Fred did was always highly complimented by his cook and personal assistant.

"Too close why?" Fred turned and shielded his eyes with his hand as he looked up into the man's kind face that now sported a scowl.

"Sahib work many day to keep the snake out of the bungla, then sahib put this, this, and this alla way up to front door." His hands swept the air to define the grand pathway Fred had in mind.

"I don't...what are you saying?"

"Snake like pygmy hen egg, yes?"

Fred nodded. "Yes," he said, wondering where this was going.

"What does pygmy hen like?"

Fred looked down at the flowers he'd chosen to grace the path, and a part of his mind visualized them fully grown, in full bloom, covering the border with lovely blossoms and leaves. And a half dozen pygmy hens roosting in the midst of it all. If he'd seen that once, he'd seen it a hundred times, but never in someone's dooryard.

He was about to plant a border garden that would invite every pygmy hen in the neighborhood to take up residence. And half the snakes in the province would follow.

"Oh. Oh my. Amu? What do I do?"

Amu laughed. "Not to worry, my friend. Not to worry. Put lemongrass here, here and here, and seamoon flower here, maybe here, and here, and no snake, no pygmy hen. Just so."

Fred swallowed. He was speechless. Something about that made Amu laugh. He chuckled and hid his grin behind his fist as he walked back to the laundry he was about to fold.

Lemon grass and seamoon flower repelled snakes. Who would have known?

Fred called his thanks and said a prayer of gratitude for Amu—something that was becoming a daily habit, he found. Thank God Amu had kept him from making this colossal mistake.

August 18, 1936 — From Fred to his Mother

These are trying days here. I am so lonesome for Dorothy that I have to fight every minute to keep the proper perspective on the work here. I try to keep busy from morning till night and definitely allot special times for writing to her and yet I find myself tempted all the time to break over and let my work slide. Am scheduled to return to Gauhati, leaving here on the afternoon of the 27th, and we will have three days together. I must leave there on Sunday night and get back here at noon Monday, in time to meet my class in the afternoon. If cases in the Hospital run properly, she may get to come up here for a short stay in September.

To date, the return of Dr. Randall is more or less uncertain, and definitely not before November, so that makes us all the more unsettled, for it would mean something if we had a definite date to count on. Guess we are spoiled children, for we both get just about everything we wish for, and now we are both feeling that things will break so that we will get to be together in our own home sooner than we see it possible. We have to be optimistic about the matter or we might do something rash.

One of the reasons I am getting such a kick out of Dorothy, is because I can think with her without reservation and just as strongly as I like and she can come back in the same strength. We have both decided that we will never get old but always find new things to learn. Music and literature seem to offer our first adventure and we know there are plenty worlds still unconquered, but, one at a time.

August 18, 1936
Letter from Fred in Jorhat to Mr. & Mrs. Kinney

Am enclosing a letter written to my Mother and had hoped that I would be able to write at length to you. The fact is, between the lonesomeness and the heat, I am finding Jorhat a most unsatisfactory place these days. I try to discipline my mind sufficiently to keep busy at my work but I find it is almost a hopeless task.

I know I can never be myself until Dorothy and I can be together in our own home. Those six weeks together are just intimations of the fullness that life will assume when we can work together in the same place. Had we not reckoned in advance on this present situation, I, for my part, would not put up with it a minute. But the absolute harmony and happiness of those six weeks were worth it all.

I tell Dorothy again and again that I got the bargain and I hate to think what she got but I am willing to do my best to improve what she gets. I am glad that she and I discovered the secret of our hearts before we had any reactions from friends and relatives on either side at home. I tell her she will just have to take me for what I am and not for what others think I am, or what she herself might think I might become and she seems to be of that mind. However, when I get further word from home, I get a sinking feeling inside, for I know I can never live up to the expectations of some for Dorothy's husband. Guess it will be better to stay in Assam, rather than disappoint her friends.

But there is one point on which I offer no apologies at all. If there is anyone who can love her anymore, or be any crazier about her than I am, then I would like to find the rare person. I know I have found a prize and I knew just as soon as I realized that she cared for me that there were no questions about our marriage. In fact, I have done nothing in life in which I was more sure that it was the best thing to do; and that the Lord had a special hand in it, than when I married Dorothy Joy.

The only thing I can't understand is just why she should care for me. She and I don't discuss that point and have stopped arguing over which got the better end of the deal. I feel that I have stepped over into an entirely new world and my desire to be of use to the Kingdom of God has multiplied many times. I can never be fully worthy of Dorothy's love but if I can only do my best for the Lord's Work, I feel I can approach something in that direction.

August 22, 1936 — Letter from Fred to his Mother

I am sitting on the verandah trying to keep cool and trying to keep from taking the first train to Gauhati. Between the heat and lonesomeness, I am just about good for nothing. I did not think I could ever fall so irrationally in love with anyone as I have with Dorothy Joy. Rather prided myself on my ability at self-control but this is one time when I capitulate completely. Write to her only once a day because there is but one mail a day. But from the time I waken in the morning until I fall asleep at night, my whole world is Dorothy and everything turns about her. I try to keep busy continually or I would simply go crazy. We bargained for it and I would not take back the six weeks we had together, but it is mighty hard to try to keep my mind on my work and remain in Jorhat.

If anyone in this world has all the marks of an ideal wife, then Dorothy has them plus. I marvel at her understanding of so many little things that make for perfect harmony between us. Surely God has a special purpose for us in this country and we are gloriously happy to give our best to what comes to our hands to do. We are both coming to a fuller realization of John 10:10.

"Fred, darling?" Dorothy crooked a finger at Fred and beckoned him to the window. "What do you call that flower? That one right at the step up to the verandah. See?"

Fred peered over her shoulder and grinned. Dorothy pointed to one of the plants Amu had recommended.

"Sea moon flower, dear. Don't you like it?"

"Oh but I do, darling! It reminds me of...of morning glories back home."

Fred drew her into a hug. He'd never tell her why the sea moon flowers were planted strategically along the front walk. They reminded her of morning glories. They reminded her of home. And that was all that mattered.

CHAPTER TWENTY-FOUR

GOING HOME

Just as Dorothy began to cope with her separation from Fred, news from home shattered the tentative joy she'd managed to recover.

Images of her father pervaded her thoughts today. How could they not? He'd been there in that first moment when Dorothy had realized her life's passion, when she'd known without a shred of doubt that somehow the practice of medicine would define her future. Each baby she delivered reminded her of it, of that day when a wide-eyed twelve-year-old girl helped her father deliver a baby, beneath a bridge in the foothills of Colorado.

He'd been every bit as present with her today.

Dorothy paused for a moment to take comfort in the quiet darkness that had engulfed the hospital. Most of her patients were doing well, and Dorothy could only give thanks for that blessing where it was due. God had blessed her with the dearest staff whose skill was as great—greater, even—than anyone could expect in a remote outpost like Gauhati. Today had challenged them like few others had. And they had risen to the tasks. Dr. Randall would find her support team ready and superbly able.

When she gets here, Dorothy thought. *If she gets here.*

She stepped into her office and poured a glass of cool water that Edna made sure was always fresh and waiting on her desk. She caught a glimpse of herself in the little Bohemian mirror and brushed an errant tendril off her forehead.

She moved closer and reached out a finger to trace the trompe l'oeil art that twisted about the mirror's frame, surprised as always at the suggestion of depth it achieved. The flowing vine was so skillfully painted that it deceived the eye with its illusion of depth and substance. But her finger proved once again, as it had each time she'd touched it since her childhood, that it was merely an artist's clever treatment of a flat surface.

Merely a deception.

Dorothy caught a sob before it spilled into the silence of her office. It was the word that triggered her unexpected reaction. *Deception.* The word floated behind her eyes. It twisted her heart with its too-fresh memory of the day's tragedy. *Deception.* Like the signs of life that seemed so strong in the young woman with the ruptured uterus.

Everything had pointed to success. The surgery went as well as she could have hoped. But the blood loss was too great, and her patient had lost her tenuous hold.

We had a young woman brought in three hours after a rupture of the uterus had occurred. Altho we operated immediately it was too late to save her. How I did long for some of the blood donors that every hospital at home has on call. Altho we typed her blood with that of three of her relatives, there was none that matched hers.

The patient was a beautiful young woman, brought in by a husband who clearly loved her. Dorothy had found herself bereft of words when he wept, begging her to save his wife.

She blinked her weary eyes and realized she still held the cablegram that had arrived on this day that was already so filled with sadness. The little mirror glimmered in a shaft of moonlight and reflected her tears that she could not manage to hold back. Bits of silver paint gleamed, nearly bringing the painted vine to life. Her mind seemed as twisted as the trailing vine tonight. Sorrowful thoughts warped into plans for the coming day, then dipped back into thoughts of Fred and then by some strange mental distortion became vivid memories of home.

How does it do that, Daddy?

She'd asked her father once how the moon could play such a trick on her eyes the way it brought the painted mirror to life at night. He'd launched into a sketchy scientific explanation until he caught her looking at him with a sort of disappointment on her face.

He'd sighed and scratched his head, then tucked his thumbs into his vest pockets, rocked back on his heels and declared, "Of course I always think a moonbeam is just God's fingertip. So it's not really a trick at all, is it, Doffy Joy? It's just God's finger painting."

Dorothy sobbed. She hadn't thought of that in years. But tonight her father's face was as clear in her mind as if he were standing right beside her.

"Oh Dad! I miss you!"

Her shoulders trembled as the emotion overtook her. As the deception of it began to sink in. She'd always had an anchor at home, a knowledge there would always be Mom and Dad to come home to.

But the cable from home this week changed all that. Even as she knew that her anchor had already been lovingly secured in Fred's heart, the anchor of her family home had not lost its place. It was merely being shared by the man in whom her faith and trust grew immeasurably day by day.

She reached out to the mirror again, placing her hands where her father once had, touching the thing that in this moment was her only tangible connection with him.

Your father has Gone Home.

The words of the cablegram had stopped her breath, squeezed her heart, and taken the strength from her knees.

Your father has Gone Home.

And Fred had come to be with her. He had dropped everything in Jorhat and flown to her side, to hold her through the devastation he knew she would be feeling. A loss he felt, as well. It had meant the world to her that he had not hesitated for a moment to come to her.

It was a comfort beyond words that her Fred had met her father before he ever met her. Fred could see her father's face in his mind as she did, hear the measure of his voice and the weight of his words as she did.

Her sobs quieted. Her heart found its peaceful pace.

For nearly ten years she'd hoped her parents would come see this new world of hers. And now her father was here, at her shoulder. Not in the way she had hoped, but he was here.

Dorothy wandered into the children's ward. She lifted the chart from the end of three-year-old Ajola's bed and was relieved to see his kidneys were showing stronger output every day. His little face had lost much of its swelling now, and she was struck by the beauty of it.

She realized she'd wakened him when he opened one eye. But the moment he saw who was standing at the foot of his bed he opened both eyes wide, smiled and raised a small hand to wave at her.

"Hello there, Humpty Dumpty," she whispered.

He giggled as he always did at the name his terribly swollen face had earned him.

"I'll just make a note here in your chart that Humpty Dumpty—" she paused and dropped him a look. "That is your name, isn't it? Mr. Humpty Dumpty?"

Ajola suppressed a squeal. "No! My name Ajola Sunny Jeem Humpty Dumpty!"

"Oh yes, how could I forget?" Dorothy turned back to her writing. "Ajola Sunny Jeem Humpty Dumpty is resting well."

Ajola giggled and let out a contented sigh as Dorothy leaned over to kiss the top of his head. His eyelids fluttered heavily, and a few light strokes of her fingers across his forehead sent him back to sleep.

Slumbering children in every bed lifted her spirits. They had come in such a variety of alarming conditions, and all were doing well now.

She stepped across into the nursery. The little row of bassinets boasted four newborns, and she stopped to check on the newest to arrive.

~~~~~~

> We have had some very interesting cases in the hospital lately. One was a little woman who was brought in from a village some 15 miles away. She had malaria, kala azar, pulmonary tuberculosis. . .and was at term with a pregnancy. Due to certain conditions, normal birth was impossible and two days after she was admitted she went into labor and we had to do a Caesarian operation. She and the baby are both doing remarkably well. She is nine days past the operation and has had no fever for two days and has gotten along beautifully in every way. Has had to have intravenous medication for both the malaria and the kala azar. The baby is an adorable little piece weighing about five pounds.

Dorothy gazed upon the infant. This was what she had wanted her father to see. This was how she wanted him to see *her*. Not as the child asking about moonbeams, but as the woman who brought new life into the world, who carried desperate women through the greatest travail of their lives and released them into motherhood.

He knew her as daughter, as student, as aspiring missionary. But she wanted him to know her as she was now. As doctor. As peer. As woman.

There was nothing for it now but to let her tears fall. In her heart she knew he had "seen" her, had grown in his understanding of who his daughter had become. Her letters had conveyed to him as much as she knew how to without seeming to brag, and surely his image of her had blossomed over time.

But for him to have stood here at her side, to have witnessed the fullness of this life she had carved out for herself—that would have been a joy unlike any she might have conceived of. To see this wee walla in her father's arms, to hear the blessing she knew he would speak over the child.

The very image of it drew a smile to Dorothy's face. She could see it so clearly. She could hear his voice as if he stood beside her. Her heart trembled with the phantom resonance of the voice she would never hear again.

Not in this world.

October 17, 1936

Dearest Mother:

How I wish I could have been with you and be with you during these days. I can't realize yet all that has happened and all that it means. The cable came so unexpectedly. I got it about 5:30pm on Thursday the 15th. I couldn't credit what I read at first. It left me feeling numb all over. If only I could have been with you and could have let you and Dad know how much I love you both. It seemed almost unbearable not to be able to go to you at once.

All Wednesday night I couldn't sleep (that would have been Wednesday daytime at home). I couldn't find any known reason for it. Had done a Caesarean Wednesday morning and altho everything had gone beautifully, thought my inability to sleep was perhaps due to that altho I was not at all worried about her. Something was wrong somewhere, but just where or what I couldn't say. Now I know the reason! Even being halfway around the world couldn't prevent my being conscious of something that was not as it had been.

I have tried to imagine what may have happened. I know Daddy was ready and for him I can feel only a deep joy for he has entered into the reward that he has won, and his race has been run victoriously and triumphantly. His going is another link with eternity and another proof of Life Eternal. Such a spirit as Dad had—the firmness of character, the integrity of it, the personality—can't be just snuffed out like a candle. There must be and is a Life Eternal. I'm surer than ever of it. I can be gloriously happy for Dad—glad that he could go without being ill a long time and perhaps helpless, glad that he could go perhaps in harness—know he would have wanted it that way, and glad that he was ready and had had such a full rich life in so many ways.

I know that letting him go on ahead was bitterly hard for you, Mother mine, and would so love to be able to help lift the load and share it more than I can at this distance. I can appreciate how hard it was better now than I could have six months ago. My thinking has raced backwards and forwards in the last two days. Have thought how much you had helped Dad to make possible his success—of the sacrifice that you both made in being away from each other so much in order that he might do the work he did. That too, I can appreciate now as never before. Oh Mother Darling, hard as the experience is and has been, I know that you are capable of meeting it in a very wonderful and beautiful way, and a way that will be worthy of Dad, and worthy of our faith. If only I could be there to help and to be near you.

Last night I lay awake from about two to three-thirty. Had been rather restless before, but just couldn't sleep. Was thinking about you all, loving you so much, and longing to be with you so, trying to know just where you were, etc.

Fred joins me in sending much, much love and the hope that the support of the everlasting arms may be very real. We love you so much, and shall be thinking of you so often. Our love, our thoughts, and our prayers will be with the girls as well as with you, Mother darling.   As ever your daughter—

Dorothy Joy

CHAPTER TWENTY-FIVE

ALL'S RIGHT WITH THE WORLD

Jorhat, Assam

December 21, 1936

At last the long six months are over and we are together in our own home and such a gorgeously happy time as we are having. Dinner tonight in front of the fireplace, tall red candles on the mantel and above them the copy of The Presence that the Guild at Calvary gave me. We both love it.

The little Christmas tree is all set up.

Dorothy dozed in the crook of Fred's arm as the tall red candles on the mantel dripped uneven trails along the bases of the candlesticks. Each exhaling breath carried with it a small sigh, without a doubt marking the single most peaceful moment of her lifetime. Knowing she wouldn't have to leave in a few days kept the lazy smile planted on Dorothy's face as she relaxed into her husband's side.

She was home.

She'd never have to be separated from Fred again.

"You're purring."

"Wha...hmm?"

"I said, you're purring." Fred tipped her chin up and kissed her forehead. "Like a little kitten."

If life could be any fuller than it is now, I can't conceive how it is possible. Certainly God is gracious to grant so much happiness and I only hope that somehow I can be of some use in bringing a measure of some such happiness into others' lives. Wish we could share our happiness with you at home, for we feel as if we have more than our share and plenty to spare.

"Well I just feel like purring, darling. Everything is so...so..."

Dorothy stopped to search her contentedly muzzy head for a word.

"Say it, my dear," Fred grinned.

"Say what?"

"The word you want to say but you think it's too utterly silly."

"Why, Fred Chambers, I don't know what word you could possibly be thinking of. In fact, I don't believe there's a single silly word in my entire— and might I add *vast*—vocabulary."

Fred laughed. "Not a one, I'm sure. So I shall say it for you. You are purring because things here are utterly *purrfect*. Hmmm? Am I right?"

"Oh Fred, it sounds so ridiculous." She poked him in the ribs. "And so utterly true."

Fred sighed and stretched. "Golly, if I could just get along with the Swedes half as well as I get along with you, my life would be simply too easy to bear."

Dorothy sat up, untucked her knees and straightened her skirt. Just mentioning the austere community of Swedish missionaries sobered her. They were the most divisive group anyone could expect to encounter in the field.

"Oh dear. What have they done now? Outlawed rugby?"

"Hmph. *That* I could probably deal with. It's worse."

"I guess you'd better tell me what it is or I might just have to stomp over there and throttle it out of them."

"Throttle them, you say?"

"Yes! Throttle! They have positively no sense at all when it comes to working with these good Assamese, and their main goal in life seems to be to make your life miserable. So out with it, Fred. What have they done?"

Fred shifted and ran a hand through his hair, a signal that had Dorothy holding her breath. He was really upset. She laid a hand on his shoulder prompting him to speak.

"They're against me, Dor. All twelve of them. Only the Tuttles, Hardings, Merrills and Huttons are in my camp. The other twelve are telling the boys they're being taught wrong."

"Wrong! That's preposterous! Fred, you know the boys won't believe it if they think about it for a second. They're doing so well in their exams. They have to know it's because of you."

Dorothy to her mother

...you were asking about Fred's degrees, etc. He got his B.A. from Franklin in 1923. Has studied at Yale and Harvard, and got his degree (M.A. from U. of C. in 1926 - History). Had two years at Yale in Religious Ed. He was ordained just shortly before coming out to Assam, but doesn't use the Rev. much as he is primarily a teacher.

Fred got a tremendous thrill out of what Dad had said about being proud of him if he was in the list whose theology was being investigated by the Swedes.

Honestly, I don't know what is ahead for the Assam mission. The Swedes are practically all of the ultra fundamentalist group and some are so narrow and intolerant that it would be hard to put paper between their ears, as Wink would say. They are out after anyone that doesn't believe and teach as they do, and some of them would stoop to almost anything to get rid of some out here.

The Swedish brethren have had it in for Fred ever since he came to the field because he studied at Yale. Another one of the Swedish men made the statement that he couldn't agree with Fred's beliefs, and when asked what they were he had to admit that he didn't know, had never talked to him about them, for Pete's sake.

From a letter we received the other day, I rather imagine that I am in for some of the same thing for having declared sides by throwing my lot in with a "heretic", but it is a grand place to be, and I didn't have to change any of my own ideas when I did it as I think we think pretty much alike.

Dorothy watched Fred wrestle with what she had just said.

"But there's more to it," he said. "The Swedes are...well, they're telling the boys they're going to build some new schools and that the boys don't have to knuckle down on their studies until the new school is ready."

"New sch—Fred, darling, I know I haven't been up here long, but from what I see, the Swedes are very long on words and very short on action. You've taught your boys well. They'll see just what I've seen. I'm sure they will."

She rubbed his back, and felt him slowly straighten. And just when she thought he was ready to make one of his philosophical statements that she so admired, he laughed. A slow, easy, surprising kind of laugh that escalated until Fred was sprawled on the divan sputtering like his sides would split.

"Well, Mr. Chambers. I take back everything I said. If the boys saw you in this condition they'd make a bee-line for that new Swedish school. If I said something funny I surely don't know what it—"

"No, no," he grinned. "Not funny, just, remarkable. How you just open your mouth and logic spills out and all of the sudden God's in His Heaven and all's right with the world." He caught his breath and stifled a last boyish giggle as his face calmed. "See, I've been so focused on the Swedes that I was losing sight of the boys. And...and I'm not here to be best friends with the Swedes. I'm here to teach the boys. The best way I know how."

Fred bounded up from the divan and pulled Dorothy with him. They stood in the middle of their new home grinning hopelessly at one another.

"I knew you'd see it eventually, darling," Dorothy smiled between slow kisses. "Those boys hang on your every word. I've watched it. They adore you."

They swayed together, moving instinctively to some invisible strain.

"They do?"

"Mmm-hm. They do. So if you change even one tiny thing about the way you manage their schooling, well I'll, I'll just..."

Fred stopped her with a long, sweet kiss.

"You'll what?" He kissed her forehead.

"I'll just have to throttle you."

"Mmm-hm. I guess you will."

Words drifted into the night and red candle wax spilled over onto the mantel. And the dimming light from the nearly spent candles was replaced by a glimmer of understanding between two souls. There would never be anything but trust between them. There would never be anything but admiration, comfort and good humor between them. There would never be anything but love.

Because God was indeed in His Heaven.

And all was indeed right in their world.

MILLIE MARVIN ON LEFT, EDNA STEVER AND LUCILE TUTTLE ON RIGHT

MILLIE MARVIN

CHAPTER TWENTY-SIX

UNDER MY HEART

~~~~~~

June 29, 1937

Tomorrow, Millie and Mrs. Kirby are having a tea supper to celebrate our wedding anniversary. It doesn't seem possible that it will be a year, but time has gone quickly. We are thousands of times more in love than we were a year ago, and it looks as though it would keep on increasing. Wish you could all be here to help us celebrate.

The amiable chatter of the dozen friends gathered in Mrs. Kirby's front room seemed to fade, muted by Dorothy's attention to a strange and wonderful sensation. Her fingers had been idly tracing the edges of the handmade organdy flowers she'd pinned to the breast of her new dress when she first felt it.

She hadn't truly planned to shape the flowers in any certain way, once she'd decided that a small posy was the perfect adornment for the new dress she'd finished just the night before this special occasion. But as she had let the fabric twine and turn of its own accord, her little bunch of flowers had begun to look very much like the Cecile Bruner rose blossoms from her wedding bouquet.

It was perfect, to wear such a vivid reminder of that beautiful day so near to her heart.

She looked across the room to find Fred where he cheerfully helped Millie serve the tea party guests. At the same moment he turned to find her watching him, and he smiled. That wide, lovely boyish grin of his.

Her hand slipped to the folds of fabric just below her waist. She wasn't showing all that much yet, but unless she was mistaken, she'd just felt the lightest flutter like a tiny flotilla of bubbles trickling beneath her belly button. Fred had caught the movement of her hand, and something in it spoke to him. His eyebrows raised in the quizzical way she knew so well, the look that said, *Something's going on, dear wife. Are you alright?*

She blinked and held back a small laugh. He knew her so thoroughly.

Oh yes, she was alright. She was more than alright. She drew her lips into the most casual smile she could summon. Their baby had just moved for the first time.

She would tell him tonight.

~~~~~~

July 7, 1937

> Wednesday was our first wedding anniversary and was a very very happy one. Millie asked us over for tea supper in the afternoon and had invited the other missionaries as well. During the day a wire came from the Hardings and Merrills in Tura with congratulations and best wishes, and that did warm the cockles of our hearts. Mrs. Kirby said that she and Millie had had a hard time deciding just what the first wedding anniversary was—wood, cotton, or what, and decided it was cotton. She gave us a dear little padded holder for the hot handle of a teapot made in the shape of a parrot, and two hot lid lifters. Millie gave us two lovely white tray cloths, and Victoria presented us with one dozen jharons (dish towels). Fred said the world began a year ago, and so Millie said that this was the beginning of the Year Two. I finished the dress (with Fred's help as he pinned the hem for me and did a jolly good job of it) made from the material Mother sent last year, and it looks ever so nice. Wore it as a celebration of the day. Made a small bunch of organdy flowers for the front.

Later when they were alone, still smiling from the party held in their honor, Dorothy had to tease her husband for his impatience.

"Well, for heaven's sake, Fred Chambers, I wouldn't have told you if I'd known you were going to pitch a hissy fit." Dorothy tried to chide Fred, but her own grin spoiled that idea in a hurry.

"It's completely unfair, you know," he whined dramatically. "He's my child too, dearest selfish wife. You shouldn't get to have all the fun."

"What?!"

"I mean, I should get to feel him kick once in awhile now, shouldn't I? Wouldn't that be fair?"

Fred reclined on the davenport with Dorothy tucked into the crook of his arm. The position had quite naturally become their favorite. She was turned just enough that his hand rested on her belly, as it had for the last half hour while he'd been waiting to feel their child move.

"*She* will kick you when *she's* good and ready and not a moment sooner, silly boy."

"She? *She*? I thought we agreed she was a *he*."

"Well of course, she is a he." Dorothy turned to give him a peck on the cheek. "You always get your way, don't you? So stop worrying. She will definitely be a—"

"Stop! Shush! Was that it?" Fred's hand moved slightly higher as the baby shifted. All she'd had to do was move and wake the little imp and her daddy got his first chance to feel his child's delicate kick.

"Yes, my dearest husband." She dropped her head to his chest. "That was it. I think she's dancing."

"Kicking a football, I think. Or maybe rugby."

"Mmm. I don't think girls play football."

"You're right, dearest. Rugby it is."

Their voices drifted off as they sat together, both hands on her rounding belly, following the child's dainty kicks across its mother's abdomen. Marveling in wonder at the new dimension this tiny babe had brought into their lives. Knowing that now, at last, in God's good time, they were a family.

~~~~~~~~~~~~~~~~~~~~~~~~~~~~~~

July 27, 1937

The "wee walla" is beginning to show very unmistakable signs of being a very active little individual and we are both getting a big thrill out of it all.

November 22, 1937—handwritten letter from Dorothy while confined in Gauhati hospital awaiting the birth of her first child

There isn't any place I know of where I'd rather be than here, and if you all could drop in and see me it would be perfect.

There are times in every family when heaven and earth conspire to reward good and faithful servants with the desire of their hearts. In November of 1937, Fred and Dorothy greeted Carol Joy, who refused to enter the world by natural means and required the surgical assistance of Dorothy's medical family in Gauhati.

There, in the place where Dorothy had set her lamp of ministry in the Satribari Compound, surrounded by those who held her in highest regard and tended with more loving care than any mother and newborn might ever hope to experience, Dorothy, Fred and baby Carol Joy began to shape their new family.

December 1, 1937
Gauhati. Handwritten letter from Dorothy

He is so wild over Carol (and so am I) and it gives me a thrill to see him with her. I think he could sit and hold her all day, and is so anxious to get us home so he can help care for her. Is crazy to learn to bathe her, etc. He's a grand husband and is going to be just as fine a father, I know.

November 28, 1937 – Fred's letter home

Dor and I have each waited longingly for a long time for a baby and we are making the most of it and I do get the biggest kick out of the little thing and an extra wallop when I see Dor with the baby. She certainly makes a lovely mother and I am sure no child will receive more intelligent care or have more love given to it than our baby. We wanted her long before we knew she was a possibility and now that she is really here we are happier than we even dreamed.

I have found a new glow under my heart that I never knew before and it never gets cool.

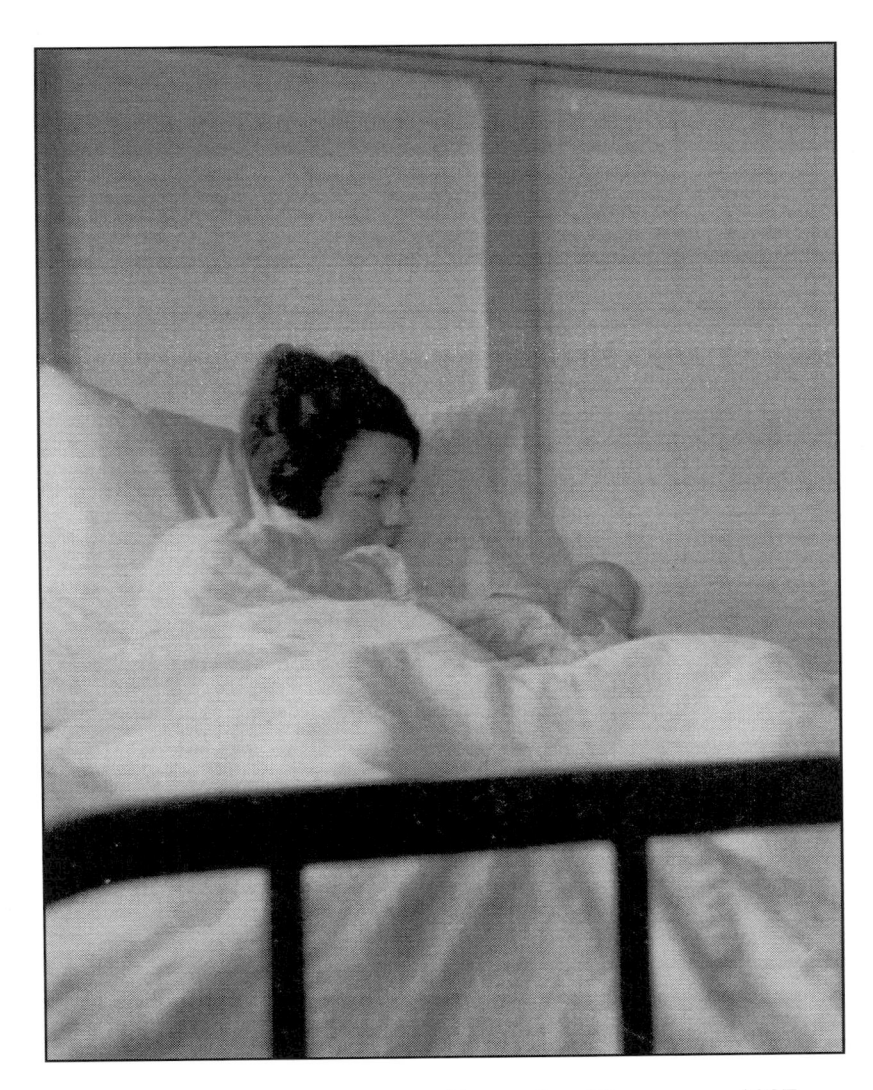

DOROTHY WITH NEWBORN CAROL JOY NOVEMBER 1937

Dr. Alice Randall delivered Carol Joy

CHAPTER TWENTY-SEVEN

WHITHER THOU GOEST

December 19, 1937 Back home in Jorhat
Fred's letter home

Dor is at church. I went for the first half and she has just gone for the second half. The church building is just across the road from our bungalow, so it makes it possible for us to plan accordingly. We thought it best not to take the baby to church this first Sunday at home and have not made arrangements for anyone to stay with her. So, we decided to "half-it". She has been a good baby and slept nearly all day, except for bath time and a short time this morning. Thus far we have not had occasion to complain for her actions and she has done very well in getting adjusted to her new home after the routine of the hospital and a long train trip from Gauhati here. Naturally we think she is the ideal child and are rather expecting the relatives to all feel the same way about her.

This is the happiest day Dor and I have had yet. The first Sunday in our own home with our new daughter.

First Sunday in our own home with our new daughter.

Life in Jorhat continued to be, for the most part, idyllic for Fred and Dorothy and Carol, measured in the length of each new phase their little daughter entered and conquered. Weeks passed with uncomplicated bliss. Dorothy and Fred cherished each other, adored their new baby, and were loved in return by the people they served.

In February of 1938, with little Carol Joy just three months old, Dorothy and Fred sent all their belongings to storage and departed India for a well-deserved furlough to the United States.

Dorothy's reunion with her mother had the most marvelous new dimension of introducing her to her granddaughter, Carol Joy. Most days that followed found the baby in her grandmother's arms, on her lap, or right next to where she was working. It became a daily experience for Dorothy and yet the mere sight never failed to tug at her heart.

The traditional six-month furlough somehow stretched into three more, and Dorothy and Fred experienced Carol Joy's first birthday in her grandmother's home.

~~~~~~~~~~~~~~~~~~~~~~~~~~~~~~~~

November 16, 1939
Dorothy's letter to her sister Carol

Dearest Carol:

Yesterday A.M. the postman brought a package which looked as though it had just come from a department store down town, but which was unfamiliar to us, and on looking more carefully we discovered that it had a San Francisco address. So, we concluded that you must have had something to do with it.

Carol simply went into spasms over the blue and white teddy bear, and "oooed" and "aaahhhed" and laughed, pointed, hugged, and admired it to the nth degree. She would love it, then hold it up to Mother and then to me to be loved. She was just as excited about it when she discovered it later on sitting on the mantel. This morning the thrills were all over again—I mean, she went thru the same performance, and when she balked at taking all of her milk, by giving some to the teddy on two or three occasions, she finished her bottle. She still has to have a bottle, as a cup is just the nicest place for blowing bubbles known to man.

We send "bohoot salaams" (many thanks). Nothing has pleased her quite as much in a long time.

The furlough extension turned into an opportune time for Fred to throw himself into his studies. But it meant leaving the idyllic conditions in her mother's home and moving about the U.S., networking, cementing professional associations, and taking delight in their little family. Reunions with family and friends lifted their hearts as they adjusted to what they felt was a temporary time away from the people they served.

The months stretched to eighteen, and one fateful day they were offered a mission post in the Philippine Islands. Fred could take a leading role in the Theology Department of Central Philippine College in Iloilo, and Dorothy could decide if she wished to work in the medical community there. Everything they heard enticed them to take the post, to serve the beautiful Filipino people in their eagerness to grow academically and to better understand God's Word.

So, with Carol Joy almost two years old and Dorothy about four months into her second pregnancy, they packed up the few belongings they'd brought with them to the States, sent word to Assam to ship their household goods to the Philippines, and once again said their goodbyes.

And sailed into a future neither could have fathomed.

A future they very nearly did not survive.

PART TWO
A SEASON IN THE SUN

ILOILO — SEPTEMBER 1939
A NEW MISSION IN THE PHILIPPINES

EMPRESS OF CANADA

CHAPTER TWENTY-EIGHT

BELLIGERENT'S BOAT

September 3, 1939, Dorothy (four months pregnant with Bobby), Fred, and 21-month-old Carol sailed on the Empress of Canada from Vancouver to Manila, with their two-door Chevrolet sedan safely stowed in the ship's hold. While at sea, their ocean liner was transformed into a belligerent's boat—one traversing waters patrolled by an enemy navy. For their protection the ship was painted battleship gray, so that it could run undetected in a U. S. naval convoy.

People were leaving the boat.

Just four days into their voyage Dorothy watched the porters carry steamer trunks down the long gangplanks and deposit them on the pier. They belonged to folks who'd changed their minds about going to the Philippines, once they'd heard the news.

War had been declared in Europe.

The newspaper Dorothy held painted a dark picture of what was happening in the world, of the threat posed by both Germany and Japan.

She lifted her eyes from the newsprint. Honolulu stretched prettily before her, its palm trees lining manicured streets that beckoned her to enjoy the respite they offered.

But the clatter of the paint crew drew her eyes away from the idyllic view. They were painting the ship while it lay in the harbor. Not a typical maintenance bit of paint here and there. They were changing the ship's color.

To battleship gray.

From Fred's memoir

Storm clouds of war were evident and war was declared the day we set sail. Many Americans aboard decided to leave the ship at Honolulu. We decided that regardless of requests to turn back, we would not. We had an uneventful voyage, filled with rumors galore. Our ship did not stop at Kobe, as scheduled, because the German Scharnhorst raider was lying in harbor there. At Shanghai, some Scotch Highlander soldiers came aboard to stand guard. A destroyer escort guarded our trip from Shanghai to Hong Kong. It was a relief to go ashore in Manila.

Once under way, the entire complexion of their journey changed. People moved about the ship in silent mode, influenced by the battle-ready demeanor of the crew. Every corner of the ship was shrouded in darkness at night, with nothing but the absolutely necessary lights allowed in the engine room.

Dorothy looked across the port side bow at the flotilla of warships that served as escort. They seemed to appear out of the gloom, then drift away toward the horizon, only keeping company with the passenger liner when they entered treacherous waters.

It was the kind of thing that should have unnerved her. It should have launched a shiver up her spine. But it didn't. Her vision of their future in the Philippines was so vivid in her mind that she could not feel threatened by this perilous passage. They were going to arrive safely in Manila. She knew it in her bones. God had seated it in her soul.

If she'd been a coward, she never would have boarded a ship bound for the middle of the Pacific Ocean—four months pregnant with a two-year-old in tow. Especially if she'd known it would be turned into a belligerent's boat before they got halfway to their destination. Had she known, she might have had to wrestle with the decision to stay safe and sound in the American setting to which, admittedly, she had grown quite accustomed.

But she and Fred had boarded the boat with complete confidence that this was the next step in the life they were building for themselves and their growing family. And when on the second day at sea they received news that war had been declared in Europe, nothing about that decision had changed for them.

The headlines alone struck fear in many a heart. It wasn't supposed to happen. The Great War, World War I, was to have been the war to end all wars. But now it was happening. Again. A less courageous or even less determined woman might have taken one look at the newspaper headlines and carried her curly-headed two-year-old onto the first boat home.

But she was making this move of her own choosing. Hers and Fred's. And she had remained committed to it, even when the lovely white skin of their elegant ship was covered in grim gray, camouflaging it to run unnoticed amid its naval escorts each time they entered dangerous waters. No use telling the enemy there was a boatload of civilians here. They were safer in their disguise. Still, they were on a *belligerent's boat*—the boat of a people who were now the enemy of those who "owned" the waters. Safer, perhaps, cloaked in gray and surrounded by military vessels. But that just meant that to part of the world they had become an enemy vessel.

October 1939—Iloilo, P.I.

The trip across the Pacific was pleasant for the most part. War was declared the day after we sailed, and with Canada entering the war a day or so later, we found ourselves on a Belligerent's boat. War precautions were taken all the way along—no running lights, deck lights practically nil, all portholes and windows heavily blanketed at night, no radiograms sent or received in order to keep position secret, the course changed frequently, a naval convoy from Shanghai to Hong Kong, and enroute the ship which is usually a sparkling white was painted a battleship gray.

Dorothy admitted to no one that she had waited for the fear to surface. It had been one thing to take herself off to India as a young single woman. But this was her family. She waited for a sign that these were waters into which she dared not wade. But none came. Quite the opposite, in fact.

With all the talk of war, a person of lesser courage might have arrived in the Philippines huddling in fear. And in that state might have seen every new place and new situation as threatening. But if there was anything Dr. Dorothy Kinney Chambers was not, it was timid, nervous, or fearful.

We left Manila on the inter-Island boat and it is a lovely thing. The trip was delightful. We arrived about ten Wednesday morning, and were met by about twelve of the thirteen missionaries here, and some thirty of the students and faculty members. It surely was a royal welcome.

Dorothy carried with her a deeply rooted internal optimism, an ironclad faith, and a commitment to serve closely held at her very core. So she'd sailed with her little family to Manila, running through the nights in blackout mode. She'd crossed to Iloilo on a little inter-island shuttle boat to set up housekeeping.

In a bit of a swamp.

Overrun with red ants.

Sunday October 22, 1939—Fred's letter to his mother

...I don't know what I expected to find in this house when we moved in but I felt it was the most barren place I had ever seen. There were not even hangers or pegs to hang anything on. No light shades or globes. There are floor plugs all over the place and that helps some. No clothes closets and two places for storing things: one in shelves alongside the entrance to one of the bathrooms and some shelves in one of the bedrooms. These are just open shelves and until we got a dresser, we were liable to look up and find our favorite pieces of "round-abouts" on the living room floor where Carol had dragged it. If I remember correctly we had a guest one day and Carol came out waving one of her mother's "unmentionables". So we are making the best of it while we wait for our stuff to arrive from Assam.

Two one-burner alcohol stoves and one electric hot plate occupied the counter in the tiny kitchen of their bungalow which admittedly had seen its better days. They served as Dorothy's cookstove. Fred only marveled at her facility with the crude setup and never once disparaged the menus that had to be adapted to the quaint circumstance.

Almost instantly Fred was elevated to the deanship of the Department of Theology, and the class preparations consumed much of his time. But it was his passion, and throwing himself wholeheartedly into his work was far more blessing than curse. For both of them.

They were even getting used to the cold showers. "Shower rains," Carol called them. There would be no hot water in their foreseeable future, so best to get used to it.

One thing two-year-old Carol refused to get used to was "Nee-Nor", a local girl who Dorothy took on to help with the house and look after Carol while she studied for her medical exams. Carol refused to take direction from Nee-Nor and adopted quite an attitude about the girl.

"Carol Joy, there's still food on your plate," Dorothy remarked one day as she popped into the kitchen to put a kettle on for tea.

"I. Not. Yike," Carol pouted, arms folded and brows crouched as low on her forehead as she could possibly manage.

"Ah. Well, then, I'll just take it for my snack, then. Thank you very—"

"No!"

Carol burst into tears and threw her little arms around her plate. "No take Caro din-din!"

She wailed horribly, as if losing the food was the greatest catastrophe she could imagine. And yet a moment earlier she'd refused to eat it.

Dorothy was perplexed. "Carol Joy, please stop sniffling. I thought you didn't like it so I was going to eat it so it didn't go to waste, that's all."

"No. I *yike* dis!" she cried.

"Well for heaven's sake, little one, I won't take it if you want it. But why did say you didn't like it in the first place?"

Carol dragged her fists across her eyes and gave Dorothy a look that clearly said she was the dimmest bulb in the box.

"Yike *dis*," she said, pointing to her plate. "Not yike Nee-Nor."

Dorothy was taken aback. None of the three of them had much of a bond with the new girl yet, but she'd certainly seen nothing to warrant such a tantrum.

It stunned both her parents to see this unaccepting behavior from their bubbly daughter who already had most of the folks on campus wrapped around her little finger. But the toddler simply would not take to the moody Filipina. And once additional issues began to materialize, it seemed to her parents Carol was already a good judge of character.

"So we're letting her go?" Fred asked after dinner.

"As much as I dread training a new girl, I think we must."

Had they not, they would never have met the beautiful Rosa Caimosa whose gentle heart knitted their little household into the smoothly functioning oasis it soon became. Their little world settled into a happy routine and Dorothy was able to focus on studying for her Philippine medical certification. Tantrums became a thing of the past. Indeed, Carol could be heard singing all over the house, even teaching Rosa her very favorite song.

A sunbeam, a sunbeam
Jesus wan me fo' a sunbeam
A sunbeam, a sunbeam
I be da sunbeam fo' he!

November 4, 1939

Finally decided to make a stab at the exams in Manila now. The hospital is going to be in rather a difficult position here due to the fact that the Board of Control has elected a Filipino as acting director during Dr. Waters' absence (and there is a good deal of feeling that once in he will not be gotten out.) The European group will not go to him, and if the hospital is to keep the European patronage—including American, it will be only by having a European or American doctor on the staff. Inasmuch as they are the ones that more or less support the hospital, financially speaking, it would go rather hard with the hospital finances if they go elsewhere.

If I don't take them [the exams] now it means waiting probably until next November, and it would be still more difficult to get away than now, so I plan to go to Manila a week from Monday and will have to be there a week due to lack of daily means of transportation between the two points. The exams last only three days, but there is a holiday after the first one, and that spoils chances of getting home on time. Such a lot of red tape to go thru to get registered for them. Hope I can pass the things, as I am afraid that if I don't I'll not have the nerve to try again.

Wednesday evening Covells and Feldmans and ourselves went to dinner at the Cathedrals—Feldman is pastor here and graduate of Missouri University and Rochester Theological. We like them both very much.

Had a letter from Martha Gifford in Gauhati the other day, and from that, dated Sept. 17th, we learned that our things had not been shipped [from Assam] up to that time, and we have still had no word as to what has been done regarding the selling—that is, the amount realized—when they will be shipped, etc. Do so wish the things would arrive as it makes me handicapped in so many ways.

In the sixth month of her pregnancy, feeling both strong and well-prepared, Dorothy left Carol and Fred in Iloilo and took the island boat to Manila. In a week she would take the exams and be back in the arms of the two people she loved most in the world.

But an insidious menace awaited her in Manila. It turned her week's stay into three, nearly compromised her exams, and very nearly cost the life of herself and her unborn child.

Its name was dysentery.

CHAMBERS FAMILY PASSPORT PHOTO
AUGUST 1939

CHAPTER TWENTY-NINE

WANNA DANCE, PRETTY LADY?

December 22, 1939

I came home Tuesday afternoon—23 days in the hospital—but am gaining strength daily, and altho still trying to be careful, and not trying to do more than navigate "in low", I feel lots stronger today than yesterday, etc.

Carol is growing so fast and is developing more independence every day—both a good and a bad thing. She is sleeping in her room at night now, but our doors are in line, and so she can see us in the morning when she wakens (at five or five thirty). She is often so tired by nine that she goes to sleep again for an hour or so, and then doesn't sleep in the afternoon when Fred and I would like to have a bit of rest. Twelve to two is siesta time around Iloilo, and no one goes anywhere. Stores and business houses are all closed during those hours, and there are no classes, so------.

She is talking in more complete sentences all the time. Her interest in books continues to grow and she knows more and more of the stories. When she sees Fred coming, she frequently calls out "here come Daddy boy".

As soon as Christmas is over, must begin to get to work in earnest to make ready for February. Have to get a bassinet made, and hope to have some sort of a bath table made that will give some more drawer space. Do hope the freight from Assam will get here early so that I can get curtains, and things of that sort finished up before the "party" in February. Dr. Waters thinks that the chances for carrying thru until term are good inasmuch as I didn't lose things with all the dysentery, fever, etc.

"What's the matter, darling?"

Fred slipped behind Dorothy as she placed two half-spent candles on the pretend fireplace they'd constructed for Santa in the living room.

"Nothing, Daddy-boy, why do you ask?"

Dorothy turned her face up for a kiss.

Fred caught her chin in his hand, surprising her by the unexpected response to her signal that she wanted a kiss. "This is me, dear girl, and I've watched you wander around the living room for half an hour, picking up things and moving them here, then there, then back again. So what's wrong?"

"Well look, Fred. Just look around." She stepped away and turned a slow circle. "I mean, it's Christmas but, well, does it *look* like Christmas? Does it *feel* like Christmas?"

Three knitted stockings lay on a footstool, waiting for Santa to fill them and hang them on the pretend mantel. Paper snowflakes hung in every windowpane, and beyond them was a straggling garden of red and mostly mud. Three packing crates of varying sizes and states of dilapidation were placed about the room, one set low as a table for Carol, and one on each side of a second hand rattan chair they'd collected from a storeroom on campus. It was the only furniture in the room.

Fred clucked his tongue. "Oh my, I see what you mean. We only have stockings, and snowflakes, and wonder of wonders a whole field of poinsettias out front and your hands are full of Christmas ornaments. I mean, no, of course not, why would I think it looked like Christmas in here?"

"Poinsettias don't count. They grow here year 'round. You can't count them," she pouted.

Fred stepped close again and encircled Dorothy and her nearly-eight-month middle. "So what's missing? What would make it seem more like Christmas in here?"

Dorothy looked into his face. *A tree would be nice*, she thought. But he'd scoured the town for a tree that was even remotely affordable and come up empty-handed. She wouldn't throw that back in his face. But oh, how she did want a tree. She *needed* a tree.

"I think...I think if we hadn't had such a beautiful Christmas last year...at home...or even if it was like Christmas in Assam, it wouldn't feel so...empty. But we don't have our furniture, we don't have our usual decorations, and we don't even have a—"

She stopped herself before she uttered the word that was on the tip of her tongue.

Fred raised one eyebrow. "A what, a......" He dragged out the word as he stepped into the hall and reached for something in his study.

"A....tree perhaps?" He pulled a 4-foot tree complete with tree stand from around the corner and held it like a trophy. It wasn't as tall as the trees at home, but it was lush and full and green.

And it was already strung with lights. Bits of tinsel still clung to its needles. It had been decorated once before.

Fred crossed the room and placed it near the fake fireplace, then bent to plug it in just as Carol came bounding down the hall.

"Daddy-boy! Daddy-boy! Mommy look! Daddy-boy getta Crissen tree! Wif yites! Pitty! So pitty!"

Dorothy set aside the basket of ornaments she held, scooped up Carol and walked into Fred's arms. "Yes it is, Carol Joy. Yes it is. Pretty. So pretty." She choked out the words that seemed hopelessly bound up in her throat.

"How on earth did you..."

"Girl's dorm," he whispered, and followed it up with a kiss. "They've gone home. Don't need it now. Soooo..."

Fred cuddled her as close as he could with Carol and the baby bulge between them.

Her tears were laced with joy as they rolled down her cheeks, past her quivering smile. She'd been so homesick, felt so lost, so depleted by sickness and worn to a frazzle with late-term motherhood. So big and lumbering. And desperate that she'd failed to make Christmas.

But one perfect gift from her husband made her feel new, whole, ready to celebrate her savior's birth.

December 24, 1939

She [Carol] had to help decorate it and we had a good time. The "pitty balls" were all put on, and the "sojer bicycles" (silver icicles). The lights are attached, and "Daddy Boy" got a silver star for the top.

Everything in the room suddenly felt refreshed and right. Fred brought the family Bible from its place in his study into the Christmas room and placed it on an upended crate.

"Here now, Carol Joy, you help Daddy open the Bible." He took her small hand in his and together they turned the pages, carefully, reverently, until the Book lay open to Luke's story of the birth of Jesus.

"We open it here, kitty-kin, because it tells us how Jesus was born that Christmas Eve in Bethlehem. And when we see the words, when we read the words, it helps us carry the words in our heart."

Her sweet cherub lips took in a long breath, and then, with the grace of some-one far beyond her years, Carol laid a reverent hand on the place her father had shown her. The place on the page that told the story of a Jesus whom she already knew and loved. And then, with slow deliberation, she cupped her fingers and drew her hand elegantly to her heart.

"Caro wan words, too, Daddy-boy."

Fred smiled up at Dorothy, and drew both of them down beside him where he sat on the floor. "All you have to do is learn a little song, puddin.'"

Carol clapped, Dorothy smiled, and Fred began to teach his daughter her first Christmas song.

Away in a manger no crib for a bed...

Dorothy's Christmas doldrums fled and the three-soon-to-be-four cuddled one another by the "Chrissen" tree. She had always made Christmas happen in their home. But this year, no matter what she did, it hadn't worked. Nothing had fallen into place.

And then, in one magnificent gesture, Fred had turned their little home into Christmas Eve. This year it was Daddy-boy who made Christmas happen.

And Carol who sang it home.

Carol jumped up and took both their hands, tugging until they rose, as well.

"Moosic, Daddy! Caro wan moosic!"

Fred grabbed her up and set to tickling her. "Moosic? You want moosic? Well, why didn't you just say so?"

"Oh Fred. I do wish we had your saxophone!"

"But why need a sax, when we could just unwrap this?"

Fred moved the rattan chair and pushed a large box forward. Before either of them could stop her, Carol ripped the brown wrapping paper away to reveal the dearest gift Dorothy could have imagined. There in the waning light of Christmas Eve sat a lovingly worn, slightly scratched, second-hand cabinet Victor.

A phonograph.

With a smile that lit up the room all by itself, Fred set Carol's stockinged feet atop his own. She clamped her little arms around his leg and held fast as somehow he managed to plug the thing in, drop a 78 RPM record onto the turntable, extend his hand to his beautifully pregnant wife, and speak the four most perfect words for that moment.

"Wanna dance, pretty lady?"

DOROTHY AND CAROL JOY
CHRISTMAS 1939
ILOILO, THE PHILIPPINES

CHAPTER THIRTY

LET IT GO

New Year's Day 1940 came in with a smile and left with a tear. Dorothy had spent a euphoric post-Christmas week feeling all was right with the world. Carol spent hours at her little toy piano Santa had brought. The new girl Dorothy had hired—Rosa—was adapting beautifully to their household. She seemed to enjoy making foods in the particular way the three of them liked, and she was quickly learning to sew on Dorothy's rented machine. She had a happy outlook on life and a foresight that Dorothy truly admired. Fred practically whistled his way through each day. His work was going well.

And Dorothy shuffled through every day with immense content, one hand resting on her swollen belly, a smile planted on her face. For hours she would stroll through the house, recalling each possession that surely was on its way to them from Assam by now, picturing the way in which it had been acquired, and then deciding where it might best be placed in their little home.

Wedding gifts, tablecloths, handmade curtains, the little nesting tables, all would fit beautifully in their cottage. Her medical books would go with her to the hospital once she got word she'd passed her exams. *If* she passed her exams. Their record collection would fit right into the record nook of their Christmas Victor phonograph cabinet.

And she knew exactly where the colorful Bohemian mirror from her childhood bedroom—the one that she'd hung in her office in Gauhati—would go. She would hang it in the front hall just above an occasional chair, so both she and Carol could check their appearance each time they headed out the door.

Life in Iloilo was good. The baby was kicking up a storm. God was in their hearts. What more could they need?

And then it came.

Dorothy was startled out of a half-doze by someone knocking at the door.

"Fred? Fred, can you get that?"

She waited to hear Fred's footsteps heading out to answer it, but there was silence. Through the window she saw him in the back yard shoveling more dirt. New Year's Day and he was shoveling dirt. It made her smile. He was determined to elevate their yard so it wasn't a constant mass of puddles.

Dorothy heaved herself out of the rocking chair and waddled to the front door. It was a postman. They never came to the house. It was Fred's habit to collect the mail from the post office on his way in to campus.

She opened the door.

"Mabuhay!" the breathless young fellow said as he politely doffed his cap. The wheels of his bicycle still spun where he had dropped it to its side out in the poinsettia lane.

Such nice manners he had. She would never tire of hearing the lovely Filipino greeting. *Mabuhay! Cheers! Welcome! May you live!* Always delivered as a cheery command. You *must* be cheerful. You *must* feel welcome. You *must* live. *Mabuhay!*

He held out an envelope with a smile. "It say oo-gen, so all us say bring it hurry-like." He turned to step back onto the planked walk but Dorothy stopped him with a thank you and a coin from her apron pocket.

It did indeed say "urgent". The word was stamped in red on the front of the envelope.

Dorothy checked the post mark. It was a month old. Well, at least this fellow took the urgent marking seriously. But the letter had clearly taken its sweet time getting here.

~~~~~~

January 1, 1940

We got word about our freight from Assam—it has gone down to the bottom of Singapore Bay on the S.S. Sirdhana which struck a mine sometime in the first half of November. It seems the Captain (it was a British boat I think) didn't know the mine fields that had been laid out.

I do not know if lives were lost, but pray they were not.

Well, we don't have to wait for it now, and Fred won't have to spend two or three days getting it out of customs, and there were probably many things that we didn't really need, but it included about $250 worth of my medical books, all my uniforms, curtain materials that I wanted for upholstering cushions here, and curtains, dishes, aluminum wear, two table lamps, toaster, little vacuum cleaner, all of Fred's books, and the ones that we wanted to keep just as old friends, about thirty lovely Victrola records, some brass wear, extra sheets, pillow cases, towels, vases and our lovely pictures.

All her worldly goods. At the bottom of Singapore Bay. It pinched her heart to think of the loss. The pictures. Fred's books. Her sewing machine. The priceless bundle of medical sketchbooks.

As her mind ticked off the things that had been lost, she relegated most of them to the past. Much of it could be replaced. But the thing that had a tear slipping down her cheek was her oldest possession. The piece from her childhood that had reflected images of her at every stage of her youth and adult life. The piece that had captured that first fateful image of her own face hovering near Fred's.

The piece she would miss most had her swallowing hard. She would never see it again.

Her lovely Bohemian mirror.

HOCKING C., DICTIONARY OF DISASTERS AT SEA
DURING THE AGE OF STEAM

The steamship Sirdhana SS, Capt. P. Fairbairn, was leaving Singapore harbour on Monday, November 13th, 1939, with a large number of passengers on board, of whom 137 were Chinese deportees, when she struck a mine some three miles offshore and sank in 20 minutes. Twenty Asiatic deck passengers were killed.

CHAPTER THIRTY-ONE

THESE HANDS

Dorothy found herself avoiding the living room. The furniture she'd intended to use was at the bottom of Singapore Bay, and that was that. But each time she saw the crates occupying the places where her furniture should be sitting it made her out-of-sorts. And sad. Until she finally took matters in hand to do something about it.

Their shopping expedition to the market district had proven fruitless so far, except for the second-hand wicker baby carriage that had certainly seen its better days. But it would do, and now that the buggy was partially filled with packages she was awfully glad she'd bought the squeaky thing.

But it was furniture that she craved today, and the furniture she liked was beyond her price range. The furniture she could afford was hardly a step up from the crates. She gently pulled Carol's fingers from the baby carriage and set them on the buggy's handle. Perhaps if Carol could help push she might—

"Mommy!!! Yook!"

Carol jumped away from the carriage and dove into the little shop they were passing. There was nothing Dorothy could do but hurriedly park the baby carriage in front of the window and follow her daughter inside the tumbledown second-hand store.

When her eyes adjusted to the dimness, she found Carol gazing up at the ceiling with a look of awe on her face as if she'd seen Santa Claus himself, just coming down the chimney.

"Oh my!"

Now Dorothy's own eyes flew open. Amid the jumble of things hanging from the ceiling of the little shop was a rattan loveseat, very like the chair they already had. On the floor below was a tall torchiere lamp with a lovely glass bowl. It was chipped in two places, but they were close enough together that the chips and the hairline crack could easily be turned toward the wall and hidden from view. She could see how perfectly suited the loveseat and lamp were, and how marvelously well they would look in her living room.

"You like?"

A little clerk appeared from nowhere, hovering now that she saw how taken Dorothy was with the two pieces.

"Well, they would certainly do nicely," Dorothy said, marshalling her enthusiasm so as not to show too much interest. "Do you have the cushions?"

The small Filipina looked confused.

"Seat cushions? Pillows?"

"Ah!" the clerk cried. "Pillow! Yes. Here."

She swept aside a pile of used clutter and pulled out two horrid purple and pink cushions, both sadly ripped and water-stained.

"Hm," Dorothy sighed disappointedly as she fingered the cushions. But it truly didn't matter that the coverings were unusable, because what she felt beneath her fingers was a good solid cushion. She'd be changing the covers anyway. And bringing it closer to her nose revealed an odor she was fairly certain she could banish.

"I yike, Mommy! Peez!"

The Filipina clerk smiled at Carol, then turned her hopeful face up to Dorothy. "I give you plenny good deal," she said. "Twenty peso. I bringa you house."

Ten dollars. The lamp was cracked and she had no idea if the loveseat was sturdy. It looked sturdy. Would Fred like it? Of course he'd like it. But ten dollars. There must be something wrong with it.

These thoughts flew through her mind as she paced a couple of steps, craning her neck to examine the loveseat. How could one tell if it was a broken down frame when it hung from the ceiling like that?

"Peeze, Mommy?" Carol fairly danced around her.

Dorothy fished in her purse and handed the woman a twenty-peso bill. The woman responded by hollering at the top of her lungs to summon two boys to the front of the store. They scrambled up on precarious piles of this and that to untie the loveseat. Moments later they had it down. Dorothy was about to sit to test it out when one of the boys laid the torchiere lamp across the seat and the two picked up the loveseat, clearly waiting for her to lead the way to her home.

She felt defeat all the way to her toes. They hadn't wanted her to sit, which meant it was a broken down bit of trash. How would she explain it to Fred? Their entire grocery allowance for the month spent on a worthless piece of furniture.

But once inside the house, the boys placed the loveseat where she asked them to and set the floor lamp beside it. One of the boys produced a dusty light bulb from his pocket and screwed it into the socket.

"La-deez and gennamen!" The second boy made a great show of finding the plug at the end of the cord, and with a grand flourish he plunged it into the socket.

Dorothy held her breath as the first boy reached for the switch.

But when she heard the small click she saw no puff of smoke. No popping of ruined light bulbs. She merely saw the soft glow of a perfectly good lamp lighting the room.

Without thinking, she sat down on the loveseat to enjoy the glow. The seat beneath her did not so much as quiver. Strong and well made, it showed itself worthy of her little family.

They were second-hand goods. And to her, they were good as gold.

· · · ·

The delivery boys were long gone and Dorothy still sat in the loveseat with no cushions, enjoying the transformation to her living room, when once again urgent mail was delivered to her doorstep. But this time it set Dorothy dancing about the kitchen. She squealed, let out a whoop, and trundled off to tell some-one—anyone—the wonderful news. Carol Joy was the lucky recipient of her ebullient hug.

It felt as if she'd been holding her breath for two months. But at last—at long last—her medical exam results had arrived.

Dorothy took a deep breath and exhaled her silent prayer.

Then she tore open the letter to find that she had passed. Very nearly at the top of her class.

~~~~~~

January 8, 1940

> Got my grades from Manila today. They weren't too bad—an average of 80.63 for the seventeen exams. I got 90, 90, 91, 93 in Anatomy, surgery, gynecology and obstetrics respectively, and was quite tickled with a grade of 88 in their sanitation and hygiene (the exam where they wanted plans for sewage disposal for a municipality, plans and sketch for a cemetery for another community, plans for a village for 2,000, etc.) Got my lowest grades in physiology, histology. Considering everything, it wasn't too bad. The highest composite score was only 82, which makes me feel even better.

Things were starting to fall into place. Her friends organized a remarkable surprise shower for her, having somehow received from Fred a list of many things that were lost in Singapore harbor. Carol had found the wonderful new loveseat and lamp for them. There was a position waiting for her at Iloilo Mission Hospital. And now that she'd passed her exams she would waste no time at all getting back to work.

After the baby, of course. It was one thing to waddle about her own home, but quite another to do the same in a hospital corridor. It would be completely frowned upon.

But was passing her exams enough? Would her hands remember what to do? Was her mind quick enough? Had she lost too much time to step back into that arena that required razor sharp instincts?

Dorothy lifted the lid of the box where she kept her medical supplies, careful not to disturb the mothballs she'd arranged around its perimeter to keep the red ants at bay. She slipped the letter from Manila into a folder she'd tucked along the side.

The corner of a folded page caught on her ring as she withdrew her hand, and curious, she pulled the page from the box. The handwriting brought a flood of Gauhati memory. The brief note from her fellow missionary in Gauhati had meant a great deal to her at the time. But now, on the eve of beginning her new practice in Iloilo it meant even more.

With tender care she unfolded the familiar stationery.

Letter from Ethel Nichols — Gauhati, June 28th, 1936
Dear Dorothy:

This morning in church as I looked at your hands, I suddenly thought of what those hands did for me nearly six years ago and that, with all the happenings of the last few days and the fact that you'd be leaving us all in a few months, etc., caused me not to be able to "keep all of the salt on the inside". . . .

I do hope there will be some way for those hands of yours to go on saving lives. You have my very best wishes for your future.

With much love,
Ethel Nichols

She'd completely forgotten Ethel's note, so uncharacteristic for a woman who held her feelings close. And how very odd that she'd found it now, when spirals of doubt were prone to twist their way into her thoughts. Here, now, at this moment, it spoke to her with open conviction.

These hands, her healing hands, were about to go back into service. Any doubt was banished with Ethel's simple, direct message written nearly four years past.

Dorothy took a last look into the box.

Her white coat lay folded on top. Pristine. Starched. Ready.

"This is Mommy's special coat, babykins," she whispered as she rubbed her straining back. "One day I'll model it for you. Soon, I hope. I probably couldn't get it buttoned at the moment, many thanks to you, my big beautiful baby belly."

Carol bounced into the room singing, "We getta baby boy, we getta baby boy" over and over with the insurmountable joy only a two-year-old can express.

"I hope so, sweet pea. I surely do hope so."

Dorothy opened the case of the rented sewing machine thinking she'd set in the sleeves on another uniform and then changed her mind. She'd already sewn two new uniforms to wear once she got back to work. What she really wanted to sew was a new dress. Something that might make her look less "increasing" when she went to tea at the Iloilo Club next week. Once the baby arrived and she went to work at the hospital her social opportunities would take a dramatic dive. So she would lumber over there to tea and endeavor to enjoy. And try to remember not to use her baby bump as a tea tray.

~~~~~~~~~~~~~~~~~~~~~~~~~~~~~~~~~~~

February 12, 1940

Have a tea at the Iloilo Club on Thursday and hope to meet quite a number of folks there. Am rather up against it for afternoon dresses. My bemberg has proved to be a white elephant. The thing has stretched (it was cut on the diagonal) until there is no fullness around the waist in front and the result is that it cups in under my "forwardness" in a most revealing fashion and there is nothing I can do about it except let it hang in the closet.

Thanks so much for the shirt for Fred. I am thrilled with my powder—it is lovely (only Carol would like to use it all in one day if she could have half a chance.) Plan to take it to the hospital with me and feel luxuriously scented up. Thanks heaps, one and all.

Had another check up this A.M. and everything seems okay. B.P. 108/88 and feeling pretty good. The baby still rides very high, and cannot be enticed into the pelvis. Dr. Myers of Capiz is coming down next Friday to help Henry Waters with the Caesarian, and I am looking forward to getting this little acrobat into another bed.

CAROL JOY AND ROBERT BRUCE
OR AS CAROL SAYS, "WAHBOOTS BOOS"

CHAPTER THIRTY-TWO

BABYKINS

A baby boy. Yes, that's wonderful.

Dorothy felt Fred's euphoria even though she couldn't fully react to it. The druggy haze was still full upon her after the long Caesarean, making her limbs heavy and her mind dull. But the babe was here. All fingers and toes intact and happy to nurse at the first opportunity.

She knew she'd held the baby, kissed his sweet little cheek, cooed something which had meant a great deal to her at the time but now she couldn't for the life of her remember what she'd said.

It was her own fault they'd had to give her a heavy pain med. She'd tried to go too long between medications, against her good doctor's recommendation. Then when the rolling, pitching pain was too much for even a stoic Colorado girl she'd had to beg, to put a night nurse off her routine in order to get the injection ready. She'd wasted the girl's time with her silly pride. But once the pain had truly taken hold, pride went out the window and she humbly accepted what they'd been trying to give her all along.

She'd promised to be a model patient from that moment on.

As the buzzing in her ears ebbed and flowed she caught a word or two of Fred's excited monologue—which she knew he considered dialogue but she was completely bungling her end of it.

Buzzzzz "college" *buzzzzz* "dean".

What did he just say?

Buzzzzz "not to worry" *buzzzzz* "double duty".

She heard him laugh and then he leaned close and kissed her. For a moment the scent and taste of Fred over-ruled the antiseptic smell and she thought she was home. He brushed a kiss across her lips and the warmth of it had her swimming to the surface, forcing her drug-calmed mind to open her eyes, lift her head, reach out a hand.

But he was gone.

What did he just say? Double duty?

She was bringing a new baby home and he was pulling double duty of some kind? How was she going to manage that?

Fred. Come back.

~~~~~~

February 15, 1940
Fred's letter home

Dear Folks:

The refrain goes like this: "It's a boy!" The little tyke weighed 8 lbs. 8 oz. He looks a lot like Carol, has a mouth like his Mother, is a husky little tyke with a well shaped head, more hair on his head now than Carol had in a long time. He rolled his little blue eyes at us, squinted a bit, yawned and seemed quite contented with the world as he found it up to the present.

Love to you one and all and know we are mighty happy in our new son.

Fred

Once the initial pain was managed and Dorothy began to recover, she took greater notice of the goings on about her. It was strange, watching a hospital go about its business and not being part of it. The nurses were taking extraordinary care of her, and yet there was nothing she'd seen them do or say with her that they didn't exhibit with their other patients. She was getting no preferred treatment. Every patient got preferred treatment.

There was a kindness here, an order, and she knew she'd thrive within it. The insights she was gleaning from her days in hospital would go far in helping her engage with the staff in a couple of months when she began to work among them.

It was strange watching Fred, too. He was thriving already here in Iloilo, fulfilled in ways she'd not witnessed before. He cherished her and Carol Joy and was completely smitten with the wee walla. But his professional side was being honed and nurtured here. He'd needed that for such a long time, and it warmed her heart to know he was in his element.

She'd be going home soon, back into the bosom of her dear ones. Only now there would be four. Each time she thought of it, something nudged a memory that she couldn't quite grasp. She'd been worried about going home, but couldn't fathom why. It was something Fred had said. But try as she might, she could not frame the context in which he could have said anything that might have alarmed her.

February 19, 1940

Dearest Mother,

Robert Bruce (Wahboots Boos) has just been in for his breakfast. He is a darling. It was a surprise to all that he weighed so much as Friday before he was born I asked Henry (Dr. Waters) how big he thought he was and he said 'not over six or six and a half'. I didn't think he was much bigger myself, altho I knew he was much more "filling" than Carol Joy was. He is 22" long as against C.J.'s 20½" and has two or three times as much hair as C.J. and it is darker. Hair has a suggestion of curl. Fingers are beautifully tapered. His eyes are as blue as Carol's ever thought of being. All in all he is a darling and I'm sure you'd think he was a worthy Grandson to bear the name of Bruce.

Fred is getting an awful wallop out of it, and you should hear Carol talk about "my big boy" and "my baby brudder". She told Fred the other day "new tiny baby nes nike Daddy (just like daddy)". Felt my arms and announced, "Mama hasn't got any fever."

Twelve days into her hospital stay, Dorothy sat up in bed knitting a third pair of booties. The robin's egg blue yarn slipped across the needles that clicked softly in the most satisfying way. She was once again productive.

Even with the wonderful hours holding and nursing her newborn, her mind had begun moving forward, nudged from its pregnant doldrums to begin anticipating getting her professional feet beneath her once again.

Each day her mental list became longer. There were uniforms to finish, laid out by the sewing machine at home, and two white coats to repair. There were the children's clothes to get in order and the matter of training Rosa to look after both Bobby and Carol now.

Rosa was so congenial that she had bonded with Carol rather swiftly. Now Carol would have to share, and that could be a bit of a bumpy road.

And there were things about infant care that she needed to be certain Rosa understood and would carry out.

~~~~~~~~~~~~~~~~~~~~~~~~~~~~~~

February 25, 1940

All my stitches are out and I'm sitting as straight up as I want to in bed and am to dangle my legs tomorrow. Up in a chair the next day (Tuesday is the 12th day) and home on Saturday. My, but it will be grand to get home.

Have to begin again on C.J.'s clothes and put away or give away some as she's growing so fast that most of her things are too short. Have material for a dress for her, and at least two of her other dresses can be lengthened. Have to get my maternity dresses revamped so I can wear them and also get about six uniforms made—all of mine were in the Assam freight.

If they had only gotten things done sooner we wouldn't have lost the freight. Then the rate of exchange in Rupees is up, so we are losing about $20 on the $100 from the sale of our furniture there. If only—

But take cheerfully the spoiling of your goods.
[HEBREWS 10:34]

Fred said he guessed this was about the only time we had really been called out to do it, and we've so much to be thankful for, and we're so rich with C.J. and a son. Guess we can't complain.

Am beginning to feel so well that I'm really getting pepped up over the idea of doing some medical work again. Hope I can help them out here. They've been so grand to me here. (Made no charge for my 3½ weeks in the hospital when here in November-December because I was "on the staff" altho I hadn't done a lick of work for them.

The mental list was making her tired now. The whole uniform issue would have been a moot point if the freight from Assam had not been lost. She chastised herself for resenting the hours it would take to replace the lost uniforms. She would just have to get as much sleep as she could in the next four days, so she could leave here in the blush of good health with energy to spare.

The needles stopped their clicking, and in the silence her thought swung home. Energy to spare? With two wee ones to care for now? And a medical practice to boot?

It made her eyes droop just thinking of it.

But it was all she'd ever wanted in her life—a place in the medical world to do the work God had intended for her, and a little family to share it with.

Both of her dreams had taken her so far beyond her imagining that it nearly stole her breath away. The very thought of it turned her face toward the window, where the golds and blues of a perfect sunset filled the sky. There was nothing muted about that sky. It wasn't a quiet setting but more of a dramatic scene change in a celestial drama. Golds leap-frogged across rosy hues, challenging them to rise and run higher and higher. The vivid colors streamed across the sky as if rather than settling for the night they were headed toward some glorious dawn.

She absently dropped her knitting into the basket at her bedside. It would be a dawn for which Dorothy Kinney Chambers was more than ready.

ILOILO MISSION HOSPITAL - PANAY

CHAPTER THIRTY-THREE

ICE CREAM AND ANTS

How narrow her world had become, and yet how broad. Existence seemed to encompass the distance between the smiles of the three people who made up her universe. Bobby. Carol. Fred.

March 1, 1940

Do wish you could hear Carol sing. Her voice is very true. Has been singing "Ha-ya-yu-ya, don de gory, Ha-ya-yu-ya Amen" (Hallelujah, Thine the Glory, Hallelujah, Amen).

Being home again and feeling mostly recovered from the Caesarian, Dorothy delighted in returning to "normal". In fact, this was the best she'd felt since before Carol was born. She had energy. She had motivation. She was surrounded by love.

March 12, 1940

We have been home from the hospital eleven days. Bobby is sleeping sweetly. He is the most active little tyke—is all over his crib and one doesn't dare leave him on any surface where there isn't a pillow or railing to keep him from rolling off. Laid him in the center of Carol's crib the other day as it was cooler in her room in the afternoon than in ours where I have his bassinet. Went into the bathroom for something, and when I came back in about three or four minutes he had turned himself clear around and his feet were sticking out between the bars at the head of the bed. He holds his head up very straight for about a minute at a time.

The tiny wee ants are so bad that I have to keep Robert's bassinet legs sitting in tins with mothballs in them in order to keep the ants off the sheet, etc. I think that one of the hardest things to put up with in this country are the ants. They were bad enough in India, but much worse here. If you want to keep ants off your clothes, you have to keep your dressers and everything else in the same thing (tin can and mothball feet). It is getting to be habitual to first inspect any garment from a drawer or taken off a hanger for ants before putting it on. Any bit of elastic that goes "phut" seems to be especially attractive to them, and girdles, elastic shoulder straps, etc., are usually more or less infested with them.

Was cleaning off a shelf the other day and that rubber lined diaper bag that I used for Carol was folded and lying on the shelf. Found that it had several million of the little pests in it—

Like it or not—and she certainly did not—ants were a part of the new normal. But today even the ants couldn't steal her thunder. She had very good news to share.

Dorothy put the last pile of clothing in its safe place and prayed the ants wouldn't find it. Laundry had been infinitely easier once they'd had a frame made to hold two buckets with a wringer stand between the tubs. But as it was later in her pregnancy when they installed the thing, bending over long enough to get all the family wash done had been too much for Dorothy in the sweltering heat. So she had reluctantly agreed to hire a "lavendera" to help. The woman was worth her weight in gold. But even sharing the work, getting the laundry done was a consuming process.

And yet today it had gone particularly well, and left time to make a special dessert for Fred. For the celebration.

First she boiled two cans of Carnation Evaporated Milk, unopened, still in the cans, for twenty minutes. Then the hot cans went into the Frigidaire for twenty minutes before she opened the cans, poured the thickened milk into a bowl, and whipped it with a Dover egg beater.

"Caro hep Mommy? Peez?"

Dorothy smiled at her daughter who seemed to dance through her days now that she was a big sister. Any qualms about her sharing their amah Rosa with

Bobby had been put to rest.

"Of course you may help, my little cook-in-the-making."

"What a cook-a-make, Mommy?"

She laughed. "Why it's you, Carol Joy. You are going to make a very fine cook one day."

"Yay! I cook-a-make!"

"Yes, you are. And now, Carol cook-a-make, I need for you to crush these graham crackers."

She knew it was a risky business, handing a rolling pin to a two-and-a-half year old on a stool. And she was right. Once that experiment went awry and half the crackers ended up on the floor and another good bit of them in Carol's tummy, Dorothy kept the job of measuring and pouring the one cup of sugar and the splash of vanilla for herself.

And when they were done, with the concoction safely in the fridge's freezer compartment and the counter and floor reclaimed from the ants who'd plundered the mess, Dorothy handed the last sticky spoon to Carol.

"Oh! Oh-oh!" Carol smacked and licked and moaned in pure delight. "Tase yike fosting. What it, Mommy? What Caro make?"

Dorothy wiped bits of goo out of her daughter's hair. "You, mistress cook-a-make, have made your Daddy's very favorite dessert in the whole world."

Carol looked up at her mother, eyes wide with wonder as she licked the last bits off her fingers. "Wha dat?"

Dorothy bent and whispered in a dramatic fashion in Carol's ear.

"Ice cream."

"Did I hear someone say ice cream?" Fred stood at the kitchen door grinning at his two girls. He held Bobby to his chest, but facing away from him so the baby could see his mother and sister. Bobby's feet pumped and his little fists waved happily.

Dorothy straightened. "We're celebrating."

"Celebrating what?"

"I cook-a-make!"

"You what?"

Dorothy laughed. "She's a cook-in-the-making."

"Ah," Fred smiled. "And why are we making ice cream on this particular afternoon?"

"Because it's a beautiful day." Dorothy took a tentative step toward Fred. "And we have a beautiful family." She advanced another step. "And the most perfect husband-daddy-boy." Another step and she was as close as she could get without crushing the wiggly bump they now called Bobby.

Fred tweaked her nose. He clearly saw in her eyes that there was something more, something that had lit a fire within them.

"You remembered." He smiled, suddenly pleased.

Dorothy blushed, not having a clue what he meant.

"Well, it's a special day, so of course your ladies would want to celebrate it." She was fishing now. "With you."

He laughed. "But I thought you were so loopy from the drugs that you didn't really hear what I was saying."

She brushed her hands on her apron, too embarrassed to admit she couldn't remember. "That just shows you the vast ability of my superior mind to work under the most difficult circumstances."

"Indeed it does, Doctor Chambers. Indeed it does." He moved into the kitchen. "I'll have to take lessons if I'm going to manage all this."

All this.

Dorothy remained silent, hoping for a better hint.

"It was a good day, though," he sighed. "Being Dean of both colleges is going to be tough, but they are my first and second loves. Academically speaking, of course. And I do find the new History faculty quite stimulating. All in all, it will be great working with them."

Dean of both colleges.

Double duty.

He was going to be Dean of both Theology and History. It would be a huge load. That's what had worried her.

But it was a high honor to be entrusted with the deanship of not one but two major departments.

Dorothy busied herself putting dinner on the table, seamlessly hiding the fact that the little celebration was supposed to be for something else entirely. She'd crafted the ice cream celebration to reveal the fact that the hospital had finished her new office, complete with a black glass above the door inscribed with her name.

Dr. Dorothy Chambers.

~~~~~~~~~~~~~~~~~~~~~~~~~~~~~~~~

April 1940

They are getting an office fixed up for me at the hospital. It is small, but will be big enough, I think. They are putting in a lavatory, electric fan, and building an examining table, bookcase, etc. Have a nice desk.

Expect to begin about the first of May, and hope to be able to confine my work mostly between 9:30-12:00 in the mornings. Will have a class in Gyn and Ob. (review stuff) with the senior nurses during the first semester from 4-5 on Tuesdays.

Finally got my certificate or diploma from the Examining Board and Fred has left it to be framed. Had the other two diplomas (National Board and University of Colorado) framed for me.

An image of the gleaming black glass name plate came vividly into her mind. How it had stolen her breath just seeing the gold letters perfectly lettered above her door. It seemed a lifetime since she'd had an actual office of her own. And now it was here, ready for her to officially resume her practice next week. A week when Fred would be finding himself busier than he'd ever known. He'd be celebrating in formal and informal settings for days.

She felt like the celebratory rug had just been pulled out from beneath her feet.

But she couldn't resent it. Truly she couldn't. She saw how proudly he wore his new mantle. Her news could wait for another day.

Dorothy quieted herself and put both her arms around her boys.

Carol wriggled between them to take her spot standing on her daddy's toes. Fred kissed Dorothy on the forehead and messages flashed between them.

Are you ready for this?

The rapid blinking of her eyelids couldn't hide the tears that welled behind them. There was no sorrow at all in them. They carried pride in her husband's accomplishments and pride in her own. In truth, she'd been too long away from healing. She knew without a doubt that she was a better mother, a better wife, a better person when she let her personhood as a healer join hands with marriage and motherhood.

It felt right. It felt good. It was time. Just not time to celebrate it.

She held her breath hoping he wouldn't read her thoughts.

Fred kissed her again and swallowed hard, his eyes misting with an emotion she rarely saw. "Your children have a remarkable mother," he said.

She fell speechless at the conviction in his words. Even with twice the work on his plate he could still draw a circle that drew her into the heart of it.

Neither of them could move or speak, and left it to their daughter to break the moment.

"Okay, evvybody."

Carol jumped up and down on Fred's toes until he winced.

"Time fo' eye-keem!"

CHAPTER THIRTY-FOUR

PRESS ON

Dorothy shut her eyes against the face that kept floating before them. Beautiful big brown eyes and a dimple in his left cheek. Soft pre-pubescent lips that would never smile again.

So many little lives had already come into her keeping, and she'd barely been at work in the hospital for a month now.

The boy she'd just lost was only ten years old. A handsome child. His fatal folly was to try and emulate an older neighbor as they all celebrated one of the many local fiestas.

He'd had the ingredients right. It was the proportions he botched. And when he packed a heavy charge of powder into his homemade canon and stuffed it with sticks and stones and touched a match to it, his abdomen had taken the brunt of the blast. It was devastating, catastrophic, unsurvivable.

To heap sorrow upon sorrow, she had come out of surgery to find out that her four-month-old pneumonia case had died. It had looked as if the infant had made a turn for the better. But not so.

Dorothy let Fred tuck her into bed and brush the hair back from her face. She hoped he didn't see the tear she struggled to hide. How could she explain to him that this was a necessary part of the brutal joy she derived from practicing medicine. The hardest part. The part that shredded her even as it kept her whole.

~~~~~~~~~~

Fred's letter home:

Have just put Dor to bed where I hope she gets a much deserved rest. She has had a hard day and one that has brought considerable sorrow to her because of loss of two patients. These experiences take almost as much energy as the hard labor she put into the work.

There is a sunny side to her work and I think she is getting off to a good start. They have already adopted her technique for sewing up an incision. Then there was a case in where the wound was not healing and the patient had been in for some time, so Dor put her hand to the difficulty and the case went out within a few days in good condition. Her handling of a number of children patients has met with almost immediate success. So, with the losses there are the gains.

Losses. Gains. He was always totting them up for her, hoping it might somehow help. Like keeping score. It seemed such a clinical assessment. How did one tally a life lost against a life saved?

Dorothy fought sleep, trying to pull her mind back into the kind of order she'd prided herself upon all those years in India. She'd weathered her first hysterectomy here this week, feeling slow on the uptake as she worked her way through it for the first time in nearly four years. But the patient was recovering beautifully.

The four-day-old child with the imperforate anus came through surgery with flying colors. It was an easy reconstruct. Still, things in a delicate newborn could easily go awry.

She had already lost two cases to tetanus in her short tenure at Iloilo Mission Hospital. Both died about six hours after admission. But the cleft lip surgery on the lovely twenty-year-old had gone splendidly, all done with local anesthesia, because for some reason Filipinos tolerated local anesthesia exceptionally well.

Scenes flashed and split and patched themselves together in disjointed fashion as her mind labored to shut down. She tried to recall each surgical procedure, each stitch, each clamp, searching for a mistake.

Had she been too long away from the practice of medicine? Everyone had advised her not to go back to work so quickly after her illness and the trauma of a surgical birth. Had she not been healthy enough to stay on the razor edge she needed to inhabit when holding dear lives in her hands? An infant and a mere boy?

"No mistakes," she muttered. "No mistakes..."

The images swirling in her head became muzzy, slipping away as did the familiar sounds of the house settling down for the night. Dorothy's breathing finally slowed, relaxing her limbs and letting the jumble of words fall into a pattern she recognized. A verse. A passage she'd written down just the day before and shoved into the pocket of her white coat.

> *But one thing I do: forgetting what lies behind and straining forward to what lies ahead, I press on toward the goal for the prize of the upward call of God in Christ Jesus.* PHILIPPIANS 3:12-14

I press on. That was it. Just press on. That was all He asked.

She could do that. She could get up in the morning, mother her children and let them feed her soul. She could hold their tiny faces in her heart as she walked the wards, reassuring her patients, tending to their needs, putting their bodies back together.

She would see to them in the surgery. In the nursery. In the new office with the black glass above the door that read *Dr. Dorothy Chambers.*

The door with the hook on the back of it where at the end of the day she would hang her white coat and know that in a few hours she'd don it again.

And she would press on.

ROSA CAIMOSA
CAROL AND BOBBY'S AMAH [NANNY]

CHAPTER THIRTY-FIVE

NONSENSE AND NUISANCE

"Fred, this can't be right."

"Hm?"

"I mean it, Fred. Look at this?"

Dorothy handed him the newspaper and within a moment he was putting down his coffee cup and grasping the paper with both hands.

June 13, 1940

The war news is surely terrifying these days. Today's report was that the fall of Paris was imminent, but that German gains were being had at the terrific sacrifice of men. Just where it will all end is a mystery.

"So many lives. And Paris! It's unfathomable." Dorothy growled.

Fred shook his head slowly. "And in the end what will it achieve other than the obliteration of families and two decimated countries."

"What deshy-mate-a, Daddy?"

Carol's inquisitive voice brought them back from the world's turmoil.

"Decimated? It means ruined. Broken. Like when you accidentally dropped Mommy's pitcher and it broke, right?"

"In alla-hundered-many pieces. I sorry, Mommy."

Dorothy laughed. "I know, precious. I'm just glad you didn't hurt yourself. We can always buy another pitcher, can't we?"

Carol clapped her hands. "Maybe get wubber?"

Now Fred joined the laughter. "A rubber pitcher. My stars, wouldn't that be a grand thing to have?"

"Den Caro not deshy-mate-a Mommy's wubber pitcher!"

"Too right, little one. When in the world did you get so smart?"

"Oh I smaht alla-time, Daddy-boy."

Those words were truer than her almost three-year-old little self could have known. And as the days passed, Dorothy and Fred found themselves being more and more careful in the conversations about the war that was escalating far beyond their imaginings in Europe.

Their experience aboard a belligerent's boat had made them fully aware of war tensions in the world. But when Japan began to creep more visibly into the picture, they took grave note.

July 4, 1940

So far war conditions surely sound bad, altho there is not much doing here as yet. Some 5–7,000 British and Americans—women and children mostly—have landed or are shortly to land in Baguio and Manila from Hong Kong. Papers here say there is no immediate danger there, but that they have been advised to get out now rather than waiting until the emergency arises. It will surely put a strain on Manila. Everything seems so screwy!

In fact, tensions were now visible even in their own community as 'friend or foe' choices began to creep into the minds of Filipino and foreigner alike.

"Rosa, be a dear and see what Bobby is hollering about, would you?"

"Hollering?" Rosa looked up from the pot she was stirring.

"Yelling...bellowing...shouting..." Dorothy coached.

"Ah, yes! Shouting! Yes, I understand."

Rosa wiped her hands on her apron and hurried to the nursery to check on the baby. If the strength of his voice were any indication, he was just a hungry, healthy nine-month-old.

Normally, Rosa would have been off in a flash to look after him. But she'd been unusually upset today, and in the last few minutes Dorothy had discovered why. Rosa had taken in some sewing from one of the Jewish ladies new to Iloilo.

November 14, 1940

Papers announced lately that it was not considered necessary now for further evacuation from Hong Kong—but that those who had gone home would not be returned for a while. Today's news about the fact that the convoy of 39 ships was not entirely sunk but that thirty had already reported, and the damage done the Italian Naval base, seemed to indicate that Britain was keeping her head and shoulders well above water. Just what Russia is going to do, and what Japan will decide to do, is yet to be seen. Don't worry about us, however. We are all well—I haven't felt so well in years as I have since Bobby arrived, —are getting our salary regularly, have plenty to eat, and if Japan does strike we won't be any worse off than millions of others—but I rather doubt if Japan really goes thru with it—she is biting off an awfully big mouthful with Britain sending reinforcement with the fortification of the Islands here.

"Mommy? Mommy?"

Dorothy answered absently. "Yes, darling?"

"Mommy, I want to wear your watch. Now, peez."

Dorothy refused to let the unexpected request completely break her concentration. Not when she was poised on the brink of illustrating a medical clue that often eluded her nurses.

She lifted her small paintbrush from the page. What a simple thing it would be to wave the child off, or slip the watch off her wrist and let Carol wear it for a bit. But that would take all the fun out of the gift Santa was bringing Carol. In fact, it should be arriving any day now. She'd ordered the little girl-sized watch in September.

"Perhaps if you would ask Santa, he would give you one for Christmas." Oh, how smug she felt. It was getting harder and harder these days to stay a step ahead of her precocious daughter.

When Carol had no hasty comeback, Dorothy had to look up from the drawing she'd been studying with a critical eye. Carol stood before her with her arms crossed in a most familiar pose that spoke of extreme consternation.

"Santa not my frien'. He *old*. 'Cuz I saw him picture."

Dorothy laughed. Last Christmas she'd been too pregnant to completely immerse herself in making Christmas for Carol. This year, if she wasn't careful, immersion in her work at the hospital was threatening to do the same. And that she could not allow. She dropped her brush in the tray.

"You are so right, my little elf. Santa is very old. You see, it takes a long, long, very long time to become as clever as Santa. Why don't you get a piece of paper and pencil and I will write a letter to Santa for you. How about that?"

"I will write myself."

"Oh. Well, then, that's even easier. You find the paper and you may use my pencil."

In two shakes Carol was back with a piece of paper. She lifted the pencil from the table and oh so politely looked to Dorothy for permission to use it.

"Dear Santa." She spoke the words as she scribbled in nonsensical but surprisingly straight lines across the page. "Mommy not yet me wear her watch. Peez make her give me it."

Oh dear. The best laid plans...

~~~~~~~~~~~~~~~~~~~~~~~~~~~~~~~~~

November 29, 1940

Dearest Mother, I get so hungry for you to see the kiddies sometimes that it seems that I would have to bring them home, or cable you to come out here. They are such a precious bunch of nonsense, nuisance, and indispensableness.

Dorothy held out her hand to receive the letter to Santa that Carol had so carefully penned and folded. Her former childish pout was replaced with complete trust that by handing her letter to Dorothy, it would get to the North Pole and into Santa's hands without mishap.

With her answering smile Dorothy pushed her war worries so far below the surface that even a German submarine wouldn't find them. They were not going to intrude upon Carol's Christmas. Not this year. She would see to that.

CAROL JOY CHRISTMAS 1940
ILOILO, PHILIPPINE ISLANDS
WITH CHRISTMAS DOLLIE AND TOY PIANO

BOBBY, DOROTHY, AND CAROL, 1940

BOBBY AND CAROL'S BEDROOM IN ILOILO
Dorothy painted the Aesop's Fables illustrations on the
windows. By the time she was done, all twelve panes were filled.
Bobby sits smiling on the window seat Fred built.

FRED WITH CAROL AND BOBBY
ILOILO 1941

CHAPTER THIRTY-SIX

INTO THE FIRE

January 3, 1941

> 1941 is here and I can't help but wonder what it is going to bring. Everything is quiet here, but papers indicate that Roosevelt is getting more and more in favor of getting into the thick of things. Guess his promises can be easily broken in the "face of national emergency". It all seems to be so senseless, and so beastly.

"Oh, don't touch, Bobby, Mommy's not done with this yet."

Dorothy caught Bobby's little hand before he could smear the wet paint she'd just applied to Bobby and Carol's nursery window.

"These pictures are from Aesop's Fables, and they will always remind you of very important values." She pointed her finger like a stern teacher and held his startlingly blue eyes as long as she could before collapsing in laughter. His remarkable eyes could change from the most impish, sparkling blue to a sage and mystical, wistfully wise gaze faster than she could say Aesop's Fables.

But today, they simply said, *okee-dokey, mommy...I get it...I won't touch the window thing again.* Oh, she was going to be in so much trouble when this one learned to talk!

> As I wasn't having to go to the hospital every day I have tried to get some of the forty-leven things around the house done. Got the third coat of enamel on the kiddies beds and also the decals—and they do

look adorable. They are ivory enamel with varnished mahogany panes in the center of the head and foot and it is on these that the decals have been placed. Got their toy box enameled and a row of little black silhouette figures around the bottom of it, their table and little chairs re-enameled and decorated with some cute animal decals and then put some little black silhouettes on the dresser drawers. Have ten of the Fables done and only two more to do. The room does look cute and even Bobby seems to love the pictures. Then I got the new piano bench varnished and stained, and the three panel screen for the guest room enameled and the soft plain reversible chevron cloth in jade green tacked in place. Have also begun to make our own bread and am having ever so good luck. Have been getting it from the hospital, but think I can make it cheaper and it is hard to get it now when I am not going down there regularly. Can get the Fleischman's yeast.

Last Saturday it was storming terribly—terrific rain, wind, and had been most of the day. It was hard enough to hear with the wind and the rain, but due to the heavy rains, the low ground in front of the Baptist Missionary Training Seminary which is just across the street from us was a regular pond and several hundred thousand frogs were going at it for all they were worth. I felt as though I had about sixty grains of quinine at one dose, my ears roared so.

Sunday and Monday were busy trying to get ready for the heavy part of the week. The College was conferring an honorary degree upon one of the men who has done fine work on the revision of the Bible into Visayan. I made the hood for him, and it came out very nicely. The scarlet band with the lining in the lovely shade of blue and gold.

Then we have exchanged guests with the others (here to attend Baptist conference) so have guests at many of the meals. Today the Rounds are here for lunch, and as the Missionary group is meeting for two days, we will be busy until Monday. There is a picnic out at Arevella this evening for the bunch, and a get-together supper tomorrow night.

Her days at home were constant reminders of where her true heart lay. Never a day went by that one or all of her three loves didn't do something that had her bursting into laughter, singing at the top of her lungs, or choking on some poignant, unexpected expression of childish wisdom.

The blessing of it was that these days seemed to move at a slower tempo, a smoother rhythm, a gentler pace. Days at the hospital always proved the opposite. Fast paced, hurried consultations, sweeping rescues and emergency surgeries made the hours disappear in a flash of healing art.

Tuesday I took out Alice Covell's tonsils and she has done beautifully. Had a phone call from one of the missionaries on the campus on Tuesday saying that there were girls who wanted to have their tonsils out on Thanksgiving morning (it had been recommended at the time of their annual checkup), and that one wanted to have her adenoids out. When they came down Wednesday morning, I found that two of the girls were having one of the other doctors, and that the third was coming to me. Imagine my surprise when I picked up her card and found that her complaint was pain when she moved her bowels. Instead of adenoids it was hemorrhoids. When I told Fred about it, he said, "You'd be surprised where your adenoids are". She doesn't need an operation, I think, and will do well on treatment.

War tensions played havoc with emotional balance in every household, and no two people experienced it in the same way. It moved things daily toward a tipping point that nobody wanted to recognize, nobody in Washington wanted to confirm, and nobody in the Chambers household wanted to either dismiss or over-react to.

When the U. S. military began to leave the islands, Washington told the missionaries to sit tight, to reassure the Filipino people they were not being abandoned. Besides, Washington said, if anything happened it would be a three-month dust-up at best and things would be back to normal.

An interruption of three months seemed manageable. So, life went on much as it had, with one delightful exception. Fred's work as Dean took a surprising turn and elevated him to the position of college president. And as president, the college decided he should have a home near or on campus.

And they proceeded to build one.

April 14, 1941

Opinion is divided out here as to what will happen. Many feel quite sure that Japan will not be foolhardy enough to try getting in any deeper with the U.S. than she is already. Others think she will make trouble, and still others think that if things do happen, Manila will be the only target. We are continuing to live one day at a time and enjoying life. The Board has inside information from the State Department and up to date feels that everything is safe.

Sayre spoke recently here to a big gathering of Red Cross workers and expressed the opinion that while he thought it would be very foolish not to be prepared for some emergency that he did not think there was much chance of any invasion. To date there has been absolutely no word either thru the papers or thru the High Commissioner's office of advice to Americans here in the Islands to evacuate so that we feel that the probabilities are that things are pretty safe. In Japan and China, evacuation, especially of women and children (and men also in Japan, I think) has been advised, but that is not true, so far, of the Islands.

Tuesday afternoon I got a permanent wave in the ends of my hair, and it is now done much as it was when I left Denver—much to the joy of most of the people here. I think that the girl gave me quite a nice one, and that after it has been washed once will be quite natural looking. Fred thinks it makes me look younger. I felt that I needed a bit of rejuvenating before becoming the President's wife!

· · · ·

Dorothy darling, pack your kit. We're going on holiday.

That was all Fred had said. Without warning he'd come home early one day and began to pack. No amount of poking and prodding could get more out of him, so she and Rosa scurried about collecting the necessities for a trip into the country, giggling like schoolgirls the whole time.

His command had them in high anticipation of a great vacation. But it was mostly the way he said it that had tantalized.

His words said *holiday*. His tone said, *Dorothy, my ravishing wife. Time for some fun. Get your sunsuit and prepare to be wined and dined in exotic ports.*

~~~~~~~~~~~~~~~~~~~~~~~~~~~~~~~~~~~~

June 23, 1941

We have taken Siebe's radio and Radiola (lovely toned one) and have sold our Victrola. Then Alma gave me a very good offer on her electric sewing machine, and so we have gone in for that.

Tonight's report is that Germany has declared war on Russia and we are wondering what effect that will have on Japan. Will she think her treaty with Germany is worth not much more than Russia's was; will she fight Russia, or side in with her because of the non-aggression pact, or what.

It is grand to have such a lovely Radiola.

In light of the troubling war news brought to them on the new Radiola, the suggestion of an exotic getaway was completely unexpected. Dorothy watched Fred unpack the car she'd just carefully arranged. He'd been so secretive about this sudden excursion that she'd had to guess what to bring along.

"May I ask...?"

Fred lifted the Radiola over his head. "Not allowed where we're going, darling girl." He winked as he trotted it back into the house.

Not allowed? Ridiculous.

She guessed now that they were going up to the little cabin in Calinog. A week without war reports from distant corners of the world would be quite bearable in Calinog. It was a quiet, serene place—a humble spot for them to center themselves in preparation of the hullabaloo that would ensue now that Fred had been installed as college president.

Clever fellow.

Fred trotted back out, hoisted her typewriter from its position of honor atop her luggage and turned back toward the house.

"Wait!" Dorothy cried. "I'll need that!"

Fred grinned. "Where we're going this is the last, I mean the *very* last thing you'll be wanting." He chuckled, clearly pleased with himself.

She folded her arms in exasperation and watched as he methodically reduced the things she'd packed to one small suitcase apiece, her medical bag, and the gear they'd need to cover the cabin windows in case of an air raid.

It was too much. More than she could stand still for. She was never without her typewriter. It was practically her right arm. Where would she spill her thoughts? How would she record memorable moments before they were over-trodden by the events of a new day?

"Fred Chambers, I call for a compromise." She felt strange putting her foot down, and folded her arms more tightly even as she lifted her chin.

He stopped in his tracks, turned, and came toward her. "Darling Dor, can you just trust me on this? I guarantee you won't even think about your typewriter once we reach our destination."

She huffed. "Yes of course, but I see no reason why it can't sit in the trunk. Just in case, don't you see? It's a meager compromise."

He lifted her chin with his forefinger. "In case what?"

"In case...in case, oh I don't know...in case we get captured by marauding pirates and there are no pens in sight and I have to type a message and put it in a bottle. Don't you see?"

Fred laughed. "Pirates, you say? Well, I hadn't thought of that. How clever of you, wife, to think of every precaution. The typewriter shall come along. But," he said, juggling the typewriter as he moved closer for a kiss, "I'll wager $5 it never leaves the trunk."

Dorothy contemplated the wager. It was a week's household allowance. A foolhardy wager. But a safe one.

"Done."

In minutes they were all in the car and passing the outskirts of Iloilo. When Fred ignored the turn north to Calinog and veered onto the coast road, Dorothy knew she'd been wrong. The tails of her scarf flew jauntily in the wind as they sang their way up the coast. Fred's joy was completely unleashed, and it lifted her with it to an unfettered place of sheer anticipation.

Six hours and two stops later they pulled off the road into a lush oasis of palms and jungle greenery. Within minutes they were installed in two small huts separated by a flower bedecked outdoor shower. Fred had brought her to the place every matron in the city spoke of as the most romantic spot in the islands.

He'd brought her to Antique.

~~~~~~~~~~~~~~~~~~~~~~~~~~~~~~

September 14, 1941

They had their first Blackout practice here last night but we were in Antique so haven't heard how things came out. We hear that they are planning them for all along the Pacific Coast. They have been having them regularly in Manila and especially in Corregidor and Cavite.

Divine Antique!

Fred had been told this was the perfect place to spend their respite holiday, but the folks had completely understated its beauty. Dorothy and Fred had arrived with the children and Rosa just the day before and already Antique and Iloilo seemed to be galaxies apart.

Dorothy sat back in the kawa bath and gave a great sigh. Rosa had put the children to bed in their hammocks after a brisk climb along the easier trail at Bugtong Bato Falls. It had been glorious. Beautiful sun, cooling mists and now this heavenly warm bath.

She sighed heavily and inhaled the wafting fragrance of the flower petals that had been strewn across the water. Why did they not do this everywhere? Why did she have to come all the way to Antique on their respite week to find such heaven on earth in this steaming bath?

Her toes brushed against the rough walls of the immense iron cauldron in which she sat. It was round, like a cooking dish, and she was cooking in it. Slowly. Blissfully.

Below her, small fires heated the great rock, and it in turn heated the cauldron, which kept her bath water at the perfect temperature to make her celestially unaware of her surroundings other than the parrots that chattered in the trees that sheltered her canopied bath.

She lifted her hand and lazily waggled her fingers. As yet, the typewriter had not left the trunk. Her warm, languid hands would be hard pressed to type a word, anyway. As quickly as the thought came into her mind, it flitted away on a breath of steam.

Here she could feel no sense of worry. No urgency. Here she could scarcely remember a schedule. Here there didn't seem to be a word for emergency.

"My turn?"

Fred called from below, waiting his turn to ascend the ladder and take her place in the heavenly stew.

"Mmm. Perhaps."

"Perhaps?"

"Mmm. Perhaps I'll let you have a turn. If you'll do something for me, that is."

"What? Throw you up a towel? Help you climb out?"

"No dear. I want you to build me my own kawa bath."

. . . .

The feeling of idle bliss stayed with Dorothy for about an hour as they navigated the road out of Antique at the end of their idyllic stay. Then, on a stretch of road they remembered as wide open and with little traffic, they encountered their first road block. It was a military installation, hastily set up but adequately manned by two Filipino officers. Cars were stopped right in the driving lane, waiting their turn to be searched.

Fred and Dorothy kept up a cheerful front, telling Carol stories, playing pat-a-cake with Bobby, and quietly singing. But in the front seat they held hands, suddenly aware that in the space of a week the world as they knew it had changed.

Joyful, raucous voices from a week ago had now turned quiet, cautious. Hands reached for identity papers, shaking a bit for no reason other than the fact that moving freely had suddenly became a thing of the past. Hushed explanations for the typewriter in the trunk were greeted with skepticism.

They were stopped two more times in the six hour drive, usually near larger towns or villages that had navigable inlets. Silence had fallen between them, and the children slept most of the way home.

And once they were home, the air raid drills began.

October 13, 1941

War conditions seem to be about the same as far as the Far East is concerned. Had another two hour black out last Wednesday evening. Wish that there was something useful that one could do in a blackout, but there doesn't seem to be much except listen to the radio. Apparently the present Japanese cabinet is pretty conservative, and not much will happen until another cabinet gets in, but who knows.

Fred has talked some of my taking the kiddies home on the Clipper (to Honolulu and Matson line from there on) but I can't see it yet at least. Neither can Ann Waters when Henry suggested the same thing. Somehow it seems easier to face uncertain situations together than apart. Guess we will continue to live one day at a time and trust that we will be guided in doing the right thing at the right time.

Kawa baths would remain a thing unique to Antique. Once the air raid drills began to escalate, Dorothy neither had time nor interest in luxuries like bathing in a steaming cauldron. There was too much to do. There were too many questions crowding her mind. Too much fear beginning to creep into the fringes of her thinking. But she kept it largely at bay.

October 19, 1941

The way things sound over the radio, it looks a bit stormy. Will send this by air to Manila and hope that it will catch one of the President boats as it leaves for the States. Will let Mother forward them to the rest of you. The radio report said last night that American Merchantmen had been ordered to go to friendly ports—and that applied especially to those going and coming from the P.I. So, mail schedules may be disrupted for a while. However, as Dad used to quote "sposin agin it shouldn't".

We've been expecting something to break since last January, and it hasn't altho things do look more ominous than they have before. However, we are not worrying and are taking one day at a time. It would be very difficult to get out of the country now if we wanted to, and somehow I can't feel that that is the thing to do anyway.

The Filipinos are Americans in the same sense that Canadians are British, it doesn't seem just fair for us to try and get out when they have to stay by. The Army and Navy folk seem to feel that Japan wouldn't have a chance now in trying to invade the Islands, and that we are well protected.

So, even if the mails are a bit slow and irregular, remember that no news is good news, and that we are writing regularly, and you will get a lot at a time. We can listen in to the "Mailbag," and get some news that way.

Air raid!

The words screamed in Dorothy's head as loudly as the warning screech of the air raid horns. They'd been practicing for weeks. But the unbroken blare of the horn told her this was no rehearsal. Enemy planes had been sighted!

Dorothy breathed a prayer of thanks that she was home today. The shrieking horns sounded clearly more ominous today.

"Rosa! Get Bobby!"

She heard Rosa's feet running toward the playroom as she helped Carol into her long pants. With one hand Dorothy grabbed a rubber mattress cover to put on the floor of the dugout shelter Fred had built in the sloping side yard. There had been enough rain that the wooden pallets that covered the floor of the dugout would most likely be wet.

Her hands felt sure and steady, even as the horns pulsed in the distance. "Hurry now." She'd heard the alarm in her own voice and purposely softened her tone.

The four scrambled into the shelter that was minimally supplied with a few provisions. It made no sense to keep blankets or any fabric of any kind in the dugout. It would be soaked, moldy, and useless to them.

They had just hunkered down on the rubber cover Dorothy spread on the pallets when Fred tumbled in to join them.

"Thank Heavens!" Dorothy tried to put a smile in her voice, but it was hard won.

"You made it in record time, I think," Fred praised. He held her eye and in the silent communication that they'd always shared she read the same fear she held in her own heart.

This was only going to get worse.

"I was sure you'd be taking cover at the college. Or in the cave, or—"

Fred shook his head. "We knew something was up. Planes all over the sky this morning, flying sorties all directions out of Cavite, we think. Something's up for sure to have that many planes aloft. So we piled in the car and beat it back here."

He stopped and took Dorothy's hand. "It's...it's true."

Dorothy's brow wrinkled. "True? What's true?"

Fred tossed each of the children a slice of orange candy from his pocket to distract them, grateful their little ears were plugged with twists of cloth.

"Pearl Harbor."

"You mean it's—"

Fred nodded his head slowly. "They're saying it was catastrophic, darling. I think...I think the entire naval fleet isn't there anymore."

"But where would—"

He shook his head more vigorously, a look of loss and disbelief shadowing his face. "I think they didn't make it out."

· · · ·

Pearl Harbor!

They had seen Pearl Harbor two years ago—several of America's greatest naval vessels had been moored at regular intervals along what she now heard was called Battleship Row.

The Arizona.

The Oklahoma.

Smaller warships had circled the island in a most orderly way. Instruments of war, merely awaiting orders to deploy. Stretching as far as the eye could see. But the atmosphere at the time had been positively jolly.

Dorothy had clenched her teeth at the very sight of it then. They'd left the ship during the Honolulu layover to put their feet on dry land for a day, to have a bit of a frolic with Carol before having to get back on board the reprovisioned ship. Their belligerent's boat.

They'd joined a couple of sailors to motor up the coast a bit. American servicemen were everywhere. Smiling. Calling their hello's. Sweet-talking the girls in the most salacious, almost comical way.

It had been a bit of a contradiction then, missionaries sharing a holiday with soldiers. But in recent months, with Japan threatening a more invasive stance, the mental image she carried of the majestic scene at Pearl Harbor—with all its able young men—had brought her comfort. She had felt protected.

And now that protection was gone. All those fresh young faces lost because Japan wanted New Guinea, and the American presence in Pearl Harbor stood in the way of that.

They'd heard General MacArthur himself on the Radiola just the night before declare that the Philippines were "the key that unlocks the door to the Pacific."

REPORTS OF GENERAL MACARTHUR:
THE CAMPAIGNS OF MACARTHUR IN THE PACIFIC VOLUME I
PREPARED BY HIS GENERAL STAFF. LIBRARY OF CONGRESS 66-60005

The Japanese understood this completely, for the islands lay directly athwart their path of future aggression.

Close to South China and the island stronghold of Formosa, they were not only an obstacle to Japan's international ambitions, but they could be made into a powerful strategic springboard for their drive south and eastward.

Flanking the vital sea routes to the south, they were the hub of the transportation system to Southeast Asia and the Southwest Pacific; from the Philippines, lines of communication radiated to Java, Malaya, Borneo, and New Guinea. Economically too, they were necessary to Japan's grandiose scheme of the Greater East Asia Co-Prosperity Sphere.

As a thriving democracy, the Philippines were a living symbol of American political success in Asia and a direct negation of the

CHAPTER THIRTY-SEVEN

LOOK TO THE HILLS

From Fred's memoir

The first baptism of "fire" came on December 18th. Forty heavy Japanese fighter planes came over the Campus, then turned and leveled off to strafe the Cadre (two transports unloading Filipino soldiers on the wharf and a Dutch Oil tanker). We had no way of knowing at the time what their targets were. For forty minutes the planes circled, dropped their empty shells over the Campus; we could hear them hit the plantain leaves as we took shelter in previously dug air raid shelters.

Strong, damaging blasts that she knew had to be taking life and limb persisted near the port. It wasn't the first time Iloilo had been hit, but the succession of blasts and the trembling house told her this was going to be bad. Dorothy crouched in the shelter and kept the children occupied, although Bobby managed quite well on his own.

"A pane! A pane come make-a fonny noise!"

Even with wads of cotton stuffed in his ears, the child still tracked every sound he heard coming from every side. Coming from places too close for comfort.

The ground trembled in one long, continuous shudder, sending small rivers of pebble and dirt streaming to the dugout floor.

When the all-clear sounded, Dorothy helped Fred load the car with the emergency bags they always had ready before she rushed off to the hospital. He would take the children and Ann Waters—now close to full term in her pregnancy—upcountry to Bagong Barrio, a missionary rest house on the northern tip of the island of Panay, about a five-hour drive.

Dorothy and Dr. Waters had already begun the process of moving the hospital to Calinog in the center of the island, but there would be many to care for at the nearly abandoned mission hospital in Iloilo after a bombing raid of this magnitude. And Dorothy knew that is where she was called to be. She left her little family preparing to flee to safety while she headed into the thick black smoke of the scourged city.

Rosa had proven to be a master at packing, and due to her special gift, there was room in the car for more provisions than they had originally expected. The young Filipina amah ran with Fred back into the house and together they shoved canned goods and anything reasonably non-perishable into flour sacks. He was just closing up after his last trip to the car when the telephone rang, its urgent peal freezing him for a moment before he shot the key back into the lock and opened the door to snatch up the receiver.

"Fred! Why are you still there!" Dorothy's voice held an unfamiliar edge that sent ripples of unease along his spine.

"Just leaving, darling. Car's packed, kiddies are stowed and I'm just locking up. Where are you?"

"At the hospital, darling. Lots of injured. Henry and I should get to Bagong Barrio before morning, I think. But Fred! You have to go now! They say a Japanese warship has entered the harbor!"

Fred was stricken with fear. Not for himself, but for Dorothy who was miles closer to the danger than he was at the moment.

A Japanese vessel of war in the harbor. The very thought of it froze the blood in his veins.

"Darling. I love you. Go now."

The line went dead.

· · · ·

From Fred's memoir

The report of the Japanese warship proved to be a rumor.

Dr. Waters and family and we, with our children, shared the same house near the hospital in Calinog. After a time, General Chinowith, USAFFE (U.S. Air Force in the Far East) official in charge of the Panay area (they were building runways for military use) asked me to serve as an adviser to the recuperating Filipino soldiers and to plan for rehabilitation camps on the islands of Panay and Negros. General Christy offered me a Commission, but I preferred to serve as a civilian. His remark was, "I envy you".

On Sunday, before April 15th, the missionaries held a conference at Bagong Barrio to discuss plans for action in case of invasion. Rumors of the imminent fall of Bataan and Corregidor kept coming in.

Among the ideas suggested was that Mrs. Covell and I go to the Campus and be there if and when the Japanese invaded to explain that the College was a Filipino Corporation and therefore, not subject to destruction as American property. Because she spoke Japanese fluently, Mrs. Covell agreed.

However, it was the opinion of the majority that the Japanese might come in "fighting" and overrun the Campus, with no opportunity to talk with high officials. That proved to be the case later. The final decision of the conference was that half the group would go into the "Hills" and try to be of help where possible and the other half, related to institutions, would remain in their respective hospitals. The Capiz Hospital had been moved down from the north coast.

Dorothy slipped through the bamboo curtain that separated their side of the nipa hut from Ann and Henry Waters and their children.

"How's the patient?" Fred asked.

"Remarkably well," Dorothy replied as she stowed her instruments. "She's close, Fred. The baby will come soon."

"I guess that's...good?"

Dorothy sighed heavily. "Good. Yes. I suppose."

Words had come hard in recent days. Dorothy had always known her mind, her heart, her mission, her course. That surety had kept communication clear and open and free.

But she and Fred had not settled their future aloud, and now she was doubting the decision they'd all but verbalized.

I want to go to the hills. It just feels safer.

Or maybe not.

How would I keep watch for them? Where would I look?

Which way will they be coming from, when they're ready to kill us?

And they will kill us, Dorothy thought, not for the first time.

I'd be the example of why not to run from the Japanese. A martyr, maybe. But architect of my children's end?

I can't do that.

Dorothy folded the children's clothes she'd just taken from the laundry line and placed them in the "gotta go" bag. There was going to be a day when they would once again need to gather their things quickly. Not in minutes, but in seconds. The gotta-go bags were always ready. Always. With bits of money and medicines spread between the bags so if they lost one, they didn't lose it all. Dorothy already carried their birth certificates in a small pouch hung around her neck.

The tacit agreement between Fred and Dorothy seemed to indicate internment was their plan. They would be found by the Japanese in the hospital and taken into custody.

Internment!

Walking right into their arms?

How do I do that?

How do I take my babies by the hand and say, "Here we are, unwelcome army. We'll stay in your 'confined community'. We'll carry on with our lives at the point of your guns every day."

I can't do that.

The hills are so green and dense. How could they find us there?

Surely we could hide! Just for a few months. Surely it can't take more than a few months. Our president promised us that.

I can live in a hole in the ground for a few months. I can make it an adventure for Bobby and Carol. I can do it.

I should do it.

I have to keep them away from the guns.

"Dorothy?"

Fred's voice came to her from a great distance. Farther away than the front porch, farther away than the yard of the little Philippine nipa hut. Much farther. It came from beyond the green hills, the ones so clear in Dorothy's mind that she had felt for a moment that she was already there. Farther than "the hills whence cometh my help".

"Hey, pretty lady. You all right?"

Fred's arms encircled her waist. Strong, steady, comforting, safe.

"Say it, Fred."

"What?"

"Say it. We have to say it. We have to speak it out loud."

Fred touched his forehead to hers. In the way it had always been in their marriage, he knew what she meant.

"If I say it, I'm not speaking for you. You have to say what your heart tells you, too. Deal?"

She nodded.

In his quiet, measured voice, Fred repeated their strategy.

"We know that if we run to the hills, the Filipinos will help us hide. But we know, too, that if they're caught helping us, they won't survive. We know that. Right? So we must stay with the hospital. Hope the Japanese will honor our Red Cross. When we think they will be upon us soon, we'll move our things to the hospital. We'll burn the military pass and hide the car. We'll live at the hospital however long it takes for them to find us. We'll submit to their questions. We'll shelter our children. We'll go where they take us. We'll manage."

Dorothy listened, and with each word her heart began to calm.

"We'll manage," she echoed. "Yes. We'll manage."

She looked up into his face and knew that he saw resolution in her eyes. At last she was fully on board.

DR. HENRY WATERS, HIS WIFE ANN AND CHILDREN BILLY, GEORGE AND
MARY ALICE WHO EXPERIENCED THE CAMPS
ALONG WITH THE CHAMBERS FAMILY

NIPA HUT OF RUTH HARRIS, LIBRARIAN
CENTRAL PHILIPPINES COLLEGE

CHAPTER THIRTY-EIGHT

CALINOG

"I wish you wouldn't, Fred."

"I have to, darling. We have most of the college's administrative papers moved to the cave already. Just a few more trips and we'll be done."

"But—"

He pecked her on the cheek and picked up his car key. "Just a few more trips. We'll be starting the college back up as soon as all this is over and we'd just be in such a mess without the records. I know you understand."

"But—"

He was halfway out the door. "But what?" he called back over his shoulder.

"Just you wait a minute, Fred Chambers."

That halted him in his tracks, but at the same moment Bobby, who was at the table eating his morning porridge, heard a rousing song come on the radio and decided to wave his spoon in time to the music.

The result was widespread, and porridge flew in forty-leven directions about the eating porch of their little Bagong-Barrio nipa hut. And a particularly large glop landed on Dorothy's cheek.

She stood stock-still, wind taken out of her sails, becalmed in a sea of porridge.

And sighed.

"We'll talk when you get back, darling. Be careful. And—"

Fred caught the glop of porridge in his hand as it began to slip from her cheek and kissed her on the relatively safe top of her head.

"I know, I know. Get back before dark."

Dorothy huffed. "Don't you dare try these roads without running lights. I absolutely forbid it. Promise me, Fred."

Fred kissed her again and instead of his usual flippant "scouts honor" salute he put his hand over his heart. "I promise."

Fred sprinted out the door and Dorothy turned to clean up the mess.

"Oh Bobby. You're a sorry little mess! But I will say that your sense of rhythm is tickety-boo."

. . . .

Fred navigated the roads as quickly as he could. There was too much to move to the hidden cave in one trip. He'd have to make two, if not three. Load the car with just the critical files, banking papers, student records and a dozen other types of document they'd identified. Then drive two miles to the cave in the hills where they'd stashed raised crates to conceal the valuable papers. It was the coldest, driest cave he could find.

He was college president. He took his personal charge to safeguard these things very seriously. In a few months when this was over, they'd do the reverse. Bring the documents back down to campus

The final trip to the cave went without a hitch, but he'd cut the time shorter than he'd planned. Still, he needed to check one more time for any mail that might have made it through. Dorothy needed word from home so desperately, and he desperately needed to make that happen for her.

He raced down a side street and whipped around the corner. The Post Office lay straight ahead. Quiet. Unoccupied. Bombed out.

There would be no word from home. Not by mail, at any rate.

The crescent moon that skated behind scattered clouds gave him just enough light to get himself back to the Calinog campsite. Still, each time he sensed an approaching vehicle his heart was in his throat. In the dark he could no longer discern friend or foe.

. . . .

REPORTS OF GENERAL MACARTHUR
THE CAMPAIGNS OF MACARTHUR IN THE PACIFIC

"One of the purposes of the Philippine campaign is to liberate the Filipinos; they will not understand liberation if accomplished by indiscriminate destruction of their homes, their possessions, their civilization and their own lives; humanity and our moral standing throughout the Far East dictate that the destruction of lives and property in the Philippines be held to a minimum, compatible with the assurance of a successful military campaign; indications are that in some localities the Japanese are evacuating cities, leaving Filipinos in residence, either failing to warn them or compelling them to stay; aerial bombing causes the greatest destruction; our objective in areas we are to occupy is to destroy totally hostile effort in order to insure our own success; in other areas we neutralize, to weaken any hostile effort which may tend to increase resistance to our occupation objectives; in the latter areas, our attack objectives are primarily airfields and shipping, not metropolitan areas or villages or barrios; to the extent possible, we must preserve port facilities that we plan to use. The Commander Allied Air Forces will, and CINCPOA is requested, to issue general instructions in consonance with the above objective of minimizing destruction of life and property of Filipinos....."

CAROL AND BOBBY
1942
TWO MONTHS PRIOR TO INTERNMENT

CHAPTER THIRTY-NINE

PRAY THAT WE MAY NOT FALL SHORT

~~~~~~

Last letter out from Dorothy and Fred, and
ONLY letter out prior to three-year imprisonment:

Calinog, Iloilo
April 15, 1942

Dearest Families:

Have just found that there is a possible chance of getting a letter
thru to the States, and am I taking it! I was feeling particularly like
having a visit with you all and so had sat down to write to you when
this friend came in. I decided to do it all over again on the machine
so that I could get more in, and tell you more. Of course this will
be censored, but think I am not very full of information other than
family, so don't worry if something is deleted.

It has been such a long time since we heard from you altho have
taken it for granted that had anything special happened that if the
Boards knew about it they would have cabled us as we have had several cables from them as a group and have sent several back to them.

I think the last letters we had were dated about the first week of
November. How we would like to know what is happening to each
and all of you—Fred and Wink, Carol, John Martin, Johnny and
Ruby, Midge, Vi, the two Mothers, Marian etc. We have wondered

and wondered. Have also wondered about Bill Reardon. Would love to be able to write to Helen. I wrote to him as soon as I had word of his arrival in these parts, but communications were interfered with shortly after that so know nothing.

Shortly after war was declared the schools all closed—students just began going home. So, within a few days, the College was closed. We stayed on and I was carrying a rather heavy schedule of Red Cross First Aid classes and was teaching about four or five hours a day.

Had just started a new class of forty students when the big bombing raid on Iloilo occurred. That came about one o'clock. We went into our air raid shelter at once—picking Bob up from a sound sleep. Carol hadn't lain down as yet. Grabbed a big bed pad off the line as the dugout was wet and muddy from recent rains. Bob was a brick, and took it as a big game. Carol didn't seem at all alarmed altho was quiet.

I hadn't taken any plugs for ears or mouth (to keep the mouth open) so tore up a hankie that Fred had. Bob lay on the pad, face down, propped up on his elbows, plug ravelings hanging out of his ears, a wad like a ten cent cigar sticking out of his teeth, a grin from ear to ear and saying over and over "A pane come, a make a fonnee noise" (Airplane come and make a funny noise).

When the raid was over, Fred took me to the hospital where I worked the rest of the afternoon and part of the evening helping out in the emergency room. There were a great many casualties due to the machine gunning largely, altho some were results of bombs. Not too much damage was done, considering the number of planes taking part.

Fred then went back to the house and packed some things up and took the Covells, the Waters youngsters and ours with the amahs up to Bag-ong-barrio very near the center of Panay Island where Erle Rounds has a camp site. It was just a tiny one with two small rooms and a very tiny cook house. He came back the next morning, (lighted cars were not allowed on the roads at night), and Ann and

I went up with him that afternoon.

I doubt if we would have left Iloilo had it not been for Ann. She was due to deliver in three or four weeks, and it was not considered safe for her to stay in Iloilo. That meant that I more or less had to go with her as otherwise she would be without help when the time came. We were awfully crowded at first with so many in such small space, and so took a small Nepa house by ourselves—Ann and I and the kiddies, and Fred came when he could. The kiddies loved it, appetites became enormous and they are brown as little Filipinos.

Christmas was rather hectic, but they had a good time. I had made quite a bit of furniture for the doll house of ply-wood just in case the other didn't get to us, and of course practically none of the Christmas mail arrived—Got a letter from Mrs. Beaver with a five dollar check in it which we haven't been able to cash as yet, and a book from Santa Ana, but haven't been able to acknowledge either of them so far (please do for me, Mother). She has enjoyed her play house, altho with her companions being all Boys—Billy 5½, George 3, and Bob, the games have been very war like.

We were quite comfortably located in our little Nepa house but it was hard being so far away from the men folk. Later however Fred and Henry came up to Calinog as their work was going to be here rather than in Iloilo, altho Fred goes back and forth once or twice a week.

On Jan. 11, we came down here to Calinog to attend church and see about getting a house here. We found a nice one, went home to pack, and that night about 2 A.M. Ann called me to say that labor had begun. We didn't waste any time but brought her down here to the hospital and I delivered her at 5 A.M. of a lovely 8 lb 13 ounce girl. Fred and I were back in Bagong by seven-thirty, finished packing and were all down here, bag and baggage by ten-thirty.

We have a much more comfortable house here—has an 8 x 10 front porch, a sala [living room] about 12 x 20 with two 10 x 10 bedrooms opening off of it—one for each family—separated by a thin bamboo partition. There is a dining room, kitchen, back verandah where we do dishes, an enclosed place for bathing, —pouring baths are the order of the day—and an outside toilet.

We have an electrolux and have been able to use it so far and that has helped. How much longer we can use it due to shortage of kerosene is another matter. Probably for another month or so and then perhaps there will be more oil available. Since coming here have helped out some with the teaching—have a class in Ob. and have been giving about two hours a day in work in the B.P.D. May start some First Aid classes soon.

Have done a lot of sewing—practically all of it by hand and can imitate machine stitching pretty closely now. Have made a shirt for Fred, have a plack shirt almost finished, a dress for myself, three for Carol, four suits for Bob as overalls—all by hand, also three bras and a slip. Also made a pair of P.J.s for George and a pr. of overalls for Bill. Ann and I take turns running the house—she is doing it now as I did it for two months straight after Mary Alice was born.

Fred felt for a while like a man without a country when the college folded up so completely, but there has been a good deal to do to keep it going—teachers' salaries to be paid in part, invoices to be made so that in case of loss or damage, we would know what the proportionate loss was—it is divided between the two Boards and the Philippine Bapt. Convention. Then recently he has been acting as Educational Director trying to get the Veteran's Rehabilitation Camp established. He is doing this voluntarily—is not in the army, and receives no salary and is free to leave it whenever it is possible for the college to reopen. When that will be no one knows altho we have hopes that perhaps it can open for the second semester next October or November, but time alone will tell. He has managed to keep busy, and is awfully busy just now. Flora and Olive are here, and we see the other missionaries with the exception of the Mungers who are in Negros rather often.

Just now we wonder what is going to happen next as Cebu is being attacked, Bataan has fallen, etc. This of course you know—probably know as much as we do. We have a small radio which belongs to a friend—it is complete with collapsible aerial, battery, etc. and we have enjoyed it as we can get local stations, London, San Francisco, Australia, etc. Helps to keep us informed as to what is taking place. Our radio is of course no good up here as there is no electricity. We have a good Coleman light and are enjoying that.

We had thought about going into the mountains in case of invasion, but have decided that one place is about as good as another and will probably stay right here and keep at our jobs. Neither Fred nor I liked the idea of running and would probably have stayed on in Iloilo until now had it not been for Ann and now I feel that perhaps it is better for the kiddies to be away from the coast in case of trouble.

I am not too much worried as to what will happen—perhaps we are overly optimistic, but think with Fred that the key to the situation is to keep at the work in hand and try and make our Christian witness as effective as possible. That is the main thing we have at stake and pray with us that we may be worthy of it.

Carol and Bob have grown so much and are so adorable most of the time. Carol and Billy have kindergarten with Olive Buckner for an hour every day and love it. Carol would like to have it every morning and afternoon every day. Bill isn't quite so keen but looks upon it as a necessary evil, I guess. She is doing very nice hand work—coloring, cutting, mending on cardboard, etc. She talks a blue streak at times, loves stories as always, writes a good deal, knows all of her letters and can print many names by herself. Can print almost any word spelled for her. She can count to twenty, and doesn't do too badly from there on. Bob can count to eleven.

Carol said the other day "I know the first part of the 'Star tangled banner'". Says "restroy" for destroy, and "reinfreshment" for refreshments. Was much interested when Mary Alice arrived and asked many questions. Wanted to know if I was sure that I didn't have anything growing inside of me. Would so love to have a baby. Wanted to know the other day if Jesus and God were one and I said yes. Said "Well why don't we have two Gods. I want a lot of gods and I want a lot of them to be interested in war".

Carol weighs about thirty-five pounds and is up to my waist and a bit above it. Loves to do certain things—help cook, wash out stockings, etc. Bill is a regular fiend on the question of war and would rather play that than anything else. Talks constantly about guns, bombs, subs, planes, tanks, etc. Carries out raids on Singapore, Manila, etc. Carol joins in most of the time.

Bob also talks the language of war. When he hears a sound he will say "Evyboddy be kite" (quiet) and then will listen. Perhaps will say "At a pane—no, at not a pane, at a chuck (truck)". He leaves off his initial s's and all of his l's. Said the other day about Mary-Alice "She a coot baby—she got a pink nice egg (leg)". Loves anything mechanical and was talking the other day about having sat in the seat of the ambulance. Said "I sit in a army-ance and I pull a gadget and make a car go". He knows where everything is, and Fred keeps his keys carefully out of Bobby's way. He says just about anything now, and talks about "chine guns" and tanks, and bolos, etc. Says his own blessing at the table frequently and it goes "Fahk ee faddy for my night, and for my sood (food) and my mamee, and my pidgeon". (George always uses this last word for some unknown reason.) If someone else starts to say the blessing and carries on a bit long, Bob starts saying "Amen, Amen, Amen, A—MEN" until they finish.

He is full of play, loves the story of the Little Red Hen now and asks for it several times a day. He weighs about thirty pounds, is wearing the shoes that Carol started to wear on her 3rd birthday—and they could be a bit wider, altho are not too tight. Carol is lucky in that when Beverly Spenser was here last fall she left two good pairs of shoes with her that she had outgrown. I would be in a hole if it weren't for that, altho she can still wear the last ones that Carol sent to her. They are just the next size to what Bob is wearing, however.

His hair is very light yet—almost white, still short enough so that a cut hasn't been even indicated, very curly. He looks so much like the snap of Fred when he was five.

I have cut Carol's hair again so that it is a Dutch Bob and very becoming—is much cooler than her curls. She was biting her finger nails rather badly for a while but has stopped now and so has her own bottle of nail polish as a reward. Bob is very boyish and even in his talk. There is nothing feminine about him. Has stopped calling me Mamee most of the time and it is just "Mom" and "Dad". Adores his Daddy and is constantly saying "I want my Dad to help me do dat". Tonight he wanted his Dad to pat him when he went to sleep. Had a bit of fever the other day—probably due to some teeth he is cutting as there was no other apparent cause—he was most explicit as to what he wanted done "wub my back, wub my tummy, wub my knee". He is a darling, and I do wish you could see him.

Put up some five quarts of jackfruit jam today and it is quite good. Am learning lots of things about the foods in this country. We can't get butter now, altho have had butter up until very recently. However, with the electrolux we make butter from coconut milk, and it is good.

The kiddies drink coconut milk often and love it, and we use coconut milk in most of our cooking—tapioca pudding is much better made with it than with regular milk. We can whip the cream from it, etc. Take a ripe coconut, grate the meat and add to it the water from the coconut. Put this thru a potato ricer to squeeze out the juice and let it stand where cool and the cream comes to the top and can be whipped to butter, salt added, etc.

Cocohoney is a prime favorite with the kiddies—one cup of coconut milk, 2 cups brown sugar, and about a tablespoon of Karo, cooked until thick syrup. It really is swell. We are corning pork and having some good baked hams as a result. Am also trying some dried meat this week just to have it on hand in case of a shortage. Have been glad that I learned how to make soap altho the ingredients are hard to get now. Conditions along that line are better, though, and we will probably be able to buy it soon. Don't worry about us for a while at least as we are not uncomfortable, starving, short of cash, or anything else. Inconveniences are the greatest difficulties and they are minor when one considers the difficulties millions of others are undergoing.

There are so many things that I know I will wish that I had put into this letter,—have been writing every two or three weeks, but can't send them all, so will keep them and later perhaps can send them. Am sending this one copy, and trust that Mother will pass on the information. Will enclose two or three of the tiny snaps of the kiddies taken just before war broke out, which were in a letter mailed just before war was declared, but which was returned several weeks later as it had never left the Island.

I hope you folks at home will keep all pictures that we have sent, if you haven't already destroyed them, as it is possible that some of our things out here may be lost. We might be able to make up some of the books again with those you at home might have. We are thinking about you all loads, and would love to see you, and reassure you that we are O.K. thus far. Don t worry about us.

Just pray that we here may do that which we find to do and do it well, and that we may not fall short of the challenge of this work out here. It will take a long time to replace all the hate in the world with love, but I have an idea that people are going to be more ready for it when this is over than they have ever been before. Surely this terrible war must bring to the mind and heart of every individual—especially Christians—the terrific need for the Love of God in the heart of every individual.

Loads and loads of love to you all— Dor, Fred, Bob & Carol

PART THREE
INTERNMENT

Iloilo Provincial Jail
April 20, 1942 - June 14, 1943

Santo Tomás Internment Camp
"STIC"
Manila, Philippine Islands
June 21, 1943 - February 3, 1945

CAROL JOY IN 1942
ONE MONTH PRIOR TO INTERNMENT

CHAPTER FORTY

WHAT HAVE WE DONE

~~~~~~

From Fred's memoir

...pandemonium broke loose in Calinog. Raids were made on Chinese and military stores. Stores, especially rice, were loaded on corrossa (bamboo sleds drawn by carabao) and taken into the Panay Hills. As they ran by our house, they cried to us, "Run for your life! The Japanese hate a 'white' skin. Remember Nanking!"

However, we waited in faith. That night we decided to sleep in the Hospital. We had stored supplies near the house and felt if the soldiers came they would loot.

About 6:00 PM on Friday, Captain Chavez came in from Passi, ten kilometers away. He said, "The d___ Japs will be here by midnight. Destroy all gasoline and autos!"

We hid the auto in a shelter, destroyed the military plates and my pass from General Cristy. A battle had been fought at Passi and the soldiers were moving toward Calinog. We took a few things and went to the Hospital. About midnight there was a burst of automatic rifle fire. Two of the three sentries at the bridge behind the Hospital were killed on the main highway from the south. Then all was quiet.

The family huddled on the hospital bed made available to them. The children slept fitfully, twitching in their sleep each time a spate of machine gun fire disturbed the night.

At dawn Dorothy slipped from the bed to peek from the window. The hospital was situated on a small rise and overlooked a lovely market square. Blooming bushes framed the lantern posts and lined the quaint pebbled walks.

But what should have been a tranquil scene was now dominated by a machine gun nest in each corner of the square.

A chill penetrated her white coat and lodged deep in the marrow of her bones. Bobby's first stirring noises pinched at her heart. She turned to look at her little family, just as Carol Joy swung out a sleepy arm to settle Bobby back down.

She'd brought them to this. She would bring them through this. There was no question of whether her children would survive. She would allow no other outcome. *But what, dear God, had they done?*

Dorothy buttoned her white coat. She would make her rounds, just like any other normal day. She settled her stethoscope firmly around her neck, like a badge proclaiming her neutrality. The Japanese soldiers who were beginning to stir in the square would find nothing sinister here. Merely doctors. Doing the work to which they were best suited.

Saving lives.

She stepped into the corridor and halted. Across the hall three Japanese officers paused from eating their breakfast. They looked at her, assessing her as she assessed them until she turned away and began her rounds.

They had taken over her hospital. Apparently without incident. In the hours before dawn.

She circled quickly through the closest ward, then hurried back to the room where the children slept.

"I didn't know where you were," Fred said, his voice weary from the night's ordeal.

"Checking the ward," she smiled. "Greeting the three officers who seem to be enjoying the cafeteria food."

Fred swallowed. "So you've met the Japanese."

"Mm-hm."

"Well then."

By midmorning the main body of troops arrived. Hundreds of Japanese soldiers swooped through the village on bicycles, a startling and unexpected image amid the tromp of feet and rumble of tanks that drowned all else. Japanese soldiers descended from the backs of trucks. Some entered the rear of the Hospital and asked for quinine. Clearly, they were no stranger to malaria.

A Japanese officer who seemed to be in charge told Fred that if the family remained within the bounds of the Hospital compound, no harm would come to them.

From Fred's memoir

I talked with a Japanese officer who appeared to be a medical man. Our conversation might well have been other than captor and captive. He regretted, as I did, that we had to meet under such circumstances. It was evidence of what we were to experience during the next three years: Japanese soldiers who had no heart for the War but wished to get home to their families. Many seemed to wish to help us in any way feasible.

Dr. Waters was taken upcountry to try to help the Japanese locate the USAFFE (United States Army Forces in the Far East). He knew little or nothing.

Dorothy asked permission of a sentry for us to return to our house to get some toys for the children. He accompanied us and when he saw the mess in which our house was left by raiding soldiers he exclaimed apologetically, "Good and bad soldiers!"

While we were away at the house, Japanese officers came looking for me to question me. It was fortunate that I was away (perhaps, another Providential fact) for with my knowledge of USAFFE headquarters, etc., they might not have let me off lightly if I had not given them the information they needed. However, they never came back to question me.

Late Sunday morning two Ford trucks drove up in front of the Hospital in Calinog. Dorothy and Fred, along with the other Americans and foreign nationals present, were told they had one hour to get ready to leave.

One hour. They had nothing but the gotta-go bags. But the one-hour warning gave Dorothy time to rethink things.

She hurried to the Pharmacy tucked away in the hospital's interior and filled her medical bag with a variety of drugs and things for the children. If this was outright theft, then she prayed God would stay her hand.

A doctor went past. Two nurses stepped up beside her to get medicines for patients. The short Filipino nurse turned to go and then caught Dorothy's eye.

"You know, Dr. Chambers," she said, and Dorothy held her breath. "You're going to need this."

She pulled a key from the pocket of her uniform and opened the double-locked cabinet, pulled out three full boxes of sulfa tablets and dropped them into Dorothy's gotta-go bag.

With a flick of the key she locked the cabinet back up, laid a hand on Dorothy's arm and said, "God be with you."

Shouts echoed down the hall now.

"You get in trucks!"

Their captors made a great show of loading their rifles before pointing them at Dorothy and Fred as they were hustled into the trucks. Henry Waters climbed in next and took the baby from Ann before helping her into the truck bed with their other two children. Americans and Filipinos who were ambulatory patients at the hospital crowded in after.

Bobby scrambled off his mother's lap and perched atop a pile of luggage, and there he stayed as they were driven south through the battle-scarred country. Through the bomb craters and cratered vehicles. All the way to Iloilo City.

And the whole way, little Bobby clutched his "nye-nye" teddy bear and sang at the top of his lungs.

· · · ·

Two hours later the truck rumbled up to the doors of the hospital Dorothy and her staff had fled just days earlier. Beyond it Iloilo burned, thick black smoke coiling up from the bomb-ravaged port city. Nothing about the hospital grounds looked the same. Foliage had been crushed into the mud by what looked to have been tanks. Here and there a door hung off its hinges.

Dr. Waters was first to jump from the truck. He was stunned as he took in the changes war had wrought so swiftly. It took him a moment to register that the Japanese guard with a bayoneted gun pointed at his chest was getting angry.

The fellow clearly wanted him back on the truck.

Around him, Filipino nurses, patients and doctors were ushered into Iloilo Mission Hospital, but all Americans and Brits were kept at gunpoint aboard the two trucks.

Once personal possessions were sorted, the two trucks took off with a jerk and proceeded to the Provincial Jail, where those still on the trucks were forced out and into the jailhouse.

It made all sorts of sense to Fred. He'd come twice to the jail in hopes of bringing aid or comfort to Japanese nationals who had been interned in this very jail by the Philippine government. Now the Japanese would use the same jail to house their Allied prisoners.

"What do we do?" an English businessman asked, frustrated at the prospect of sleeping on the hard jail floor.

Dr. Waters laughed, then spoke in a suddenly serious tone.

"Men and rats adapt."

Fred blanched. It was a shocking statement, and yet he'd already witnessed evidence of just that very principle. He'd seen the English businessman before, on several occasions. Always impeccably dressed. But today he looked weary and disheveled, in nothing but dirty shorts and sneakers.

Men who had spent most of their adult lives behind a desk were now showing a bit of muscle from the physical work recent weeks had demanded of them. They were adapting.

"Dink, Mommy! Needa dink!"

Bobby was wailing now. Parched by the dusty ride.

Dorothy stepped into the lavatory and turned the tap, not really expecting anything, and not getting anything. The city water system had been destroyed by the Americans when they evacuated Iloilo.

"Thank you ever so much, fellas," she moaned.

A Japanese guard had followed her into the lav, and above Bobby's screeching she managed to get the fellow to understand that they needed water, and they needed it now. He forced her to take Bobby back into the cell and then closed the door on the women. Within minutes she understood why. He was rounding up the men and barking orders to them.

He was taking them in search of water.

BOBBY'S TEDDY BEAR

Bobby's blue and white teddy bear was originally a baby gift to Carol from her Aunt Carolyn. When Bobby was born, Carol passed it on to her baby brother. In 1966, when grown-up Bob was serving in Vietnam, his wife Mame felt the responsibility of preserving his precious mementos from the Philippines. She bronzed the little bear so it wouldn't deteriorate further. While Dorothy was a bit dismayed, Bob saw the bronzing as the act of love it truly was.

CHAPTER FORTY-ONE

NINETY-POUND BATTALION

Nights were the hardest, when they were confined to the cells. Men in one cell, women and children in the other.

Bobby seemed to have suspended his need for sleep, and more than one internee threatened to box his ears if he didn't keep quiet. But they underestimated the child. Now, instead of just singing, he moved around the cell on his rubbery two-year-old legs. Dancing.

Carol was another matter. Overnight she'd become mother to everyone in the cell.

"Mrs. Lady needs a blankie, Mommy."

"It's okay, Mrs. Sojer Wife. We'll help you wash that tomollow."

"No, Mr. Big Person, you alla-ready had yours."

The remarkable thing was that whether she was commiserating or scolding, people for the most part smiled and accepted her pronouncements.

And on the first Sunday of captivity, Carol Joy led the singing.

Fred quietly organized a worship service, and much of the group of internees convened in the jail chapel. Fred delivered a sermon from Dr. H. E. Fosdick, reading from a book he'd refused to leave behind. It was a treasured volume, one that Dorothy had gifted him on their first anniversary. It would not be abandoned.

The makeshift little chapel offered a familiar setting, under unusual circumstances and with a good deal of tension, and most heads remained bowed, even while Fred spoke. When he announced a hymn, they joined tentatively in a lyrical whisper, casting glances from the corners of their eyes to see the reaction of their Japanese guards.

With one exception, that is.

When Fred called the name of the hymn, little Carol Joy immediately stood up, walked to the front to stand beside her Daddy-boy, and sang in her pure, sweet treble. Her perfect melody emboldened hearts that were beginning to feel cowed. And when she concluded the final verse, there were twice as many Japanese guards at the chapel door than when she started.

. . . .

That same day, they met Loreto Tupaz.

The mood of the camp was still quiet. Guarded. Most of the one hundred internees were still keeping to themselves, organizing a spot for their things, and keeping a suspicious eye on anyone who came uncomfortably close.

Internees had to fend for themselves in all things, and especially where food was concerned. The preparation and cooking over open fires consumed a good bit of time in the middle of the day for many, not just in rounding up food, but in collecting firewood and something to use as a cooking pot.

At first, mealtime was "every man for himself". But on this first Sunday, several of the internees contributed canned meat, and two had baby potatoes to boil. And they all ate together in the jail yard. It was satisfying and left most of them feeling that two meals a day were going to be okay. But more than that, the communal meal seemed to birth the fledgling idea that cooperation might be the best path to survival.

Just as the Sunday meal was being cleared up, they heard a commotion at the front of the jail. One voice rose above the rest—clear and honey-laced—and captured the attention of the internees.

"How you doing today, officuh?"

The chipper voice could be heard moving from place to place in the outer room. "Oh, you betta get dat fix, officuh. Not good it get infect."

They could hear her clucking and chatting with the Japanese guards, and all the while the chatty voice came closer and closer to their enclosure.

It was mesmerizing. Japanese growls turned to polite responses, and there was even a chuckle or two here and there.

Eventually, the door to the cell block was opened by a Japanese guard who held it ajar and nodded respectfully to the small woman who smiled her thank you. But before entering, she turned back to the crowd of soldiers in the front room and whispered something in a soft, respectful tone and elegantly bowed.

Loreto Tupaz stood about four-foot-nine, and was more than engulfed in a navy blue woolen nurse's cape with a red cross emblazoned on her left chest. The cape was of the old style and flowed to her ankles. On her head she wore a crisp white nurses' cap that must have dated to the 1920s.

Loreto Tupaz
The Ninety-Pound Battalion

Ms. Tupaz was a hero of the guerrilla movement in the war-torn Philippines. In postwar years, Miss Tupaz worked with Dr. Henry Waters to develop Central Philippine College of Nursing (later the Central Philippine University College of Nursing) into a college of distinction, recognized both in the Philippines and abroad. Loreto D. Tupaz Hall now houses the College of Nursing and Allied Health Sciences.

She moved around the cells, making greetings quite similar to those she'd made to the Japanese. Her tempo seemed the same, never tarrying longer with one internee or hurrying away from another. But all along the way she would catch the eye of each internee, and as she moved away, her foot would slide a small cloth-wrapped package toward the internee as she passed along.

By the time she'd circled the cell block, there were thirty small packages quickly concealed by the internees, each package having magically fallen from the internal folds of the petite young woman's voluminous cloak.

Within weeks the internees had dubbed this tenacious little lady their "ninety-pound battalion", for nothing less than a battalion could have walked right through those Japanese guards as she had.

Loreto came weekly to the jail, always managing to bring the very thing someone was needing. Vegetables, bandage rolls, aspirin, canned milk.

Gradually, her tempo changed. She asked to see the internees first, spending a little more time with each visit.

Once she'd checked on each internee, she spent equal time with the Japanese soldiers. They never once wondered why she wore the huge woolen cape, many sizes too large for her, in the humid heat of Iloilo City.

Whether or not she had anything to do with it, they would never know, but after a month in the jailhouse, a Japanese officer came to the men and made a startling announcement.

"We busy fight war. You take burned building. Make fence. Go round three school building. Move there."

Move out of the jail!

There was no question they wanted to do that very thing, and that afternoon the men were taken out by a Japanese lieutenant and set about collecting materials and erecting the fence.

For days they were marched around the neighboring city blocks and set to ripping sheets of corrugated tin from the rubble to carry back to the schoolyard. The metal sheets offered about two seconds of welcome shade as the men hoisted them overhead for the trek back. But within minutes the heat they'd collected lying in the beastly tropical sun was strong enough to penetrate the men's makeshift gloves and sear their hands.

Once they'd collected as much as each man could carry, they were marched in a group, under guard, about six blocks away from the jail to a small schoolyard with three small buildings where they set about erecting a very sturdy fence.

Fred gloried in the freedom of being away from the jail. He would stride along, deep in thought, or mentally embracing some particular challenge he needed to think through. His mind was miles away one day when he nearly bumped into the person in front of him as the group suddenly came to an abrupt halt.

It took a moment for Fred to get his bearings, and to assess what the devil was going on as they were quickly formed into ranks as if ready for inspection.

A Japanese officer came striding across the street from the guard post he'd been inspecting. The man's arms flailed angrily as he approached the small group of internees. Without warning, he strode behind the front row, slapping each prisoner in the back of the head until they realized he wanted them to bow. When he reached the end of the row, he knocked the cap off Fred's head.

The small group of men looked at one another confused until Fred turned toward the soldier and brought his posture to full attention. Under his breath he urged the group to follow his lead.

"Bow. Now."

The Japanese officer paced back and forth in front of them in full rant. As Fred began his slow bow, the man stopped mid-rant and stared as the entire small group of white men bowed low from the waist.

A smile crept across his face as he took in the 'honor' they paid him, and answered their bow with a full bow in return.

A new fact of their internment was learned that day. If one came near any Japanese officer, one had better be prepared to bow. Nothing inflamed them more than to have a prisoner pass by without bowing.

But true to the Japanese code, the officers would always stop to acknowledge the bow. It was one of the many contradictions they had seen already. The Japanese army could show horrific disregard for human decency, even for human life. And then turn around and offer some kindness or gesture of politeness or good will.

It kept the internees in a constant state of uncertainty.

But it wasn't easy for the men, enduring the intense physical labor it took to build the fence that would free them from the jail. The substandard nutrition conspired with the heat to take its toll on the men—enough so that their guard adopted the habit of giving them frequent rests. When shade was not available, the men would take turns standing behind the others seated on the ground, offering impromptu and most welcome shade with their bodies.

One particularly hot day Fred found himself seated not far from that day's duty guard and drew him into conversation.

"Your English is excellent," Fred said as they passed around water to fill their tin cups. Only one inch of water per internee was allowed on these work breaks. Never more.

The guard nodded and attempted to hide a satisfied grin.

"Chicago."

Fred looked at the fellow. "Chicago? You're from Chicago?"

"Six month. I study there."

Fred was aghast.

"Oh my! You went to school in Chicago? What did you study?"

"Agriculture."

Fred studied the man's face. He'd been gruff with them at times, but fair. Always fair. Clearly it was their good fortune that the guard assigned to their work detail had spent time in America.

· · · ·

By the end of their first month of captivity, the fence was completed and everyone moved their things into the schoolhouse camp. It felt luxurious, compared to the cramped quarters of the Provincial Jail.

The entire elementary school compound was forty by eighty yards, not quite as large as a football field, but it was space. Space to move about, space to grow things, space for the children to play.

Of the three small buildings, one was used for dining, one for men and women without children, and one for families with small children. Beds were made from whatever they'd been able to collect on their daily sorties for fencing material.

To their surprise, the gates were left open for a short time each day. Friends among the Filipinos, Spanish, Swiss, and the Swedish Salvation Army were permitted to bring food, fuel, ten-gallon Standard Oil barrels in which to cook and so on, as gifts for the internees or oftentimes for sale.

One morning mid-week of the second month in captivity, Dorothy watched the bartering and tried without success to tamp down her envy. People were buying things.

"Fred, look over there." She pointed to a vigorous bit of haggling that was going on in front of the dining hall. "That fellow has glass jars."

"Hm? Oh yes, I see. And a jug, too."

"I'm going to buy those glass jars."

Fred raised a curious eyebrow.

"I can sterilize things. Put them in the glass bottles and boil them. Here, look after Bobby while I do this."

She handed Bobby over to Fred and pulled a small pouch from beneath her clothing. She turned a bit toward Fred in order to obscure the view of the pouch as she pulled a roll of one-peso bills from the pouch.

"Dorothy!" Fred exclaimed, but she shushed him. "Where did you get those?"

He knew that roll alone was more than they'd been able to bring in with them. And he had their money stashed where no one would find it.

"The Chinaman," she whispered.

"He gave you—"

"He *loaned* me some money. I'll pay him back after the war. Now keep Bobby from following me."

They all knew that arrangements for cash could be made through a certain local Chinaman, but Fred had not entered into that type of clandestine arrangement. He preferred to think that God would provide.

And of course, God had. By way of Dorothy's resourcefulness and a Chinaman's generosity.

Dorothy approached the busy vendor and waited her turn, hoping nobody ahead of her had their eye on the glass jars. They were in better view now, and she'd inspected them closely. The rubber gaskets that sealed the lids when they were latched looked nearly new.

She really had to have them.

But just as she was about to begin her transaction, the woman who had just completed her trading turned back.

"Oh, and how much for those glass jars?"

"Ten peso," the fellow said.

"For all five?" the woman asked.

"Ten peso each one. All five fifty peso."

The woman blanched and Dorothy cringed.

Fifty pesos for five glass jars. It was a fortune. And as badly as she wanted them, she couldn't countenance it.

The woman turned away and Dorothy stepped up. And as she did, she saw that the man had a badly blistering burn on the back of his hand. She fished in the pocket of her white coat for the tube of Unguentine she knew was there. It was nearly spent, but there was enough in it to treat the fellow's wound a couple of times over.

"Mabuhay, sir," she greeted. He looked up, surprised that this white woman used the familiar greeting in such a comfortable manner.

"Mabuhay," he responded. Its meaning generally meant *I hope you are well* or something like it. But its literal meaning was *may you live*. And that is what she intended to do.

"Your hand needs to be treated, sir."

He looked at the back of his hand and sadly agreed.

"I can see that it pains you," she continued.

He nodded.

"I have Unguentine. For you. If you give me the five glass bottles for ten pesos."

A look of overwhelming gratitude came over his face, and he reached out to take the small tube.

But Dorothy didn't let go.

"There are two treatments in this tube. One today and one two days from now."

He nodded and tried to accept the tube, but still she held on to it.

"And I will take all five glass jars for ten pesos. Total."

He blanched and began to withdraw his hand. But she moved her hand slightly forward, keeping him in contact with the offered medicine. And at last he relented.

The tube disappeared into his pocket, along with Dorothy's ten pesos, and she collected the five glass jars, along with a small roll of wire she'd gotten him to throw into the bargain. It was enough, she hoped, to fashion wire handles for each of the jars.

It was a small victory, but went miles toward buoying up Dorothy's spirits. She'd never been good at bartering. Always paid the first price asked. But today she'd acquired a new skill.

And it seemed she was very good at it.

She'd had the Unguentine in her pocket because the partially-used tube had been in the parcel Loreto Tupaz had dropped into her pocket last week. And a gift from the "ninety-pound battalion" was not to be wasted.

~~~~~~~~~~~~~~~~~~~~~~~~~~~~~~~~~~~~~

From Fred's memoir

Two times daily a front gate was opened for thirty minutes and vendors were permitted to bring food to give or sell. Sometimes the firewood bundles contained notes from the guerillas upcountry giving news of the War. Money was provided secretly by a local Chinese merchant. An internee could pass a note to a certain fellow internee containing his name and amount of money desired. Within a few days that internee would give the person the amount in pesos. A record was kept and the total amounted to thirteen thousand five hundred pesos. (Peso = $.50) After the War, when I returned to Panay to help reopen the College, I went to the Chinese merchant to repay and arrange for repayment by others, only to be told that all was cancelled because of his gratitude for the winning of the War by the Allies and his safety.

CHAPTER FORTY-TWO

RUPTURED

Dorothy returned from the well where it had been the women's turn to bathe. The saltwater well was inside the compound, but for bathing only. Drinking water had to be carried from the San Augustine Mission next door.

Use of the drinking water station at the Mission had been hard won, however. Initially, internees were expected to use the well on the grounds of the elementary school prison. But that, of course, was out of the question.

Commandant Yano finally agreed to provide a tank for drinking water. When it arrived weeks later, the internees found it riddled with holes, top to bottom.

His reply when the camp committee complained about the leaking tank was simple. Fix it.

But how? No one in camp had the skill or materials to repair a steel tank.

After punishing weeks, Yano at last agreed to allow the camp to use the drinking water from San Augustine. But bathing could only be done at the seawater well.

"Oh, that feels better," Dorothy sighed as the cool water trickled down her spine.

The constant state of wariness was taking its toll. Her back and shoulders ached from the tension, and merely letting the water stream across her shoulders worked like a balm. She stood in a metal washtub, dressed in a thin nightshift. Not every woman in the group felt the need for such modesty.

As she washed, Dorothy looked across to the playground and watched one of the older girls help Carol with the swing. Bobby remained under Ann Waters' watchful eye. Ann would get her turn at the well when Dorothy returned to watch Bobby and precious baby Mary Alice.

The children were thriving better than one might expect, thanks mostly to the resourcefulness of Nurse Tupaz. She helped Ann supplement her nursing well enough that baby Mary Alice was growing at a normal rate for a four-month-old.

Not that it was easy. But at every turn someone's inventiveness would provide a fairly effective substitution for ordinary conveniences they'd all taken for granted. Whether it was a rat trap or a device to secure the nipple on a baby's bottle, someone in camp would always invent a clever solution.

Still, each time the camp forged some new way to improve their status, Commandant Yano would find a way to set them back. He was cruel in his choices, sending in rice and fish but denying them wood to build cooking fires. Or when they asked permission to sell furnishings from their homes to buy food for the camp, he granted the request with a smile. They discovered all too soon that he had already sold most of the furnishings. And no money for food was ever returned to the internees.

Dorothy gathered her things and headed back to the living quarters with a half dozen mental notes swirling in her head. There were wounds among the internees that she needed to check on, and a small list to make for Loreto.

Fred was seated on the crude bed he'd created for them out of a sandbox confiscated from the schoolyard, and when he looked up at her, she gasped. His face was drained of color.

"Fred! What's wrong!"

Fred shook his head slowly and winced. He reached a hand to his lower right side and winced again. "It's a lot of pain, Dor. I don't know—"

Dorothy whisked around to kneel in front of him, certain she'd see bruises if he'd been injured, or punched by a guard. But there were none.

Her practiced fingers probed gently until a quick tap over his appendix told the story. If it hadn't ruptured yet, it would soon.

"Fred, we've got to get you to a hospital. Now!"

In a mad scramble, Dorothy called to Ann. She felt a rush of guilt that Ann would have to wait for her bath now. But Ann saw immediately the urgency and hurried her on her way.

"Go with him, Dorothy! I'll watch the children," she called as Dorothy sped away.

It took precious minutes to convince the guards she needed to see Commandant Yano, and then a half hour to convince the man that her husband needed emergency surgery. The commandant was still in a state of agitation after the guerilla attack the night before. Just a few blocks away his men had fought off the guerilla force for hours when they'd tried to get close enough to liberate the internees. He'd barely managed to keep them from breaking down the gate.

Now he was suspicious of everything.

From Fred's memoir

One night an attempt was made by guerillas to rescue us, but they were driven off. Perhaps it was to our good, for at that time there was no refuge except in the Panay Hills, and no means of escape from the Island.

The irony of it was that Yano had known Fred before the war. He was a local Japanese businessman who had been conscripted to serve as commandant of their little camp. He and Fred had been teammates on an inter-island tennis team that played a tournament with the adjacent island, Negros. Now he was in charge of keeping Fred imprisoned. Or as the Japanese persisted to call it, "in contained community".

He acted as if he wanted to help Fred, but his suspicions could not be allayed. Eventually, he agreed to transport Fred to the hospital and insisted on staying in the operating room throughout the surgery to ensure the patient had no opportunity to escape.

But Dorothy was not to go.

If this was an escape plot, he was going to be certain husband and wife were not together. Nothing she said could convince him that since she was a doctor she should accompany her husband. Leaving her children in camp should have guaranteed her return, but he would have none of it.

The guards roughly helped Fred into a truck and forced Dorothy back inside the gates. But not before she saw Fred's white face turn to the window of the receding truck.

She knew what he was thinking. It might be the last time he saw her. His burning eyes conveyed to her everything she meant to him.

And she prayed. *Please God, bring him back to me!*

. . . .

Once Fred was suitably incapacitated by surgery and drugs, the commandant allowed Dorothy to spend a night at the hospital to attend him.

It was strange sitting at his bedside in a hospital where she'd functioned as a practicing doctor for two years. She knew the people. She knew every corner of the building.

It was all familiar. Except for the one thing in which she had taken so much quiet joy. The piece of black glass above her office door. The one that had read Dr. Dorothy Chambers. It had been taken down. And behind her desk sat a Japanese official.

Dorothy walked the halls while Fred slept. A stranger in her own bailiwick. On the second morning she stood outside her office door and watched the Japanese officer. So strong was the need to let him know he trespassed. So strong was the need to let him know how dramatically he had disrupted her life, how dangerously perilous he had made her children's world.

She swept her eyes across every corner of the room, and that's when she saw it on the hall tree just past the open door.

Her white coat. The one she'd left thinking she'd be back to get it in a few months after a temporary move to Calinog. The one with the slip of paper in the pocket.

...I press on toward the goal for the prize of the upward call of God ....

Whatever the message had been those months ago when she'd written down the snippet of scripture, it held a world of difference from the meaning it carried for her today.

I press on.

Her whole being shuddered at the thought of those special words in that special coat in her special place, but out of reach. Hijacked by the foreign presence.

But why should they be? Why should they be out of reach? The coat was her property. He may have confiscated her office, but the coat was hers.

Dorothy drew a long breath. It sang along her ribs and bolstered her spine. It lifted her chin and chased the tremor from her hand.

With resolution flowing in her veins she stepped forward. One step. Two. The Japanese officer looked up. His face held no emotion. No curiosity, no resentment, no welcome, no hatred. He just looked at her.

Three steps. Four.

His eyes followed her progress, watched her hand reach for the coat. They moved from her hand to her face and back again. She waited for him to command her to stop.

He put his pen down. The movement froze her for only an instant, and then she reached out to touch the coat. The familiarity of it overwhelmed her. The history stamped within its fibers flooded her senses. Gauhati. Jorhat. The women. The children. The years it had hugged her shoulders through every victory, through every crisis.

Her fingers gathered it and lifted it from the coat hook. She turned her eyes toward the Japanese officer. Was the line of his mouth a bit more severe? Was he going to call her out?

She drew the coat into both hands, and without taking her eyes from the man behind her desk, she slid it on. Left arm, then right. The instinctive roll of her shoulders settled it perfectly, and her hands smoothed the lapel, then dropped to her side.

Dorothy tipped her head a bit.

This is mine, her eyes told him. *And I'm taking it.*

· · · ·

The coat stayed put on her shoulders throughout the next few days as Fred began to recuperate. The hospital took excellent care of him, and she even had the unexpected pleasure of a three-course meal, most of which disappeared into her medical bag. Thanks to their father's appendicitis, Bobby and Carol would eat very well this week.

Fred's recovery took a very normal course, until a rumor began to circulate regarding the fate of several of his former companions.

During the brief months in Calinog, Fred had been approached by General Cristy of the USAFFE to work as an advisor to injured Filipino soldiers. He had even offered Fred a commission.

But Fred preferred to serve as a civilian. And that decision was now proving to have saved his life.

Several of the fellows who had worked with him had been taken by the Japanese, interrogated, and put aboard a ship bound for hard prison time in Japan.

Somewhere in the Pacific, American warplanes spotted the unmarked ship and sank it. With its hold packed with prisoners. If Fred had accepted the commission offered by General Cristy, he would most likely have been on that doomed ship. The knowledge of it both weakened and revived him.

Fred knew he'd been led to the decisions he made, and when confirmation of the rumor came via Miss Tupaz that the ship had indeed gone down, his faith stuttered for only a moment, and then lifted him to even greater levels of devotion.

~~~~~~~~~~~~~~~~~~~~~~

From Fred's memoir

From the beginning, for me, there was never a feeling of being imprisoned. I have an unusual tendency to claustrophobia. However, the high walls of the Provincial Jail had no effect. Two reasons may have contributed. From the time Dorothy and I made our decision at Calinog to remain with the Hospital, because we felt it was what the Lord would have us do; and because there was always something to do to help somebody, since we were all in it together. There was a peace and an assurance that carried throughout the internment.

THE OROKU MARU SANK IN SUBIC BAY AFTER BEING BOMBED BY
AMERICAN PLANES WHO COULD NOT HAVE KNOWN ITS HOLD WAS
FILLED WITH AMERICAN PRISONERS OF WAR

Fred's resolve remained rock solid when he and Dorothy returned to the schoolhouse prison camp. Keeping busy kept his mind off the pain, and as a member of the camp committee, he had little trouble keeping busy.

From Fred's memoir

Each morning the "executive committee" (a Scottish banker, Dutch Roman Catholic priest, and myself) sat under a tree near the outside fence and listened to "complaints" or suggestions. The complaints ranged from "burnt rice" to "crying babies". When a British Captain of a tanker—who along with some of his crew were interned—complained that the babies got all the milk that came into camp, Fred pointed out to him the "law of the sea": women and children first. The fellow was never able to agree that the law of the sea should be observed in camp, particularly if it meant he wasn't going to get any milk.

The committee handled all manner of complaints and helped facilitate all kinds of camp events. But the event that most dampened the spirit of the schoolhouse camp was its first funeral.

From Fred's memoir

A local merchant who ran a lighter (flat-bottomed barge) service between ship and shore had hidden much of his machinery when the American forces withdrew. The Japanese were determined to find it, and took him from Camp for interrogation. He was brought back shortly thereafter, but apparently had been beaten severely.

He took to his bed and whereas before he had been a strong spirited individual, he seemed to have lost it. His only remark was, "They didn't get anything from me."

Shortly thereafter he died of internal injuries from the beatings.

I learned more years later after the War, when local Filipinos who witnessed the interrogation said the soldier pressed him until he struck the Japanese officer. Then they tied him up and beat him, as the Filipinos said, like they'd never seen an animal beaten.

We were permitted to hold a funeral service and buried him near Camp.

Not long after the funeral the usual routine was broken by unexpected visitors to the camp. It was the middle of the afternoon on a Thursday. The camp was quiet, moving slowly after the midday siesta. Two men in white business suits stopped for a moment to speak with the commandant. A few moments later the commandant nodded and pointed. The two men turned to see where the man pointed and began moving that direction.

Dorothy clamped her teeth together and couldn't stop her heart from lurching wildly in her chest.

The commandant's finger unmistakably pointed to Fred.

The two approached Fred and introduced themselves, and Fred led them to seats at the makeshift dining table in the camp "commons". Dorothy joined Fred and nodded politely at the Filipino who wore the clerical collar of a priest and who identified his companion as a Japanese clergyman. They sat in disbelief as the priest disclosed to them that he had been sent in behalf of the missionaries who were hiding in the hills. They sought Fred's opinion as to whether or not they should come in. The Japanese chaplain wished to help because he had known Howard Covell at the Berkeley Baptist Divinity School before the War.

The clergyman knew things about Howard that Fred felt could only have been known if they had truly been acquaintances. But Dorothy wasn't so sure. The questions the second man plied were making her suspicious.

"Why did they come together?" she whispered to Fred. "If this Filipino knows our people at Hopevale, why couldn't the Japanese fellow have just asked *him* about Howard instead of taking time to find us? Why did they come here? To ask us questions they could have answered themselves? It doesn't feel right."

Fred's knee began to jitter up and down as it did when he was working out a problem. He looked at her, then at the two men, and knew they dared not say anything that might disclose the location of the missionary party of nineteen that had fled to the hills.

If he said anything at all that might unintentionally give them a clue where to find Hopevale, he might walk his friends right into a trap.

But what if the missionary group truly wanted to come in? What if they sought internment? What if they *needed* internment? Could he deny them?

"So all *five* of them are still together?"

It was a trick question, and Fred watched the faces of the two men.

"Yes, yes, they've stayed together. All five."

Fred's heart sank.

"We would certainly have room for them," he said, hoping to look agreeable.

There was little to go on but instinct. If he gave them no information would he be denying his friends safe harbor? That would be on his head for the rest of his life if he were the reason they were denied sanctuary.

But would it be safe harbor? Or a Japanese death trap for them?

~~~~~~~~~~~~~~~~~~~~~~~~~~~~~~~~~~

From Fred's memoir

All we could say to the two was that we had seen the missionaries before the invasion of Panay by the Japanese forces and knew only that they planned to go into the Hills. One or two were sure they were "marked by the Japanese before the War" and would have no chance if caught.

As it developed, they were caught between American-Filipino gue-rillas led by Colonel Peralta, and the Japanese forces. If they helped the one, they would be considered "bandits" by the other and killed.

The trick question settled it. Either the Filipino clergyman was loath to pro-vide the Japanese chaplain with more information than necessary, or he truly didn't know there were nineteen in the missionary group, not five.

Fred stood to shake hands with the two clergymen. "Please do give our most sincere greeting to them when you see them."

Dorothy handed the Filipino a small packet she had quickly prepared. "Would you be so kind as to give this to Rachel when you see her?"

The Filipino priest smiled, "I'm sure Rachel will be most grateful for your gift, Dr. Chambers."

Dorothy smiled and stepped back.

There were eight women among the Hopevale missionary group of nineteen. And not one of them was named Rachel.

CHAPTER FORTY-THREE

BITTY-BITS

Summer was taking its toll. Dorothy's skin was parched and red, thanks in part to the broken-down, ratty hat she wore most days. It did little or no good fending off the sun's hot rays. Carol and Bobby were brown like little Filipinos. Energy levels were visibly lower than they had been five months earlier, if you knew what to look for. A man's stride might be shorter. A woman's knitting needles might click less vigorously. So when Alice Waters came running across camp one afternoon, Dorothy dropped what she was doing and hurried to close the distance.

"Dorothy! Come quickly!"

Alice turned and snatched up Dorothy's hand.

"Do I need my medical bag?" Dorothy asked, already a bit breathless as they hurried toward the gate.

"No! It's her! It's Rosa! She's come to see you!"

Dorothy stopped, stunned. "Our Rosa?"

"Yes!" Alice's face broke into a smile Dorothy hadn't seen for some weeks. "Our Rosa!

It was nearly four o'clock and the gates would be closing. They ran harder, hearts pounding, breaths sounding ragged in their chests. But as they rounded the last building the sound was drowned out by the heavy padlock clanging into place on the gate's chain.

On the far side of the gate a Japanese guard stood facing them, his gun at ease but his face set. And beyond him at a safe distance they could see the lovely slim figure of the children's amah, Dorothy's friend Rosa Caimosa. Her familiar brown eyes showed no fear.

"Rosa!"

"Doctuh Kinney! I have supplies for you!"

"Rosa, it's really not safe for you to come here. But how wonderful it is to see you! Is your family well?"

"We have gone north and I could not get a cart to bring me here until now. But I have come! I have sewing needles. And thread. And custard apples and a chicken!" She paused, then added, "I know how you love chicken. Especially chicken legs!"

Rosa started to walk forward but the guard, who had turned at the sound of her voice, held his rifle out warning her to stop.

Immediately Rosa hunkered in the dirt and tore the brown paper and string from her package. She held the paper and string up for the guard to see, then crushed them into a ball and lobbed it over the gate for Dorothy to catch.

The guard was clearly uncertain what to do, and to Dorothy's great joy she could see he was going to do nothing.

Next came the cleaned and plucked chicken, re-wrapped in a soft cloth once Rosa had shown it to the guard. Dorothy thrust the paper-and-string ball at Alice just in time to catch the chicken.

One by one Rosa tossed the things from her package over the fence for Dorothy to catch, and by the time they had it all only one egg had been sacrificed to the hard-packed dirt.

Dorothy and Alice had been squealing their thank yous with each item that cleared the top of the gate and now they stood hugging the treasure with tears in their eyes.

"God bless you, Rosa! God bless you!"

The guard was forcing Rosa back onto the road, back the way she'd come, but she paused and pulled the lovely broad-brimmed hat from her head.

"I come tomorrow," she called. "Early! I come early!"

Dorothy couldn't contain her joy. To lay eyes on the dear girl was wonderful. But to receive her bountiful gifts was almost more than Dorothy could handle without dissolving in tears.

And then with a wave of her hand, Rosa launched her pretty hat into the air. It sailed toward the gate, nearly too low to clear it. But in the last moment it skidded across the uppermost bar of the gate and landed at Dorothy's feet.

Dorothy scooped it up and held it to her heart and stood waving until they could no longer see the girl. Only once Rosa was truly out of sight did a tear slip down Dorothy's cheek. She hadn't been able to get the one thing she needed more than anything.

A hug.

Maybe tomorrow, she thought. Maybe tomorrow.

• • • •

Rosa did not appear the next morning and Dorothy was stricken with an immense sadness. She had been so intent upon getting that hug. And she needed to let Rosa know that she'd found the hidden surprise.

After stowing Rosa's precious gifts in her bunk area, Dorothy had set about preparing the chicken. First she cut it into quarters, with one quarter going to Alice and Henry Waters. She removed the skin from the meat of two of the quarters, cut the meat away from the bone, and sliced it into strips to fry in coconut oil. It would make a savory hardtack that would last several weeks. The skin was fried separately to make something similar to pork crackling. The fourth quarter would be that night's dinner along with a crunchy round chunk of custard apple for dessert.

Custard apples were a far cry from the sweet, juicy, red apples of home. They were tart. Almost bitter. But most satisfactory in a pie.

It wasn't until she was preparing to boil the bones of the skinned portion that the thought had struck her. As she was about to toss a leg bone into the boiling water, the memory of Rosa's comment stayed her hand.

I know how you love chicken. Especially chicken legs.

It was an awfully strange thing to say because Rosa knew Dorothy didn't care for the dark meat of a drumstick. So why...?

Dorothy rotated the bone in her greasy fingers, then turned it end for end. She had to bring it close to even see that something was hidden there, but with a slight wiggle the nubby end of the drumstick bone came away. Too easily. And there, rolled up in the hollowed-out bone was a worn and tattered 50-peso bill.

. . . .

By August 1942 there were nearly a hundred internees at the school compound. Most of the cooking was done by men now, in a cooking shed near the dining room. The women prepared much of the fixings, and the men did the heavy work. They carried wood for the fire, kept it stoked, and heaved around the heavier pots. The cooking vessels of choice were 5-gallon Standard Oil tins.

There weren't many ways to cook rice, mongo beans and pinakas (dried fish). At first the men had tried to do some creative things, but spices were hard to come by. Now the only surprise in the daily fare was whether or not there would actually be fish in the soup.

Those who didn't cook took their turns at washing up after dinner, and of late, the camp had become surprisingly quiet during cleanup. Early on, banter was common, but now, after months on a pretty skimpy diet, effort went more to the task of cleaning up than any attempt at being sociable.

One October evening six months into captivity, Dorothy finished drying the family's tin plates and stowed them beneath the sandbox bed. She never left their plates for the kitchen crew, but kept four plates in her own area. She doubted really hot water ever touched the plates the men washed.

Her sterilizing jars were still too hot to touch, but she carried them carefully by the crude bark handles she'd attached to each jar's wire hanger and lined them up at the foot of the bed. The handles were smooth now, softened by steam and molded to fit her hand.

The jars stood in a row, like little soldiers, reaffirming to Dorothy that she was maintaining a good sense of orderliness.

But there were only four.

There was a good bit of envy in camp over those jars, and experience had taught her not to leave them untended. Dorothy looked about her area, then knelt to look under the bed. She breathed a sigh of relief when she saw the fifth glass jar tucked in with their belongings.

But it looked odd, not empty, as she would expect, and not filled with clear boiled drinking water, either. She pulled it toward her, lifted the lid and sniffed.

Soapy water?

"Mommy, don't dwop it!"

Carol Joy rushed to Dorothy's side and held her little hands below the jar to catch it if Dorothy happened to lose her grip.

"Sweetie, what is this?"

"I made soapy-soap for you."

Dorothy grimaced. "But sweetie, we have to be very, very careful with the soap. We need to make it last."

"I know," her daughter said with a look of disappointment that her mother would think she didn't know such an important fact of life. "Not *our* soap. I made it from bitty bits."

"Bitty bits?"

"Mm-hm! Like these ones." Carol pulled a small cloth packet from her pocket and carefully opened it. In her palm lay a tiny collection of soap slivers, the remnants of bars of soap that had been used until the sliver was too small even to be held.

"Carol Joy, where did you get these?"

Carol smiled, delighted that she'd surprised her mother. "At the bathtub," she beamed.

"You mean, the bathing well?"

"Yes! You know, Mommy, when it's really hot and evvybody sleeps?" Dorothy nodded. "I go to the bathtub and it's all dry, alla round. And I save 'em. I save the little bitty-bits. Just like this!" She held the cloth up for Dorothy to look closer.

"And den—!" With a triumphant look she pulled the glass jar toward her and unlatched the lid. "I put 'em in...I shake-a shake-a shake! An' look, Mommy! Soapy-soap!"

Dorothy was aghast. It was so clever, so resourceful of her little daughter to preserve the soap bits and repurpose them into her liquid soap. But there were a hundred people in camp, many with questionable hygiene or obvious symptoms of bacterial diseases. She knew it, because she helped to treat them.

She started to tell her daughter that they couldn't under any circumstances use soap other people had used. It just wasn't safe.

But what if it was?

What if she provided Carol with a jar of boiling water in which to drop her bitty-bits? Would that be enough to kill anything that might be lurking in them?

She oohed and ahhed over Carol's soapy-soap as she wrestled with the dilemma. It should be safe enough. And Carol seemed so thrilled that she had done something helpful for her mommy that Dorothy simply couldn't squash her enterprising little heart.

"I'll tell you what, sweetie. This is a really, really wonderful thing you're doing for me. So I'm going to let you use my tweezers next time. Would you like that?"

"Yay, Mommy! Yes! Yes!"

"But you should probably use them just like a doctor would, don't you think?"

Carol became very serious and nodded her agreement.

"So next time you're going to collect bitty-bits I want you to come get me and we'll go together. You can use the tweezers, and the game will be to try and collect them without ever touching them yourself. Want to do that?"

Vigorous nodding.

"Then we'll bring the bitty-bits back here, and we'll boil some water in two jars. One will be yours to put your bitty-bits in, and then when it's all cooled down, you can shake it up."

"But what about the other jar, Mommy?"

"The other jar? Well, that's the jar we'll use to disinfect the tweezers. Every time. Just like doctors do. Right?"

"Right!"

Carol clapped for joy and ran off to tell her daddy-boy about the new plan.

And Dorothy stowed the jar of soapy-soap. She'd have to get rid of this batch. It was most likely swimming with little villains ready to take her family unawares. So it had to go. Then she'd boil the bottle. Twice, maybe.

So Carol Joy could have her soapy-soap.

~~~~~~

Letter to the Ministers and Missionaries Board From Kenneth Stapp
September 9, 1988

In the late 1940's, while a student at the University of Colorado, I
had the privilege of becoming acquainted with Dr. Fred Chambers
and his wife. One Thanksgiving, the Chambers had invited several of us students over for dinner. Their girl, about nine or ten
at the time, came in to ask if she could have some scraps of soap.
Permission was granted. Soon she returned, shaking a glass jar
which contained a bubbly soap solution. After she had gone into
another room, Mrs. Chambers said that when they were in camp,
the tiny girl thought that she could help the family by making the
tiny pieces of soap grow in this fashion to augment the meager soap
supply. The parents were willing to sacrifice some of the precious
soap to allow their daughter to have a sense of contributing to the
family's welfare, when they had so little to spare.

At no time in our acquaintance did I sense that the family was
resentful because of their wartime experience or harbored the
thought that with their background, some prominent place of
labor was their due. They were grateful to God for His watchcare
and desirous to serve humbly wherever they felt led. Faith was not
announced by visible trappings nor proclaimed by pious words but
rather evidenced by an unpretentious life characterized by adher-
ence to principle and the willingness to give of self in love.

PREWAR ILOILO, ISLAND OF PANAY, PHILIPPINES

CHAPTER FORTY-FOUR

THE PURPLE SHOES
CHRISTMAS 1942

It could never be said that the internees became complacent, but after many months in confinement, most had a sense that food supplies would continue at the rate they'd been experiencing. It wasn't a lot, but it sustained them at a level where they could do the work necessary to maintain the camp. In short, though vestiges of malnutrition were evident in many of the internees, at that time no one in the camp suffered symptoms of actual starvation.

But one particularly challenging day, when the gates were not open to trading as they had come to expect, the internees were startled to find that camp supplies were not adequate to provide dinner. How they let it happen, no one could explain. The prospect of no food virtually silenced the camp. They moved around stunned, completely demoralized that they could find themselves going to bed on an empty stomach.

The next morning was not so quiet.

When no breakfast could be had either, people rummaged in their private stashes for a crumb of any kind. Coming up empty made them frustrated and angry. And anger made them noisy.

The camp committee refused to meet. They had suffered no food for twenty-four hours the same as the rest, and they weren't about to become the "whipping boy" for such a disaster.

Just as the noisiest internees were working themselves into a frenzy, providence stepped in to avert a wholesale riot.

From Fred's memoir

...a man came to the gate and spoke to myself and one of the cooks. A quarter of meat was brought in and hung up in the kitchen for all to see. Everyone looked forward to the beef-feast the next day. After the meat was consumed with relish and appreciation, apparently by all, our small daughter was heard to remark, "My daddy said it was horsemeat".

And so it was.

A calesa (small two-wheeled buggy) pony had been killed in an accident. The animal was butchered and a hind quarter brought to the Camp by a Filipino who guaranteed it had been prepared under sanitary conditions and that the pony was healthy.

No one recanted his words of praise for the meat and, so far as is known, no one regurgitated.

It was often that way. The good hearts of the Filipinos filled many needs, seen and unseen, in the most compassionate outpouring of love for the Americans they counted as their neighbors, their friends.

• • • •

Dehydration was a constant problem in the camp. Despite Dorothy's many cautionary words, people consumed less and less water. It was so far across the compound to the San Augustin College and its drinking-water source, and the containers of water were so very heavy to carry back, they said.

And she certainly understood their complaints.

"But good lord, Fred. It's so simple. They should just buck up and do it. And why hasn't someone rigged a wheelbarrow, for pity's sake?"

At least she didn't have to worry about her children. Fred never failed to keep them supplied so that every day she could boil two gallons of water in her pickle jars, just for her family's drinking and cooking and cleaning. And at the end of every day, the jars would be bone dry.

Dorothy was managing to keep herself and her family from experiencing dehydration, but getting enough rest was quite another matter. As was her habit, Dorothy made herself available day or night to treat any health problems, and people seemed not to care that they were waking her from a sound sleep to tend to their minor ailments. But because she never made them feel they should have waited until morning, they continued the practice.

The most worrisome problem among internees was caused by bluebottle flies. Mosquito netting kept insects at bay through the night. But in the daytime, as they moved about the camp, everyone did constant battle with the flies.

Any small scratch was an open invitation to the bluebottles. And with the horrid sanitary conditions that existed in Iloilo City, it was an open invitation to disease.

The simple solution was to use plenty of soap.

But often there was no soap.

And a small scratch visited by even one fly quickly became a tropical ulcer. They occurred most often in the lower legs and feet, and in no time at all the flesh would begin to deteriorate and refuse to heal.

Dorothy knew that once the ulcer got to the deep tissue and muscle, amputation was a high probability for the patient. So when Fred came sheepishly to her and showed her a well-established tropical ulcer, she was more than a little miffed.

"Fred! How did you let this happen?" Dorothy's face screwed up in the worried expression with which he was most familiar. He'd really screwed up this time. But they'd been on work detail under Japanese guard, carrying the camp's refuse to the dump site two miles away when he stepped on a piece of shrapnel. It flipped up and caught him just above the ankle.

He'd cleaned it when he got home, but the beastly flies had already done their damage.

Dorothy's supply of sulfanilimide was put to the task, and eventually his ulcer did heal. But she was going to have to find a way to get more if they stayed in this disease-ridden place much longer.

She didn't even care that she'd put the fear of God into her children. If they got a scratch, they were to use Carol's bottle of soapy-soap immediately, then come to see her. No matter what.

From Fred's memoir

Life seemed to move at a healthy pace in general. Soap was a prize item but seemed to be available when needed. However, everyone in Camp suffered from tropical ulcers due to flies from unsanitary conditions in Iloilo City and lack of soap to keep sores clean. The writer still bears scars of the ulcers. Fortunately Mrs. Chambers had some sulfanilimide which hastened cures.

While a major concern was for the health of the body, the mind was not neglected. Daily, we made a trip, under guard, to the San Augustin College, next door, for drinking water. Our guard, a local merchant before the War and very cordial toward internees, followed well behind to give time for our American Augustinian priests to pick up the news from their Spanish colleagues and to be given books. Father Monte, Italian (Augustinian Priest) from Philadelphia, taught Spanish to those who desired it. A teacher internee taught some of the children, with the result that our daughter was a year ahead in her reading when she returned to school after the War.

· · · ·

"This is a stupid book!" Carol threw the book down in disgust.

"What book?" Dorothy was startled and dropped the skein of yarn she'd been rolling. Bobby had outgrown his cotton sweater and the first step in making a new one was to unravel the old one into orderly skeins.

Carol dodged to her left and scooped up the ball of yarn before it rolled out the door and restored it to her mother's lap.

"What book?" Dorothy asked again.

"This one," Carol said, kicking the book further under the bed.

"Carol Joy, that is no way to treat a book," Dorothy scolded. "Books are precious! The things we can learn, the places we can visit without even getting out of our chair are wonderful." She cocked her head toward the book and cocked an eyebrow toward Carol who immediately got the message. She begrudgingly retrieved the book and dusted it off before plopping it down on the crate next to her mother.

"Oh my! *Little Black Sambo*! Carol, do you know where this story takes place?"

"Under a tree," she sulked.

"But where is the tree?"

Carol thought for a minute. "In little black Sambo's town."

"Well, maybe, but the tree is in India! Where you were born!"

"In India? Really?"

"Yes, sweetie-kins. In India. And it's sort of like a fable. You know, like Aesop's fables."

"I don't care," Carol pouted, "it's still a stupid book."

Dorothy was about to launch into an explanation of the moral of the story, that the tigers each wanted to be the most grand tiger in the jungle, and how that was their downfall. But something stopped her. Carol wouldn't have minded that. It was the kind of thing she was likely to preach to Bobby once she'd read it in a book. And she definitely knew the difference between truth and fiction. The story itself wouldn't have upset her.

Dorothy put down the yarn and pulled Carol into her lap. She was getting taller now, her legs a bit gangly and her curls a bit less unruly, but she was not too old to sit on her mother's knee.

"Tell me what made you angry, sweetie."

Carol's lip trembled and she played with the collar of her mother's dress while she worked up the courage to speak.

When the reason for her upset finally came out, Dorothy nearly cried. Little Black Sambo's mother made him a beautiful red coat. Then got him a pair of beautiful blue trousers and a pair of lovely purple shoes. The remarkably colorful illustrations showed Sambo in all his fine new clothes, beaming and strutting through the jungle.

Her fingers caressed the pictures as her sadness tumbled out.

"He looks so pretty," Carol said quietly. "And Mommy, he has purple shoes!"

Ah. Purple shoes. A red jacket, blue trousers and purple shoes.

He was full of color. Full of life. And her little daughter had not had colorful new clothing for longer than she could remember. Everything was drab off-white or washed out colors faded by the merciless sun. And shoes that were really too small, so the toes had been cut to make them into sandals.

Of course the child would want colorful clothes. *Of course* the illustrations made her sick with envy.

Dorothy fingered the yarn she was retrieving from Bobby's little sweater and knew what she had to do. Somehow she had to find purple dye. Maybe eggplant? She'd dye the yarn and make it into a sleeveless bolero vest for Carol. The bolero would add color to whatever she was wearing.

The shoes, however, were a different matter.

For several days Dorothy stewed about the shoes. She did her daily chores and tended to the medical needs of the camp, but always, in the back of her mind, was the problem of shoes for Carol Joy. Preferably purple.

At night, after Carol was asleep, she worked on knitting the bolero. It was coming along beautifully. The pattern she decided to knit into the bottom border created just the kind of puzzle she needed to absorb her interest until the night cooled off enough to sleep. The pattern made the going much slower, but that was the joy of it.

She had a list of things she wanted to ask Loreto Tupaz about when she visited the camp that week, and front and center on her mind was shoes for Carol. But when the opportunity arose, Loreto merely scrunched up her face at the request. Little Filipina girls went barefoot or sandal-footed. Western shoes were hard to come by. For children, at any rate. And impossible with a war going on.

"And buttons," Dorothy added. "Any bright, big, colorful buttons. Can you find any?"

Loreto patted her hand. "If they here, I get. You see. Not to worry."

"And eggplant. Don't forget eggplant!"

She sounded so needy, so uncharacteristically demanding even to her own ear. But somehow it had become the most important thing in the world to Dorothy, to bring some color into her dear daughter's life.

The days seemed to dawdle on as she waited for Loreto's return visit. When "market day" came and the little ninety-pound battalion sadly shook her head, Dorothy began to despair of getting a pair of shoes for Carol.

Still, Loreto did find two big, luscious-looking eggplant, which cheered Dorothy no end. She quickly set about preserving the "meat" and when she had the beautiful purple rinds ready, she found an out-of-the-way place to let them dry in the sun. Then she watched them like a hawk for three days, fearful that some wayward bird would swoop in and steal her purple treasure.

But they remained safe. And they dried beautifully.

A piece of screen laid over a tin can worked perfectly to shave her eggplant rinds into powder. A little water would turn it into a regal dye. She had saved back a half jar of banana-peel vinegar to set the dye. Everything was ready. If only she had a pair of shoes.

By Saturday she had finished knitting the bolero. She'd changed her mind about dying it purple. She would save the dye for shoes, mostly because she had visions of the tropical climate turning the upper half of her daughter's torso purple—despite the banana-peel vinegar—to say nothing of staining whatever dress she had on underneath it.

A strip of red cloth, though, solved her challenge of making the little vest full of color. She pieced it together from an old bandana, then gathered it to make a perfect bright ruffle around the bottom of the short vest just below the carefully worked border. Marching up the front were three giant red buttons Loreto had managed to find. A small bow at the neckline made from a pair of denim overalls Bobby had outgrown completed the truly sassy look.

She'd been on a mission to bring color into her daughter's world, and the colorful bolero did just that.

"Mommy," Carol gasped when Dorothy presented it to her just before bedtime. "Mommy!"

She hugged the bolero to her heart, then held it out, then hugged it again. She could scarcely let go of it long enough to put it on.

There was no question that it would fit perfectly.

And unlike any other event in Dorothy's memory, it rendered Carol Joy speechless.

It was the range of emotion that startled Dorothy. Carol wasn't a child to covet things. It was clearly her grief over the absence of color in her life that had initiated her anger over the innocent book. But is that truly what she mourned? Or was it a greater loss that haunted her?

That night Dorothy watched her little daughter sleep, the new bolero laid out just above her pillow. Still within reach. In that moment it was impossible to "keep the salt on the inside", and the tears flowed freely. Not from sadness, but from the knowledge that she'd been able to bring some joy back into her sweet daughter's face.

It was the kind of thing her own mother would have done for her. A lifetime ago. Just thinking of her mother caused her heart to pinch, and made her fingers twitch for the typewriter keys. There had been no typewriter, no spare paper or ink to write with for eight months now. And in truth, she dared not write even if she had the wherewithal to do it. The Japanese guards tolerated many things, but not the keeping of a journal or the writing of a letter that might be spirited out of the camp and into the hands of the enemy. So she had not even endeavored to write.

But tonight, with the poignance of her daughter's joy still wrapped around her, Dorothy wrote. In her heart. The words she would write to her mother, if only she could.

Dearest Mother,

Dorothy found her fingers moving on her knees, typing out the words. As they came faster and faster, her fingers took on more speed, writing into thin air the words that she willed to take wing and find her mother.

This war, this senseless, crazed mania that has swept the whole of civilization into something nobody can even recognize, has for a moment taken a back seat to a small child's delight.

· · · ·

The Sunday morning before Christmas there was no question what Carol would wear, and she literally danced all the way to chapel, so happy was she to have some color restored.

Christmas in captivity. It didn't feel like something to dance about, but to keep the smile on her daughter's face, Dorothy danced alongside her. Carol's giggle was balm to her heart, and for a few more precious steps Dorothy kept up with Carol. But all too soon the effort was too much, and Dorothy slowed to a walk, resigned to merely watching her dancing daughter.

When they reached the chapel space, Carol instinctively slowed and they walked together to the front of the outdoor chapel, to the bench that was "theirs".

Dorothy walked on to the makeshift altar and placed an arrangement of poinsettias she'd gathered from the ones that grew like weeds along the fence. It was satisfying in its simplicity, comforting in its rich color.

And it spoke of Christmas.

She took Bobby from his daddy's arms and turned, expecting to see Carol already sitting in her favored spot.

But she wasn't.

Carol stood to the side, her hands clasped over her mouth, trying hard not to shriek in this place she knew was to be honored with a quiet voice.

She stood because the place Carol sat every Sunday morning was occupied. By a slightly used pair of dirty white canvas boaters.

Just Carol's size.

Just waiting to be transformed by Dorothy's eggplant dye.

Dorothy looked at the people filing in. They were all looking at one another with sly smiles and winks. But no one, not one single person, would own up to having gifted Carol with her soon-to-be purple shoes.

WAR-SCARRED PHILIPPINES

CHAPTER FORTY-FIVE

LEAVING ILOILO
JUNE 16, 1943

"We can't take it all, Dorothy. There's no room."

Fred and Dorothy stood at the sandbox bed and took inventory of the things that had not yet been packed. For six months they'd planned this, ever since the January day when the commandant strode in, stomped his booted feet to get their attention, and said to prioritize everything they owned, and left.

They'd all figured that meant they were going to move. But they'd been here fourteen months now, and until today, they'd had no word at all as to when it was going to happen.

Twice they'd had false alarms, seeing indications from their Japanese guards that they would be moving. But both times rumor had it that American submarines had been seen in the harbor and when rumor evaporated, the threat of moving went with it.

When the word finally came, it became very real in a hurry. The announcement cast a troubling pall over the group of one hundred mismatched souls who somehow had managed to maintain a civilized community under completely dire conditions. But there was no time to complain. Or insist on an explanation. Or ask where they were going.

An intimidating cluster of Japanese officers and civilians armed with pistols and military rifles strode into the camp on the morning of June 16, 1943. In as few words as possible, the commandant announced the entire camp must be ready to leave by eleven. And take only what they could carry.

Time and again Dorothy and Fred had planned and re-planned what they would take when the time came. But now that it was upon them, with less than two hours to manage it, they could not find a way to get everything in the few travel cases and flour sacks they owned.

Nor could they carry it all.

"Bobby can carry the children's clothes. Take them out of the rucksack and put them in his bag." Even as she spoke, Dorothy began to do just that. "Then I'll put the glass jars in the rucksack."

With a determined grimace she worked the five jars into her rucksack, padding them with things already inside.

"There!" She felt triumphant. But Fred didn't share her enthusiasm.

"Pick it up," he said.

"Well let me just finish this first, then I'll—"

"Pick it up, Dorothy." He lifted the rucksack and dropped it heavily into her open arms.

She looked at him, worry lining her mouth. "I can do it." She hefted the bag so the bag's strap was over her shoulder. "See?"

"Walk to the well and back."

"Oh Fred, don't be ridiculous."

"Dorothy, do it now."

Even the children shushed when they heard the quiet command in their father's voice.

She pulled a face at him, shifted the bag higher on her hip, then turned and walked away from her family, out into the courtyard, across to the dining shed, then on fifty yards to the well.

With each step her knees threatened to buckle. Her back screamed, her neck would hardly hold her head up so she could see where she was going, and her feet refused to do anything but shuffle.

This bag was nothing compared to loads she'd carried time and again in Gauhati. This should be a breeze.

And yet it was not. Her heart was pounding before she was halfway to the well. Her whole body shrieked for her to drop the bag that weighed down her bones.

She realized now that she'd been subconsciously lightening her loads in recent months, splitting the wet laundry into two loads instead of one, and so on. Because her body was beginning to tolerate less and less, and poor nutrition was solely to blame for it.

Standing still, Dorothy was the picture of slender good health. Moving under the weight of the rucksack she'd turned into a decrepit old woman. When had she become such a ninny that she couldn't carry forty pounds across the yard and back?

Dorothy turned to start her way back and bumped into Fred. He had followed her. With a sad sort of grin he pulled the bag from her shoulder and hiked it over his own, and drew her into a hug.

"Oh Fred," she cried. "I thought I—I mean, I didn't know it would—oh Fred!"

"No tears now, darling girl. It's only things. You know that. If it were Bobby you were carrying, why, you'd be walking right along and whistling Dixie, too. But this? This is just things."

She knew he was right. Knew it with every screaming joint in her body. But she'd left so much behind. Her India things, gone to the bottom in Singapore Bay. Her Iloilo things, ransacked by the Japanese in Calinog. She'd been stripped of everything but the minimum necessities.

And it was happening again. Again there was no time to organize it well. No time to fret. No time to say goodbye.

What would Rosa do when she found out they'd left? She might slip down from the hills for a visit to bring vegetables and find them gone. Poor dear Rosa! It wasn't right to just disappear from her life like this!

Dorothy turned toward the bunk that was now stripped of its bedclothes. Slowly she drew four of the five glass jars from her bag and lined them up on the sandbox bed. She would keep one, but the other four had to go. They'd done their job, and now she would leave them for someone to find, maybe someone who needed them worse than she did. Maybe Loreto would find them, and know what to do with them. Her heart pinched at the thought of never having the chance to thank the beautiful little Filipina nurse who had made her life so much more than bearable here in camp. To never again hug Rosa who had taken the Chambers family into her very heart.

But this time the salt stayed on the inside. Anger had a way of drying her tears and today not a single tear escaped.

There was space in her rucksack now and she turned to Bobby to retrieve the clothes she'd shoved into his little pack.

But he scooted away from her.

"I carry it, Mommy!"

"Oh sweetie, it might be too heavy. Let Mommy check it, will you?"

"No!" He backpedaled further away. "I carry it. I a sojur. See?"

He threw the bag over his shoulder like a sack of potatoes and marched up and down the path to the dining hall, his head high, his chin up, and the bag with the children's entire wardrobe and his old worn out teddy bear bouncing along on his back.

His three-year-old legs were spindly, but strong to the task. And his determined face won her heart all over again, unleashing tears to wash away her anger.

At eleven o'clock sharp the little family of four was lined up and ready to go, each with a pack they could carry a good distance if they had to, and none looking back over their shoulder at the pieces of their life they were leaving behind.

· · · ·

It was days before they knew where they were being taken. All one hundred of them were driven in trucks to the wharf, then loaded onto an inter-island steamer.

From Fred's memoir

On June 16, 1943, some Japanese officers and civilians came into Camp, very evidently armed with pistols. Some of us wondered if "this was it". They told us that we should be ready to move within two hours. The Camp was literally cleared of every personal belonging. We were herded into trucks, like cattle, not told our destination, and taken to an inter-island steamer docked in the harbor. The ship had been a tug sunk in Manila harbor and had been raised and put into service. We went aboard, about a hundred of us, and found our places wherever we could. The ship was already loaded with sugar and raw carabao hides. Fortunately, Dorothy, the children and I were together. Some not already interned were put aboard.

The trip to Manila took a week and demonstrated running between "Scylla and Scherybides" . If our ship moved too close to shore there was liability of trouble from guerilla bands. We might be rescued! If our ship moved too far offshore, there was liability from American submarines. Thus it took a week for the trip that in peacetime would require twenty-four hours. It was a wet trip, sleeping on deck, and it rained five nights out of seven.

Dorothy stretched her legs out in front of her, trying not to jostle those around her. She hadn't sat in a chair in nearly a week. Here, on the deck of this ancient steamer, there was scarcely room to sit and almost never room to lie down.

Her clothing felt strange, stiff, after having been rained on each night and dried in place the following day. She needed a bath. She needed to wash her hair and clean her teeth. She needed to walk!

It was impossible to dispel the sense of disorientation. She couldn't shake the dazed, disconnected feeling that came over her while sitting on the deck of a steamer that clearly had spent some time at the bottom of the harbor. It creaked and groaned, and gears that had evidently received minimal restoration after the sunken vessel was raised screeched their displeasure day and night.

While it could never be accused of running silently, the inter-island steamer nevertheless threaded the intricate course that kept them just far enough from enemy American submarines, and not quite close enough to guerillas on shore who might mount a rescue attempt.

A handful of overcooked rice and a kind of hardtack biscuit were given to each of them twice a day. And trying to get more than one-half cup of water per day was a challenge that not even Dorothy's kind, persuasive medical charm could manage. Their guardians weren't so much mean and threatening as disinterested. Clearly, they'd done this before.

Early morning on the seventh day the engines throttled down and an eerie silence descended. Dorothy roused from sleep and could not get her bearings. Carefully she rose to a kneeling position and fully absorbed the scene before her.

On every side loomed broken masts, blackened hulls and the tangled rigging of scuttled boats. Each stark mast, whether broken or bent, seemed to mark something more than merely the grave of a once-proud boat.

The steamer slipped silently along the narrow portion of the channel that had been cleared of wreckage. All around her people began to rouse. Fred shifted his sleeping children so he could kneel beside his wife. She took his hand, and felt the tension in his sinewy arms, the rigid self-control he was demanding of himself.

For the first time in her life, surrounded by the horrible evidence of a world gone awry, she felt they were alone. Whatever lay ahead was going to take every resource they had, every shred of ingenuity and every ounce of courage they could summon.

The burned out shoreline revealed their destination. This damaged shell of a once-thriving port was Manila harbor. They were being taken to the internment camp at Santo Tomás.

It seemed as though the night had robbed them of their place in the world. Dorothy reached for Rosa's hat. But it, too, had been lost in the night.

MANILA BAY

From Fred's memoir — The trip was uneventful, but the harbor at Manila was a sight with masts of sunken ships all over. Corregidor looked as if it had been burned out. We were taken to Santo Tomas to begin another chapter, with new friends and a greater challenge. At that time, Santo Tomas was a small "town" of 4000, with Los Banos housing 2500 and Baguio 500.

UNIVERSITY OF SANTO TOMAS
ESTABLISHED 1611 - MANILA, LUZON, P.I.

COMMANDEERED BY THE JAPANESE TO HOUSE PRISONERS OF WAR.
OVER 7,000 INTERNEES PASSED THROUGH THE CAMP, WITH NEARLY
4,000 CONFINED UNDER ARMED GUARD FOR THREE YEARS –
JANUARY 1942 THROUGH FEBRUARY 1945.

COURTYARD SHANTIES AT SANTO TOMÁS

CHAPTER FORTY-SIX

SANTO TOMÁS

JUNE 21, 1943 — 250 DAYS INTO INTERNMENT

Dorothy and Fred had barely spoken since they'd crossed the gangplank and set foot on solid ground. Occasionally she carried—or rather dragged—Fred's pack so he could carry Bobby on his shoulders.

"Wha's at, Dad?"

Bobby would point to some grand landmark that rose above the palm trees in the distance, and it was usually Dorothy who replied. She was the one who'd spent time in Manila, and it helped to focus on those lovely vistas—many still undamaged by the war—and ignore the blackened harbor behind her.

They shuffled and stopped, shuffled and stopped with their group of one hundred and nine until they reached an open area on the wharf and without ceremony were ordered at gunpoint into waiting trucks.

Bobby clutched his frazzled teddy bear close to his chest, clearly remembering their departure from Calinog when a Japanese soldier nearly ripped it apart to check it for contraband. But this time his precious buddy was ignored.

It was Carol's doll they were interested in. Her little five-year-old face was rigid with anxiety as the gruesome-faced guard turned and twisted, rattled and shook her sweet dolly that had come to her all the way from the USA two Christmases ago. When he held it out to another guard to examine, the child nearly fainted.

"It's fine, sweetheart," Dorothy cooed. "The soldier won't hurt Pippa." She prayed she hadn't lied to her daughter.

And she hadn't. At last they were satisfied it was just what it looked like. A little girl's dearest friend. Once they'd given the doll back, Carol clutched Pippa fiercely. Dorothy reached for words to give her back her smile but came up wanting.

All along the bone-rattling route, Filipinos stopped to watch the small convoy. They nodded surreptitiously to those on board, careful not to be seen making eye contact with any particular person among the internees. A barefoot Filipino who was not so careful received a wicked slap to the head from a guard he hadn't been aware was watching.

They were everywhere. Watching.

When the trucks finally lurched to a stop and they were told to get out, Fred collected the family and moved them into the queue that was forming at the gate of Santo Tomás University. This would be the first of a thousand different lines that would dictate their lives in the coming months.

The square tower of the main building stood grandly in the near distance, a five-minute walk from where they now stood. The children could see little through the fence that was woven with strips of weathered bamboo to purposefully obstruct the view from both directions. But Dorothy could see enough. Enough to know that life had just changed immeasurably for them. The barbed wire that looped ominously along the tops of the walls and massive iron gates told her that. And somehow she was going to have to summon the courage to immerse herself in this strange new world.

The urge to disappear into the city behind her was strong, but the line moved her ever forward. She felt a tug on her arm and looked down to see which of the children it was. But it was not one of her children. It was not one of the two precious souls she'd brought through so much and now thrust ahead of her into this new strangeness.

It was a Japanese guard. And he was tugging on her medical bag.

So far she'd managed to safeguard the medical supplies she'd collected over their months of internment. And now her bag was full, thanks to Loreto's final donation just the week before. She had quinine, sulfanilamide, aspirin powder and more.

Would they let her keep it all? Or would her meager collection be confiscated? Would she be allowed to practice medicine? Or would that be forbidden? These questions joined the others that had been circling in her brain in recent days.

Would the family be housed together? Would they have to pay for every meal? Would they find funds like the lifesaving Chinaman in Iloilo provided? Her heart raced and she felt her smile quiver as she released her hold on the bag.

So many unknowns.

After asking several questions regarding the contents of her medical bag, the guard closed it, sealed it with a tag on a knotted string, and nodded to her. Dorothy peered at the square red stamp on the tag but as usual, the Japanese "chop" told her nothing at all. She reached for the bag but the guard stayed her with a warning hand.

"Izza yatuh," he said.

"But—"

"No now. Yatuh," he insisted.

Later. Not now. Later.

Dorothy withdrew her hand and tried without success to calm her racing heart. She'd never yet been forced to give up her bag. So far in their internment she had been allowed that small courtesy. Now the prospect of losing it seemed catastrophic. She had hidden half their money in the lining of the worn leather bag.

She knew her eyes would betray her if she looked at the guard, but she had to. She had to read his intentions. Was he confiscating it? Would he report her for having something in there she shouldn't have?

Dorothy raised her head and forced herself to look the fellow in the eye. "For me later?" she asked.

He nodded and cocked his head toward the bag he was just setting on a cart behind him. "Yatuh."

The dry mouth of panic made swallowing hard, but Dorothy forced herself to put it in God's hands. She would leave it to Him as to whether or not she would ever see her medical bag again, the bag whose leather grip fitted her hand so perfectly. The strong, sturdy bag her father had gifted her when she graduated from medical school.

Her fingers kept reaching for it, searching for its familiar grip. It was like a phantom limb, gone but still felt in the familiar way it rocked against her palm.

"Dorothy? Dorothy Kinney! Over here!"

They had barely reached the halfway point of the "intake" area when she heard someone calling her name. She and Fred turned toward the voice. It came to them like a lifeline, like a branch to hold on to until they could find purchase for their feet.

"Over here!"

A familiar face smiled at them from beyond a rope barrier.

"Louise? Louise Spencer?"

Dorothy started to moved to the barrier, pulled like a magnet to the woman from home, from Colorado. But a bayonet lowered in front of her, stopping her headlong rush to the safe harbor of a friend, and she crept back into the slow-moving line.

Over her shoulder she could see Louise moving parallel to her, pointing to a spot beyond the end of the building. That was where they would meet.

The beastly intake process took two more hours. Questions, statements, signatures—all demanded with suspicious tone. Dorothy was sure that Louise would tire of waiting, and for some reason that seemed devastating to her.

But once outside the long "intake shed" Dorothy ushered her family around the corner, and into the arms of the first face from home she'd seen in more than two years.

· · · ·

Dorothy sought a quiet place to distance herself from the shock of the day. In this jungle of people, though, a place of solitude was not to be found. She blessed their good fortune that Louise and Dick Spencer had been there to guide them through the bewildering rules of life in Santo Tomás. But it was almost too much. Too much to try and be sociable when all she wanted to do was strip down and wash and sleep for about a month.

Of course, there was no bed yet. No mattress. No place to rest her head until Fred could build something.

Somehow she managed to not embarrass herself, and to show Louise the courtesy and gratitude she truly felt even though she was too tired to properly express it. It seemed that tears were more ready than words. But Louise understood.

"Dorothy, go easy on yourself," Louise whispered. "I know what you've been through. They took you and your children away from camp, not telling you where you were going. I can't imagine you didn't wonder if they were going to shoot you all." She patted Dorothy on the arm, her understanding shocking yet complete. "The soul doesn't recover from that overnight, you know. Give yourself some time."

The soul doesn't recover from that overnight.

The words spun in dizzying relief in her head, making the world recede as if she and Louise were the only ones left in it. She sensed an almost physical adjustment of her heartbeat, a resumption to something that nearly approached normal. But then, normal was a "relative" state of being these days.

A few minutes alone was all she needed, just a few minutes to collect herself, then she could face things.

But how she expected to find a place to be alone almost made her laugh.

Four thousand internees carried out their daily business here. Four thousand people brought to the small college campus by the red "chop" of Imperial Japan. Into "confined community".

They stood in line for food, stood in line to wash hands, another line to wash hair, more lines to get into the bathroom to receive a single sheet of toilet paper doled out to each person in need of it. They reported twice each day for roll call, some of which lasted a grueling two hours. And they were not to be missed upon pain of—

One third of the internees were over the age of sixty. They took the standing in line less well, but better than the ones who were under the age of sixteen. Some four hundred children were imprisoned here, if the information she'd received was correct. And many of them had been here well over a year now.

They were mostly the children of foreign nationals—children of diplomats or bureaucrats from Sweden, Germany, England, America, Australia, or children of businessmen attached to major international companies—children whose parents had found the Philippines to be a satisfying place to live and rear their families. She doubted it felt so satisfactory now.

Some of the singles were military wives separated from husbands who had been caught in that devastating surrender of Bataan. Some were army nurses. Some were mining engineers or rare gem salesmen or oilmen here on assignment from Standard Oil. There were musicians here, and artists. They were an amalgam of society—the good, the not-so-good, the demanding, the compassionate, the arrogant, the meek, the cowardly and the courageous.

And all were here against their wishes.

SANTO TOMÁS INTERNMENT CAMP
LIMITED PRIVATE EDITION - FREDERIC H. STEVENS
© 1946 - PAGE 415

June 22—Iloilo internees arrive after seven-day trip—109 men, women and children experience exhausting journey.

THE WAR DIARY OF PAUL ESMERIAN
TRANSLATED BY ROBERT COLQUHOUN

18 June 1943
It's less painful perhaps to go to prison flanked by two policemen in a police van than to turn oneself in alone, in a hired vehicle going at a gentle trot, on a lovely sunny afternoon. A small piece of paper, covered with a tiny red Japanese stamp, bearing characters I don't even understand, will make of me a prisoner, as surely as would have done men in helmets and jackboots. Twentieth-century bureaucracy has so conditioned us that a small typewritten note is enough to make us hand ourselves over to our enemies.

We drive past the camp railings, covered by woven bamboo laths to prevent internees and passers-by from seeing one another. There's still time to tell the driver to turn round, still time to ignore the red stamp and try to hide in the countryside, and perhaps join up with the guerrillas. But for a white man, the chances of escaping pursuit by the Japanese or avoiding denunciation by the Filipinos are practically nil. The red stamp is stronger. - PAUL ESMERIAN

CHAPTER FORTY-SEVEN

RESTORED

On the seventh morning in camp Dorothy woke with a start. She'd slept the night undisturbed, a blessing for which she was beyond grateful. She flung the mosquito netting aside, hopped from the bed and peered over the bunk above her head. Bobby's slumber was deep and peaceful, and his teddy still lay within reach. Carol lay at the other end of the bunk, her head on one arm, Pippa in the other, a half-smile on her face.

Fred had done the impossible and managed to beg borrow or steal—she didn't actually care which—enough planking to fashion a bunk bed for them. The first week he'd only scrounged enough wood to fashion a single bed, so Dorothy had spent challenging nights sharing the bed with two children. But yesterday he'd found enough to complete the second level and she'd had a blissful night's sleep...on a plank bed with no mattress. But without four additional little restless legs.

It was a huge gift, because they'd been allotted space for two single beds in a former classroom crowded with the beds of six other women and their ten children. The other women and children slept on iron beds provided early on by the Red Cross. But now there were no more beds, so Fred had scrambled to correct the problem. And his solution was ingenious. He'd made the two beds in a bunk style, leaving one of the spaces free for the children to move about in.

God bless her brilliant husband!

But how had he slept, she wondered? She and the children had been assigned to the Annex for women and children. Fred had been assigned to the gymnasium balcony where the men and older boys slept. He could spend time with them here in the Annex during the day, but at night he had to be at the gym before curfew at nine.

She wasn't at all surprised that the Japanese did not want more children to be born in camp...more mouths to feed, more crowding in the Annex. But their hopes that they could keep pregnancies from happening merely by separating the men and women at night while still letting them mingle throughout the day was laughable.

From Fred's memoir

Because some internee couples were permitted to live together during the day, some pregnancies resulted. When the Japanese learned of these they sent the fathers to the old walled city prison: Fort Santiago. Because the Catholic Fathers in Santo Tomas Seminary were permitted to remain in their quarters on Campus but outside the walls set up for the Camp, they learned that "fathers" had been imprisoned and went to the Japanese officials to protest. However, the Japanese cleared up the matter by stating that it was not the "Catholic Fathers" but the "pregnant fathers" who had been locked up.

Dorothy gathered her kit and moved through the maze of beds that populated the room to which they'd been assigned. Counting herself, seven mothers and twelve small children made this classroom in the campus Annex building their home. Each bed was creatively draped with its own netting, and underclothes hung drying from some of the rigging. Many of the beds at this time of the morning were still occupied.

The room monitor—herself an internee—was still asleep near the door. Dorothy had taken seriously the woman's admonition that nothing happened in the room without her knowledge. And absence at roll call was a dire offense. The monitor answered directly to the Camp Committee for every transgression among the women for whom she was responsible.

Her assigned room was no different than all the other classrooms, Dorothy had been told. But some folks—like the Spencers—had built shanties, creating whole neighborhoods of makeshift housing and staking out their own little plots about the campus. Neighborhoods took on clever nicknames: Jungletown, Glamourville, Garden Court, Foggy Bottom, Southwest Territory, and Out

Yonder. One found them by navigating 'streets' which were little more than footpaths named MacArthur Drive, Papaya Lane, Hollywood Boulevard, Camote Road, and of course, Fifth Avenue.

Whether or not one owned a shanty, all were required to sleep in the assigned buildings and could only occupy the shanties during the day. And no shanty could be enclosed with walls that might hide one from the watchful eye of the Japanese guards. In these open-air neighborhoods, privacy was a relative thing.

The idea of a place of their own was certainly appealing. But to Dorothy it seemed to be something available to the wealthier internees, and she doubted there would ever be a shanty in her future.

The cloying smell of multiple thunder pots scattered about the room made her wish for an open-air shanty. Louise had alerted her to the fact that many folks used covered "toidies" in the night, and now the mingled smells of full thunder pots and unwashed bodies made her wish mightily for ventilation of any kind.

She stepped into the hall and turned right, bound for the bathroom. The hall provided just the ventilation she was looking for, open to the air on one side and covered by a long, low roof. But the sight before her elicited an unguarded groan. She'd forgotten about the lines. She would have to rise earlier tomorrow. A thirty-minute dawdle in the hallway waiting her turn to wash up was simply not going to pass muster. She'd heard about the meager handful of toilets for a community of four thousand internees and reminded herself to be grateful there was even one in her building.

To her surprise, the line moved quickly, and when she discovered the reason for it, Dorothy had to wrestle with her modesty. There was one showerhead, shared by no less than eight women grouped in a tight circle of sorts, some facing modestly away, some still dressed in underclothes, but rotating with their little circle to take a few turns beneath the trickling showerhead.

She'd been granted privacy that first night, perhaps out of courtesy to a new internee, or perhaps because more women availed themselves of the shower in the morning than the evening. She wasn't to know. But this morning's rude awakening as to how the camp's meager water supply was handled seemed cruelly crushing. She doubted she'd ever become accustomed to it. Like the crude sign on the wall reminded her, *if you want privacy, close your eyes.*

Dorothy dressed carefully, pleased that her white coat looked halfway respectable after having been hung up for the night on the pegs Fred had built into the bunk. She was going to work today. They'd assigned her to the medical staff of the children's hospital, and she was eager to report.

SANTO TOMÁS INTERNMENT CAMP
LIMITED PRIVATE EDITION - FREDERIC H. STEVENS
© 1946 - PAGE 116

> The Children's Hospital continued at its original location until October, 1944, when it was transferred to the Model Home on the ground floor, Main Building. This move was considered necessary in view of the air raids and expected bombings, and the new quarters were safe and convenient. Drs. Ream Allen and [Dorothy] Chambers were in charge of the hospital at various times, assisted by volunteer nurses.

The washroom line had taken long enough that now she had less than ten minutes before Fred would arrive to look after the children, to get them dressed and take them to breakfast and explore the camp. That was the plan.

She reached for her bag to polish her stethoscope, then remembered that the bag had been confiscated. Pray God they had spare instruments at the hospital.

· · · ·

At least they hadn't taken her white coat. Dorothy flexed her spine and shifted her shoulders, reassured by the coat's familiar hug. It was barely a five-minute walk from the Annex—her new home for the duration—past the outdoor kitchen and dining shed to the small hospital established for the particular care of interned children. No trees blocked the sun, and Dorothy's first mental note was to somehow obtain a hat.

The hospital was arranged in one long ward with a small wing on each end. Her quick assessment as she walked to the receiving area estimated twenty beds, more than half of them occupied, but room for a few more, if needed.

The beds were lined up in ranks of ten along two long walls, with plenty of room between for both medical staff and parents to offer their special brand of care. Clever rigs were affixed to the head and foot of each bed, with hooks for medical charts and lashings to hold mosquito netting out of the way during daylight hours. The nets themselves hung from a crosshatch of thin wires that had been strung throughout the entire room, about fifteen inches down from the ceiling. Every sleeping area she'd seen here in camp had these crosshatched wires, and a corner of her mind registered the practicality and ingenuity of it.

But that's where the similarities ended. No two beds had the same linens, and some had no pillowcases, and one merely had a threadbare sheet thrown over the gray-striped ticking of the mattress. Still, every threadbare sheet was neatly tucked.

Two little girls were out of bed and sat barefoot on the floor playing an almost raucous game of jacks.

Dorothy smiled at them, and caught the eye of the older girl whose turn it was. It threw the child's coordination off and the rubber ball went flying. Without thinking, Dorothy lunged and caught it before it rolled away down the long expanse of the ward.

With a sheepish grin she restored the ball to its owner. "Oh dear, that was my fault! Does she get a do-over?"

Both girls laughed and simultaneously said yes...and no.

"Which child are you looking for, may I ask?"

Dorothy turned toward the sound of the pleasant voice.

"Me? Oh, I'm not looking for a child...I mean, I'm here to work."

The woman turned to address her and for the first time noticed Dorothy's white coat. The look on her face revealed she did not think the white coat was quite appropriate. Her next words revealed why.

"Ah! Wonderful. I thought the new nurse was arriving tomorrow."

"Well perhaps she is. You see, I—"

"We've already cleared breakfast so if you'd just start with temps and vitals we'll be right on schedule. I'm Noell. Sue Noell. And you're—?"

"Chambers," Dorothy replied. "Dorothy Chambers."

"Goodness me, Chambers, that's not the name I was given. Although—"

Noell stopped mid sentence, with a screwed up face that made Dorothy laugh.

"Yes, it's Dr. Chambers, I'm afraid."

"Oh shoot. Oh heavens to betsy. I am so sorry! I knew there was a new doctor and all they told me was D. Chambers, and I was thinking...well, you know...but mercy me! Welcome!"

"Thank you, Noell. And may I say you seem to have things in fine order here."

"Well, you may say that now, but you would have shrieked a year ago." Nurse Noell did a half turn and swept her arm to take in the ward that lay before them. "A year ago this was a monkey cage, and over there were the guinea pigs. Just a roof, no walls. And look at it now!"

"Monkey cage?"

"Animal experiment lab for the university's medical students, dontcha know. But don't worry, they cleared it all away. Built this new, thanks to Mr. Verlinden. Donated it all. Nice fella. Now let me give you the nickel tour."

Nurse Noell walked Dorothy to the far end of the ward, showing her the supply room woefully stocked, the dispensary minimally supplied, the linen cubby, the outpatient clinic, and a small desk and chair that were to be hers, if, according to Noell, she managed to find time to utilize them. It was the kind of whirlwind tour that fed Dorothy the very thing she'd been starving for. It spoke of routine, and beckoned her in such a way that it made her palms fairly itch to grasp hold of it. In less than ten minutes Noell had swept away the ill-fitting mantle of survivor and restored Dorothy to the woman who belonged in the white coat.

The tour ended back at the supply room where Noell had promised to retrieve a stethoscope. Dorothy stood in the hall, taking in the smells that carried messages of healing. Alcohol, merthiolate, sterilized bandages, freshly laundered towels. And thankfully, no smell of monkeys, guinea pigs, or lab experiments.

"Here you go."

Dorothy turned back toward the supply room and held out her hand for what she thought would be a stethoscope. But instead, Nurse Noell stood there beaming as she brought from behind her back an item that stole Dorothy's breath.

She reached for the worn leather handle and tried unsuccessfully to keep a tear from spilling.

They'd given her back her medical bag. It was hers, alright. She knew every crack and crease in that dear leather. She'd have known it even if it didn't have those small gold letters embossed just below the catch.

D. Chambers, M.D.

. . . .

Just before sunset Dorothy stepped out of the Children's Hospital side door and had to think a moment where exactly she was going. The mall area between the hospital and the Annex which had been fairly quiet this morning was teeming with people scattered along the trampled dirt boulevard. It was an unorganized procession of sorts, moving toward the Main Building and beyond. Some carried a chair or crate or blanket. And most of them wore hats.

With a sigh of resignation she began "excusing" her way through the crowd and made it across the human traffic. She picked up her pace as she entered the Annex hoping the crowd wasn't headed to some required meeting and she would come up absent.

It had been a grand day, by all accounts. The twelve little hospitalized patients were doing well, and the fifty or so she and the nursing staff tended in the outpatient cubicle would all be fine in a day or two. Only three had required stitches. Much of what she saw could be attributed to vitamin deficiency, malnutrition, or accidental injury. But one symptom had her concerned.

Several youngsters had presented with stomach ills that seemed unlikely for dysentery, amoebic or otherwise, but presented a similar type of pain. Her questioning hadn't been able to get to the bottom of the matter, except for one commonality among two of the small boys. They admitted to eating the leaves of a plant they couldn't describe and didn't remember where they'd found it.

She mulled over the problem and had to double back when she realized she'd passed the Annex room to which she and the children had been assigned. The moment she entered she heard Bobby's gleeful laughter and grinned. With renewed energy, she sidestepped her way through the maze of beds until she reached their corner of the room. She was removing her white coat as she rounded the end of the bunkbed and stopped, startled by the little scene.

Carol and Bobby sat tucked as close as they could get beside a slender young woman who sat on Dorothy's bed talking in an animated voice. Her auburn hair curled prettily around her youthful face. She was telling the children a story.

Dorothy cleared her throat and the girl jumped from the bed, clearly embarrassed to have been caught unawares.

"Mommy!"

The happy greeting was laced with ebullient smiles as Carol and Bobby jumped from the bed.

"Oh! Doctor Chambers! Hello!"

Carol and Bobby threw themselves at Dorothy, an energetic greeting to say the least.

"This is Jeanne, Mommy," Carol said.

"She's nice!" Bobby interrupted. "And she's mine!"

"Hold on a minute, kiddos." Dorothy dropped a kiss to both their heads and turned what she hoped wasn't too disapproving an expression toward the young lady. "So you're Jeanne, then?"

"Yes! I'll be watching the children for you. That is, if it's alright with you. That is, you see, Mr. Chambers will be teaching some classes and needs someone to look after the children when you're at the hospital so he—oh, dear, I'm nattering on, aren't I!" Jeanne seemed clearly flustered.

"Not at all, Miss—, um—"

"Travay! Jeanne Travay! I'm so glad to meet you. Your husband told me all about you. I mean, that is—"

Dorothy assessed the slender girl with the lovely brown eyes. What was he thinking, barely a week in camp and Fred was already leaving their children with a stranger. She'd have to put an end to this.

"Yes. Well. Miss Travay, I believe that will be all for today. I shall—"

"Oh, golly, that's great, Doctor Chambers! There's entertainment tonight and I really want to get there before it starts."

Ah. So that explained the crowd on the boulevard.

"Entertainment?"

"Yes! The *Little Theatre Under the Stars.* They play something special on the Victrola on Thursday nights. Sometimes camp people perform. Tonight's a movie, though. It'll be a lot of Jap propaganda, but it's a movie! I can just make it if I leave now." She reached a hand to chuck each of the children under the chin. "Shalom, my littles!"

And she was gone.

Dorothy felt herself succumb to any number of peculiar emotions. Fred had left the children in the care of someone he couldn't possibly know much about.

She was pretty. She was young. And she was Jewish. Her youthful loveliness seemed undimmed by the circumstances.

And Dorothy's children were clearly in love with her already.

But was she responsible?

Dorothy's thoughts were drowned out by the children's litany of the wonderfulness the magical Miss Jeanne had brought into their day. She had shown them the whole camp, taught them how to hold both their tin plate and tin cup without spilling while they found a place to sit in the dining shed, and let them take their afternoon nap in her friend's shanty in Foggy Bottom. She'd even taught them which of the Japanese guards they should be sure to bow to and how to pick the weevily-weevils out of their mush.

They couldn't wait until they'd see Miss Jeanne again tomorrow.

And Dorothy couldn't wait until she could bend Fred's ear about that very thing.

But Fred wasn't here, and wouldn't be until tomorrow morning. He was already safely ensconced with the other men in the gymnasium. Or had he gone on to the movie?

She doubted he knew how lucky he was to be there and not here, watching her try ever so hard not to boil over.

It took longer than usual to settle the children for bedtime, but their happy chatter calmed her in a way she hadn't expected. For the first time in months they'd done things about which she'd known nothing, had spent their day away from her watchful eye, and their passion for telling her every tiny detail was remarkably refreshing in its unfamiliarity.

"They're going to let me try out for the fly-swatting club, Mommy."

"Me too!" echoed Bobby. That sent him into a paroxysm of karate moves around their tiny area.

An annoyed voice from across the room shushed him quicker than the threat of an early bedtime. "Hold it down over there!"

"Sorry!" Dorothy said quietly. A finger in front of her lips silenced her two and they spent the next half hour pantomiming and giggling as they slowly unwound and got themselves ready to be tucked in.

At precisely nine o'clock, almost like the flick of a switch, the noise level in the building shifted to hushed whispers. The snicker of mosquito nets dropping into place seemed to signal 'lights out', though no lights burned in the building.

Dorothy tidied their space and double-checked the children's netting before sliding into her own space. The netting closed around her as if drawing a line between the events of one day and the next. She was tired to the bone. Weary in a good way, but weary nonetheless.

She stretched to ease her bones into a more comfortable position and heard her own stomach growl. For the first time today she realized she'd been so immersed in her work that she'd completely forgotten to eat. She'd forgotten her own rule: keep yourself healthy so you can be the help others need.

Tomorrow she would do better. But she should have asked that girl Jeanne where she might find a hat.

Her eyes fluttered heavily shut.

And whatever did the children mean by weevily-weevils in their mush?

Surely not.

Oh, surely not.

AERIAL PHOTO SHOWS THE CAMPUS OF SANTO TOMÁS UNIVERSITY
COVERED WITH NIPA HUTS AND SHANTIES
WHERE INTERNEES WHO COULD AFFORD THEM LIVED.

PHOTO COURTESY OF JOHN TEWELL

EXCERPT FROM MANILA GOODBYE BY ROBIN PRISING
© 1975 BY ROBIN PRISING. PP 151

THE HUNGER LINE

First the three meal tickets were taken by the kitchen staff and I waited, outwardly patient, while they were inspected for forgery, the correct date found and each ticket punched—Father's, Mother's and mine. Then a scoop, made from a can half the size of a Campbell's soup tin and wired to a stick, dipped—so very slowly—into a big iron pot. The scoop was then scraped carefully level and our ration of swill was poured into the pails. The swill was rotten, soupy rice or rice cooked with cornmeal, sometimes with bits of meat or greens, but if these slightly savored the saltless slop, they could not be seen. The boiled white worms and tiny stones, however, were easy to see.

If a drop of gruel or a grain of soggy rice dribbled to the rough-hewn wooden table, I stretched out a finger to wipe it up, but if I reached for anything that spilt to the ground, the person behind me would stay my hand, warning me against dysentery. At last, a generous dipper of tea, coffee or ginger water, with flies and bugs afloat in it, filled up my largest pail.

On rare occasions, Sundays or the Mikado's birthday, a small thumb of banana or perhaps a quarter-cup of coconut milk or the liquid waste from soybean cattle feed might be included with our fare. These were so delicious that the mere taste of them hurt.

MEAL PREPARATION AT SANTO TOMÁS

WHITE BUILDING TO RIGHT OF CENTER IS THE ANNEX
WHERE DOROTHY, CAROL AND BOBBY WERE QUARTERED. MIDDLE
LEFT IS THE CHILDREN'S HOSPITAL WHERE DOROTHY WORKED.

CHAPTER FORTY-EIGHT

TREAD CAREFULLY

"You're awfully quiet, Dor. Are you feeling alright?"

Dorothy felt Fred watching her as she encouraged the children to eat their morning mush, even though it was barely palatable. If she had any place for a campstove she could have fried it into mushcakes in a bit of coconut oil. But in their tiny quarters there was no chance of that.

It wasn't until Bobby fished a weevil out of his bowl and hucked it over his shoulder with his spoon that she remembered last night's cautionary tale.

"Bobby, don't throw—"

She'd barely uttered her reprimand when a dour-looking matron loomed at her shoulder.

"I'll be the one to break my neck in this slippery muck if your child continues to disregard the rules," she spat.

"The rules?" Fred inquired.

"No weevils on the pavement. Gets slippery. Too many falls. Either eat them or put them on the table, then back into your bowl when you're done. Scrape them in the buckets by the water spout when you rinse your bowl. See that he does it."

She gave a curt nod in Bobby's direction and sailed away.

Dorothy cringed while Fred instructed Bobby in the collection and disposal of weevils. She'd been biding her time, waiting to question Fred about the nanny arrangements when the weevil-wafting episode interrupted her pent-up irritation.

It hadn't been easy holding her tongue while Fred dominated the conversation. He'd opened their morning dialogue with fifteen straight minutes of exuberant monologue. Apparently he had been welcomed with open arms into the camp's academic community yesterday. In the space of an hour they'd outlined a plan for him, allotted him a teaching space on the top floor of the Main Building and given him a list of college-bound students' names.

Once he was finished with his weevil warning he turned to her again.

"I'm serious, Dorothy. Are you not feeling well?" His hand on her arm tried to leech the anger out of her, and she felt guilty clinging to it as she offered a meager smile.

"No, I'm fine," she answered without looking at him. "Collect the buckets like I showed you, Carol, so they're ready to wash." Carol jumped from her bench and gathered the four wire-handled tin buckets that served as dinner plate and breakfast bowl all in one. "And do the...the weevily wash like the lady said. Scrape first, rinse, then wash, okay sweetie?"

Carol nodded and skipped off to do a chore Dorothy had no doubt she would be hating by the end of the week.

"I like your hat," Fred said, buttressing his smile with a wink. "Quite the high fashion chapeau, I would say."

Dorothy huffed. She'd stopped at the camp's unofficial recycled clothing vendor—not much more than a ragman right out of a Dickens novel—on the way to breakfast with Fred and the children. Several hats hung on a rack that rose above the fellow's cart. But the brim of the hat he'd foisted upon her was particularly wide and the "bowl" was an open weave that would keep her from getting too hot, so she had gratefully adopted the sad thing. It had cost her one outrageous half peso.

"I met Jeanne," she said.

"Excellent! Wonderful girl! She'll be in my class."

"So...the children will be with her? In your class?" She heard the disapproval in her voice and didn't like the sound of it.

"Oh no. Her brother will watch Bobby while Jeanne's in class, and Carol will be in her own class."

"You have it all worked out then."

She felt bitter words rising to her tongue, and it was so foreign to her that it nearly made her ill. From what she could see he was practically giving their children the run of the camp.

She'd never spoken a harsh word to him in their entire acquaintance, yet this morning she could barely hold back a seething tirade. This was their children he was talking about, and he seemed so cavalier as to their care. She'd taken on the work at the hospital safe in the knowledge—or rather, erroneous assumption—that the children would be safe in Fred's company throughout the day.

"Actually, I do have it all worked out," Fred smiled. "Jeanne is a lovely girl. Her brother bunks in the Gym balcony not far from my spot. She plays violin and was a college student when all this began. Her parents have a shanty in Glamorville, one of the shantytowns on higher ground here. She's articulate and highly regarded by several of the faculty. She doesn't require remuneration...sees this as one of the ways she can be of help in the camp. I will pick up the children and breakfast with you every morning. Then I will take Carol to the Kindergarten class where she will be for two hours, and Bobby will come to class with me. Miss Travay will arrive a bit early along with her brother, Saul. The brother will entertain Bobby while we have class. After class, Miss Travay will collect Bobby, then get Carol, get their noon meal at the children's kitchen and settle them for the siesta. After siesta I will collect them, since I will be done with my teaching and camp duties by then."

Dorothy blinked.

"What?" Fred seemed finally to have noticed her annoyance.

"Well, I...that is, I thought they might..."

"Might what?" Fred reached across the table and took her hand.

Dorothy stilled. All night she'd worried that it would fall to her to work out proper supervision for the children. She had mentally railed at Fred for leaving them yesterday with the first person who came along. But now she saw it was nothing like that. Nothing like that at all. He had come up with a very satisfactory solution, one with which the children clearly were thrilled. Just because Bobby and Carol's *mother* didn't know all the details didn't mean their *father* didn't.

"Oh, darling girl, you miss them, don't you? Going back to work in a hospital after being constantly with your children these fourteen months has been hard on you. I should have thought of it, sweetheart. I could have brought them over to see you, or waved through the window or something. Would you like me to do that this afternoon?"

Now she really *was* going to cry. He'd completely misinterpreted the reason she was out of sorts. And she was grateful for it.

Dorothy managed a weak smile. He was so generous with her when she had just been practically wicked with him. This damnable war was making her doubt everyone around her. She looked into his eyes and put her hand atop his that was still caressing the back of her other hand. She would never doubt him again. Not ever.

"No, darling, that won't be necessary. You've worked out your schedule and you don't need to complicate it by gathering everyone up to pay me a visit. I'm fine with it all, truly I am."

He beamed. "Then I must be on my way." He blew a discreet kiss from across the table, the only kind of kiss either of them would be comfortable with in a public setting. "I'll go fill their little minds and you go save their little boo-boos." He saluted as he moved away from the bench and turned toward the Main Building.

Dorothy stared. Surely she'd heard him wrong. Little booboos? Is that really how he thought of her work? He of all people knew better than that. It was an utterly careless thing to say. Booboos indeed. He couldn't have forgotten already how she'd saved his own foot from the tropical ulcers that very nearly required its amputation. She dared him to call *that* a wee booboo.

Dorothy watched him go as her emotions jostled about and at last began to untangle themselves. The prospect of teaching again had restored a small bit of Fred's radiance, and despite his cavalier dismissal of her healing art, she thanked God for that. She'd very nearly tarnished his bright mood with her unbridled fit of pique.

Well, it wouldn't happen again. She'd see to that. It was work that kept them sane, after all. She would tread more carefully in the future. And perhaps drop a hint that Fred might do the same.

She sighed, welcoming the release from her former angst. Now it was time to don her white coat. And go save some little boo-boos.

· · · ·

She'd been afraid. That's what it boiled down to. Afraid she wouldn't be able to manage her little family in this teeming compound. She'd never really felt that kind of worry before, and had dealt with it in the least satisfactory way. But in the space of a conversation with Fred and a whispered prayer as she stood washing her coffee mug, she felt renewed.

Dorothy threw herself into the clinic routine, anxious to shake off the morning's emotional unrest. It was only minutes before an emergency presented itself in the form of a ten-year-old boy. With a knife sticking out of his foot.

He was bravely hobbling toward her, helped on either side by two other boys of similar age. Had it been a parent helping him, Dorothy doubted he could have held back his tears. But caught up between two friends, he was doing a remarkable job of pretending that having a blade sticking out of his foot didn't scare him to death.

She would ordinarily expect them to have pulled the knife out as soon as it happened. But the blade looked to be fairly well embedded in the bone. It was going to take a bit of doing to dislodge it without breaking it off. And it was going to hurt like the dickens. Without eggs and milk in his diet, his bones would knit slowly. And she'd have to bind him well because a boy his age wouldn't be likely to stay off his foot through the long healing process. He'd have to come in regularly for disinfectant, or tropical ulcers at the wound site would be his next battle.

The boy pushed himself up onto the examining table and used both hands to lift his foot up. He seemed to know the routine as if he'd been here before.

Dorothy put a solemn hand on the boy's shoulder.

"Let me guess," she said gravely. "Mumblety-peg?"

The boy grimaced. She was right. He'd tried just a bit too hard to win the game of flinging a knife into the dirt to see who could come closest to his own foot. The upside of it was, if the knife went into your foot, you automatically won.

· · · ·

Several hours and three dozen patients later, Dorothy found a moment to sit down. Camp rules had each internee working four hours a day. In the state of malnourishment in which they existed, four hours was the maximum expected. Dorothy had been on her feet now for six hours.

She had barely taken a deep breath when a hand reached in front of her and dropped a biscuit with a dollop of jam onto the desk.

"Bomber bread," the voice said.

Dorothy looked up into the gaunt but kind face of a woman she'd seen working around the ward.

"Frances Lloyd," the woman said. "We're awfully glad you're here, Dr. Chambers."

Dorothy smiled and scooted over to make room for Frances Lloyd to sit. "Happy to know you Miss—"

"Mrs.," the woman offered. "My husband and I were some of the first ones here."

"Ah. A dubious honor," Dorothy smiled. "Thank you for the...what did you call it?"

"Bomber bread. Some call it a 'battle biscuit'. Rice flour, salt, shortening, soda, vinegar, and water. Easy as pie. Make it ahead and it doesn't spoil, so there's always something to eat if there's an air raid and we can't get to the chow lines."

"Do you use banana vinegar?"

"Whatever we can find. There's always somebody making up some vinegar from bananas, or even prune pits if you can get them. Bomber bread tastes like a whole lot of nothing, but it does make a nice lump in your stomach. Try it."

Dorothy picked up the flat biscuit and took a taste. The biscuit itself was just as she'd said. A whole lot of nothing. But the jam on top was out of this world. It stimulated taste buds that had long since gone dormant.

"What *is* this," Dorothy asked in wonder.

Frances grinned. "Mrs. Oftendahl's 'strawberry' jelly."

Dorothy was shocked. Strawberry was not possible. Out of the question. Even though it tasted exactly like her mother's homemade strawberry jam.

"You have to tell me. How could it taste like strawberry?"

"Eggplant, calamanci, and brown sugar. Pretty terrific, hm?"

Dorothy nodded. She took another small bite, then wrapped the rest carefully in a bit of paper, tenting the top so it wouldn't disturb even a smidgen of the scrumptious 'strawberry' jelly.

Frances frowned. "Don't you like it?"

"Oh! It's wonderful! Too wonderful! I'll save the rest for Bobby and Carol.

They will be in heaven."

"How old are they?"

"Bobby's almost three and Carol just turned five."

"Such sweet ages. I remember when my boys were that age," Frances said, her smile turning wistful.

"I'd love to meet them."

"And I would give anything in this world to see them right now," Frances said softly. "Anthony and Samuel are in Australia."

"How very hard for you!"

Dorothy put out her hand to console the young woman, and in a few quiet words, the Lloyd family's story spilled out. Frances, her husband and two boys had made their home in Hong Kong, and when war threatened, her husband Samuel insisted she and the children evacuate to Australia, which they did. Her husband stayed at his job with Asiatic Petroleum in Hong Kong.

When it seemed calm enough, Frances and her husband Samuel met halfway for a brief visit in Manila—on December 8, 1941, the day of the first attack. Stranded in Manila with their boys still in Australia, they were among the first to be interned one month later on January 8, 1942.

As the final words of the wrenching story penetrated Dorothy's heart, the young woman was called to assist a nearby patient. They stood, each reacting with a caregiver's instant response. But before they moved, Frances and Dorothy shared an embrace, a hug that went beyond the moment to encompass the heartache one mother sensed in another.

The entire fourteen months that Dorothy's family had been confined together in Calinog, Frances had been here. Listening to the bamboo telegraph report news of Japanese forces advancing on Australia. Not knowing if her boys were alright. Never hearing their voices. Never touching their faces.

So she came here to the children's ward every day, offering aid to some other mother's child because her heart was breaking for her own.

A familiar tingling set Dorothy's fingers typing against her thigh.

Dearest Mother,

I'm so bound up in surviving this ordeal that I fail to remember how this war is affecting other mothers...how it must be affecting you. I forget about that ache that must live in the pit of your stomach, wondering every day if we're all right. Worried about little Bobby, a child you've never met but who lives with all his rambunctious glory in your heart. Forgive me, Mother, for forgetting that this is your war, too.

. . . .

A minute of peaceful seclusion was all she asked. Just one minute. One minute to feel a snippet of breeze that might cool the sweat from her brow. One minute to soak her feet in a luxurious bath of Epsom salts.

Just one minute.

But at Santo Tomás, that was an impossibility. Today the muted, lethargic thrum of activity in the yard assailed Dorothy as she headed for the laundry tub. If it was a good day, waiting in line for the tub would take about a half hour. If not—well, it wasn't unusual to lose a good two hours just waiting your turn in one line or another.

So the inevitable conversation trickled out. Johnny was teething again. Sarah had a crush on the Baker boy. Why wouldn't the camp committee talk to Commandant Konishi again about the dwindling food supply. Had Charlie Winters successfully hidden the food bundle that had come over the wall to him the night before. The usual.

Dorothy turned away from her grousing neighbor and scouted for a bit of shade where she could wait her turn. Fred knew several men who had spent endless hours warning Charlie to slow down his deliveries. But selling the contraband was keeping his family alive. So Charlie persisted.

Hundreds of internees seemed to have an unlimited supply of money. Consequently, there were always buyers for anything Charlie could bring in. In some cases, company VIP's had lines of credit that were guaranteed to be paid in full the minute the internees were released. In other cases, internees provided needed services that garnered them an income.

"I understand your Fred has joined the Thespians for this week's comedy," a cheerful low voice said in her ear.

The intern who introduced herself as Josie came around to stand beside Dorothy near the line, a bundle of laundry hitched high on her right hip.

Dorothy grinned. "Ah, yes, it's true, although I do believe Thespian is a rather grand label for the kind of acting he'll be doing in their little skit."

"Well, it is a comedy, after all. One wouldn't expect anything too Shakespearian," Josie laughed.

"Oh, forsooth, you misapprehend me, fair maid. Shakespeare he can do! It's contemporary man that he finds a bit of a challenge."

Josie hooted. "They should have cast you in the play, Dr. Kinney. You're a natural!"

The two women shared a laugh that almost lit their eyes before they parted and stepped up to the newly available tub. It was early in the day, and the water wasn't too brackish yet. Still, doing laundry in someone else's dirty water was an abhorrence Dorothy was quite ready to be done with.

Sweat trickled down her back, sending up the sour scent that reminded her this dress needed laundering as desperately as the ones in her bundle. If only there was a tree to offer some shade.

She doubted they had to stand in line—in the sun, no less—in Hopevale. Dorothy closed her eyes and pictured the mythical canopy of palm trees she'd conjured up in her imagination, the canopy of trees that kept the little paradise of Hopevale in a perpetual state of coolness. It was jungle, wasn't it? Vast, over-grown jungle. There had to be plenty of shade.

Were her friends who had fled to the hills cavorting happily in their little inland paradise today? She shoved a damp lock off her forehead, trying to shove the envious thoughts away, as well. They most likely had to beat their clothes against a rock in a mountain stream rather than experience the luxury of an actual tub.

But to Dorothy's imagination, it seemed that nobody must ever go hungry in Hopevale, with fresh mangoes on every branch and plenty of good jungle vegetation to go around.

Nobody ever got weary in Hopevale, with the spirited little cadre of missionaries to keep God's Word on the tip of every tongue.

Nobody ever snapped at their neighbor or coveted someone else's dinner plate.

Blessed are the poor in heart, for they shall find Hopevale.

Blessed are the meek, for they shall inherit all the mangoes.

Blessed are the peacemakers, for they shall be home by Christmas.

Blessed—

"Dr. Kinney?"

Dorothy looked up, startled by Josie's hand on her arm.

"I hope you have lots of dresses, ma'am," she said, "because if you keep scrubbing like that, there's going to be nothing left of this one!"

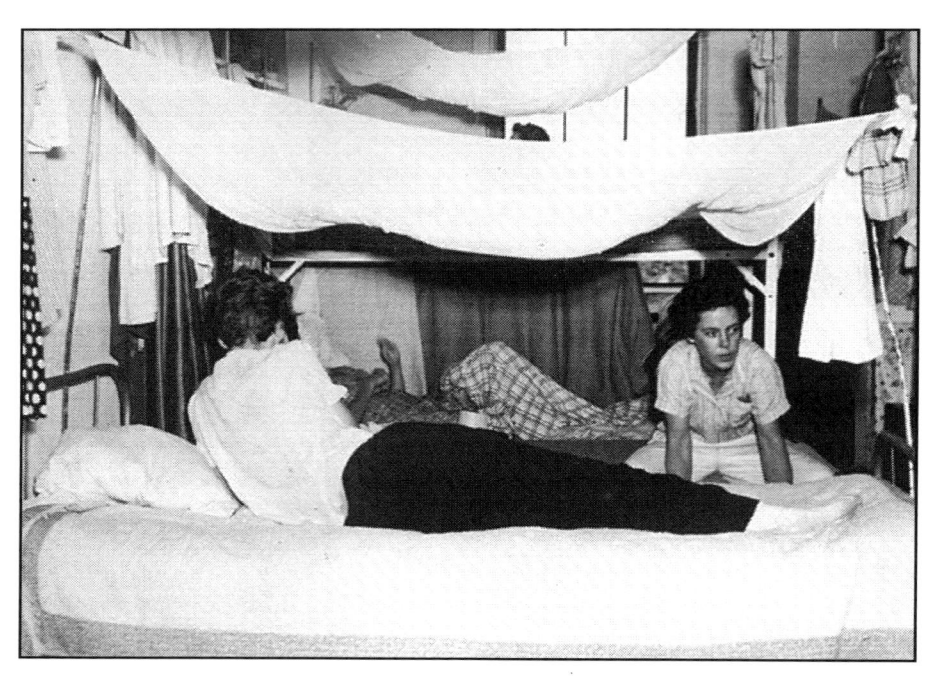

ABOVE, WOMEN'S QUARTERS. BELOW, OUTDOOR HAIR-WASHING TUB

CHAPTER FORTY-NINE

SAY SOMETHING

Dorothy's dress was sticking to her shoulders. She shifted, wishing the stifling humidity would lift. It was like breathing through a cloud as she paid a house-call on a very sick woman.

"I believe your mother has acute enteritis," she told the son.

Dorothy turned to the boy who had led her to his mother's bedside. He was so distraught that she put a comforting hand on the teenager's shoulder. He'd come to her begging that she persuade his mother to get medical help.

"Not dysentery?" the boy asked. His bony hands twisted at his frayed walking shorts that had long ago given up any resemblance to their original fine quality. Clearly, they had been an expensive purchase at some point in time. But from the looks of his mother's spartan area, they were no longer people of means.

The woman was thin. Too thin to sustain much of an illness. Dysentery might have taken her through death's door. But Dorothy felt this bout of enteritis would not—if they could get it quickly under control.

The boy bunked with other teenage boys and some of the men on the balcony of the gymnasium. It was Fred who had seen the boy's worry and found out that he hadn't been allowed into his mother's room in the Annex. All he knew was that she was sick but wouldn't go to the hospital.

At Fred's urging, Corbett Conklin had waited around the children's hospital until Dorothy was finished with her outpatient clinic. When she heard his plea she had not hesitated to escort him past the protesting room monitors who guarded the door of his mother's quarters. She found the woman weak and dehydrated on her bed.

"No, not dysentery. It has similar symptoms, but enteritis is more like a food poisoning that sets in and sticks around to cause trouble." Dorothy was pleased to see the boy relax slightly. "Because she's dehydrated, I'm going to ask Dr. Waters to admit her to the hospital. They'll get her fixed up just fine. And then..."

Once again Dorothy battled with the severe shortage of drugs the camp was currently experiencing. Nurse Noell was absolutely brilliant at getting her hands on the most commonly needed drugs. But there was never anywhere near enough to treat every condition. Not in a camp where half the population suffered some tropical malady and all the camp suffered some nutritional deficit. It would be a miracle if the hospital had any of the drugs that might give Mrs. Conklin speedy relief.

What she contemplated now was a simple non-medicinal aid for minimizing the symptoms of acute enteritis—a homeopathic recipe that would have been swift and inexpensive if her patient were anywhere but here in Santo Tomás.

"Then what?" Corbett began to fidget, upset by Dorothy's hesitation.

"Well, then she'll be strong enough to leave her room so you can spend time together. And whenever you can get hold of an egg, make a sort of eggnog for her. That will do wonders to keep the enteritis from setting back in."

She smiled, regretting how easily her words could either plant fear or relief in the boy. But perhaps it wasn't all that surprising. Fred had told her that Corbett's father had not survived the death march on Bataan. He was a much-loved traveling magistrate and word had been carried along the bamboo telegraph to inform Mrs. Conklin that he had been killed. He had joined the guerilla forces and had fallen in the first days of the march. By getting word swiftly to Mrs. Conklin, the guerillas honored the man they regarded so highly.

Corbett's mother was all he had left in the world. His anxiety would understandably rest on tenterhooks.

"For now, take this note to Dr. Waters in the main hospital. I'll wait here and look after your mother until—"

"I'll be right back!" he said as he snatched the note and disappeared..

Dorothy settled on the edge of the bed to wait for Henry Waters to arrive. If he was in surgery, it could be awhile. But she knew he would admit Mrs. Conklin to the main hospital once he saw her deteriorating state.

The woman on the bed beside her was too weak for conversation at the moment, so Dorothy simply rested her hand lightly on the woman's shoulder, mostly to remind her someone was here, that she wasn't alone.

"You have a lovely son, Mrs. Conklin."

The woman's eyes fluttered and she opened her dry lips to speak. Dorothy had to lean close to hear the woman's words...words that broke Dorothy's heart.

"He's not my son," she whispered.

"But his name—"

"I gave him the name Corbett. And my last name. He doesn't...he doesn't remember his own name."

The surprise Dorothy couldn't keep from her face must have led the woman to continue her story.

"A year ago, while his family was still hiding in the city, he saw his mother shot, and his father..." Mrs. Conklin paused. Not so much because it was hard for her to speak, but because it appeared difficult to say the words. "Beheaded," she whispered.

Dorothy pressed her fingers into the woman's shoulder, finding no words to express her horror at the woman's revelation. Moments passed before either of them could speak.

"It was just after I received word of my dear Patrick's death. I found the boy standing in the road. His mother was...horribly damaged. But I know that she saw me before she...before she died. But his—" A tear slipped from her eye and traced a line down her temple and onto the pillow. "His father's head was...was... gruesomely displayed." She choked. "Corbett was staring at it. He...he wouldn't speak to me. He wasn't crying, he was just...looking like he expected it to...to say something."

Dorothy's own tears flowed freely now. The woman gripped her hand just as Dr. Waters stepped into the room.

"No one...no one knows. He doesn't remember a thing about it now. He thinks he's my son. Don't..."

"Hush now. I won't say a word. Mrs. Conklin, you can be sure his story is safe with me. And my husband will look after him. They bunk near each other, you know. Let's just get you better now," she urged.

But Dorothy knew already that somehow, without breaking her promise, she'd find a way to enlist Fred's help with Corbett. If he'd suppressed his memory so significantly, it could be cruelly catastrophic for him if the images came flooding back too swiftly.

This boy might very well be a ticking time bomb.

· · · ·

An astonishing ten months disappeared in a haze of humid days and airless nights, tended wounds and minor surgeries, weary lines and endless roll calls. They were marked by mounting alarm over the progress of the war, an incredible shortage of materials of any kind, and failing health in most of the four thousand internees. Ever so quietly, a group of special squads were organized, made up of one hundred and three hand-picked men. They would spring into action if the camp fell under a state of emergency and lives were threatened on a large scale.

Once the package lines were permanently closed and food and goods no longer came regularly into camp, the chow lines nearly doubled, making short rations even shorter. The commandant confiscated all unused building materials, making future shanty repair an impossibility. All privately owned electrical and gas appliances were ordered to be surrendered to the Japanese authorities.

SANTO TOMÁS INTERNMENT CAMP
LIMITED PRIVATE EDITION - FREDERIC H. STEVENS
© 1946 - PAGE 445

July 17—Japanese sergeant with small camera begins photograph-ing all internees in groups of five, each with number displayed across chest.

Occasionally Dorothy had the opportunity to visit the nipa huts, though due to weather her outdoor ventures were often severely limited to dash-ing from the Annex to the children's hospital and back. For three days in November, torrential rains and hurricane-force winds battered the campus. When it finally calmed, shanties were in shambles, some blown completely down. Portions of the boardwalk lay scattered about the garden area, and walking through the camp was made treacherous due to debris that littered the grounds.

Twenty-seven inches had fallen in three days, water-logging possessions, destroying perishables, and contaminating the camp's water supply.

Satisfied that her outpatients were all safe and doing well, Dorothy headed to Glamorville to collect Carol Joy from Jeanne's shanty. The family called it the *Travay Chalet*. She looked forward to these times, always pleased when Jeanne invited her in to sit for awhile and chat.

It was the nicest nipa hut she'd seen, with rattan rugs on the floor and cleverly woven shades with open spaces to let the light in. They lent a feeling of privacy even though the open squares were large enough and placed strategically enough that the Japanese guards could get an adequate look inside whenever they felt the need.

The Travays always seemed to have funds, and had hired others so that their 'chalet' was one of the first shanties to be restored after the monsoon.

"Have you talked to Mr. Chambers this afternoon?" Jeanne handed Dorothy a china teacup with some sort of cool, fruity tea. Impeccable manners shown through her every movement, yet in such a natural way that it was like chatting with a school chum. Now she was sharing with Dorothy the wonderful cool tea she'd made for herself on this blistering afternoon.

The fact that it was cool was as surprising as the fruity taste, and the two sensations fostered an immensely satisfied smile.

'Cool' could be achieved by carefully covering an earthenware jug or pitcher, then partially burying it in the shade beneath the stilted shanty. It was an extra step requiring a tiring bit of work, which made it all the more touching that Jeanne had shared this hard-won cool tea with her.

She took a sip, marveling at the brilliant explosion of taste in her mouth. She held it there, savoring the way it seemed to refresh and revive her. It was gloriously, maddeningly sweet.

She often enjoyed what she thought of as delicacies here at the chalet. Sitting in the very civilized space she could almost forget where she was.

Jeanne's father was—or rather, had been—a prominent businessman in Manila. In fact, he owned one of the Philippine's larger businesses before the war. He had resources beyond those that most here enjoyed, though there were many ways in which his family suffered as hers did. Especially now that the gates had been closed to Filipino tradesmen.

Somehow, though, probably via the camp's black market, Mr. Travay was still able to get small quantities of supplemental food. She knew Jeanne shared bits of food with Bobby and Carol. From the looks of it, they were probably from her own rations, as Jeanne was as lean as most of the young women her age in the camp. There was no end to the blessings the girl had brought to the Chambers family. And the cool tea seemed heaven sent.

Now it was Jeanne's lovely voice that brought Dorothy back from her brief reverie.

"No, I actually haven't seen Fred yet today. Is something—"

"Oh no! Nothing's wrong. If anything, something's very, very right."

She was beaming, clearly enjoying being the one to share a titillating piece of news.

"Well then, out with it," Dorothy smiled. "You look like the cat that ate the canary!"

Jeanne laughed. "I'll be eating more than that by this time tomorrow!" She grinned. "The Red Cross Comfort Kits have arrived!"

Dorothy's heart leapt at the thought. They were intended to get one relief box per prisoner per month, but to date no person in camp had ever seen one. Was it possible they were actually on their way?

SANTO TOMÁS INTERNMENT CAMP
LIMITED PRIVATE EDITION - FREDERIC H. STEVENS
© 1946 - PAGE 422-426

Nov. 5 — *Teia Maru* [French ship formerly known as the Aramis seized by Japanese and renamed] bringing in relief supplies, medicines, and mail due tomorrow on return from Goa.

Nov. 10 — From official minutes: "Contrary to the original understanding. . . the Japanese military have been withdrawing considerable quantities of these (Red Cross) supplies both direct from the piers and also from the warehouses, with the stated intention of storing same for distribution among war prisoners. In particular, the indications are that a large proportion of the medical and surgical supplies and shoes have been withdrawn, together with a little less than half of the comfort kits . . . .

Nov. 30 — Red Cross Relief kits from *Teia Maru* come into Camp for storage until examined and approved for distribution.

Dec. 16 — Special meeting of Executive Committee hastily called to consider too rigorous inspection of Red Cross relief kits received in Camp on November 30. Fifteen Japanese military inspectors open all kits, remove all cigarettes (due to unacceptable printing on one of the brands), take out and examine contents of kits, open some cans and damage two kits beyond repair. Verbal protest at once made to Commandant, followed by written protest to be sent to Swiss Minister in Tokyo.

Eight hundred kits given out to internees today. Daily deliveries to continue until Camp distribution completed.

"You're serious?"

"Absolutely positively!" Jeanne could hardly contain herself. "My dad and brother and Mr. Chambers and a bunch of fellows were assigned to go to some dock and load relief boxes onto trucks this morning. I can*not* wait! What do you suppose is in them?"

"Oh my."

This was stunning news.

"Protein, please. Plenty of protein."

•   •   •   •

The next thirty days were torture. The entire camp waited with bated breath for the relief boxes, but by the first week of December the kits had still not been dispensed.

There would be tins of potted meat, some said. Others felt they'd be full of army k-rations, but who cared. If it was good enough for their boys, it was good enough for them. Others scoffed. It was just another rumor, they said.

But Fred had carried them into the trucks with his own hands. He knew they were real. Whether the Japanese would actually release them to the internees was impossible to know.

To dispel some of the tension caused by waiting for the comfort kits to appear, the Camp Committee accepted a challenge from the Japanese officers. They would suspend anything other than necessary work details for a day and meet one another on the baseball diamond.

Internees began a feverish round of betting. Foolish stakes of entire comfort kits were waged. Most bet that the STICS—Santo Tomás Internment Camp team—would crush the Japs.

Fred was hesitant to play, but joined the team anyway. He was their best shortstop. They needed him, they said.

"I wish you wouldn't," Dorothy had sighed. "It's too much running. Besides, you know you'll win and the Japanese are not going to take that well. Not well at all."

"Exactly," Fred had countered. "And that's why I have to play, even though I know our boys are going to raise holy ned when I suddenly get very, very clumsy."

"Clumsy? You?" Dorothy raised her eyebrows, then turned to him with stunning realization. "You're going to throw the game."

"We have to, darling girl. No choice there, I'm afraid.

Beating the Japanese was the very last thing they could afford to do. The only possible end to this game was a clear Japanese victory or the entire camp would suffer. And the best way he could help secure that outcome was to be on the field.

· · · ·

Game day arrived, every bit as hot and humid as every day that had preceded it. Straws were drawn and the Santo Tomás team drew first 'at bat'. Things got off to a shaky start until Corbett Conklin hit a home run. The spectators cheered feverishly for the scrawny boy as he loped around the bases, bringing in another runner. It was an auspicious start.

Fred grimaced and shook his head when Corbett shrugged his shoulders, as if admitting he'd done just the opposite of what Fred had counseled him to do. The kid had agreed to help throw the game. But his grin proved he hadn't been able to resist showing off.

As whispered suggestions to tone it down filtered through the crowd, the cheering died rapidly. It wouldn't do to celebrate a victory over the Japanese. Not unless they wanted a cut in rations. Or double work for the week. The Japanese officers seemed to know the things that were coveted by the majority of interns, and those would be the first things restricted if they felt the need to retaliate.

Fred got the team into a huddle.

"We all know we'll clobber them," he said. "But the only way to end this day is a Japanese victory dance." He looked them each in the eye until their expressions showed they understood.

The huddle broke and the team's next batter stepped into the box.

The crowd murmured quietly as the much-hated Lieutenant Abiko took the pitcher's mound for the Japanese. He taunted the crowd, who knew enough now not to take the bait. There were no catcalls. No derisive sounds. No indication of any kind that the wiry officer was getting their goat.

But Abiko would not give up so easily. He seemed intent upon giving them a show. With a sly grin he put the baseball on the ground, exaggerating his movements so everyone would see what he was doing. In a series of great, sweeping motions he reached into his sleeves and pulled something out. Then another and another.

And after a comical wind-up that at last had the crowd snickering, he began to juggle.

With eggs.

The crowd gasped.

Eggs.

How could he be so careless with an egg? With *three* eggs?

It was horrendous. The Japanese team laughed and crowed as Abiko sent the eggs higher and higher until at last he exceeded his own abilities and the eggs eluded his hands.

Splat.

Splat.

Splat.

"Strike one-two-three you out!" Abiko yelled with glee.

The STICS were dumb-struck. Many of them had not been able to get their hands on an egg for months, or if they had, it had come at a high cost. Salt could be had for $25 per pound on the camp's black market. Fred knew of a woman who had traded a fine quality engagement ring for eight pounds of rice. Loans could be had at exorbitant interest. By 1944 a $1,000 check would garner $30 in cash. Japanese guards eagerly traded small quantities of food for jewelry, stealing pride, sentiment, and family history in one swift exchange.

But eggs? Priceless.

Corbett Conklin began walking slowly to third base as the Japanese team danced toward home plate. The STIC team had not played their third batter, but it was clear Abiko considered his egg joke to have turned the game. He could cheat all he wanted, and the STIC team could do absolutely nothing about it.

Fred headed out to take his position at shortstop. He watched the boy, taking in the sudden change in his demeanor as Corbett scuffed each foot angrily. The egg incident had triggered something in Corbett. He was brooding, casting hooded looks at the Japanese team.

The Japanese were terrible at the game and their first two batters went down one after the other, no matter how easily the STIC pitcher lobbed the ball.

Their incompetence didn't seem to assuage Corbett's angst. He stood straight up, pounding his fist into the palm of his hand.

Third to bat was Lieutenant Abiko, but when he took his place in the batter's box he reached once again into his sleeve. Fred watched as the next move seemed to play out in slow motion. Yoshi drew an egg from his sleeve and tossed it high. It tumbled as it rose, higher and higher. Yoshi's gleeful grin seemed almost diabolical as he raised his bat and swung with the flailing motion of a very bad strike.

Corbett's eyes followed the bat's path as the prancing officer laughed and kicked dust toward the STIC team.

The egg landed in the center of home plate and shattered.

From the corner of his eye, Fred registered the cruel antics in the batter's box. But his eyes were fixed on Corbett, and the moment the crazed look broke on the boy's face, Fred took off running.

Corbett crouched, then dug his toes in and launched himself for home base. He was going to tackle the Japanese officer.

No, he was going to kill him.

Fred dug in harder and ran for his life. He had the angle on Corbett, and half-way between third base and home plate, Fred tackled the boy. They tumbled to the dirt and rolled over and over. Fred's shoulders scraped across the pebbled ground. His hips recorded every bruise.

Corbett raged. His dilated eyes looked as savage as the gibberish he was screaming. His fists pummeled Fred until two of the team pulled him off.

Fred scrambled to his feet and somehow dragged the frenzied boy from the field. Once out of sight of the others, they collapsed to the ground.

The boy gasped. Long, wrenching gasps. He dredged them up from the very pit of his soul, and then broke into desperate, heaving sobs.

Fred cradled Corbett and let the violent tremors shake loose all the memories the boy had denied for months.

Behind them, the game resumed as if nothing had happened. As if a boy had not just made a journey beyond himself and found his world to be even more cruel than he'd thought it to be.

· · · ·

"I've never known someone so utterly devastated, so...so ripped from his foundation."

Fred sat with Dorothy, their foreheads touching, knees interlocked, hands clasped together in a pose they'd used for years when approaching prayer.

"I couldn't prepare you, Fred. I wanted to. But I promised his...I promised Mrs. Conklin I would keep Corbett's secret. But if I'd known—"

"I know, darling. You told me enough, though, and I understand it all now. Witnessing the killing was unimaginable trauma for that poor boy. It was just so terrible when he started to remember...so terrible the way he began to describe things he saw in that street, with his father...his mother... the way each word tore itself from him. It was so physical, so desperate, so...I don't know. So excruciatingly mournful."

Images of the boy's soul-searing crisis began to churn in Fred's mind and set him rocking. Together they swayed, expanding the boundaries of their undividedness as if stillness could not hope to contain the magnitude of the experience.

"He was so exhausted. But then...he just kept muttering the same thing. Over and over and over."

Dorothy lifted their joined hands and kissed her husband's knuckles. She slid her arms around his neck and he clasped his hands behind hers.

"What did he say?"

"What?"

"Over and over. What did he say?"

Fred sighed. "Oh. Just...it didn't really make sense."

"What did he say," Dorothy prompted, although she knew it would be just two words.

"He just kept staring into the distance and muttering... 'Say something.'"

RESIDENTS FLEE AS JAPANESE BURN MANILA
PHOTO COURTESY OF JOHN TEWELL

CHAPTER FIFTY

THE BAMBOO TELEGRAPH

As prisoners of war, Dorothy and Fred—like everyone in Santo Tomás— lived by the charity of the open-hearted Filipinos. Many relied on bundles left for them at the package shed by former Filipino employees, or small offerings hoisted over the prison walls in remote corners of the campus compound. These gifts had to have come at great sacrifice for many, as conditions in Manila were dire.

Dorothy and Fred had no friendly network among the Filipinos of Manila. But the bamboo telegraph stretched across the islands, and in some indefinable way, word traveled from village to farm, from guerilla to tradesman, that there were missionaries without resources in Santo Tomás. And now and then an anonymous package had shown up at the package shed marked for delivery to the Chambers family. They were rare, they were unexpected, and they were life-saving. With the permanent closing of the package shed, the loss of that source of food was devastating.

Yet, while foodstuffs sustained their bodies—minimally—it was news that kept them all for the most part sane. And somehow the news kept trickling in, no matter how stubbornly the Japanese tried to isolate them.

News came by way of the bamboo telegraph. It might be a small note someone received, rolled around a few pesos and stuffed inside a chicken bone, or a few cryptic words sung in passing. But it was news, and everyone in camp craved it. And passed it on. And within minutes news would transform into rumor and it became impossible to know what was real news and what was wishful thinking. And yet the camp would cling to it as if it came directly from God or General MacArthur.

It was frightfully true that if you were found receiving communications from outside the formidable fences of Santo Tomás, the punishment would be horrific.

Yet still the news came.

It was impossible to keep the Japanese from knowing that news had come into the camp, and it drove them crazy. The camp tempo, indeed the entire camp personality, changed when news was received.

Radios were forbidden, but that had not kept an enterprising internee from building one—right under the noses of their captors. Each time a significant victory by the Americans seemed to be celebrated in camp, the Japanese made a mad search of each bed and box, every bundle and bag, determined to find the guilty party who harbored it. But Tom Poole's precious homemade radio would elude the Japanese for the entire war.

On a late Saturday afternoon in December of 1943, Dorothy sat with Fred on a blanket he'd spread on a ratty spot of ground cover that was halfway dry. The large tin can he'd rigged over a skimpy bed of charcoal was heating up nicely. Earlier in the day a package containing fresh heart had appeared on Dorothy's desk at the hospital. The exact variety of the *donor* was difficult to tell—too small for a dog, too big for a chicken, and the pigeons had gone missing from the roof of the Main Building several months ago—but it was fresh. She would cook it, shred it, and make a gravy of it. The children would be over the moon having gravy on their rice. And it was better than a tonic for Carol.

The Red Cross comfort kits that had been hauled into camp two weeks ago still had not been distributed. Rumor had it that the Japanese guards weren't done opening the boxes and taking what they wanted. It was all the camp committee could do to keep some of the camp hotheads from actually rioting. But to Dorothy's mind, it would be an awfully short riot, what with the depleted energy of most internees.

Fred had practically swooned telling her all the foods he'd seen in one of the comfort kits that had fallen open. The Klim powdered milk alone would be manna from heaven.

Dorothy poked the coals to encourage the flame.

She hadn't told Fred yet that she was worried about Carol. She'd examined the child thoroughly and had turned up nothing, but it couldn't quiet Dorothy's fear that some malady was preparing to rear its ugly head.

By the time the heart was sputtering on the makeshift tramp's stove, the camp loudspeaker began to sputter to life.

"My friends, in a moment we'll begin our evening's entertainment, but first, a word from our host."

The loudspeaker crackled again and the harsh voice of the camp commandant, Mr. Kodaki, shattered the ears of internees in every corner of the camp. Speakers wired to trees throughout the campus made certain that no internee could miss any directives delivered by their Imperial guardians.

Dorothy groaned. "What infraction will he scold us about tonight, do you suppose?"

Fred chuckled. "Pay no mind, my dear. Life will go on as it has whether Kodaki likes it or not. If the Americans have made inroads in retaking the islands we'll get our ears boxed. If the Japanese have taken another flyspeck in the ocean, we'll get a treat on Sunday. Life will be as it always has been here, ruled by the Japanese tit for tat."

EXCERPT FROM MANILA GOODBYE BY ROBIN PRISING
© 1975 BY ROBIN PRISING. PP 120

No one could escape from the loudspeaker. It reached the farthest corners of the camp and governed our action through the day. At sunrise it would burst out as the needle struck the groove of a worn recording, often of a trio of girls crooning 'Good Morning', which played so loudly that the words were indistinct. Then, like the staccato rasps of Hitler played backwards, came the Nipponese blasting orders to their sentries. An American voice followed, a radio voice washed in soapsuds, bubbling with folksy familiarity as it gave us our orders for the day. At ten- or twenty-minute intervals the LOUDSPEAKER would switch suddenly on, ordering someone to report to the commandant's office, repeating the order, giving instructions to labor squads, repeating the instructions, paging doctors and telling mothers to fetch their children from begging the Japanese soldiers for food.

Apparently this time life had 'crossed a line' and Kodaki saw fit to punish the entire camp. As of this week the last Japanese food vendors would be banished from Santo Tomás.

The prospect of losing the Japanese vendors was met with mixed emotions. There would be no more of the coveted items like peanut butter. But those in camp who couldn't afford it anyway would never miss it. If only peanuts could be had, Dorothy could make her own peanut butter.

If only.

Kodaki's droning voice was finally silenced and the always-too-cheerful *Voice of the Philippines* Don Bell—whose real name was Clarence Alten Beliel, Sr.—took over the microphone.

Dorothy listened to his announcements with half an ear, then looked up with a start.

"F. C. Chambers? Who is that?"

"Me, darling. He must have misspoken, and meant to say F. R. Chambers. I've been elected by the camp parents' group to represent them on education matters in the Camp Committee."

"Oh that's grand, Fred. I'm not surprised they would look to you."

She smiled and reached for his hand. It felt odd beneath her own. Where flesh normally touched flesh, the hardness of bone was felt. When had that happened?

Their diet was woefully inadequate, but somehow the loss of flesh had simply happened outside the scope of her awareness. She looked at her own hand, surprised to see that it looked much the same. She looked at Bobby and Carol who played quietly at the edge of the blanket.

That is exactly what had been worrying her lately. They played quietly. *Quietly.* Bobby wasn't full of his fifty questions, and Carol had no urgent stories from school to relate.

"Fred, I think I should—"

"Shh! Did you hear that, Dorothy? Did you hear what Don just said?"

"No, I was just—"

"He said Reno, Dorothy. Reno! He asked if any of us have visited Reno and then said Reno was closer than we thought. Don't you see? It's code!"

Dorothy tried to make sense of what Fred was muttering below his breath, but it was just a bunch of nonsense. Was this another sign? Was the poor nutrition taking a mental toll that even she had not suspected? But Fred saw her confusion and hastened to explain with covert whispers.

"Reno, Dorothy. It's what MacArthur calls his plan for retaking the islands. Don Bell said 'Reno is closer than we think'. He means the Americans are closer than we think! Closer to retaking the islands!"

Fred's face glowed with understanding of what this might mean for them. MacArthur's plan was working. The Japanese had taken the islands in ninety days. And everyone knew the Americans could do things much, much faster than the Japanese.

Could it be true?

After two years of a confinement that was supposed to last only three months, Dorothy had refused to allow herself to contemplate liberation. While she had never given up hope, she had marshalled her thinking to expect many more months of privation. But now, with Fred's excited words, for the first time her mind expanded to allow the dream of liberation.

Please let it be true.

Scattered applause brought Dorothy back to the moment. The braised gravy was done cooling on the cookstove, and she was exhausted. She began to gather up her things, ready to trudge back to the Annex while Fred took care of the cooking paraphernalia. But a movement at the front of the *Little Theatre Under the Stars* captured her attention.

The Little Theatre was the camp's attempt to boost morale. Plays, small skits, and talent shows were chief among their offerings. But in recent weeks there had been fewer presentations. And the folks that had managed to make it to the stage showed less and less energy and more and more wariness. The edgy Japanese listened to every word of every script, even the lyrics of every song. Their misunderstandings were gargantuan, and more than one 'playwright' had been harshly dealt with because the commandant didn't understand irony, exaggeration, understatement, or the many interpretations of words like 'battle'.

Tonight a thin, willowy woman walked slowly across the crude outdoor stage, her violin tucked beneath one arm. She moved with the elegance of one who had made the same walk hundreds of times, in concert halls and opera houses, in lovely gowns to complement a tuxedoed orchestra behind her.

It was Mrs. Nash. Grace Nash. She'd brought her sick little boy to the hospital with a fever that had made even Dorothy fear that they might lose him. The poor woman had been distraught, beside herself with fear just a few weeks earlier. Now she gave her audience a decorous nod. Then, like an elegant ballerina, she tucked her violin beneath her chin, closed her eyes, and swept her bowing arm in a wide arc to hover an instant over the strings. Dorothy felt herself holding her breath as the tension built a moment longer, and then Grace lifted the tip of her instrument, almost as if it were taking a breath itself, and then plunged into an enthralling toss of taunting notes.

One note skidded into another, some impossibly high, others gliding to rich, low depths. Just as Dorothy felt the music was going to surge into its climactic notes, it dipped again, and Grace added more fever to the ripening scales before dropping to a sustained note. Her long fingers rocked the strings in a slow easy vibrato, and Dorothy found herself dreading the moment the sound would stop.

But when the moment came, the gifted violinist let it sail away with a quickening of her trembling wrist that spun the toppling final note out into the night. And with infinite delicacy, she tiptoed into the gypsy strain that was the joyous, mystical meat of the piece.

If the ringing prologue was its gemstone, this precocious dance was its heart, and Grace's eyes remained closed as she played. But her eyebrows danced their own expressive motif as she leaned and stretched her upper body through the haunting rigors of the piece.

It was as if every note extracted energy that Grace could not possibly afford to expend, and the sheer gift of exhausting herself in behalf of this audience's evening entertainment overwhelmed Dorothy. It became too much, and Dorothy silently begged her to stop. She strained toward the stage and implored the woman to cease, to save what small store of energy she had. Did she not know that she needed every ounce of it merely to survive?

But Grace played on, seeming to draw from some fortifying well that lived deep within the melody.

The music dipped into languid hollows and then taunted with a maddeningly slow progression toward the ripping tempo with which it raced toward its finale. It was not until Dorothy felt her own heart might burst that the woman drew from the instrument a final note. It wavered, spun, and then melted into the starry heavens, taking with it the fears of a people who had been robbed of their own music.

CHAPTER FIFTY-ONE

SWEET JESUS

The haunting core of the music stayed with Dorothy through the coming days. It breathed into her soul a promise that whatever effort was required of her, she would rise to the task.

Dearest Mother,

There are no words to describe captivity. It's akin to being suspended inside a heartbeat. For weeks. For months. And then something comes along that bumps that heartbeat into a steady stream of heartbeats. That opens eyes and restores smiles and makes life seem actually normal.

You never know when it will come, that bump that will jolt you out of the desperation that lives behind your eyes, carefully guarded. But you long for it in your sleep, in every minute of the day. You can't really put a name to it, or shape your want into terms that don't sound completely ridiculous if you voiced it out loud. But it's there.

Always.

Waiting.

Relief boxes from the American Red Cross provided that bump on December 17th of 1943.

~~~~~~

From Fred's memoir

Because the Japanese Imperial Army recognized no authority but its own power (Japan had not signed the Geneva Accord) they did not permit Red Cross supplies to be delivered to Santo Tomas.

369

However, a clerk in the Japanese headquarters in Manila, who was friendly to the USA, stacked some papers so the Commandant would sign them without realizing he had signed a permit to unload Red Cross Comfort Kit boxes in the Manila bodega for the Camp. Once signed, there could be no changing, so some of us were taken in trucks to the bodega and brought the supplies into Camp. They contained everything from food and cigarettes to sulfa drugs. There was considerable exchange of contents among the internees, some insisting on receiving their share of cigarettes, although they did not smoke, in order to exchange them for food. The most valuable outcome was that with an epidemic of measles and whooping cough, not a death resulted because of the sulfa treatment.

The comfort kits so long awaited were more than food and medicine. They were more than shoes and cigarettes. Not that long ago the boxes had sat in front of American workers. On American assembly lines. On American soil. Packaged and labeled by American hands.

Dorothy sat with her hands on the open box, making contact with home in the only way she could.

The contents of the box were safely stowed now. But the box still sat in a place of honor in their tiny cubicle. Carol made the box into a home for her dolly. Bobby crawled inside and turned it into a ship. Or a plane. When he took a nail and started to scratch pictures in the side of the box Carol stayed his hand.

"This is a special box, Bobby."

Dorothy had dealt for two days now with the aftermath of the wealth that arrived in those special boxes—the physical injury that occurred when internees squabbled with one another, claiming someone had stolen their tin of potted meat. Or that someone had swiped their tin of butter and replaced it with a smashed one. Or a starving internee who defended her relief box with fists even though she had willingly wagered it against the Japanese in the infamous baseball game. But mostly it was the painful indigestion, diarrhea, or bloating from having over-indulged in the contents of the box that Dorothy had to contend with in her patients.

When a person is on a path to starvation, pacing oneself can be the challenge of a lifetime. And it was a challenge that many internees lost and the children among them couldn't comprehend.

For Dorothy, the challenge was keeping her mind on her work instead of dreaming about the special treat she'd give her family to supplement that evening's meal. She'd never had this dilemma in her entire life. When she was on duty, her work had always fully occupied her attention. But now the distraction of food revealed a weakness she hadn't expected.

She smiled, thinking of the reverent way her children had unpacked the long-awaited box. Bobby and Carol had no idea what some of the items were. They'd never seen a whole cardboard canister of KLIM before. For them it was a sweet drink. For her it was a miracle drink. Sweet powdered milk packed with protein and Vitamin A and D. If she could bathe her family in it she would, so great was her belief that it was key to their survival. And Bobby couldn't wait to get his hands on the canister once it was empty. It was the most engaging 'toy' he'd seen in months.

Now that they had a whole canister, Dorothy's challenge was making it last as long as possible. If she mixed it quarter-strength it would last six months. Part of the ongoing dilemma was the two-and-a-half ounces of water allowed per child per day. That was certainly not enough to get any good quantity of KLIM into the children.

But there were ways around that particular stumbling block. KLIM could be mixed into the watery *lugao* of rice and weevils and talinum weeds and brought to a boil. If it wasn't boiled, the KLIM just stuck to the talinum leaves that floated on the surface of the sadly unpalatable soup. But once boiled into a bit of a mush with KLIM, the children quite liked it.

It was the people who drank the KLIM full strength that found their malnourished stomachs rebelling. If she paid good attention to it, she could give the children a good bit of nourishment every day for half a year. Bobby would just have to wait a good long time to get his hands on the empty container.

· · · ·

"Sweet Jesus, that was good."

A startled silence swept over the small family that crouched in a circle on the floor of the Chambers cubbyhole.

Dorothy, Fred and Carol turned as one and stared at Bobby as he licked the chocolate from his fingers, the sound of his inappropriate comment still ringing in their ears. Fred had judiciously rationed each family member one-half of one square of one of the chocolate bars the kit contained, and with great pomp and ceremony they'd each popped the small treat into their mouths on the count of three.

Too many in camp had already learned the hard way that these chocolate bars were packed with more than just good sweet chocolate. They were the D-ration bars, made to last a downed pilot several days, his only sustenance while waiting to be rescued. Eat them too fast, in one sitting, or even in one day, and misery knew no bounds. The groans coming from the restroom areas were clear and ominous testimony to that fact.

Sweet Jesus?

Dorothy darted a glance at Fred. Which one would field this bit of discipline? It was such a joy having something to celebrate. It had been months since anything like this had captured the enthusiasm of the camp, had fostered such an undercurrent of swapping and neighborly dickering, even though jealous hording was the primary reaction of the day.

Neither parent wanted to spoil this moment with a reprimand. But *Sweet Jesus*? That kind of language simply could not be overlooked.

"Robert Bruce Chambers, you watch your mouth!" Carol's little voice broke the silence, her scolding tone muted by her own smacking lips.

Bobby slapped both his hands over his mouth and raised his eyebrows, darting a wild-eyed look at his mother and father. Then confusion settled on his face and his hands fell away.

"What?" He looked at all three, then scrunched his scrawny shoulders. "What did I say?" His tone was incredulous. One could almost see his three-and-a-half-year-old mind replaying the last few moments and finding nothing that begged for a scolding. "What did I say?!"

"You said 'Sweet Jesus'!" Carol pointed her finger at her brother, saw a bit of errant chocolate there, and set about to lick her finger clean.

"Well, you just said it, Sissy, so you watch *your* mouth!"

"Did not!"

"Did too!"

"Did __"

"Hold on, now, you two." Fred's voice of authority squelched the squabble. Both children fell silent, hands dropped in their laps, faces suitably chagrined, awaiting judgment.

"Bobby, why did you say those words? Sweet Jesus?" He stared Bobby down, crinkling his brows a bit to soften the inquisition.

Bobby looked to his mother. Maybe, just maybe she was going to intercede for him. But Dorothy just lifted one eyebrow and cocked her head a bit as if to say 'Better speak up, son'.

"I'm waiting," Fred urged.

Bobby squirmed. He was in trouble and he didn't have a clue why. People said 'Sweet Jesus' all the time. Then realization dawned and he knew just how to fix it.

"Well, I meant, um, what I meant was...was..., 'Sweet Jesus, that was good. Amen!'"

Bobby's face brightened in victorious jubilation as he watched his mother and father sputter and spasm. For some reason his comment had reduced his parents to suspicious gurgling coughs.

At last his father managed a serious expression, gave him a swift lecture on the appropriate use of the Lord's name, and they folded their hands and bowed their heads to give thanks for this bounty that had come all the way from America. And in their prayer—underscored by rumbling tummies—they named each precious bit of food individually, rolling the words around on their tongues as if the words themselves were the appetizer.

> One pound can of KLIM powdered milk
> One pound can of oleo margarine
> Half-pound package of cube sugar
> Half-pound package of Kraft cheese
> Six-ounce package of K-ration biscuits
> Four-ounce can of coffee
> Two D-ration chocolate bars
> Six-ounce can of peanut butter
> Twelve-ounce can of salmon or tuna
> One-pound can of Spam or corned beef
> One-pound package of raisins or prunes
> Five packages of cigarettes
> Seven Vitamin-C tablets

Two bars of soap

Twelve ounces of C-ration vegetable soup concentrate

Dorothy picked up each item, feeling joy in the need to ask God's blessing on the bounty. How long could she make it last?

She would puree the Spam with a splash of carabao milk to make a paste and spread it on the bomber bread she would bake in the little tramp oven—if she could find some fuel to burn. It would go much farther that way. The coffee she would trade for powdered milk from someone else's box. The vegetable soup concentrate would show up in everything, bit by bit, adding unexpected flavor. Her mind clicked off the possibilities as she organized the little cache. She reached for the last item, the four-ounce tin of coffee that Fred had cradled to his chest. He resisted, his eyes beseeching her to let him hang on to it a moment longer.

"Fred," she whispered. "Don't."

His face fell. "Couldn't we just..."

"No!" She hadn't meant to be so sharp with him but for heaven's sake, he knew it had no nutritional value whatsoever. He knew there were those like him who craved it, who didn't have children to feed and would willingly give up their ration of powdered milk for it. He knew it. Why was he challenging her?

Rations had fallen dramatically again. Breakfast was a mere cup of thin, watery mush and a quarter cup of hot water. Lunch was served only to the children and very elderly internees. Supper was mush or sometimes mashed Philippine sweet potato. Never satisfying. Never rejuvenating. Never enough.

How hard it was each evening to lead the children in asking God's blessing on their food without railing silently at Him for letting her feel so helpless to fill her children's tummies.

She raised an eyebrow at Fred, then slowly cocked her head, her lips pressed tightly in disapproval.

With a heavy sigh, Fred handed over the precious tin. He'd embarrassed himself and he knew it.

Oh, how she would have loved to tear open that tin right now and brew him a cup of coffee. Oh, how she wanted to see that euphoric face he would make as he savored each sip. Oh, how she desperately wanted to make him smile.

Dorothy reached up a hand to cradle his face. She would make it up to him one day. When they got out of here. If they got out of here.

Dorothy composed her face, hoping that thought hadn't written itself too plainly in her eyes.

God would provide. God would give them the strength and courage to do the hard things that might ensure survival. She knew that. She did.

But today, even in the face of this unexpected bounty, it was becoming harder to feel such rock-solid assurance.

It was odd how easily thinking of another half year in captivity had infiltrated her thinking. For the first two years she'd felt every month would be the last. Surely they would be liberated soon.

But now some part of her had become resigned to the reality of their situation. MacArthur seemed no closer than when they'd celebrated his Reno victories on the lower islands. This would be their second Christmas since he'd uttered the famous words, "I shall return". It had become the rallying cry throughout all the islands. It was scrawled in the sand, painted on the sides of buildings throughout Manila, and even written upside down and backwards in chalk on a Santo Tomás classroom blackboard. It showed up less and less these days. Erased from the board now. Faded from the sand. But the message was not forgotten.

WORLD WAR II ONLINE DATABASE
C. PETER CHEN, FOUNDER AND EDITOR OF THE DATABASE

Though rather casually noted, "I shall return" became the powerful symbol which was the spiritual center of Filipino resistance. "It was scraped in the sands of the beaches, it was daubed on the walls of the barrios, it was stamped on the mail, it was whispered in the cloisters of the church", recalled MacArthur. "It became the battle cry of a great underground swell that no Japanese bayonet could still."

CHAPTER FIFTY-TWO

TOO RAW FOR WORDS

There were two things, besides her precious family, that Dorothy always found energy for. Looking after her dear little patients, and staying ahead of the bedbugs.

Today the smell of prune-pit vinegar was particularly strong in Dorothy's corner of the room, giving testimony to her ongoing battle against the minute beasts.

The last time she had treated her mattresses was early fall. It was nearly the new year, and time to do the job once again.

December 20th 1943. A day marked in history by banishing bedbugs.

It was a task that left her breathless and aching even though it was a simple matter of sprinkling vinegar on their mattresses and stuffing them with a certain bug-repelling weed that grew behind the hospital. Gathering weeds for personal use was forbidden and could have landed her in the women's jail every time she did it. But she'd always begun by gathering enough for the thin mattresses on the hospital cots. Once she and Nurse Noell had moved each patient and treated each mattress there always magically seemed to be enough left over for four more mattresses—hers, Carol and Bobby's shared bunk, Fred's cot, and Sue Noell's. It was something they did every few months.

Like clockwork.

They would sneeze for three nights, but there would be no bedbugs in the Chambers bunkbed. She would need to remind Fred that it was time to treat his cot. She'd used all the prune-pit vinegar, though. He'd have to fend for himself on that part of the venture. But she'd saved a small bundle of weeds just for him.

She knew he'd appreciate that. Maybe she'd even get a wink out of the gloomy-gus today. He'd been blue about something for nearly a week. Or maybe agitated was a better word for it. Now that she had a bit of time she went in search of him.

"Ah. There you are."

Fred hailed her from his perch in front of the hospital where he often waited if she didn't join him in the chow shed for breakfast. He was going for something cheerful, but fell woefully short.

"Good morning, darling. I have a present for you!" She softened her smile, conscious that she was trying a bit too hard. But the look on his face had her worried.

Fred rose, and lifted his hand in greeting. But before dropping it to his side, he kissed his extended fingers and then waggled them at her. It had become habit once they'd discovered a public peck on the cheek was going to get them a disciplinary warning.

His smile seemed tentative and an unmistakable air of sadness about him sent up small warning signals to Dorothy.

"What's wrong?"

Fred put a hand beneath her elbow and ushered her around the corner of the hospital to sit on a pile of stones.

She waited for him to speak, and though he tried several times he couldn't seem to dredge up words. Each time he opened his mouth and closed it without speaking, his emotions plummeted further toward desolation.

He dropped his elbows to his knees and pressed his palms into his eyes.

"You're scaring me, Fred. What's happened?" Dorothy dropped the bag of weeds and put a hand on his arm.

He drew a breath, but no words came.

"Someone died." She said it softly, so softly that it barely registered in her own ears.

He nodded.

"Here? In camp?"

He shook his head.

"Then—" Her hand flew to cover her mouth. Fred didn't react to death in this fashion. His deep faith served him well in finding the peace that follows pain and death.

But not today.

If it was someone outside of camp whose death had moved Fred so deeply, then it could only be one of their missionary group—someone from the group hiding out in the hills...in Hopevale.

A tear slipped from her eye. Those who went into the hills were as young and vital, full of life as Fred and Dorothy had been two-and-a-half years earlier. Even the oldest were hale and hearty. And the children—

"Oh Fred!" she choked. "Not one of the children!"

He nodded and tried to stifle a cry that breached his throat in a strangled moan.

Dorothy grabbed his arm with both her hands. "Tell me who!"

Fred sat up straight, uttered a horrid gasp, and collapsed with his head in her lap. "All of them, Dorothy," he choked. "All of them!"

. . . .

As Fred became able to relate his news, sorrow drained all color from her world. The bamboo telegraph was rarely wrong. Rumor running rampant through camp could never be trusted. But this had come to Fred directly from a trusted source who had received the dire news from the guerillas.

It was unspeakable. Too raw for words.

The Japanese army had been led to Hopevale by a downed pilot the missionaries had previously harbored. The Imperial officer had promised the pilot that none of the missionaries would be harmed. He just wanted to question them. But once they reached Hopevale, everything fell apart. The pilot had twenty-four hours to grieve his failure to protect the men, women and children of Hopevale before he shared their fate.

The knowledge of it splintered Dorothy's conviction that her own children would be safe here in Santo Tomás. The Japanese liked the children. Most of them had children at home they were sorely missing. If they chose to show kindness, it was often toward the children.

But the Hopevale tragedy revised Dorothy's thinking. She would have to make a plan. A plan with a place where Bobby and Carol would be safe if things turned treacherous.

A True Post-War Account
AS TOLD IN A MILITARY HEARING

Iloilo City 1945

I, Paterno M. Eñano, 23, Buena Vista, Iloilo province, Panay, Philippine Islands, was employed by the Imperial Japanese army as an interpreter beginning Nov. 1, 1943 and ending April 19, 1944. I escaped from the Japanese garrison in Miagao, Iloilo province, Panay, after I had killed with a bayonet one Japanese soldier and overcome another Japanese soldier. I suffered one wound on the right arm above the elbow and one wound on the left arm near the wrist, both as a result of bayonet thrusts. I volunteered for Filipino guerrilla forces in the mountains and was accepted. I was promoted to sergeant Aug. 15, 1944, a rank which I still hold.

Above 9 a.m. on Saturday, Dec. 18, 1943, I left the township of Libacao, Capiz province, with a Japanese force estimated at 500, including officers and enlisted men, under command of Capt. Watanabe to proceed to Iloilo city. Next morning by walking through the mountains we reached the American camp, Hopevale, three kilometers west of Katipunan.

About 9 a.m. Capt Watanabe ordered that the American camp be searched for Americans believed to be hiding. A Filipino mountaineer whom the Japanese had captured the previous day told Capt. Watanabe that Americans were living near Katipunan. The mountaineer, a civilian, had no connection, as far as I know, with any military organization whatever. The Japanese threatened the mountaineer with his life if he refused to talk.

Approximately 250 Japanese soldiers surrounded the camp, while the remaining Japanese force, including Capt. Watanabe, entered the American camp proper. Japanese soldiers captured 16 Americans, most of whom they found in their homes. The Japanese collected the Americans, took them to a house one-half kilometer southward, where the prisoners were placed under guard and kept until the next day. Japanese soldiers confiscated canned goods owned by the

Americans. They gave the Americans neither food or water.

The Japanese previously had captured three other Americans, including Lt. Robert King of Iloilo city and two others, probably engineers, who I couldn't identify. These men also were placed under guard in the house.

I knew most of the 16 Americans captured in their camp near Katipunan. I remembered them as being on the faculty of Central Philippine college, which I had attended before the Japanese invaded Panay.

About 3 p.m. the Japanese escorted 12 of the Americans, one by one, from the prison house to the house in which I was staying at the time. Mrs. Covell was the first person escorted to the house. I was standing an estimated five meters from Mrs. Covell and Capt. Watanabe. I heard Mrs. Covell beg Capt. Watanabe for mercy. She said in Japanese, "Capt. Watanabe, why you kill us all. We are Christian missionaries." Capt. Watanabe smiled, said nothing.

I saw Capt. Watanabe draw his sumarai sword, and Japanese guards stand by with bayonets fixed. Then, I turned my head. I couldn't bear to watch it. Mrs. Covell screamed. I walked from the house until I could hear no more. The remaining 11 Americans were brought into the house - one by one.

Although I didn't see the execution with my own eyes, I am positive beyond a doubt that Capt. Watanabe beheaded with his sword 10 of the 19 Americans. Capt. Watanabe was the only Japanese in our party who possessed a sword. Japanese soldiers bayoneted the two Clardy sons rather than cut off their heads. The other seven Americans were killed elsewhere in the vicinity.

I returned to the house - scene of the execution - an hour later, about 5 p.m. The house already was in flames. Bodies of the Americans burning inside could not be seen through the smoke and flames. After the roof had fallen in and the house reduced to ashes, I looked carefully amid the ruins. The odor of burning flesh was strong. I noticed particularly that none of the heads of the American men and women, 10 of them, were attached to the bodies. But heads of the two children were still on the bodies.

It is my belief that Capt. Watanabe is solely responsible for the death of these 19 Americans. I believe he killed 10 of them with his own hands. Japanese soldiers, perhaps, bayoneted the two boys. I do not know who killed the other seven, but I know they were killed.

It was the policy of the Japanese army at that time here that Americans found hiding in the mountains would be captured only. None were to be killed without orders from officers.

Paterno H. Eñano

Signed before me the 4th day of June, 1945
R. Fred Chambers
President, Central Philippine College
Sgt. John Garland Smith
Press Relations Office
49th Infantry Division
APO 46 c/o Postmaster San Francisco, California

Missionaries Lost in Hopevale
Miss Jennie Clare Adams, nurse, Nebraska
Professor James Howard Covell and Mrs. Charma Moore Covell
Miss Dorothy Antoinette Dowell
Miss Signe Amelia Erickson
Rev. Erle Frederich Rounds, Mrs. Louise Cummings Rounds and
      son Erle Douglas Rounds
Dr. Francis Howard Rose and Mrs. Gertrude Coombs Rose
Dr. Frederick Willer-Meyer and Mrs. Ruth Schacht Meyer

Other Americans killed at Hopevale:
Mr. Mark Walsh Clardy, Mrs. Fern Clardy and sons Johnny and Terry
Lt. Robert King

HOPEVALE

Dorothy stumbled from behind the hospital, then slipped across to a little-used path. She couldn't go into the hospital. Not now. Not yet. They would see her distress. They would ask questions.

They would know.

And if the Japanese suspected Fred had been in contact with guerillas—

She prayed he'd be careful. He could tell no one. Not the other missionaries in the group. Not anybody. One careless word and he—and the person he spoke to—could be singled out for retribution by the Japanese.

It was all too much to carry. Her heart couldn't bear it.

Dorothy knelt in what they'd come to know as the Fathers' Garden. This part of the Dominican seminary—though part of the campus—was technically out-of-bounds. But she needed a moment. A moment to grieve for those dear people.

Their names scrolled through her prayer as she sought to memorialize her lost companions. She lingered in sorrow over Howard and Charma Covell, friends who had shared their home, eaten at their table, supported Fred in his work at the college. Their own children were grown and scattered at boarding school and university. Safe, she hoped, perhaps not yet knowing of their terrible loss.

Images of their smiling faces fused with the faces of the others lost in the Hopevale massacre. Jennie Adams—a young nurse from Nebraska—Dorothy Dowell, Signe Erickson, Francis and Gertrude Rose, Ruth and Fred Meyer.

She prayed harder. The faces that tore wrenching sobs from her were the families. Fred and Louise Rounds and young Erle. Mark and Fern Clardy and little Johnny and Terry. Such wonderful little boys.

It was too much. Too much. She couldn't bear it. Each time she looked at Bobby and Carol she would see those sweet children playing together, their carefree laughter lost forever to the horror of this wretched time.

The loss. The loss. It weighed so heavily, dragged her spirit to a depth she'd never experienced, and threatened to hold her there. For the sake of her sanity she had to shrug off the brutal malaise that sought to destroy her will. She had to press on.

Press on. Those were the words that at last nudged Dorothy to her feet. She would carry the names in her heart today and every day.

But for now she would merely press on. And pray no one found out Fred had brought her this devastating news.

HOPEVALE MONUMENT

SIEBE FELDMAN

At the outset of the war, missionary Siebe Feldman returned to the United States on furlough, taking two of the Covell children with him, unknowingly saving them from their parents' fate. It was Siebe's Radiola that Dorothy and Fred listened to in Calinog, just days before they were taken by the Japanese.

CHAPTER FIFTY-THREE

THE GHOST OF CHRISTMAS PAST
CHRISTMAS 1943

In Dorothy's experience, deep within the human spirit that has been bruised and bent in the most cruel ways is the capacity to love. So it was no surprise that for many of the souls chasing survival in Santo Tomás, the Christmas Season offered an opportunity to fan that tenuous flicker of love.

December of 1943 found much of the camp involved in some sort of Christmas preparation. Wives knitted string socks for their husbands. Women made rag dolls and men fashioned small trucks and cars—all to be distributed to the camp's four hundred children.

Each toy was made by way of sacrifice. The legs of one internee's favorite chair were cut short and the pieces yielded wheels for twelve small cars and trucks and planes. Women sacrificed blouses that were being saved for liberation day, each providing enough fabric for about four small dolls. Partially-used cosmetics were packaged for the teen-aged girls, tied prettily with hair ribbons tenderly washed and pressed between the sheet and mattress of an internee's bed.

Carol was thrilled to be on the Children's Inter-Camp Mail Service for Christmas Day. For weeks she'd been counting down the days until she could go about the camp—accompanied by an adult—and distribute greeting cards. The adults on the committee would have completed nearly four thousand Christmas cards to be distributed personally to each internee by smiling children. Just like her.

For most internees, days were essentially repeats of the day before. Work assignments were carefully scheduled so that for the most part they shared the burden equally. One might be scraping camotes in the kitchen, another might be scrubbing up a toilet or handing out toilet paper, while yet another burned trash. These jobs might rotate week to week.

MEMORY FROM CHILD INTERNEE
SASCHA JEAN WEINZHEIMER JANSEN
100 MILES TO FREEDOM BY ROBERT B. HOLLAND PG 145

One of the men we called "the exterminator" because his job was to keep track of rats. He was diligent in his duties until the prisoners ate the rats. Earlier, we had garbage, but later on there was no garbage because we were *eating the garbage!*

Consequently, those who were inclined to help with the Christmas preparations had energy and time left to do so after completing their assigned tasks about the camp.

Dorothy had no such definition to her daily work. The special card she carried in her pocket allowed her to be on the grounds after curfew, if she was answering a medical emergency or taking night duty in the children's ward.

She would slip through the blackness, savoring the small breezes that would never quite reach the sleeping quarters. The rest of the world rested behind blackout shades, so with conscious effort she would lift her shoulders and lighten her step so as not to waken anyone.

SANTO TOMAS INTERNMENT CAMP
NO. 219
DATE Feb. 8, 1944 SPECIAL PASS

DR. D. K. Chambers   ROOM NO. Annex
IN THE EXECUTION OF HIS DUTIES AS Doctor
                    IS AUTHORIZED TO be out
of her building any time day or night

                    Valid Until Revoked
Dept. of Patrols   THE EXECUTIVE COMMITTEE

BY _____ BY _____
C. E. LIVINGSTON   W. A. CHITTICK

Everything about Santo Tomás was different at night. Nobody stopped her in the middle of the path to press a medical complaint. The clattering sounds of the camp were replaced by the soft call of night birds and the whisper of the large banana leaves as she passed by.

These silent passages in the dead of night offered the only time that Dorothy could draw within herself, to meditate. To ponder. To breathe. Still, some small part of her would always remain on guard against shots that might ring out in the night. And they did. The next morning she'd hear all about it. She wore her white coat like a shield against some weary Japanese guard who might suspect she was violating curfew or undertaking some nefarious errand.

It was fruitless to keep track of her hours spent in the pursuit of healing. Whether it came to a forbidding number or not, she would endure them.

But it was more than enduring the work. For Dorothy it was *embracing* the work. She had asked God to make her an instrument of His peace, and He had given her healing hands.

Nobody had to tally her hours. Nobody had to watch to make certain she contributed her full four hours to the camp's welfare. There would have been no need for such monitoring.

~~~~~~~~~~~~~~~~~~~~~~~~~~~~~~~~~~~~

From Fred's memoir

...some who seemed to have a purpose to help others, although they themselves were starved to the point of invalidism, gathered or tapped unrealized sources of strength. This was true of Mrs. Chambers who continued to give medical help to any and all who called on her. She started out with heavy step but returned with a spring in her step.

.... never during the internment did she seem to lack the necessary strength to carry on. On the night the camp was taken over by American troops, she, with other doctors and nurses, was on duty for hours without experiencing loss of strength to do what needed to be done.

So, on Christmas Eve of 1943—615 days into captivity—it was not quite midnight when Dorothy tumbled into bed. She harbored a fleeting moment of jealousy that it was Jeanne who had taken the children to the Christmas Eve gathering. Perhaps taking the children to the event herself might have rejuvenated her. But her patients had to come first. There were no two ways about it.

Her head pounded from the day's demands. All she wanted to do was put her head on the pillow. But tomorrow was Christmas, and she had one more task before she could rest.

In her heart of hearts Dorothy knew that her little family suffered dearly for lack of her attention. Though never intentional, it was always regrettable, merely the insidious byproduct of being the loved ones of a woman whose unique skills demanded that she spend large parts of her day in service to others.

But for the next few moments, Dorothy would resist her pillow long enough to do something about that.

From beneath the pillow that so wickedly beckoned she retrieved the small rag she had selected earlier from her wash line. It was threadbare, badly raveled, and long ago bleached of any color it might have had. She held it up in the darkness, looking for some sign of its former self. Had this been one of Carol's sundresses? One of her own camisoles? She turned it this way and that, searching, her fingers willing themselves to recognize the scrap.

It seemed important, necessary, to identify it. She'd brought so few things into the camp, how was it possible not to recognize every thread of every ragged garment?

She rolled it lazily over, barely feeling its thin presence against her slender fingers.

"Whatever you were, little rag," she smiled, "it didn't hold a candle to what you shall become."

· · · ·

Dorothy threaded the last string through the placket of the little bag she was fashioning and tied it off. The drawstring worked perfectly. The two little cloth bags she'd just made out of the ravaged camisole would hold her Christmas presents to the children. On the smaller one she embroidered a small dinosaur before placing inside it the three marbles she'd been saving for Bobby's marble collection. On the larger one she embroidered a cheerful elephant, then placed within it three hair bows and one doll dress for Carol's baby doll Pippa.

It was such meager bounty, but she knew the gifts would bring the smiles she anticipated. They were her dearest darlings, never failing to show their appreciation for any small pleasure.

Carol surely had dim recollections of the joyful Christmas of 1941, when her little voice filled their home with the Christmas carols she was learning to love. It was that Christmas when she'd received her precious Pippa, her toy piano, and so many other small treasures that now seemed like an incredible extravagance.

But Bobby. Dear little Bobby. He'd turned two years old just a few weeks after Pearl Harbor. That Christmas of '42 had been a bit less bountiful, though it lacked for nothing in the joy and delight his little family had taken in celebrating the season. But he remembered none of it.

Christmas in captivity, with its restrictions and deprivations, with its lack of color and cheer, was the only kind of Christmas he knew. Everyone here over the age of four or five had known at least one traditional Christmas, and could draw those memories as a framework for celebrating. In their mind's eye they saw the festive colors, envisioned the table laden with favorite foods to be savored, the glorious music, the joyful greetings and candlelight services in grand churches decorated with holly and wreaths.

But Bobby had none of that. The little palette of his mind was clean, fresh, and was being imprinted daily with the drab, meager existence, with the colorless, lackluster semblance of what a Christmas celebration should be.

Dorothy was aware that half the camp had been going through the motions for some weeks now, making sure the children had a Christmas celebration. But for many adults, it was somewhat of a necessary bit of play-acting. One could never say there was an abundance of Christmas cheer in the camp, however there was most definitely a wealth of gratitude among the grown-ups. Gratitude to see another Christmas.

But the actual words, the phrase that could always lift hearts and bring smiles to faces—the words that could always ignite a bit of joy in the soul—were glaring in their absence on this second Christmas in captivity. No one could say it. No one could think it. That simple phrase would be the greatest lie anyone could tell. And so the words just weren't spoken.

Perhaps next year they would return to people's lips.

Perhaps next year the words would spring from their hearts.

But tonight as she looped the Christmas surprises over the bunk's posts and peered at her two sleeping angels, Dorothy wept for the words that simply could not be said. *Merry Christmas.*

JAPANESE PROPAGANDA PHOTO TAKEN OF
CAROL AND BOBBY - CHRISTMAS 1943

• • • •

"Of course, you're going. We're all going. Now on your feet, darling girl."

Dorothy groaned. "Fred, please. Just a few more minutes." She yawned heavily and shifted the weight off her right hip that hadn't stopped burning while she tried to nap.

Bobby threw a pile of mosquito netting over her so he could scramble under the bunk for his marbles that seemed to perpetually roll that direction.

Her Christmas gifts had been a success. Carol sat at the end of the bunk trying out the three new bows on her dollie.

"You have to wear this one, Pippa," Carol scolded. "It's Christmas. And this one is red." She carefully stowed the two other bows in the little washed out bag.

"See there? Even Pippa's getting dressed for the party. Now you, too, Dorothy. Up and at 'em."

Fred gave her a gentle tug, and it was enough to set her upright.

They'd had the loveliest little celebration this morning. Fred had arrived with gifts of his own and warmed her heart with his orchestration of their Christmas sharing.

Now he was insisting they go as a family to the Camp celebration. Of course she would go. But nothing could compare to watching her dear husband work the story of the first Christmas into their morning, using Bible verses and family singing to prolong the anticipation of gifts. It had been the best possible Christmas under the circumstances.

Dorothy had taken special care dressing, arranging her hair in a more elaborate style and fashioning a rosette from a handkerchief to perch in her hair. Now all she had to do was freshen it up a bit and she would be ready.

Minutes later they walked hand-in-hand out the Annex door and followed the crowd of families to the intersection of Bodega and Annex road. A fully decorated Christmas tree had been placed in the center, its branches laden with handmade ornaments tied on with patchwork bows.

They stopped, unable to simply walk with the flow of people past the tree. It seemed a radiant gift meant for them personally, a promise that Christmas could be extravagantly beautiful in the most humble of circumstances.

"This one's a little bigger than your Chrissen Tree, isn't it, Carol Joy?" Fred asked.

Dorothy looked at him, then down at their daughter, just in time to see the smile spread across her face.

"It's beautiful, Daddy. Sooooo beautiful." She folded her arms and looked toward the angel at the top of the tree. "I think if our Chrissen Tree went to Heaven, then maybe it could have turned into a great, tall tree like this one." Then her eyes flew wide and she gasped. "Maybe! Oh, maybe! Could this be our tree come down from Heaven to be here for us?"

She looked to Dorothy and Fred with wonder in her eyes, and they knelt to draw Carol and Bobby into a hug. There were all sorts of answers they could have had for their imaginative daughter. But none that could be voiced over the tears in their throats. How else could a six-year-old expect something so beautiful to have arrived in the middle of this deprived community, if not sent down from Heaven?

As the crowd thickened, they were forced to move along, certain nothing could make this Christmas day more perfect.

Until they stepped around to the other side of the tree.

The whole plaza ahead of them had been taken over by several dozen plank tables radiating out from the tree. And each table was piled high with the gifts handmade by the craftsmen and craftswomen who'd labored in secret for weeks.

At each table an elf began distributing gifts.

Trains, hobby horses, kiddy kars, scooters, metal and wooden boats, jig-saw puzzles, rulers, stilts—all were joyfully received and immediately put to use by the four hundred children of Santo Tomás.

The pleasure of it all brought spikes of pain to Dorothy's heart. It was nearly too much, seeing this outpouring of Christmas generosity. People who she knew had no children of their own sought out children who'd received the gifts they'd made in their secret toy shop. The joy and love on their faces brought excruciating delight.

But it was the words they had for each child they hugged that brought Dorothy to scarcely controlled tears. There was no hope of keeping the salt inside when she heard them.

Over and over.

Honest. Sincere. Heartfelt.

The words she'd longed to hear.

Merry Christmas.

BACK VIEW OF SANTO TOMÁS EDUCATION BUILDING
SHOWS SHANTIES, GARDEN, AND LATRINES.
PHOTO FROM COLLECTION OF ROBIN PRISING, AUTHOR OF "MANILA GOODBYE"

CHAPTER FIFTY-FOUR

DESCENT

While it was unlike Dorothy to doubt MacArthur's word, she was slowly becoming convinced that the lauded general had met his match. Each new sunrise found her memory of the hope his rallying cry had engendered long ago fading further and further.

As the days passed it became a mounting mystery to Dorothy how time could manage to slip by without her noticing, accumulating weeks in the blink of an eye. In her mind, the new year had barely begun. But her makeshift calendar on the wall said otherwise. There were always too many patients and too little energy. Too many daily living chores and too little energy. Too much need to spend time with Carol and Bobby and Fred. And too little energy. But at least she was with her little family. That was a blessing that some might never know again.

SANTO TOMÁS INTERNMENT CAMP
LIMITED PRIVATE EDITION - FREDERIC H. STEVENS
© 1946 - PAGE 62-63

On February 27, 1944, four internees—S. R. Barnett, J. H. Blair, E. T. Ellis, and Everett B. Harris—the first three living with their wives and families in Camp and the last an elderly man, were taken into custody and removed from Santo Tomás Internment Camp, by the Japanese Military authorities. A few days earlier these four men had been questioned about bringing news into Camp. In the course of this questioning, Mr. Blair had been so badly beaten that he required hospitalization. A day or two later another internee—Earl

H. Hornbostel—was also removed from Camp. Neither the Internee Committee nor the families of these men were informed as to the reason for the arrest. The Internee Agents wrote the Commandant on March 9th requesting him to use his kind offices in obtaining information on this matter, but no reply was received to their letter. They wrote again on April 14th invoking the provisions of the Geneva Convention of 1929. There was no reply to this second letter. A stone wall, a grave, could not have been more silent. These men seemed to have disappeared from the face of the earth.

Some time afterwards—on May 25th—the Camp was notified that E. B. Harris had died at San Lazaro Hospital on May 9, 1944. On August 3rd, news was officially received in Camp that the four surviving internees had received sentences for imprisonment as follows: E. T. Ellis, four years; S. R. Barnett, J. H. Blair, Earl H. Hornbostel, three years. These sentences were to start July 1, 1944.

The whereabouts of these four internees was not definitely discovered until the Arrival of the U. S. Forces of Liberation. They were found by guerilla troops in the insular prison at Muntinglupa, weak, emaciated, at the point of death. Months of suffering, both physical and mental, had been their lot. They had finally been condemned to death and the firing squad had already set the date for the horrible orgy. Had the rescue been delayed for only a day or two longer, they would undoubtedly have been executed.

Their offense? Bringing news of American victories into Camp and thus making it harder for the Japanese Imperial Army to win the war.

· · · ·

CLOSE VIEW OF SHANTIES ON THE BACK SIDE OF SANTO TOMÁS CAMP.
Much of the life-saving food and morale-boosting information from
loyal Filipinos came into the camp over this wall.
PHOTO COURTESY OF JOHN TEWELL

An inglorious spate of rain greeted the spring of 1944. One day stretched into the next, one catastrophe narrowly averted before yet another descended upon the small hospital and clinic Dorothy managed. She was both physician and director of the children's hospital now, which meant not only tending to her patients but having her skill at diplomacy tested daily.

She hadn't the energy for it any more, and yet she could never allow herself to abandon her duties. One hundred forty-one cases of measles, three cases of diphtheria, forty-two cases of bacillary dysentery and sixty-two cases of asthma had been reported in camp for March.

This particular morning had been unexpectedly harried as more and more patients began to turn up with symptoms of whooping cough. They'd no sooner seen a decline in the measles epidemic than the signs of pertussis began to appear. An alarming statistic had been bandied about in the monthly meeting of the medical professionals at Santo Tomás. It seemed that when pertussis patients were living in a barracks situation, a death rate of 15% to 35% could be expected.

How much higher would the toll be if those patients were children? Might they lose between sixty and one hundred-forty children? Unfathomable. She would not let that happen. The isolation procedures she'd put in place had to work. Stoic parents of the little patients agreed to boil the family's clothes and bedclothes, even though a number of the most threadbare items might disintegrate in the process. If she could just round up some more sulfa, it seemed that the villainous whooping cough might just have met its match. But first she had to address the very sick child she'd just sat with through the night.

Dorothy scanned the small darkened ward beyond the bed of little Eirik Solden. His temperature of 105° was not abating. So far a diagnosis had eluded her. For three days she'd been battling his fever, bathing him with cool water laced with alcohol. His glands were terribly swollen, but there were no signs of inflamed or infected tonsils. It was frustrating not to know what was going on in his small, fever-ravaged body.

This scrawny four-year-old was losing even more weight daily. Ounce by ounce his ability to survive was slipping away. Something had to be done or she would lose him. Her three previous checks of the little boy's throat had shown no evidence of infected tonsils. Yet she knew that infection lay at the root of the boy's malady. But where?

She sat by his bed, one hand cooling his brow and the other paging through a thick, well-worn medical book. As always, she was drawn to the illustrations and very nearly turned the page. But two words caught her eye.

Hooded tonsils.

Could it be? She'd never seen a case. But the enlarged lymph nodes behind his jaw were tender to the touch, and other signs were consistent. The tonsils could be infected even though they showed no outward sign.

Now she knew what to do. He needed a tonsillectomy. But that would be impossible until the child's overall health improved. In short, surgery right now would kill the child.

Eager to build the child up quickly, and to raise his blood coagulation to a level that would allow him to survive a surgery, Dorothy summoned Nurse Noell.

"Keep him cool until I get back."

"Where are you—"

"I'm going for a cocktail!"

Dorothy succumbed to giddy relief as she hurried off to the supply room. Noell most likely thought she'd flipped her noggin. But she hadn't. She'd never been more clear about anything.

It took her an agonizing three hours to collect what she needed. Dr. Waters had a bottle of calcium powder; Jeanne had one package of gelatin and knew where she could get two more; and Dorothy had a bottle of iron tonic in her bag.

For two weeks she plied the boy with extra milk and her tonic cocktail. But at the end of the two weeks Eirik's lab test still showed his blood coagulation to be deficient. Anyone could see that the boy was rallying, but until the coagulation level improved just a bit more, no doctor would expect the child to come through surgery.

For one more week she continued the protocol, then held her breath until the lab results came back. And when they did, the boy's mother collapsed in a puddle of tears, clutching Dorothy's hands and whispering, "Bless you! Bless you!"

It seemed half the camp knew when the boy was taken out of the camp for surgery. They stopped her in the halls, found her in the chow line, just to ask about the little boy they thought was going to die. The first child the camp would lose. But Dorothy would not allow their gloomy prognoses. At every turn she silenced them, reproved them for giving up so easily on the boy.

It was with the greatest relief that she was able to report three days later that the tonsils had come out, filled with poison.

And the boy survived.

· · · ·

Once Eirik was stabilized and out of the woods, Dorothy found renewed energy to deal with the pertussis.

She breezed past the medicine cupboard and took quick stock of the sulfa supply. If more whooping cough patients were admitted they'd be in trouble. There was barely enough on the shelves to keep up the current doses for the children already hospitalized. In their seven hundred seventy days of captivity, Dorothy had not lost a single child. But without sulfa, they could come perilously close to that 15% to 35% mortality rate everyone dreaded.

The supply of sulfa powder that had arrived on the mercy ship *Teia Maru* a year ago was nearly gone. But the heroic camp committee always managed to scrape up medical supplies when the need was greatest. And they knew that sulfa was their only hope of escaping a morbid outcome.

Camp scuttlebutt had it that a supply of sulfa had been brought into the camp just the night before. If true, it was God's timing at its best. But how long before the commandant would release it to the hospital? Any slight infraction of the half million rules he'd imposed on the camp might encourage him to withhold whatever he thought was most needed in camp. And the most needed thing right now was sulfa.

Once it was released to the camp, it still had to be pressed into pill form.

She was at the door about to leave, the sulfa dilemma uppermost on her mind, when a low whistling sound stopped her. She turned in time to see Jeanne Travay's younger brother entertaining one of her little patients.

"Goodness, Saul, I was just leaving. Everything okay with you?"

"Hunkee-doree, Doc."

Dorothy smiled, noting the small bundle he was tossing up and down. He caught it easily behind his back, then tossed it again, though this time he had to fumble for it.

The children loved it. Saul came up breathless.

He was an understandably scrawny fourteen-year-old with a winning smile. He lobbed the package one more time, raising his arm high enough that his shirt exposed some angry purple marks marching up his bony rib cage.

"Hold on there, Saul. Those are some nasty bruises."

His smile turned sheepish. "Oh they're fine, Doc. Not to worry."

Something in his tone told her there was a story behind his cavalier dismissal.

"Out with it, young man. Did you fall?"

Saul stopped tossing the small package and held it out to her, clearly intending to change the subject. "These are for you, Doc. Sulfa pills. Not a full supply but I thought you'd want what we produced last night. Soon as the Japs released it we pulled a shift together to press 'em."

The medicines received in camp came in their raw, lumpy powder form. Saul had evidently worked a shift grinding the powder to its finest form with mortar and pestle, then hovered over the ancient copper pill press to produce the round tablets. No wonder the boy looked weary.

He dropped the packet on the desk beside her.

"Well, you certainly didn't get those bruises punching pills, did you."

"Nah. Had a little dust-up with a guard last night."

"You were out after curfew?"

"Had a pass, though. All on the up-and-up. Makin' the pills for ya."

"Well then?"

"Guard didn't like it that I snagged a handful of turnips from the Jap stores on my way home, dontcha know."

"He caught you stealing? Saul! You could be—"

He grinned. "Yeah, but I'm not. Ernest Stanley came along and saved my bacon." Earnest Stanley was a translator on the Camp Committee. He spent so much time with their captors that some internees liked to call into question his loyalty. But those who knew the information he reaped from those informal chats with the Imperial Army understood how very valuable his hours among the Japanese soldiers truly were.

"But the bruises?"

"Ah," he sighed. "Knocked myself into a stack of crates when that Jap guard jumped out at me with his bayonet. I think I woke him up. Scared the willies outta me."

Dorothy shuddered at the thought of where Saul might be this morning if Stanley hadn't come to his rescue. Whatever the British translator was doing out late at night was certainly good fortune for young Saul. It was God's good timing all over again.

The boy saluted and ambled out the side door. But something about the rhythm of his exit was wrong. His shuffling gait surprised Dorothy. The boy was always on the run. But today he walked. As if he weren't in any hurry. As if he *couldn't* hurry.

Dorothy called him back.

"Up on the exam table, young man," she ordered. He made a good stab at grumbling but gave in too easily. If she was reading him right, he *wanted* her to examine him.

She kept up an easy banter with the boy as her fingers traveled across his bruises. They were deep, but the damage beneath wasn't critical, and to her relief she detected no internal bleeding. And no cracked ribs.

Dorothy covered the worst of Saul's bruises with a poultice of brown paper soaked in hot sambong vinegar. It seemed to bring the boy measurable relief.

He and the other teens who liked to work the pill press had done her a huge service by working a night shift. But it was just too risky for them to be out at night. She would talk to his sister about his night's escapade as soon as she had the chance. Jeanne was worth her weight in gold, and Dorothy would return the girl's loyalty by looking after her brother.

• • • •

Jeanne Travay had become one of the stabilizing cogs that kept Dorothy's world working. She washed the children's clothes so Dorothy only had to look after her own and Fred's. She found a ball of string so Dorothy could knit new underclothes for Carol and Bobby. Each week she came up with some small morsel that gave the children a meager addition to the horribly deficient line chow.

She had even introduced Dorothy to a woman who owned a washing machine and made it her personal mission to clean the rags that women had to use when "Aunt Flo" made her monthly visit. It was an act of kindness that meant more to these women than any could express.

But recently, many of the women had stopped visiting the kindly woman who laundered their bloodied rags. They needed fewer and fewer of her pristine, boiled, cleaned, folded and freshly stuffed rags as two years of malnutrition gradually robbed their bodies of that natural cycle.

For Dorothy, the day she no longer needed to visit the rag basket came and went with little notice. If she insisted on answering the call of her little patients at all hours of the day and night, her malnourished body would simply do what it had to do. It began shutting down unnecessary functions.

The fatigue she was feeling now intruded upon everything. It slowed her down, made her think twice, double checking every decision. Fatigue made every chore take longer.

Dearest Mother,

I'm whingy (whin-gee) today. That's what my British friends call it.

Means whiny. Please don't think badly of me, but I've been whining a lot lately. Maybe not out loud. At least I hope not! But all I want to do is lie down and take this weight off my swollen ankles. I admit I've never been too empathetic with women who complain of swollen ankles. Now I take back every word I ever said. These huge clubs at the ends of my legs are sapping my energy and making me feel downright ugly. And the fatigue... Mother, sometimes I don't know how I can put one foot in front of the other. And then I get caught up in looking after my little patients and I somehow forget about it. Until the next time I sit down, and it overwhelms me.

CHAPTER FIFTY-FIVE

WHINGY

Santo Tomás Internment Camp
Limited Private Edition - Frederic H. Stevens
© 1946 - page 454-460

September 21—The great day arrives at last! U.S. planes raid Manila.

September 23—Commandant's office warns of greater bombing activities to take place in near future. Urges internees to continue constructing shelters.

September 24—Annex (children) has two meals a day plus rice and milk for lunch.

October 12—Internees warned not to enter closed area in front of Education Building or look at packages being stored there.

Internee Committee submits letter to Commandant asking for information regarding activities taking place on front campus, where soldiers are quartered and army stores being deposited. Point made that this is internment Camp and should be kept from becoming a military objective.

After a sweltering summer, the appearance of American planes in the skies turned every internee into a mixed bag of hopes and fears. Surely liberation was imminent. But the constant explosions on the fringe of the city and incessant air raids intruded upon every task now, throwing any kind of schedule to the wind.

The children's clinic was moved to the first floor of Main. Dorothy began hording small bits of food for her most critical patients, determined that when the skies turned brutal with smoke and flak and brought the kitchens to a screaming halt, her little ones would still eat. Parents of the little patients followed her example and somehow kept bits and pieces of shredded banana skins and the occasional batch of bomber bread appearing in the clinic's small larder. There were even a few camotes, the Philippine sweet potato that had been a staple in the first years of captivity and now were nearly non-existent.

She kept Bobby and Carol with her during the daytime now, knowing they were safer on the first floor of Main than they were in the one storey Annex. She had to keep them as safe as possible from the bombs that seemed to come nearer every day. She had to keep them safe from the Japanese guards who threatened harsh retribution to any prisoner who dared to look at the sky in search of winged heroes.

EXCERPT FROM MANILA GOODBYE BY ROBIN PRISING
© 1975 BY ROBIN PRISING. PP 146

Nearly a month went by before the American planes came back to bomb Manila. When the raids started up again in mid-October, we were strictly forbidden to watch them. Lieutenant Abiko made certain that the rule was enforced as he and his soldiers knocked about the camp trying to catch anyone looking at a plane. If caught, you were slapped and hustled roughly to the guardhouse near the Main Gate, where you were made to stand with folded arms, looking straight ahead, out in the open—despite stray bullets and shrapnel—for a twelve-hour stretch. As the raids persisted, glancing up at the sky at any time might incur such punishment, and some people grew so furtive that whenever they left their rooms they kept their eyes on the ground.

It seemed to Dorothy as if it took twice as long now to do everything. Even knitting a pair of string undies for Carol. She could no longer sit for a couple of hours, knitting through the evening's enforced blackout. She was simply too tired.

She would sit on the bunk with her feet up, giving the edema in her ankles the ghost of a chance to recede, and then she'd wake up an hour later with only a half row of stitches done. And the last few stitches were such a cobbled mess she'd have to pull them out and start again.

The unorthodox knitting string was thin and coarse, but with the right stitch it made a reasonably comfortable pair of panties. Within minutes of starting to knit, Dorothy's shoulders would begin to complain and she'd shift about trying to get comfortable. Moving without pain was a distant memory these days. The aching persisted, whether she was bending over a patient or harvesting her family's meager share of weeds.

They weren't really weeds, though in civilized times they were treated as such. No self-respecting yard or garden would tolerate what some called Philippine spinach. But here they were carefully grown greens, the only edible greens available now in the compound. Nobody would forego collecting their weekly allotment of talinum weed, no matter how much their shoulders hurt. An internee would no more leave talinum uncollected than a prospector would leave gold in the mine.

Knitting at night made gathering talinum in the afternoon that much more painful. And gathering talinum made knitting a simple pair of undies take an extraordinarily long time. But one day the process came to its successful conclusion and Dorothy tiredly but joyfully presented Carol with two new pairs of panties.

Carol held them up, then folded them to her chest. "Thank you, Mommy."

"Change into one of them now and put your panties in the basket for Jeanne to wash tomorrow, sweetie pie."

While Carol changed, Dorothy laid back on the bed. The effort of finishing the second pair had worn her out. She prayed she wouldn't get an emergency call over the camp loudspeaker to report to the hospital. She doubted she'd make it across the yard.

Dorothy reached for the laundry basket to stow the old pair Carol had just stepped out of.

"Wait, Mommy."

"What, dear?"

"Wait. I need those back." Carol's sad voice came as little more than a whisper. But a poignant note caught Dorothy's attention and she sat up and turned to face her little daughter.

Carol stood in the narrow path between the bunk and the wall, a tear running down her cheek and her new panties hanging down around her knees.

Dorothy had made the very same size she'd made three months earlier. She was sure of it. But this pair was easily two sizes too large. And not because they'd been made differently.

They were too large because her precious daughter was losing weight more rapidly. Too rapidly. And now her tiny behind didn't carry enough flesh to keep her panties from slipping to her knees.

The realization of it devastated in a way that sent Dorothy struggling to draw a breath. The sight of it broke her heart.

But she refused to let the truth of it break her spirit.

"Give them here, sweetie-kins. Mommy can fix them."

• • • •

She watched Carol even more keenly these days. The happy child who had memorized every verse of every hymn rarely sang now. Her hair was thinner and curled less eagerly. Her brother's antics no longer annoyed her, but simply passed without comment.

Carol's plump baby cheeks had lasted well into her fourth year. But today there was no trace of them. Today they lived only in Dorothy's memory.

Dorothy's reaction to that realization was incredibly physical. She knew now that it was possible for one's own heart to literally quake if the news were dire enough.

And the evidence of her daughter's decline set her in motion. Within minutes of arriving at the children's ward she began to examine Carol and Bobby thoroughly. Every vital sign and every limb, palpating carefully and listening intently.

"Does this hurt?"

"Nope."

"This?"

"Nope."

She kept eye contact with Bobby, searching to see if his answers matched the message in his baby blue eyes.

"Does this hurt?" Bobby asked as he poked her back.

"Nope," she smiled, though in truth it had. He was a tough little tyke, resilient, like a marathon runner. Painfully scrawny but tough.

"Well, Bobby Chambers, you are the most fit four-year-old I've seen in a month of Sundays. I declare you champion of the universe."

Bobby beamed and jumped down from the examination table. "What about Sissy? Is she champion of the girl's universe?"

Dorothy laughed at his enthusiasm. "She may well be, brother bear. You run over to my desk and get the treat I left for you."

"Salt?" he asked hopefully.

When she nodded he shot off toward her desk. She watched him wet his index finger, then roll it across the few grains of salt she'd placed in a metal dish. He stood there a moment, just looking at his finger, then with reverence he put his finger in his mouth to suck away its saltiness. Seconds later he plopped down cross-legged on the floor, then dropped his head back, eyes closed, his tongue licking his lips over and over so as not to miss a single grain of its goodness.

She turned to Carol, already sensing what was to come.

Before she even put the stethoscope to Carol's chest she felt she knew what she would hear. The dark circles under her daughter's eyes, the listlessness, both warning signs of the murmur she feared.

And it was there. Carol's heart was literally beginning to break.

Dorothy's own heart tripped over itself, thudding ominously in her breast. Carol's little body had devoured all the fat it could find, every little morsel, and now, on the edge of starvation, it was starting to attack her heart muscle.

·　·　·　·

Once she had confirmed her diagnosis, Dorothy sent an urgent message to Henry Waters. He was here, now, and Dorothy felt her nerves calm merely by his comforting presence in the examining room.

"Open your blouse, Carol Joy. Let Dr. Waters hear your heart."

Carol complied, her motions listless, her eyes dull. That was the hardest for Dorothy, seeing the inquisitive light dimming in her precious daughter. In the past, Carol would have been on a keen edge, begging her turn to listen herself, asking all manner of questions about hearts and veins and lungs and how did God know to make it that way.

But not today.

Today it wore her out just to undo the buttons on her blouse. Her little frame was birdlike, delicately boned, so fragile. When she exhaled on an exhausted huff, her ribs stood out in skeletal detail.

A panic she'd never felt before swept over Dorothy, thwarting her usually calm diagnostic process. She had to get more protein into this child. Starting now. Today. And every day she had to find more.

"Do you hear it?" Dorothy watched Henry's face as he listened.

"I do!" he chimed. "Do you want to listen, Carol?" He didn't even wait for her to answer and already had the stethoscope plugged into Carol's ears. Once she was distracted listening to her own heartbeat he turned to Dorothy.

"You're right, Dorothy. It's a murmur. A fairly significant one, I'm afraid."

He patted her hand, sympathy written fully on his face. He had known Carol since she was a toddler, and had delivered Bobby under perilous circumstances. Dorothy trusted him like no other with her children.

And he'd just confirmed her fear.

"Have her take meals at the hospital for three weeks. Bobby, too, I think. Then—"

"Henry, it...I...what I mean is...could you—"

"Oh goodness, yes! What was I thinking. You can't really prescribe extra rations for your own children, can you? People will talk. Sorry! I'll arrange Carol's prescription and we'll take a look at Bobby down the road. How does that sound?"

Relief covered her in waves of emotion that threatened to set her trembling. There was no doubt in Dorothy's mind that he'd just saved Carol's life, giving her permission to eat the more nutritious food that the hospital kitchen was allowed to prepare. In truth, hospital food was only marginally better. But better was better.

Henry pulled her into a bolstering hug, turned a smile toward Carol, and ambled off to tend to his other patients. The dear, dear man! A hoard of patients awaited him, but he'd come at her hurried request to the children's ward to see Carol rather than force the child to walk the greater distance to his office in the camp's main hospital.

Dorothy returned the stethoscope to her kit. She would put Carol on bed rest. No activity that would cause her emaciated body to gobble up more calories than necessary would be allowed. Hopefully the special kitchen prescription would halt the deterioration.

Dorothy knew the progression. Though they had not yet lost a single child, she'd seen the progression on too many faces in this camp, faces that gradually acknowledged the slow death that was starting to number their days.

And then the faces would be gone.

At first the camp had shown a kind of collective reaction to the deaths from starvation by exhibiting a modicum of concern for others who might also be in peril. They'd shown concern by offering a morsel here, a tidbit there to those who looked desperate.

But no longer. Because the morsels weren't to be had. Almost nothing came over the walls anymore. The Filipinos in Manila were as challenged as the internees, and the risk of discovery was simply too great now, bringing the clandestine deliveries to a trickle.

Some had tried, of course. They'd sneaked away to find food for themselves or their families, only to be shot or jailed trying to return. The realization that nothing would be coming in had left many in the camp very nearly defeated.

As she wheeled Carol and Bobby from the Main building exam room back to the children's ward, Dorothy conceived a plan to make a game out of her daughter's recovery.

"Carol, darling, I've decided you're going to have a mattress holiday."

Carol looked up, mildly interested in something she'd never heard of before. "A what?"

"A mattress holiday," Dorothy repeated. "It means you get a holiday from all your chores. It means you don't even have to dress yourself. You will be the princess and we will be your slaves. Your wish is our command, your highness." Dorothy swept the best kind of curtsy her beri-beri-bound joints would allow. Once settled in one of the empty cots, she removed Carol's blouse and shorts and pulled on a loose-fitting pajama smock. "You are Queen of the Bedpost now!"

She forced a smile as she arranged the bedding and lifted Carol's thirty-seven featherweight pounds onto the cot. She had weighed the exact same thirty-seven pounds two years earlier when they entered Santo Tomás, but was now two inches taller.

"Now, my lady, what is your first command?"

Carol screwed up her face in concentration. Dorothy waited, wondering how she'd tell her she couldn't even sit up in bed except for one half hour in the morning and one half hour in the afternoon.

"I shall think upon it," she quipped, showing that she wanted to participate in the game. But she was clearly too tired to think of something. Too tired to want anything to occupy her time. Too tired to do anything but just lie there and rest.

"Mommy?"

Bobby had been very interested in this new development, and now he hopped up onto the cot and crossed his legs. "Sissy didn't get her snack. Maybe it would make her feel better." He turned to Carol. "And if you don't want it all, it's okay if you share it with me."

Her son's request tortured her. She couldn't even provide her children with a small snack other than a couple of grains of salt. The contents of the relief box were gone. She'd made things last a good seven months, but had she been too stringent? Could the stress to Carol's little heart have been avoided if she'd supplemented the children's meals more liberally?

Common sense told her no. And her medical mind agreed. The 'crash and burn' after a short period of normal eating would have had just as debilitating an effect.

Bobby rustled impatiently on the cot, just enough to remind her that he was waiting for an answer.

What to do?

She was about to go back to her desk to get the few grains of salt she'd set out for Carol when she remembered the small empty butter tin in her pocket. The relief box butter that she had doled out so skimpily had been the most remarkable luxury. To a starved palate, it had made the crudest foods taste like a priceless delicacy. Now all that was left of the butter was the waxed paper liner in the empty tin the butter had been packaged in. She'd scraped the last of the precious butter into the children's mush several weeks past, then rolled the paper up. She'd dropped the tin into her pocket just this morning to bring it to the clinic, intending to clean it out and use it to store small clips. But perhaps—

Without hesitation she opened the tin, unrolled the waxed paper and tore off two strips that were still slightly greasy to the touch. She twisted them gently, trying mightily to leave all the butter residue on the paper and not on her fingers.

"This, my darlings, is a wonderful snack I've been saving for you. One for you, and one for you."

"You funny mommy," Bobby quipped. "This is paper!"

Dorothy caught his little hand as he nearly threw the paper twist away.

"It's butter paper, Bobby, and it's wax. You can chew it but don't swallow. Try it!"

Bobby watched Carol put her small twist in her mouth and begin to chew. As the salty, buttery residue began to seep from the paper onto her tongue her face lit up like Christmas. That was all it took for Bobby to pop his own strip into his mouth.

The euphoric sounds clearly communicated their pleasure with this new snack. Dorothy smiled as she moved down the row of beds, surprising each of the eight little patients with their own twist of butter paper. The moans of delight were sweet music to her ears.

But bits of butter-coated paper would not supply the nutrition her daughter desperately needed.

Dorothy bit her lip.

The hospital chow would certainly be a small step up in nutritional value, but for Carol to grow stronger would take far more protein than even hospital food would provide. She thought through the short list of meager provisions she had. She could mix Carol's powdered milk stronger for the next few weeks, even though it meant the supply would dwindle that much faster. But what she really needed was protein. She'd find peanut butter or eggs or potted meat or chicken gristle or a bit of fresh heart. Somehow. Someone had to have a stash they would trade for the two or three scoops of coffee she had left.

Dorothy's heart twisted and tumbled, overwrought with the need to safeguard her children. Between the two of them, surely she and Fred could manage it.

Dearest Mother,

You of all people know how I longed for family, those long years in India, when I was fulfilled in every way but one. And God answered my need with Fred and Carol and Bobby. My dearest treasures, my heart, my all.

Did He know that these two little darlings were destined for these troubled days? For this desperate hour? Is that why He gave them to me? Am I enough?

CHAPTER FIFTY-SIX

STARVING LITTLE HENS

Dorothy slogged through the pouring rain, her wooden bakyas betraying her at every step. Their wet hemp straps stretched just enough across her toes that they slipped one way as she slid another. She may as well have gone barefoot. That certainly might have spared her ankles these wrenching twists. But if one had any hope of keeping the mud off one's feet, the thick wooden sandals were the only option. Shoes didn't have the ghost of a chance against the rivers of mud.

Dearest Mother,

It's October, and I never thought I'd welcome the rain, but now that it means the bombs stop falling on Manila for a while, I can't help but be glad of it. We don't see the American planes close overhead, but they are ours, bombing the harbor, taking out Japanese installations. Our "keepers" have moved their anti-aircraft guns close now. Shells fall on the grounds. They shoot flak at our planes, and it comes back to land about the campus as red hot bits of steel and shrapnel. In the distance we've seen parachutes fall from burning planes, burning chutes failing to open, open chutes falling slowly, swaying gently, delivering our boys—some of whom are shot as they float like cloth dolls birthed in the clouds—to this plot somewhere between heaven and hell.

She'd managed so well for over a month now, trading their relief allotment of cigarettes for small morsels of bolstering food for the children. But now she had only three ounces of coffee grounds to trade for protein of some kind. Any kind. Surely it would be enough to trade up to a small portion of spam.

414

But nobody had a thing to spare. They'd gazed longingly at the coffee before shaking their heads. She'd not embarrassed herself by appearing anxious, even though it was humiliating to beg.

She looked back along the row of shanties she'd just visited. One fellow had offered her a can of corned beef. His price? $100 American. Another would consider selling only a bundle of goods. It was all or nothing. In the bundle were two tins of meat, some bouillon powder, some firewood and a few other small items. His price? $500 American. None of that Mickey Mouse Money, he'd insisted. They all despised the worthless currency printed by Japan for their use, and no one would call it anything but just that—Mickey Mouse Money.

Buying anything was hopeless. She could only pray for a trade.

Her medical skill was the most valuable thing she had to trade. But that was never an option. It was unthinkable. It would violate everything she believed in, everything she'd built her life's work around. Any demonstrated medical need would automatically find help at her hands. With no thought of compensation. Tonight the only thing she would barter with was coffee.

Dorothy settled into a slow shuffle along the miserable excuse for a board walk that was more mud slide than walkway. The rain was coming in on a pretty good slant now, buffeted by winds that could not quite manage a typhoon, but stayed strong enough to make the going perilous.

She made one last visit to the two bachelors in the shanty at the end of Camote Road and then headed back to the Annex. It was exhausting, battling the weather, battling her sense of dignity, trying not to let slow panic overtake her. Her children needed protein. Somewhere in this camp there was protein to be had. She just had to keep asking. And she would. Tomorrow.

Dorothy stood in the rain, holding her wooden bakyas in her hands and rinsing them in the rain as best she could before entering the Annex. She paused at the door, her mind whirling through every possible source of food and coming up wanting. She stepped into the long hall that led to her room and shook as much rain from her dress as she could. Inside the room she moved as cautiously as possibly, careful not to drip on the beds she passed.

So fervently did she concentrate on her passage through the small room that she practically bumped into a woman who stood at the entrance to her own family's little cubbyhole.

"Oh! Mrs. Nash! I didn't see you. Oh dear, I've gotten you all soaked. So sorry!"

Grace Nash stood at the 'threshold' of Dorothy's minuscule abode with a small bundle in her hands. It was mesmerizing to see those hands close up, the long slender fingers that had coaxed such magical music from her violin all those months ago. She was one of those beautiful women who always seemed to maintain a dancer's pose, and while—like Dorothy—her body was beginning to betray itself, it had not robbed the woman of her innate poise.

"Pay it no mind, Dr. Chambers, no mind at all. I've just brought you a little something. It's not much. Not at all what I would like to bring. But my little Gale is doing so well, and I know it was your doing, getting him posted out to the hospital. And I never thanked you. So here."

Instead of handing the bundle to Dorothy, Mrs. Nash carefully lifted one edge of the pretty handkerchief that concealed her gift. Beneath the embroidered corner, cradled in a nest of similar handkerchiefs, were two small, brownish, eggs. With practically translucent shells.

Her voice, which had been hushed from the start, now dropped to a furtive whisper, lest the little treasure find its way into other hands in the dark of night.

"Let's keep them in their little nest, if you'll just tell me where you want me to put them," she whispered. "They are so fragile the shells are almost transparent. Poor starved little chickens can't seem to make a proper egg."

Dorothy quickly emptied her one and only small wooden bowl and held it out. The sight of Mrs. Nash's perfectly improper little eggs had robbed her of words. There was such a moving reverence in the way Mrs. Nash laid the cradled eggs in her little bowl that Dorothy found herself holding her breath, lest the eggs vanish on a careless sigh.

God had heard her prayer, and sent Grace.

SURVIVING A JAPANESE INTERNMENT CAMP:
LIFE AND LIBERATION AT SANTO TOMÁS, MANILA, IN WORLD WAR II
BY RUPERT WILKINSON. PG 123

Private money and credit helped if you had it. There was always food for sale at colossal prices, some of it brought in officially by the Japanese and some sold by profiteers from smuggling and hoard-ing. In early November 1944, [an internee] bought five cans of Campbell's soup at $10 each (about $150 today). A month later he felt guilty about buying a pound of mongo beans, for which he paid sixty prewar pesos (some $450 today).

"It is a crime that if anything can be bought it can't be obtained by the camp for the good of all," he wrote in his diary.

For people with valuables rather than cash, there were Taiwanese guards who coveted rings, watches, and jewelry to take home to wives and girlfriends. In January, a fine diamond engagement ring could fetch 4 to 5 kilos [8 to 10 lbs] of rice plus extras such as tobacco. Internee dealers who got to know "the right" guards nego-tiated the sale, taking a third or more of the proceeds in food or cash for the risk; some guards took the jewelry without delivering.

None of this stopped malnutrition.

Things were changing almost daily now. It had started with the "pig victory", an inglorious escapade in which a pig had escaped from the Japanese army's live-stock pen. It was quite miraculous how it vanished into thin air with a whole patrol of soldiers chasing after it. But vanish it had. And it's reappearance in var-ious and sundry shapes and forms was equally miraculous. Even so, the aroma of roasting pork was never once detected on the breeze about camp.

In recent weeks rumors had run rampant that the Americans had the Japanese in retreat. Camp guards taking over the first floor of the Ed Building seemed to give the rumors some credence. And now the camp loudspeaker had just issued a coded message that nearly stopped every beating heart.

"Better Leyte than never!"

Strange though it seemed, every adult knew what it meant. Don Bell had been reminding internees to replant their gardens, then ended his announce-ment by saying it wasn't too late to plant. In fact, he said, it was "better Leyte than never". He'd used the moment to slip in an announcement to the intern-ees. One they'd been praying for these many months.

Dorothy and Fred had met for dinner, the first time in nearly ten days. The meager chatter died instantly around them as internees registered what had just been said. The people around their plank table looked at one another, stricken dumb by the coded announcement. They'd been waiting for it, longing for it, for some news that the Americans were coming to get them.

But when the announcement came, in its cryptic code, they couldn't quite bring themselves to believe it. Here they were, in October of 1944, no real food to speak of, just the unrecognizable dregs of what passed for food—husks of rice, but no actual rice usually present, a few weevils floating on the top of cups of soup. Even the weevils weren't interested in mere husks, it seemed.

Yet unexpectedly, and completely out of character, the Japanese had brought in a small supply of rice.

Why? What could have prompted this overdue act of charity?

The answer lay in the announcer's quip.

Of late, camp announcer Don Bell had confined himself to mere reminders, cautioning the internees not to use other types of paper in place of toilet tissue and so on.

But tonight, after announcing that a bit of rice had been delivered into camp, and prompting people to be sure and replant what they were using from their meager gardens, he added the quip, "Better Leyte than never!" It was audacious! It was scandalous that he would make such an obvious announcement within the hearing of their armed guards.

But cautious glances confirmed that none of their captors had picked up anything suspicious from the announcement.

Better Leyte (lay-tee) than never!

"Fred! Did you hear that? Fred?" Dorothy poked him, dragging his attention from the man at the end of the table who he'd been staring at for the last five minutes.

"Did you?" she repeated.

Fred turned to her, raised an eyebrow and shook his head. "No. What?"

Dorothy lowered her voice to a whisper. "The Americans have taken Leyte! They're coming! No wonder our keepers brought rice into the camp. They've got to fatten us up in case they get caught holding us here!"

Even as she spoke the words, the truth of the matter suddenly occurred to her. The supply of rice was actually meant to demoralize the camp. Normally, extra rations were only provided when the Japanese felt victory was near. So extra rations were meant as a ruse to make the internees think the Imperial army had beaten back their boys in blue.

But Bell's announcement had just revealed the lie.

Anyone who had listened to the men's endless conjecturing on the progress of the war knew that Leyte was the key. If MacArthur could take Leyte, he could establish a firm foothold for retaking the islands, and an air base from which to mount inland raids. This was the best news they could have heard.

MacArthur was on his way.

Fred patted her arm. "It's...good news then."

Dorothy's smile faded. "Yes, darling, very good news, don't you think?"

He turned his attention back to the man he'd been studying throughout the evening meal. The man who sat quietly smoking a cigarette hand-rolled in a scrap of fine, thin parchment.

"Maybe MacArthur can get my Bible back," was all he said.

. . . .

Dorothy knew how much it had pained Fred to lose his Bible. He'd guarded it so carefully, particularly in recent months, when the very thin scritta paper used for the printing of bibles had become a surprisingly popular toilet tissue. With dysentery rampant throughout the camp, and thievery at its highest point ever, every personal bit of paper was at risk of being 'borrowed'.

So it was no great surprise that his Bible had gone missing.

Now Fred leveled the finger that had been propping up his chin and pointed it at the other table where the man, who Dorothy knew lived in the gym where Fred bunked, was just exhaling from another drag on his cigarette.

It seemed the height of disrespect. Fred had been without tobacco for his pipe for months. Now he'd lost his special Bible—possibly to this man who not only had tobacco, but now had paper in which to roll it.

He sighed. "It's not like he stole the *words*, is it? It's just paper."

Dorothy huffed. "Pilfered paper."

Fred cocked his head to the side and managed a smile. "*Possibly* pilfered paper."

She grasped his hand and squeezed it, loving him for finding humor where there seemed to be none. She knew her husband well. He would never confront this man. He would probably pray that the man might accidentally read a verse or two before he set fire to it. But Fred would never challenge the man.

Never in a million years.

· · · ·

By November, things were little different, except for the fact that now there was no firewood in camp so the mush was almost always cold. The rice was mostly husks and dysentery was at an all-time high. Curfew had been moved up to 7 P.M., and due to the air raids and falling bombs, school had been permanently suspended.

A cruel rumor sped through camp that American Red Cross boxes were on the way. When nothing materialized, Dorothy tended to agree with those who said it was a morbid hoax intended to further demoralize the camp.

On a particularly sultry morning Dorothy was headed back to the clinic after delivering Carol and Bobby into Fred's keeping for the day. Morning had come much too soon. Three children who had eaten the poisonous leaves of an hibiscus bush had needed watching through a long and worrisome night.

She knew where the hibiscus bush was now, and needed to send someone to cut it down. They'd removed all the poisonous plants early on, but somehow this one had escaped notice when it began to grow back and had nearly cost the lives of three small children. She would set Fred to the task of removing it. It would be the kind of chore that would help him work out his frustration.

Like the entire camp, Fred had been on tenterhooks since General MacArthur had landed on Leyte in October.

1944 was going to be the year of their liberation. They'd been so sure.

But it was late November now, and they'd heard nothing further. Nothing remotely encouraging had come over the wall by way of the bamboo telegraph.

Everyone knew that it had taken only ninety days for the Japanese to seize the islands. And since the Americans did everything so much better and faster than the Japanese, they should surely be at the gates of Santo Tomás by now.

But they were not. And depression was setting in.

Dorothy jumped a bit at the mechanical clatter of the loudspeaker lashed in the top of the palm tree she was passing as it came to life. She had been deeply absorbed in what she could do to help three poisoned children with her limited supplies when, from fifteen feet overhead, the camp loudspeaker began to blare.

Good mornin', good mornin'!
We've danced the whole night through,
Good mornin', good mornin' to you!

In some misguided attempt to wake folks up thinking the world was a happy-clappy-place-today, the song had become the morning ritual. And it never failed to grate upon her nerves.

The unwelcome bleating jolted her heart and slammed at her brain. *How dare they.* There was nothing good about this morning. Not for those three innocent babies who had writhed in pain through a tortured night. Not for those little ones who had seen their salvation from starvation in the form of a few poisoned leaves.

Dorothy bent down and grabbed the three closest stones piled around the base of the tree that hosted the offending speaker. In a rage she threw the first stone at the tin villain, but on it blared. She stepped back, aimed, and threw the second stone. Still the ridiculous tune spewed forth.

She put her entire body into the effort as she hurled the third stone. But her aim was poor, her arm was weak, and the speaker blared on and on. She couldn't even avenge three innocent kiddies.

Dorothy shrank back onto the walk. Her behavior was at once humiliating, horrifying, and supremely satisfying. She swept a guilty look over her shoulder as she straightened her white coat. Had she been seen?

Nervous now, she walked on to the clinic, forcibly calming her skittering pulse. If they'd seen her, she'd be on her way to jail at this very moment.

At the hospital's entryway she stopped, still gathering herself. She would never again let them rob her of her serenity. It was simply too risky.

CHAPTER FIFTY-SEVEN

THE LITTLEST HERO

Bobby swayed where he stood, just a few yards from the Main Gate, contemplating the laughter coming from the Japanese open-air mess tent that sat just inside the forbidding fence. He'd never been here by himself before. There were always a bunch of kids hanging around.

But tonight they all were staying inside, out of the driving rain. He wiped his lip where the water was running in great rivers. He had to do this.

Mom and Dad were out finding food to trade. He wanted to do the same. But he had nothing to trade. So he slipped away from Jeanne and Carol and the room monitor who kept track of them when his mother was doctoring.

He'd been here with the kids a hundred times before, hanging onto the thick posts that supported the roof, watching the Japanese guards eat. It wasn't scary. Not with all those kids around. And some of the guards seemed to really like the kids, as long as the kids followed the rules. The men would try out some of their American words on their audience. And once in a while they'd end up tossing them some food scraps.

He shouldn't be here, though. Mom would throttle him if she knew. If the air raid siren started again, he'd never get back to the room in time. He could still run, but it sort of hurt. And he could only run short distances at a time.

EXCERPT FROM MANILA GOODBYE BY ROBIN PRISING
© 1975 BY ROBIN PRISING. PP 157, 159

Starvation is taking its slow toll. Seeds of fear are sprouting quickly now: We know that we are near the beginning of the end—will the end be massacre or liberation? In the last week of 1944 I discover

422

that I can no longer run; that whenever I begin to hurry my knees knock together and my legs sag under the weight of my fragile body. I can count my bones from the collarbone down—each joint, each jutting rib. Waiting under the hot sun in the hunger lines, I break into cold sweats. Unable to keep my knees straight I grow faint, struggling against the terror that I may black out and spill the food on the ground.

The slop is more wormy and watery now and almost tasteless. By New Year's Day I have developed a habit of vomiting up, and swallowing again, a mouthful of food for an hour or so after the two scoops of gruel each day. Even the vomit tastes good. I go to the latrine as seldom as possible, trying to hold everything inside me, stingily preserving it for two or three days. And without any pity, but in cold disgust, I notice that many prisoners are losing their minds and furtively devour imaginary meals, slurping and eating the air. Men suck their thumbs, gnaw at their hands.

The entire morning of January seventeenth is spent in roll call. We stand famished and exhausted while the whole camp is counted, recounted and counted again. Last night a man called Eisenberg escaped. The Japanese threaten to inflict severe punishment on the Internee Committee, the room monitors and the rest of the prisoners. But their threats are plainly bombast. I keep wondering how Eisenberg had the physical strength to escape when I could not even manage to run.

No, if the siren went off like it had almost every day for the last month, he'd never get past Main Building, around the Ed Building, across the commons to the Annex in time. But he could hide if he needed to. In places no adult could possibly follow. And then he'd slip home.

Bobby plowed through the mud and stopped just behind one of the thick outer posts. Unconsciously, he wiped a hand across his mouth. They had meat. He could smell it. The boys could always identify each smell, and through them he'd learned of foods he'd never eaten. How incredible it would taste.

He leaned forward, trying to get a better look at their plates. But his foot slipped in the stupid mud, and his grip slipped on the rain-soaked beam. He stumbled two steps before he caught his balance. And suddenly, there he was, in the light, just below the tent platform.

The guards looked over, startled. He knew what he had to do now, so, very slowly, Bobby dropped his arms straight to his sides and began to bend.

No halfway bow would do tonight. He needed a favor from these guys, so Bobby didn't stop bending until he was parallel to the ground. He held the bow for a moment longer than necessary, then straightened.

The guards hooted and nodded, and some of them stood up from the benches and returned the bow, while others gave a nodding bow from where they sat. Others spat words that sounded pretty naughty to Bobby. That wasn't very nice.

One guy had a biscuit in one hand, another had a fork piled with greens, and still another had what the boys called a drumstick in one hand. And Bobby began to drool.

He couldn't help it. His mouth just started running with saliva, and he swallowed over and over, trying to get rid of it. Rain dripped from his hair. His clothes were soaked as if they'd just been in the laundry tub, and his shoes each dragged a clump of mud along with them. He was a mess.

Bobby ran his tongue across his lips, and heard a quiet "Ah" off to his right. One of the guards that he knew always threw food to the kids got up from his place and carried his plate to the edge of the platform. He hunkered down and held his plate out to Bobby.

Was he supposed to just take something? Was he supposed to accept the plate? Bobby stared at it, then risked a glance at the guard's face. The man nodded, held the plate farther toward him.

So Bobby snatched the whole tin plate.

A roar of laughter filled the soggy space, but Bobby didn't hear it. He had grabbed the one bite of greens that was left on the plate and shoved it into his mouth, then snatched the remains of a biscuit and dragged it through some kind of juice. He chewed and swallowed as fast as he could and then swept up a small piece of meat, the only other thing left on the plate, a sad little piece of gristle. And it was heavenly.

He looked up at the guard and signaled for a drink. The guard laughed and cracked some kind of joke that made the men laugh again. But he turned to the table behind him and grabbed a cup.

Bobby didn't even look in it. He dumped the contents, then set the cup down on the edge of the platform and ever so carefully poured the juices left on the plate into the cup. He used his fingers to scrape down every bit of the saucy substance until the plate was clean enough to put back on the shelf.

Then he picked up the cup, closed his eyes, whispered "Sweet Jesus, Amen", and drank the small portion of meat and vegetable juices.

He felt so satisfied that he knew this must be what it feels like when your soul gets to leave your body and fly up to heaven.

And then he almost threw up.

He was a bad brother. The worst! He'd come here to get food for Carol and he'd eaten it all! A tear trembled beneath his eyelid, then slid down his cheek. He had to ask for more. He couldn't go home without food for Carol.

So Bobby gave a bobbing head-bow toward the guard, picked up the plate, put the cup on it, and held it out toward the guard. But when the man reached for it, instead of letting go, Bobby hung onto it. He released one hand and pointed his finger at the plate, and at the same time wrinkled up his brow in the most pleading expression he knew how to render. It almost always worked on Mom. Maybe—

The guard laughed his head off, grabbed the plate and walked through the dining hall holding the plate high overhead, showing all the men how clean Bobby had licked it.

Bobby sniffled. He'd messed up. They weren't going to give him any more food. He couldn't go home now. He'd blown it.

He took a tiny step backward, still haunted by all the food still strewn across the table. The guard was coming back. And he didn't have a plate in his hand. Bobby gulped. The man was coming back to chase him away! He'd made him mad now!

And then the guard smiled. Like an angel reaching down from the clouds, the man leaned off the edge of the platform and handed Bobby a small packet. Food wrapped in a soiled napkin.

Bobby's heart began to hammer in his chest. His face broke into a grin so big it hurt his cheeks. He flung his torso into a wild bow, then spun around as fast as his muddy feet could manage and headed back to the room.

He'd done it! He'd found some food for Carol.

Mom was going to be so happy.

· · · ·

Dorothy scraped the mud from the bottom of her shoes. Bending was the worst, but there was no way to accomplish the task without bending. She turned to fling a handful of mud into the darkness and saw two small shoes stuck in the unforgiving muck just inches from the Annex door.

They looked like Bobby's. The little imp. He wasn't even to be out in the rain, much less leave his one and only pair of shoes out here for anyone to help themselves to.

She wrestled them out of the mire and hurled a glob of mud as far as she could toss it. Dollops of sludge and debris broke away and landed on her arm and peppered her skirt. She gasped, looking at the mess she'd made of herself. In an instant it turned her pristine white coat into prison garb.

Thoughts as dark as her dirty coat simmered up from her empty belly, and she suddenly lashed out.

I hate this!

The words she hissed into the night seemed thrown back into her face by the pelting rain. They stung her ears and bruised her heart.

She muttered, striving to dispel the harsh thoughts as she swiped another fistful of mud and cast it angrily to the ground. Rain dripped across her face, mingling with the tears that had somehow exploded from her eyes.

Leave it, Dorothy...just get on with it!

She slammed the soles of Bobby's shoes together, doing a great deal to shed mud from the shoes and a great deal more to soil herself and the annex wall. But if anything, the little shoes looked worse than before.

Again and again she clapped the soles together.

Harder. Harder.

Her muscles shrieked louder with each vicious thrust, until at last her shoulders fell in exhaustion and her mind slipped into darker territory.

This is all my fault.

As the words slid from the shadowy place where she'd confined them these many months, the stone that was lodged in her throat finally moved, letting out the cry she'd stifled for so long.

I did this.

The condemning words seemed to scorch the darkness around her, at the same time bleeding her of anger as she released them into the rain. Her breast heaved, forcing long, rasping gulps of air to rush from her with the guttural sounds of a woman whose mind was threatening to abandon her.

God help me!

The words echoed in her mind. Once. Twice. Then suddenly the self-vilification was gone. Just like that. Dissipated into the molecules of wetness that still pummeled her face.

Resignation slowed her hand as she swept away the worst of the mud from herself and from Bobby's shoes and carried them with her into the Annex.

Step by trembling step she moved away from the scene of her momentary madness. It was time for her to get a grip. She could do it. She *had* to do it. She'd done it countless times before. She could do it again. She was a problem solver. A healer. A saver of lives. A clever creator of ingenious tools. She was a visionary, a devoted Christian, a champion of the underdog, a servant. She was a mother. A parent. A warrior.

She was a failure.

The thought stopped her in her tracks, and with the greatest effort she struggled to find words that would banish that horrible thought. But it refused to release her.

She couldn't protect her children. She couldn't find the food to sustain them another day. She couldn't even clean a muddy pair of shoes.

Dorothy had never in her life accepted failure. But she had never in her life felt so tired. Thank God for the rain, because if the air raid sirens had gone off again she didn't think she had the strength to gather the children and crawl under the bed.

It must be the fatigue that got the best of her tonight. She wasn't the sort to rail at the wind. God had every right to expect better from her. She'd have strongly admonished any of her student nurses who spoke to themselves the way she had tonight. She might even have lectured her own children had they dared show such weakness.

Yes, that was it. Fatigue. It had to be the fatigue. It seemed to quadruple each day. Since they'd moved the children's ward to the Main Building it was twice as far from her room now, and she had to stop and rest at least three times every time she walked to or from the clinic. Needing to stop twice in an eight-minute walk was nothing short of shocking.

She paused a moment before entering the room, and begged her God to clear her mind, to let her creative spirit flow so she could craft a solution to getting food for her children.

In the unusual quiet she felt a tiny portion of her burden fall away. Somehow it was going to be all right. That thought encircled her mind and calmed the tremor in her stomach.

Feeling stronger than she had a moment earlier, Dorothy straightened her shoulders and arranged her face in the cheerful countenance she required herself to present to her children, and stepped into the room.

She walked quietly to the corner she shared with her two children and then stopped, a small gasp escaping her lips. She reached one hand to the wall to steady herself, and the other flew to her mouth of its own accord.

Carol was sitting up on the bed, licking her fingers and smiling more broadly than Dorothy had seen in weeks. Bobby sat beside her bed on his little stool, a bit of cloth in his hands that he now raised for Carol to make another selection.

Dear God in heaven.

Bobby had found food.

THE BOMBING OF MANILA

PHOTO COURTESY OF JOHN TEWELL

AMERICAN SINGER/ACTRESS DEANNA DURBIN
DIED IN 2013 AT THE AGE OF 91

CHAPTER FIFTY-EIGHT

DEANNA DURBIN IS DEAD

Dearest Mother,
They told us today that Deanna Durbin is dead.

Dorothy lay under the bed with the children, listening to the bombs that sounded so much closer than before. Both children were asleep, unfazed by the noise.

In the first weeks of bombing, the explosions had been so far away that one barely registered what they were. Then, over time, they'd come further into the city and now there was no mistaking the hell they were unleashing.

Manila was sustaining horrible damage as the Japanese sought to maintain their hold against the U.S. forces. Anti-aircraft guns could be heard every day now as planes dropped bombs on the harbor, seeking to decimate the Imperial Army of Japan.

Bobby had become an avid shrapnel collector. Dorothy had warned him over and over about waiting an hour so the metal would cool enough not to burn his fingers. But it seemed there was no way he could leave a fascinating piece of steaming shrapnel to someone else, and she was constantly medicating his sore fingers. The very idea of shrapnel was fascinating to him, and he would talk to any who would listen about how the Japanese anti-aircraft guns shot little bomb babies up into the air that would explode near the American planes, hoping to damage them enough that they couldn't drop their big mama bombs. Where he'd heard that was anyone's guess.

The Japanese shouldn't waste so much time trying to damage American morale, Dorothy thought. Each bit of shrapnel that plummeted through a roof and set a shanty on fire did a very nice hatchet job all by itself.

She pictured Fred in his air raid shelter on the first floor of the gym, a book in his hand or the cold pipe in his mouth. He hadn't had pipe tobacco in two years, but puffing on it was not only a comfort to him, but to her as well.

He was never without that pipe. It was something normal. Something from before.

Like Deanna Durbin.

They'd only seen a few of her movies while on furlough from India before the war, but the pretty brunette with the silver voice was everybody's icon, the girl next door. When conversation turned to movies, Deanna Durbin was the name that brought unanimous smiles. She was loved by all.

And she was dead?

Dorothy refused to mourn. Not yet. After all, the news had come from the Japanese radio broadcast. They got names mixed up all the time. Or worse, they distributed news that was patently not true.

It was no stretch at all to imagine that they chose a name all the American troops would recognize, a name that often came to a GI's lips in conversation. It was just like them to choose a name that was part of the hopes of the enemy, something they longed to return to, a symbol of the life they'd left behind. Every soldier pined for the day he would get back to the people he treasured, to the voices of home, to the movies he loved.

Deanna Durbin was part of that. Part of what was normal. Part of what was home.

So they just want us to think she's dead.

Dorothy had said as much, night before last, as her whole table had sat in stunned silence when the announcement came from the loudspeaker. But nobody nodded. As one they seemed to take the news to heart, crestfallen, dazed. A piece of what they longed to go back to was no longer there.

If it was indeed a Japanese trick, it had worked. Morale in camp had never been lower.

Dorothy had sat down beside Fred for the evening meal, weary from an especially troublesome case she'd been monitoring day and night in the children's clinic.

He looked tired, she thought. Maybe it was just the wrinkled clothing. It was his nature to be a fastidious dresser, so even after all this time, wrinkles still looked completely foreign on Fred.

There had been no water for laundry since the Japanese had bombed the nearby reservoir. If it had not been for the rainy season, Santo Tomás would have been in dire trouble.

As it was, they had to forego doing laundry. But a week didn't go by that you couldn't at least rinse things out, even if just by standing out in the rain and letting your clothes get good and soaked.

Besides, there was no longer any soap in camp, and the native bark that had been a good substitute had by now been depleted as well.

Dorothy no longer cared about the rumpled look of her clothing. As long as things managed to dry out before she needed to wear them, she was satisfied.

"I had to move," Fred said with a heavy sigh.

"What? Again?" Dorothy wondered if she'd blanked out for part of the conversation. A few weeks earlier Fred had been told to move his bed to the gym floor. The balcony was being taken over as a sort of isolation ward. Was he moving again?

"My office, I mean."

His office that had been merely one desk was now a simple circle of stones, ever since his desk had been confiscated by the kitchen for firewood. Just a simple circle now. But it was his.

Fred reached over to rub her shoulder. It hurt, his bones against her bones, but she'd never let on.

"The new commandant took over the whole first floor of the Ed Building," he said, and Dorothy's eyes flew wide.

"Why!"

"Does he need a reason?" Fred asked.

Nobody spoke. In the silence, Dorothy's mind raced to find a reason for this turn of events, and didn't at all like the conclusion to which she easily leapt. Of course they were moving into the Ed Building. The internees who lived on the upper floors would be their shield now.

She swallowed the words, refusing to give voice to her fears that those men were now in some sense hostages. But truth be told, weren't they all?

"Do your students know?" she asked, and he nodded.

"Did you find another place?"

He shrugged, then shook his head.

It was too much. Fred was a teacher, an administrator. An office was not just a place to work, it also had its own innate power. Young people came there seeking his counseling, usually of the academic variety, and sitting there in the circle with Fred puffing away on a cold pipe gave them all a sense of normalcy.

A few still came daily, even though classes had been suspended when the students became so nutritionally deprived that classes could no longer be held. And teachers no longer had the energy to prepare and present a lesson.

Every bit of energy was now focused on survival.

But a few were like Fred. If they could not find an outlet for their inquisitive, contemplative minds, they would go stark raving mad. So they would gather around Fred's circle and debate. It didn't matter what the issue was, they'd each fall onto one side or the other and discuss the issue of the day. It was not at all uncommon for several to switch sides midstream and begin debating the opposite view.

So it seemed practically criminal that his office, their gathering place, had been confiscated. The one small thing that represented some stability in their young lives was the fact that they could still meet around that circle. It gave them a place and a purpose that was uniquely theirs.

And it meant even more to Fred than it did to them. For him it was a symbol that he continued to do the work for which God had sent him into the Philippines in the first place. He was still on mission. He was still on task. His office had rooted him in this place of constant upheaval.

And it had been taken away.

"You'll find another place."

He shrugged again. "I know."

Dorothy touched his face, alarmed at the despondency she saw there. Yes, it was true that he could find another place to meet with his students. But did he have the energy to?

· · · ·

"The death toll tripled today."

If Dorothy had brought him along on her errands, hoping to cheer him up, this first stop was hardly going to do the trick. Fred watched Dorothy as she stood in the hall of the camp's main hospital staring at the numbers chalked on the wall. It served as the place of record until things could be put down on paper.

After each name, a cause of death was listed. "Old age", "Heart attack". And here the word "malnutrition" had been struck through and replaced with "unknown".

"They finally let him out of jail, you know."

Fred nodded. Everyone knew that Dr. Stevenson, who served as the camp's chief medical officer, had spent three days in the camp jail because he'd defied the commandant's edict to remove *malnutrition* from every record of the deceased in which in which it had been recorded as the cause of death. He had steadfastly refused to write anything other than the truth.

The commandant insisted that malnutrition could not be the cause of death, since they were treating the internees too well to even think that one could die for lack of food. The other camp doctors had quickly altered the death certificates they'd signed, but Dr. Anderson had dared to defy the commandant by labeling three of his patients as having died of malnutrition. After several days in jail he made the decision to bend his thinking on the matter.

Dorothy lifted a weary arm to write in the latest casualty, the mother of the little girl she had saved in the night. As he watched her shape each letter of the woman's name, Fred prayed for comfort for the grief-stricken child whose mother Dorothy said had given up.

He watched her start to write, then erase it. She started again, then flung the chalk into the tray.

"What's the medical equivalent of 'broken spirit'?" she muttered.

Fred stepped to her side and took her hand. He saw in her eyes that her great fear was that this woman was only the first of those who were giving up.

For three years they'd been sure of rescue. Now every attempt to take back Manila seemed doomed. And the transformation of the camp into a military compound had internees scurrying out of the way of squads of Japanese on the quick march through camp day and night, jeeps, trucks, and crates of ammunition stockpiled and heavily guarded, and anti-aircraft guns practicing sighting in on their targets and letting loose their horrendous volleys.

It was maddening. The Japanese had come to the brilliant conclusion that the Americans weren't going to bomb their own, that the Americans knew there were U.S. citizens down here in Santo Tomás and they would keep their bombs clear of here.

So every bit of Japanese military equipment they could muster was brought into the camp for safekeeping. Great pyramids of crates now occupied every corner, not close enough to the walls to provide a nice stair step to freedom, but close.

And there were trucks everywhere. Parked in perfect military precision, row upon row, the trucks overtook the only open areas in the camp. It was menacing. It was claustrophobic. It was noisy. And it was a perfect opportunity for mischief.

Fred walked alongside Dorothy, defiantly holding her hand. She needed his touch right now and he could not have separated their hands if the commandant himself stood in front of them with his shiny bayonet.

He steered her toward a lot filled with military vehicles. Jeeps, trucks, tank wagons, all lined up in precise rows waiting to be deployed. He smiled. She had failed to cheer him up, but he could cheer her. This very lot was the perfect place to do that.

Without looking toward the vehicles, Fred whispered to Dorothy to casually glance toward any vehicle and inspect its tires. He knew the moment she spotted the problem.

"Fred, it simply can't be a coincidence," Dorothy snorted. "I mean, look at them. Half their tires are flat! Again!"

They stood quietly for a moment, watching the crew of Japanese going from truck to truck with an air bubble. They'd suspected vandalism right away, and railed at the internees. But after closely inspecting a number of tires, they found not a single puncture in tire or valve stem.

"In two hours they'll be flat again," Fred whispered.

Dorothy giggled. Nothing had prompted a laugh for weeks, and from the look on her face Fred knew that the laughter bubbling up felt foreign to her.

"Those guards have been here all day, Fred. Our people could not possibly be doing this!"

Fred kept his face sober as he glanced sideways at her, beneath lowered conspiratorial lids. "So, you're suggesting Divine intervention?"

Dorothy poked him in the ribs, then regretted it when her finger found no cushion there. "No, silly. But really, if it is...mischief...how in the world would they do it right under the noses of so many guards?"

Fred just smiled. One day he would tell her how they were doing it. One day he might even demonstrate how they made the ingenious device that converted a valve stem into a slow-leaking vessel.

But not today. Today a little mystery was good for her. It cheered him just to hear her chuckle again. And never, under any circumstances, would any word that could possibly be used against the mischief makers ever escape his mouth. He applauded them. He admired them. He prayed for them. He almost wished he were one of them.

. . . .

One week later the trucks were gone. And they had taken their leaky valve stems with them. It didn't matter now where they took the trucks. Until every tire was replaced, they'd suffer the same rate of flats as they had during their tenure on campus.

Problems like that kept the camp commandant in a constant state of anger. During the worst of it, his mood filtered down through the ranks, and the children who usually scored handouts at the Japanese mess hall went home empty handed more days than not.

Things got so bleak that many of the kids just stopped coming. So when the vehicles were all removed and the guards began to return to their normal routines, Bobby was there with just a handful of others, the scrap of napkin cleaned and pressed, and with yet another small cartoon of thanks inked into its corners.

He was awfully proud that he'd thought of doing it. The first time he returned the napkin he'd drawn a figure of himself bowing low before the Rising Sun. An image of himself honoring these soldiers who called themselves Sons of Heaven would have been a lie, of course, had he not added the tongue sticking out between his cartoon lips. Unless their eyes were very, very good he doubted they could see it.

The same guard always watched for him, and took great delight in showing off each new drawing before tucking it into his pocket and offering yet another bit of cloth with an equally small bit of food in it for Bobby.

The first time Bobby had drawn on the napkin, the guard had tried to ask him who had made the drawing, but Bobby couldn't make him understand that he had drawn it himself.

The next time, after Carol had washed the napkin and he'd pressed it beneath his mattress, his penciled drawing had faded so badly it could hardly be seen. The Japanese guard, disappointed that the drawings might disappear altogether, left the mess hall and returned moments later with a fountain pen.

He gestured to Bobby that he wanted him to take the pen to whoever it was that had drawn the pictures. It was clear that he wanted the pictures restored, using the pen's indelible ink.

Bobby had just smiled, popped the cap off the pen, and proceeded to redraw the cartoon pictures. The soldiers had gathered round, watching the small boy with the curly platinum hair concentrating so hard on his artwork.

When he finished, the guard picked up the napkin and held it up to the amazed faces of his comrades. In an instant, three other guards had grabbed their napkins and gestured for Bobby to draw a picture for them.

Bobby just made an exaggerated frown, popped the cap back on the pen and laid it down on the tent platform. He stepped back, raised his eyebrows, made a pitiful face and pressed his hands to his stomach.

If they wanted him to draw, they needed to bring on the food.

And they did. Mere, minuscule scraps. But in Bobby's world, it was food.

Memory related by Santo Tomás internee
Dorothy Khoury Howie
100 Miles to Freedom by Robert B. Holland pg 134-135

The last Christmas in the camp, 1944, Jimmy had paid two hundred fifty dollars for a duck. He knew a man who could get things done and get things for a price. So Jimmy got this duck and killed and cleaned it. Then I cooked it for Christmas dinner.

...When I went to use the bathroom, two women were showering. One, a very beautiful redhead, was saying to the other, "Oh, yes, we cooked it and had it and it tasted like chicken. It really was good." The other one said, "Yes, I have heard that is how it tastes." I said, "What did you cook?" And she said, "A cat!"

I threw up all my dinner. When a cat disappeared in the camp we knew what had happened. Toward the end, nothing crawled or moved; anything that was alive was eaten.

16 Dec. 1944. The air raid continues. Forty-eight hours now. Sound of bombing and machine-gun fire several times last night. Few planes. They watch over Manila like vultures their prey, circling incessantly. Naturally there's talk of a landing in the south. Something must be brewing for the Americans to be trying to neutralize Manila in this way. In the meantime, for us, new practical difficulties. Yesterday we didn't get any mush and today it will only be ready at 8:30 a.m. Impossible to hear the loudspeaker, broken down. The children are touchy, especially Nicholas who bursts into tears at the slightest thing that annoys him. No lights in the evening, of course, and we go to bed at eight o'clock. Wonderful weather but strictly forbidden to leave the shanty, even to hang out the washing or saw wood. Christmas is approaching.

CHAPTER FIFTY-NINE

CANNAS AND CASKETS

This wasn't the way Christmas was supposed to happen.

Dorothy struggled to resurrect a mental image of reds and greens and Christmas holly on the windowsills, but amid the drab grays and dusty clutter of the camp it simply would not materialize in her brain.

She longed to see a door decked out with a wreath. For that matter, she longed to see a door. There had never been any doors in camp. They'd been removed by the Japanese long before she and Fred took up residence. There would be no hiding from their guards was the message, nothing in camp they could not see.

In recent days she'd heard much reminiscing over the first Christmas in Santo Tomás. The internees recalled sharing a lovely celebration, with extra food, toys made for the kiddies, and a camp choir singing the Hallelujah Chorus.

Over and over again people recited the clever dishes they'd organized for that first Christmas meal. They dwelt on the ingredients, describing the flavors in ebullient detail that spun mental images they swore they could literally smell.

Perhaps it was as they said. She'd never know, since the Chambers family had not entered camp until mid-summer of 1943 and shared their second Christmas in captivity with Santo Tomás. Even though shadows lived behind every smile, that Christmas had not been as bad as one might have expected.

Now they were about to share their third.

Just thinking of the mystical beauty of a real Christmas with soaring organ music and hot chocolate at midnight made her heart ache for her children who had no such memories.

For Dorothy, thinking of that first Christmas behind a barbed wire fence in Iloilo conjured poignant visions of purple shoes and Christmas carols. It had seemed such a meager Christmas, but even now—remembering the bounty of that Christmas meal with actual meat on the table and real milk in the children's cups—it almost seemed obscene.

Everything seemed obscene: the memory of portions of rice scraped into the garbage that first year, four whole, incredibly extravagant sheets of toilet paper doled out per use. Sugar to bake with. How could they have been so wasteful? How could they have been so naive as to think after one Christmas as a 'confined community' they'd have been going home?

Now they were facing the third Christmas in captivity, and the bleak promise that it held was this very moment disappearing before her eyes.

Fools. They were all fools to have been so trusting.

Dorothy watched the shocking scene as it played out at the main gates, grateful that she'd not let Bobby come along. She almost had, knowing he'd love watching the trucks come in. But something had told her not to mention it to him.

Now she was glad she hadn't. Everyone expected some sort of food offering to come into the camp at Christmas. Somehow, some way, someone was going to get some food in here.

And there it was.

On the YMCA trucks. The ones that were being forced to turn around and leave without delivering their bounty. The Japanese armed guard would not relent.

"Prisoners have plenty."

And when they had leveled their guns at the trucks, the drivers had no choice. They had to leave. Taking the bounty with them. Taking the life-saving food away.

Dorothy fought her simmering anger. She would not—could not—allow herself to lose her temper. Slowly, she forced her fisted hands to loosen and set her fingers fluttering shakily against her thigh to press imaginary keys. Anger would be her undoing. She knew that with every fibre of her being.

Dearest Mother,

These Japanese will do anything to save face. Today they turned away
life-saving food, because it came in YMCA trucks. Trucks made in
America. The drivers would surely report seeing emaciated prisoners

desperate to get their hands on the food. They would tell the world that the Japanese were letting women and children starve. Japan would lose face, and that would never do. I watched the trucks disappear, taking the children's Christmas with them and I thought, I thought for a minute that, that I would...

Without the expected food to rally the most desperate among them, she knew the death toll would mount. Rations had been cut yet again, to portions too minuscule to count on anyone's scale of survivability. She could no longer tell if the children's tin soup mugs had even been used, they'd become so adept at gleaning every drop and dreg.

As the last truck disappeared in puffs of dust the soldiers turned to the small crowd. They were angry, too. They would have had first choice at anything that came off the trucks. It was their feast, too.

Dorothy turned her back, not daring to let them see her burning eyes, and began to shuffle back to the Annex. She would roll through her day as she did most days now. The light-headedness had become her normal state of being. For the first time she felt oddly grateful for her swollen ankles, grateful for the weight of them that anchored her—even as they tethered her to the place she desperately wanted to leave.

Her medical bag banged brutally against her thigh as she swung around. It was too heavy today, and nearly toppled her once or twice as she headed to her room. Nothing would part her from her bag now until she hid its contents beneath her bunk. It was too precious, even more so now that the trucks had been turned away from the gate.

She could almost feel them rolling about in the bottom of her satchel, singing to her. Six sad little canna bulbs.

Christmas dinner.

· · · ·

In the days leading up to Christmas, Dorothy quizzed anyone she thought might help her know how best to use the cannas. Boil them whole or shred them first? Get them wet and roll them in rock salt and let them sit for awhile? The suggestions were as varied as the people who made them. But at last she'd set upon a recipe utilizing the best suggestions and the only ingredients she had with which to improvise.

In Her Own Words
Dorothy's Postwar Essay

Only 2 ½ oz. of water per child per day was allowed. But, we had so little to eat...and the kids stayed hungry...

Fred was very thin; both kids weighed less than they had 3 years earlier; I myself was down to 100 pounds, some of which was edema.

I recall our last Christmas before the war ended; Fred and I dug, scraped and boiled some canna roots, seasoned them with rock salt, and invited friends for our "feast" to celebrate the coming of Christ!

The Santo Tomás Story
A.V.H. Hartendorp
Page 358

Late in the month, the health committee informed the Internee Committee that, along with the increase of dysentery, there were occurring a number of cases of food poisoning in which the cause could be traced to the use of strange plants for food. On the thirtieth the internees were warned in a broadcast against the use of hibiscus leaves, canna-lily bulbs and roots, and hemp.

Instructions were given for the proper preparation of the core and heart of the root of the banana tree, a taro and cassava root, both of which had outer skins of a poisonous nature.

· · · ·

The strange taste of the canna shreds that bolstered their usual meager lugao seemed appropriate. A strange taste for a strange setting. The only familiar aspect of Christmas 1944 was the holy message that still burned clear and strong in hearts that could not countenance diminishing it.

Christ is come.

For several weeks leading up to Christmas that joy had lingered in small ways about the camp, until true to form, the Japanese army found a way to squelch it. Earlier, on Christmas Eve day, the camp's leader—Carroll Grinnell—had been thrown into jail. Most suspected it was a reprimand and he would soon be released. But on January 5th, he and three others were taken to some unknown location, and that news rocked the entire camp. Carroll Grinnell and Alfred Duggleby led the camp committee and between the two of them were responsible for nearly every decision that had kept the camp functioning and fed these past three years. Ernest Johnson and Clifford Larsen were arrested with them, all on suspicion of having had contact with guerrillas. It was an accusation that the Japanese generally greeted with the most dire of punishments.

The arrests seemed to signal a rampant paranoia among the Japanese, which sent internees into paroxysms of both fear and elation. Fear that if the men who had worked most closely with the Japanese in running the camp were not spared the wrath of their jailers, no one would be. Elation because they knew paranoia to be the best possible sign that the Japanese feared they were about to be overrun.

And they were right.

On the third day of February, a local casket maker delivered his order to the gates of Santo Tomás. It happened every week now. Because internees were dying of starvation each week.

The camp undertaker accepted the order, and surreptitiously acknowledged the Filipino casket-maker's signal that the third casket from the bottom was for some reason special.

The stack of caskets rattled and creaked as he rolled his cart to the area set aside for burying the camp's dead. As soon as his helpers lifted the casket third from the bottom off the cart, he followed, waiting for them to return to the cart.

When he saw their backs, he turned to the casket, lifted the lid slightly, and felt along the underside of the lid until his fingers touched the corner of a slip of paper sticking out from beneath a strut.

He hurriedly worked the paper free, deathly afraid that he would be seen before he was able to retrieve the message.

But it slipped free. He clutched it in his hand, stood, reseated the lid, nodding as if it had passed his inspection, and walked a few feet away. He made a show of pulling his notebook from his pocket and flipped it open, ostensibly to study the names of the departed. But inside the notebook he opened the small note and read its brief message:

Be careful. Something happens tonight.

His outside contact was rarely wrong, and within an hour, the message seemed to be validated.

For weeks squadrons of American planes had passed high overhead, dropping their explosive payloads on strategic Japanese installations.

But on that February afternoon, a small squadron of American planes approached Santo Tomás, banking in from the south, their noses pointed toward the barrage of bombs that were decimating the enemy. As they neared the camp, they dropped altitude, skimming low across stripped palm trees and crumbling houses. Just moments out from the camp one plane dipped side to side, waggling its wings.

Every ear in camp was fixed on the planes that seemed to be barreling through their space, though most dared not look. In the instant before they crossed the camp boundary, furtive glances revealed that the pilot who had waggled his wings had his canopy open. And in the next instant something fluttered past the wing, dropped by the pilot's own hand onto the camp's grounds.

It was a message.

Wrapped in the straps of his own flight goggles.

Roll out the barrel! Christmas comes tomorrow!

The carpenter couldn't know which message was more accurate—tonight or tomorrow. But he set his own hopes on tonight. And he was not disappointed.

MEMOIR OF PETER ROBERT WYGLE
THE RESCUE OF SANTO TOMÁS BY ROBERT B. HOLLAND PG 184

By this time our main preoccupation was food. We had survived without much of it for about a year, and that tends to color one's thought processes. We were pretty far down on the scale of physiological well being, though I don't remember being particularly concerned about it. Mom and Dad were slowing down considerably, and we made jokes about the beriberi. We'd stick our fingertips into our water-filled ankles and watch the holes stay there for several minutes. Any infections we got would last forever, and we'd have to force ourselves to get up several times a night to go to the bathroom because we were so weak. Nobody ran anywhere. They didn't move very much at all if they didn't have to. But this came on so slowly that I don't think we realized what was going on—at least the kids didn't. I guess that's how starvation works. One morning, instead of waking up, you're just dead.

CHAPTER SIXTY

THE HARBINGER

Dorothy was halfway between the Annex and the clinic when the low-flying squadron came bursting through above her head, barely skimming the top of the Main Building. Their thrumming engines were the same as the hundreds they'd heard overhead for weeks now, yet they seemed to vibrate like a child scarcely able to hold a secret. They pulsed and sang, and as the lowest plane waggled its wings and skated off into the clouds it seemed to take with it the tremor that had sat in her stomach for countless days.

She stood frozen, searching for the lump of fear that appeared to have vanished, expecting its return at any moment. But it did not. Instead, her breathing steadied, as did her pulse. She'd prayed for more than three years for an end to the war, and now skies dominated by friendly aircraft seemed to signal that it was finally happening.

Dearest Mother,

I know that you will catch my meaning when I tell you I have been afraid. I used to think fear was an unreasonable response made by people of weak faith, just as stage fright was only experienced by those who are unprepared. But my friend Grace has revised my thinking. She's the most marvelous violinist, Mother. Such a Divine energy flows through her, such surety that her fingers will find the sweet, pure center of each fleeting note.

I commented to her once that her gift was so remarkable that surely she never experienced anything so amateurish as stage fright. Well, she looked at me with her beautiful hazel eyes and told me that while she didn't call it stage fright, she did call it performance anxiety. She laughed, saying that one day I should ask her husband about it. And then she became serious and said, "If any performer ever tells you they are not nervous, then I guarantee that you will not hear their best performance. One needs a bit of nerves, anxiety, apprehension, whatever you want to call it, to be on the fevered pitch of your very best performance."

So I think fear or apprehension has perhaps done that for me—kept me on the fevered pitch of my best performance so that my flagging energy and wasting body didn't affect my skill as a doctor. As a parent. As a wife.

Grace Nash has her "four strings to survival", as she calls them, the strings of her violin that have kept her sane in a world gone mad. I've had my practice, the knowledge that though my hands are tied, they are not powerless, unproductive, fruitless.

Fear doesn't have to incapacitate or weaken a person. Fear doesn't make one less courageous. Fear merely exists to remind one of one's vulnerability.

I began to understand that concept early on when I stupidly challenged a Japanese guard. For some reason I expected him to address my situation logically, to see the sense of what I was insisting upon. Well, he either didn't see it or couldn't see it, and it made him angry. I know now that he couldn't help but be angry. Probably because he DID see the sense of what I was asking and was bound by unreasonable restrictions put upon him to deny my reasonable request. I embarrassed him. I made him lose face. And I felt the point of his bayonet hover inches from my waist.

My vulnerability had never been made more clear. My children might or might not have a mother, depending upon that soldier's ability to leash his anger. That was the day I first felt the leaden weight of fear in my belly.

Today an American plane swept through the camp, barely missing the trees. It took with it my fearfulness. My apprehension. My sense of vulnerability. It stripped away the sledge of trepidation and I felt my faith shining through more fully than I have ever felt it in my life.

I shall see you soon, Mother. The skies have told me so.

Grace Chapman Nash
by Judith W. Cole
http://aosa.org/documents/100 Yrs of Graceful
Living and Teaching.pdf

Grace, Ralph and their two young sons endured more than three years of internment in various prison camps including the dreaded Los Banos. They survived dysentery, hepatitis, lice, bedbugs, separation, acute starvation, and the birth of their third son. It was her violin, her four strings to survival, to which she turned for comfort and to comfort others. She received a small bag of mongo beans from one Japanese soldier for performing with her violin. This occurred just prior to the family's rescue on February 23, 1945, just hours prior to scheduled execution. Their lives had been spared and for that gift, Grace dedicated herself to living each day to the fullest.

· · · ·

They were coming. American troops were coming.

At last.

To say that the rumor mill was in a frenzy would be an understatement. The Americans were coming. The Americans were here. The Americans had been turned back outside the city. The Japanese have scheduled us for execution in three days. The Americans have surrendered.

Dorothy shut her ears to the camp's whispered joys and fears. Too many times they had seen their hopes soar, only to have them hammered back, beaten down by a vile oppressor. She would not watch for the Americans like others did. She didn't need to. It was a cruelty which she would no longer inflict upon herself. She *knew* they were coming. That was enough.

Bobby, however, soaked up all the rumors like a little sponge.

"What will they look like, Mom?"

Dorothy heard his question but had lost the thread of his conversation. "Who, dear?"

"The Americans. The Marines. The ones who're going to let us out of here."

"Ah. Well, they might be Marines. And they might be Army. They'll look just like your dad and his friends, except not so skinny. Some will be younger, some will be older. But they'll all be dressed alike in uniforms."

"Like the Japs?"

"The Japanese. Yes, dear. That's how soldiers dress. All the same."

Bobby continued to work on his drawing. He'd found a rock that worked like a piece of chalk and now the floor of their tiny space was covered in smudged sketches.

"What kind of plane is that?" she asked, relishing a quiet moment to drink in the sight of her clever, talented, winsome son as he sketched on the floor.

"It's the kind we saw this morning."

"Bobby!" Her heart stuttered at the thought of her little platinum-headed bundle standing in the courtyard gazing up at the aircraft. "You know you weren't supposed to be watching!"

That was the trouble with entrusting her children to the care of others while she was at the clinic. They thought Bobby was a perfect, sweet, angelic child who would never, ever, consider breaking a rule.

"It's okay, Mom." He sounded so grown up, trying to reassure her that his lapse was insignificant. "I stayed under a rubber plant the whole time. Nobody see'd me."

"That's no kind of shelter, young man. You are to be indoors! Rules are there for a reason, and I expect you to follow them, even when I'm not here. *Especially* when I'm not here. I need to know that you're staying safe."

Bobby thought about that for a moment. She must be losing her touch, because he wasn't even chagrined by her scolding.

And then he lobbed his arrow.

"Maybe you could quit being the doctor and just be the Mom. Then you could be here to remember me the rules."

It cut to the quick. The hardest things Dorothy ever had to hear usually came from the mouths of her babies. Bobby had no idea what he'd said. In his own way, it was a compliment. He wished for more time with his mother.

But it bruised her to the core, nevertheless.

She sat down on the floor beside him, struggling to get down now that her beriberi had taken ownership of her ankles and her bones hurt all the time. She fingered his pure white hair while he was drawing.

"Bobby?" she asked quietly. "What did you say they call this airplane again?"

"It's a B-24, Mom. A Libator."

"A Libator?"

"Uh-huh."

Dorothy leaned across him to look more closely at the sketch. He was right. It was a B-24.

The Liberator.

Bobby was inscribing on the floor a perfect image of the planes that had so profoundly moved her just hours earlier. It was a perfect image, drawn by the smiling boy who'd never known freedom, yet somehow knew the harbinger of freedom when he saw it. It should be a monument to the child's innate knowledge that in those winged chariots were men who would show him for the first time what freedom looked like. Smelled like. Tasted like. It should be etched in stone, mounted on the walls for all to see.

But it had been sketched on the floor for all of ten minutes now. Too long. It could never be seen. Not by anyone, lest they feel the necessity to tattle. And so she had to break her little son's heart just a bit and help him scuff away his drawings.

He smiled up at her.

"It's okay, Mom. I got another one."

Dorothy gulped. "What...another one? Where? We'll need to make it disappear too, you know."

"Can people do that?" His little blue eyes were wide with wonder.

"Well, that depends. Where exactly is this other plane?"

Bobby gave her a roguish smile.

And pointed to his forehead.

The other plane was already safely stowed.

In his brain.

WE BAND OF ANGELS
BY ELIZABETH M. NORMAN

The malnutrition led to a variety of ailments: neuritic pain (inflammation of the nerves), parasthesias (numbness in the hands and feet), ocular pain (sharp ache in the eyeballs and blurred sight or double vision), pellagra (raised red spots on the skin that eventually become dry and scaly, and bleed), ariboflavinosis (sores on the lips and a red and swollen tongue) and anemia (reduced red blood cells causing extreme fatigue and weakness). The lack of proteins and vitamins led to small epidemics of measles, whooping cough, bacillary dysentery, and left almost everyone else dizzy with headaches.

We lived on the second floor of Main Building. We had a stairway to the second floor and the stairs were on two levels. You went up, say, six steps, then there was a landing, then you had another eight steps to go. Well, it got to the point where you had all you can do to make the first set of stairs when you discover that you have to sit down and take a breather before you take on the next set of stairs. They had to make benches and put them there on the landing [so people could rest]. The writing was on the wall.

...starvation is a slow assault on the body, an inexorable attack. Every day brings with it some small loss of function, and with each loss, each violation, the victim seems smaller, somehow less human than the day before.

"I'd wake up in the morning and when I'd stand up I'd start urinating [on myself]," said Sally Blaine. "It was absolutely so embarrassing, it was terrible. Some of the girls really flooded themselves in front of other people. Josie went to the camp central committee and she told them we've got to have more meat for these girls."

Even the youngest and strongest of the internees began to fail. More than half the camp had swollen hands and feet. Their body chemistry was so askew from malnutrition, they were always dizzy with headaches or had toothaches, bleeding gums and sore tongues. Across campus everyone seemed to walk at a snail's pace, so anemic they had to pause frequently for breath or rest. To the nurses the camp took on a geriatric look.

Eleanor Garen "had a funny feeling that night". The Japanese soldiers on guard duty outside the wall were singing, like men having one last moment together. More ominously, earlier in the day soldiers had placed large barrels under the central staircase in Main Building.

Dynamite? Whispered a few panicked internees.

Rose Rieper snuck a look at the barrels and saw something else, some "stuff", as she put it, "soaked with kerosene". She and some of the other nurses were convinced the commandant meant to "blow STIC up".

SANTO TOMÁS INTERNEE FAMILY'S MAKESHIFT BOMB SHELTER

CHAPTER SIXTY-ONE

THE FLYING COLUMN

It should have been reassuring, watching the Japanese burn everything they couldn't carry with them. It should have been a joy, watching them prepare to leave.

But it was not. It was frightening. It shook the camp out of its lethargy, and the internees watched their captors warily. Was it true? Would they just leave, let the internees walk out on their own? Or would they do the same thing to the people that they were doing to everything else they couldn't take with them?

Over the years of captivity, Japanese propaganda had sensationalized the care they were lavishing on the people at Santo Tomás. According to the Japanese, the internees were treated like honored guests, under conditions that far exceeded the standards of the Geneva Convention.

Once the captives were free to tell of the deprivations, the tortures, the killings, the world would know they had lied. Everything the people of Santo Tomás knew about their captors told them the Japanese would never allow their lie to be found out. They would destroy the evidence first. And that meant—

A cold shiver gripped Dorothy's spine, shot through her neck and lodged as knife points behind her eyes. If it came to that, she would hide the children in her secret place. They would be frightened of the dark, but it was the only place where they would be safe. Still, how would she know when to take them there? If they were already in hiding when a roll call was demanded, there would be hell to pay. If she took them too early and the food stash ran out, she'd risk exposing them by creeping out to bring more food.

The pain behind her eyes began to throb. It was impossible for her to plan. She would have to rely on her instincts. She prayed to God she would know the signs when the time came.

Meanwhile, watching the Japanese preparations became infuriating. They clamped down on any minor infraction, real or imagined.

But so far, the only internees who had been singled out were the Camp Committee. These four men seemed to have received the brunt of the hostility. In retrospect, everyone believed that weeks before, on Christmas Eve, no less, they'd seen the first indication that the Japanese were preparing to leave. It was then that, with no warning whatsoever, the four men who had served as the camp administrators had been taken by the Japanese and not heard of since. No charges had been made, no indication why they were being singled out.

It was no surprise, however. These were the men who would know any deals that had been struck between the Japanese command and the internees. These were the men who would know any bribes that had been passed. These were the men who would know if relief supplies were distributed to the internees as intended, or the Japanese had kept them for themselves. If the Japanese wanted to get rid of any evidence of wrong-doing, it was clear that they would have to silence these four.

Everyone in camp knew that wherever the men were, they had to be suffering terribly. Few came back from Japanese custody able to walk upright without assistance.

It was possible they weren't being fed.

It was possibly even worse than that.

It was possible that they were already dead.

SANTO TOMÁS INTERNMENT CAMP
LIMITED PRIVATE EDITION - FREDERIC H. STEVENS
© 1946 - PAGE 70-71

December 23rd [1944] ..."In the afternoon (of this same day) a number of military police came into Camp and a platoon of soldiers were also brought up from the gate. The Hospital and compound were closed and thoroughly searched. Guards were posted at the doors and inside the Main Building, and most of the Main Building was searched. Mr. E. E. Johnson was arrested about 3 P.M. and presumably taken out of Camp for investigation; Mr. C. C. Grinnell, A. F. Duggleby and Clifford L. Larsen were arrested later and held in the Commandants office until after 7 P.M. when they were lodged in the Camp jail. The shanties of these four internees were thoroughly searched by the military police and soldiers and also Mr. Duggelby's sleeping quarters in the Finance and Supply office. No indication was given as to the reason for their arrests."

C. C. Grinell was one of the most prominent men in Camp, being Chairman of the Internee Committee. A. F. Duggleby, vice president of Benguet Consolidated Mining Company, had held important positions in the Camp administration since its organization; Ernest E. Johnson was the Special Oriental representative of the United States Maritime Commission, and Clifford L. Larsen was in the service of the Atlantic Gulf and Pacific Company, Manila. The arrest of these four men profoundly shocked the Camp.

THE WAR DIARY OF PAUL ESMERIAN
TRANSLATED BY ROBERT COLQUHOUN
PG 165

Two camp leaders, Carroll Grinnell and Alfred Duggleby, together with Ernest Johnson and Clifford Larsen, were arrested for being in contact with Filipino guerrillas – Larsen, who was innocent, a case of mistaken identity. All four were taken from camp on 5 January 1945. On 21 February, after liberation, their bodies were found buried in Manila. They had been beheaded.

• • • •

An uneasy quiet kept most of the internees indoors that night as everyone pondered the message dropped from an American plane. They hunkered down, not knowing what they were getting ready for. But once again Bobby braved the downpour to collect some scraps of food from the Japanese mess tent. He hardly worried about it anymore, since his grownup buddy Saul Travay always hovered in a hidden spot around the corner, keeping an eye on him. He didn't really need Saul, but if his mom got suspicious all he had to say was that he'd been out with Saul. She'd figure Saul had given him the food, and it wouldn't be a really big lie. Just a little fib.

Tonight Bobby strutted. He swaggered. He approached the tent through the muckish mud with a grin he couldn't wipe off his face. They were going to love tonight's cartoon.

He felt the scrap of cloth inside his pocket. The fabric was getting a bit limp, but so far he'd managed to keep it dry.

Bobby stopped just short of the platform, keeping a respectful distance, waiting for them to notice his presence. He caught the eye of the young guard he always dealt with, and the man grinned, raised his hand in a wave and called a greeting.

But just as he rose, Lieutenant Abiko stepped between him and Bobby. The lieutenant snapped out an angry order and all the men who had begun to wave a greeting suddenly became intently interested in their plates.

Bobby's soldier looked at the armed guard, then at Bobby, shrugged his shoulders and then sat back down. He peeked at Bobby out of the corner of his eye and gave a quick shake of his head.

He was not being allowed to speak with Bobby tonight.

Bobby's face fell. What had he done? Why didn't they like him anymore?

He pulled the napkin from his pocket and stepped up to the platform. Lieutenant Abiko leaned toward him, threatening, jabbing his gun toward the camp, a signal that he expected Bobby to leave.

But Bobby had taken a lot of time drawing tonight's cartoon. He especially wanted the friendly soldier to have it.

Sensing that he might never have another opportunity, Bobby sought and held the eye of the young soldier. He slowly bowed, and before straightening up, reached forward and placed the napkin on the platform. Keeping his head down, he smoothed it out, and then reached into his pocket for the fountain pen the young soldier had let him keep.

With a reverence that belied his years, Bobby placed the fountain pen on top of the napkin, dropped his arms to his sides, and slowly completed his bow.

The mud sucked at his shoes as he backed away, threatening to land him on his bottom. His throat tightened, but he refused to cry.

They'd liked his drawings. He'd liked their food. But the guard with the gun put an end to their exchange that night.

He squared his shoulders as he hurried around the corner where Saul waited. Walking upright just made his hungry stomach cramp all the harder. Still, Bobby felt proud that he had decided to leave the napkin and return the pen. They hadn't kept their part of the bargain. But at least he had kept his.

THE SANTO TOMÁS STORY
A.V.H. HARTENDORP - PAGE 401

Deaths during the day numbered four for the first time in the history of the camp. Men were seen, greeted casually, spoken to; they looked weak and pale—but everyone looked that way. One did not think of them as men who were soon to die, and then they were dead. It seemed that in its last stages beriberi destroys the will to live. Internees began to study each other's faces for marks of death—shamefacedly, pityingly. Men were beginning also to study these facial expressions as applied to themselves. "Does that man think I am going to die? Do I look as bad as that?" The cold fear of death gripped probably most of the weakened men and women in the camp.

• • • •

"You know what it means, Fred," Dorothy whispered. The children were already in the room getting ready for bed while she and Fred said their hasty goodnights at the Annex door. They'd intercepted Saul bringing Bobby home, and something had made Saul spill the whole story of the cartoon and food exchanges. He'd seemed worried, and they'd been too shocked to be angry with the teenager for abetting Bobby's misadventure.

"They're separating themselves from the children because they know they're going to do something bad to them."

Dorothy was adamant that she was right. Fred was skeptical, still refusing to believe the worst. Time after time he had seen the Japanese brutality, and still he refused to believe that they might exterminate the entire camp.

"Give it another day, Dorothy," he pleaded.

"But—"

"Just one more day. Then we'll see. If we need to hide the children, we will, but you'll stay with them."

"I can't!"

"You will." Fred gave her a stern look, one she rarely got from him. "I'll get food to you if it goes beyond a week."

"But they'll take you and—"

"Shh. They'll be too busy to think about finding you. And they won't get anything out of me. You have to trust me."

Dorothy watched the certainty settle over him. At least he saw now that they would have to hide the children soon. At least he was awaking from his state of denial. She would give him the one more day that he asked. If things progressed as far tomorrow as they had today, he would have to be blind not to see that it was time to hide the children.

It seemed the only way. The *only* way. To save her children's lives.

· · · ·

Just after nine o'clock that evening, a strange rumbling was heard. It had the feel of a vast squadron of airplanes coming in low. But this sound was even deeper. It hugged the ground, pounded its message mile by mile as it neared the gates of Santo Tomás. It rose from subterranean depths on velvet-footed megatons to vibrate on the surface.

We're coming, it said.

The shredded trunks of trees bombed bare shook with its approach, shedding their collected ash upon the trembling ground. Roofs of buildings destroyed in earlier bombings lost their tender hold and collapsed, as if bowing to a long-awaited avenger.

Something happens.

Inside the camp, people stirred. Confused, wary. Was it time to hide? Time to run? Run where?

The rumbling escalated. Internees cowered, reached for their emergency kits, the ones that had stood ready for three years. If they had to run, these kits held the meager things they wouldn't leave without. Passports. Birth certificates. Money.

Husbands slipped across campus to find their wives, mothers roused children from their sleep.

Something happens.

At the far end of the wide avenue, the long guns turned the corner first, then swung crazily around, the bulk of the massive tanks that carried them maneuvering in their awkward dance around the corner. Curbs crumbled, pulverized into sand by the forbidding treads of the behemoths.

The tanks advanced, their fearsome rumbling ratcheting to unnerving heights as they approached the gates. Their guns swayed left, then right, then settled into place, trained on the gates of Santo Tomás.

Few inside could manage anything but a terrified prayer. These tanks would lay waste to their buildings before they could make it to the bottom of the stairs.

This was it. And then the cry went up.

"Stars! I see stars!"

The cry was repeated, hall to hall, doorway to doorway. Cautious heads peeked from windows, and a young man broke free from his young wife's grip and ran into the courtyard.

"Stars! They have stars! They're ours!"

Dim figures walked ahead of the leading tank, and then shots rang out. The man leading the squad crumpled, and shadows of Japanese soldiers melted into the shadows of Santo Tomás, running from the army of tanks.

The young husband stood entranced, taking it all in, then whooped and threw his cap into the air as he swung his arms wide and turned his back on the looming tanks still poised outside the closed gate.

"They're ours!" he hollered.

He ran back to grab his wife and together they ran into the embracing arms of the massive guns, into the embracing arms of General MacArthur's 1st Cavalry, U.S. Army.

Beautiful, boyish faces appeared out of the tops of the tanks, and armed soldiers materialized from behind, quickly subduing the foolish Japanese who thought to make a stand.

With the speed of flawless practice, the army entered, set up their perimeters, secured new foxholes and set about reclaiming Santo Tomás. Young GIs tumbled from Sherman tanks with names like *Battlin' Basic* and *Georgia*

Peach. They made their work look easy, a sure sign of the immense skill they'd acquired amid the ugliness of this war.

After three years of waiting, the exchange took place in mere minutes. The threatened prisoners were now the protected citizenry, freed by the unabashed, brazen undertaking of General MacArthur's magnificent young men. His Flying Column.

· · · ·

As welcome as that blessed moment was, it was also the moment that the big Japanese guns that had been focused on Manila swung about and trained their killing force on Santo Tomás. The final Battle for Manila had begun. Several hundred internees who had survived starvation now perished, felled by an Imperial Army that was slow to recognize they no longer held the city.

The Japanese guards held two hundred men hostage in the Education Building for some twenty-four hours before finally demanding that his men be given an escort to the edge of the city. MacArthur's men provided the escort and transported the guards safely to the edge of Manila. And into the hands of guerrilla forces who were only too eager to exact their revenge.

Through that first long day and longer night, Dorothy worked without rest at the hospital where injured internees were brought. The water had failed again early that day, making triage challenging. Dorothy's momentary panic over diminishing supplies was quelled when the soldiers began bringing stockpiles of their own medicine and equipment into the hospital. And barrels of water.

When the bombardment finally quieted and medical personnel were able to re-establish quasi normal shifts, Dorothy slept. But her eagerness to at last celebrate liberation had her slipping from the bed earlier than she might have to seek out her children.

Now she stood in rapt silence, still feeling the tug from Bobby's hand that had drawn her to the graveled quadrangle beyond the garden. She had to look up to see his scrappy little face now, beaming atop a huge American tank where he sat on the knee of an American GI.

She had held him at bay as long as she could, keeping the children with her at the clinic while the Japanese mercilessly shelled the campus. They seemed relentless, aiming all their vitriol at the U.S. troops, only managing to kill or maim more internees than soldiers. The dust had not yet settled as the enemy guns began to discover what it felt like to be overrun by the Allies. The soldiers knew when it was safe and encouraged the internees to come out. Dorothy knew that she needed to offer her children this moment of rejoicing. And to share it with them.

. . . .

She felt indecent, nearly naked in her flimsy, threadbare cotton. The uniforms of these soldiers looked like veritable suits of armor, made as they were of thick, sturdy khaki that might still keep a crease if not so covered with the filth of the battlefield. By comparison, their very sturdiness seemed to mock her disheveled state.

These fellows looked as capable as their actions proved they were, and she had been surprised to note how small and careworn the Japanese soldiers looked by contrast when at last they had been marched out of the Ed Building.

The young men were everywhere now, and Bobby could scarcely keep from scrambling out from under his bed each time a spate of shelling resumed. A particularly friendly squad had built their small bunker just beyond the Annex, and both children were mesmerized by the easy banter that drifted through the window. And by their infinite supply of chocolate.

The soldiers' jocular tone never missed a beat as they went from "at ease" to full alert. They could sight in on a rogue gun that sought to pin them down and quickly silence it, resuming their conversation exactly where it had left off.

SANTO TOMÁS INTERNMENT CAMP
LIMITED PRIVATE EDITION - FREDERIC H. STEVENS
© 1946 - PAGE 380-381

To be shelled when every internee had that feeling of exaltation of being freed, petrified the minds of all. They were dazed, and absolutely helpless from physical or nervous shock. The horrors they had suffered in the past faded into insignificance and were beyond comprehension. Each shell had a sound all its own... They saw their comrades, their wives and children torn to fragments. They had no chance to retaliate—they could only say: "Thy will be done."

...No one knew just where a safe place was, but the opinion was that the north side of any building was the safest.

...So, now in the Camp's temporary graveyards were rows of newly dug graves and in them were the mortal remains of those unfortunate internees who had fought starvation and cruel treatment of the Japanese for over three years, only to lose their lives at the end—but they died with the knowledge that America had come back—that over them would float the flag they loved. To the survivors, there was the dimness of the future, a new life to begin from scratch.

A MORTAR ROUND HITS THE FRONT OF
MAIN BUILDING DURING THE BATTLE FOR MANILA

The second night of bombing was merciless, and the sound of crumbling masonry told Dorothy there would be scores of wounded needing attention.

But at last Fred gave the all clear and Bobby scrambled out to check on his crew. Dorothy scooted out from under the bed and brushed the debris from the back of Fred's shirt. He had stretched himself across the opening at the edge of the bed, shielding them from the chips of mortar and brick that flew in the window when the enemy gun had made a direct hit taking out the corner of the opposite building. Her fingers made swift reconnaissance and found only scratches. Carol stayed where she was, finishing up the latest entry in the notebook her "Yank" had gifted her.

Fred's arms stretched across the small living space, one hand on his daughter's foot, the other hooked through a belt loop on his son's britches.

Dorothy was satisfied. All was well.

She grabbed her medical bag and kissed the top of Fred's head before she dashed into the night. It wasn't difficult to follow the cries of alarm that would lead her to the injured.

She stopped, turned, and looked back at the window. Now all three were framed there, watching her as she sped on a mission of mercy. She blew a kiss, and they answered it in kind, and then she turned.

Soon. Soon. Soon she would just be the mommy. But right now her hands were needed elsewhere. For now, for at least one more day, she would be the doctor.

• • • •

It took weeks for everything to get sorted out, and for the most part, the problems were easy to solve, trivial and merely a nuisance.

Repatriation brought with it the blessings of food, the absence of fear for personal safety, and trepidation over how vastly the world had changed while the internees were absent from it.

By the third of March, the Allies owned Manila. The battle for the city which had originally been declared an Open City—meaning it should have remained free of military aggression—was at an end. Manila was horridly decimated.

But it was over.

What would the future hold? The future that had been so dearly longed for was now upon them. One mere step forward and they would be swept up in it. Would it demand more of them than they were able to offer?

All the possibilities and the challenges that freedom embodied lay daily on each heart.

On the second day after the soldiers arrived, news had swept through the camp that stopped every internee in their tracks, forced healing hearts to stutter and laughing lips to tremble into a muttered prayer.

That was the day, they were told, that the High Command of the Japanese Imperial Army had scheduled mass executions for every internee in camp. Every man, woman and child was to have met their death at the hands of the Imperial invaders on February 5th, 1945.

TERRY: THE INSPIRING STORY OF A LITTLE GIRL'S SURVIVAL AS A POW DURING WWII
BY TERRY WADSWORTH WARNE

During the shelling, Lt. Jerry Shea and his companion told my parents...they had seen the drums in the basement of the Main Building. The newspaper in Laramie, Wyoming, published a portion of a letter written by Robert Corey, one of our fellow prisoners who was a mining engineer, to his mother right after liberation that said the Japanese "had hidden dynamite and drums of gasoline throughout all this camp, with orders to kill and burn everyone in the camp at first sign of our soldiers."

My parents had been told that the Japanese had placed drums of gasoline in the basement of the Main Building with the intention of herding all the men and boys into the building and setting it on fire to kill all of them like they did to the American military prisoners on the island of Palawan. The women and girls were to be held as hostages and taken to the front lines for the protection of the Japanese troops.

JAPANESE POW KILL ALL POLICY
TAKEN FROM AN EXHIBIT INTRODUCED DURING THE TOKYO WAR CRIMES TRIAL. IT IS KNOWN AS THE "KILL ALL POLICY" AND WAS ADMITTED INTO EVIDENCE ON THE 9TH OF JANUARY, 1947.

2. The Methods. (a) Whether they are destroyed individually or in groups or however it is done, with mass bombing, poisonous smoke, poisons, drowning, decapitation, or what, dispose of them as the situation dictates.

(b) In any case it is the aim not to allow the escape of a single one, to annihilate them all, and not to leave any traces.

I hereby certify that this is a true translation from the Journal of the Taiwan P.O.W. H.Q. in Taiwan, entry 1 August 1944.

Signed, STEPHEN H. GREEN [American cryptographer]

This document was transmitted to every POW Command and every POW prison camp commander.

Though there was much speculation, at no time did Dorothy hear that any Japanese soldier had lit or attempted to light any of the deadly gasoline barrel bombs that had been stowed beneath the stairs in Main Building, just yards from the children's ward. Yet knowledge that they may have been ordered to do so chilled her marrow.

It seemed now that mere hours were all that had separated her family from victory in life and victory in death. A handful of minutes. That's all.

They had survived starvation, humiliation, deprivation and isolation. Blackouts, bombings, air raids and artillery shells. They had lived with courage and determination and abiding faith that they would see home again.

After surviving three years and two months of captivity, Dorothy, Fred, Carol and Bobby joined hands and walked out of the blackout and into the light—a light of a very different kind. It was the light of freedom.

〜〜〜〜〜〜〜〜〜〜〜〜〜〜〜〜〜〜〜〜〜〜〜〜

From Fred's memoir — March 14, 1945

No words can describe my feelings the morning I took a walk outside Santo Tomás. I suppose we shall never feel just right until we set foot on the USA. We have not dared even to dream of that until the boys came in for we knew what could easily be the end of our internment, altho that thought never disturbed us. One day when the full story has been written we may then fully realize how narrow was our escape. Nevertheless we shall always be grateful to those who gave all that we might live. The remainder of our lives however well invested cannot pay the debt.

CAROL AND BOBBY IN DENVER 1945

CHAPTER SIXTY-TWO

EPILOGUE

It wasn't until April 9, 1945, that Dorothy ushered five-year-old Bobby and seven-year-old Carol Joy onto the repatriation ship bound for a San Pedro pier outside Los Angeles.

Bobby had turned five just twelve days after liberation and left the confines of Santo Tomás for the first time only three days after that birthday. He'd barely turned two years old when they'd begun their years of confinement in Calinog, Iloilo, and then Santo Tomás. There was nothing in his memory of life outside a barbed wire fence or an iron gate. So everything about this immense world they called *freedom* was new to him. And not the tiniest bit of it was to go uninvestigated.

Dorothy answered every question, explained every new task in great detail. Her little son's eagerness to meet his grandparents touched Dorothy in a way she'd always known would happen but was incredibly moved to witness. When he asked if they would have to stand in line for roll call at Grandma's barracks, she nearly wept.

So it was rather a forgotten birthday, though Bobby never noticed. How could he, when he got to ride with his GIs on a troop transport, have the run of a tent city while the papers were sorted, and walk up the gang plank of the biggest ship he'd ever seen?

How could he when every GI offered him Hershey bars and every Navy nurse gushed over his beautiful curly white hair? Birthdays were nothing compared to this. Not in his experience, at any rate.

Departure for home took place under a melancholy cloud, as Fred stayed behind to find his way to Iloilo. He would retrieve the college files he'd hidden in a cave in the hills and get the college running again before he would join them stateside. The pain of separation kept tears flowing long after the ship slid over the horizon.

They'd made the trip in 1941 aboard a belligerent's boat, running silent and dark through enemy waters. The danger was not yet over, but the atmosphere among the passengers was one of nervous joy. Had the world moved too far beyond their reach while they were suspended in time?

Letter from Fred
June 5, 1945

...next week I hope to go to the place where our missionaries hid out. Yesterday, the record of their tragedy was made official and I have a copy.

[The college] seems to have fared very well: lost only 2 bldgs, but all but 10% of their library. Once I get these trips out of the way and something of an organized group set up, I am going to plan for home. Hope it will be the last of this month, but don't count on it until I have more definite ideas. [It was not until August that Fred would be reunited with Dorothy, Bobby and Carol.]

I am understanding too what a whale of a difference it makes to have the family here and not have them here. There is an emptiness that takes the fun out of work. I shall be glad when we can continue to plan things together and do them together. I am sure it was right to come here but I shall be mighty happy when I can turn my face homeward. Till then, I'm loving you one and all and am eager to be with you.

Fred

Bobby missed his dad—his best pal—sorely, so for twenty-three days at sea he made everyone on board his best friend and found more than enough time to get into mischief. The second day at sea, Dorothy stooped over to throw down a rug for him to sit on and threw a disc in her back. Now Mom was not the doctor, but the patient. Friends from camp looked after the children while

Dorothy lay in agony in her sleep hammock below deck.

But once they set their feet upon American soil, there was no holding her back. She laughed as Bobby discovered apples, carrots, and elevators. They spent hours in their own personal bathtub, reveling in the idea of one bathroom per family, personal automobiles, and pudding.

CAPTURED: THE JAPANESE INTERNMENT OF
AMERICAN CIVILIANS IN THE PHILIPPINES
BY FRANCES B. COGAN

...as some explained later, leaving fellow internees proved much harder than anyone had originally thought it would be. Who else could empathize with their experience or turn an understanding eye on peculiar, camp-related behaviors: children, for example, unconsciously sneaking food away from a meal and secreting it in a room or finishing dinner by licking the plates—a "habit that was hard to break," according to former internee Susan Magnuson DeVoe.

And then came the reunions, introducing her son to her sisters and mother for the first time, watching their instant bond, and wiping each other's tears. The generosity of their family and friends went miles toward setting them up for housekeeping, something Dorothy ferociously addressed. She would make a haven for Fred to come home to. Soon. But never soon enough. Every minute of separation was a trial, even knowing that it was temporary.

The Japanese had been so very wrong. Deanna Durbin was indeed not dead! But oh, how the world had changed. Dorothy was making decisions over things she'd never even known about before. The ration cards everyone had used during the war were new and mystifying to her, though so very welcome. 'Golly' seemed to be a word she was going to have to work into her vocabulary. Women wore slacks now as much for fashion as for practicality. And everywhere she turned there was another telephone jangling off the hook. The sounds, the smells, the smiles—all were new to Dorothy.

But there was one thing she'd known in her heart for months now. One thing she'd quietly come to terms with. She would not be returning to medicine. Doctor's orders. And it wasn't just her flagging health issues that had made up her mind for her. After one thousand twenty-one days in captivity her dear children had earned the right to her presence in their lives. Fully. Completely. Not what was left of her after sixteen hours a day in some emergency room. Bobby would get his wish. From now on, she would let someone else be the doctor and she would be the mom.

August came and went in a blur of emotions when Fred walked in the door. He and Dorothy moved everywhere in tandem, shoulders touching, hands linked, not daring to let more than an inch or two grow between them, until after weeks the anxiety began to dissipate and they could smile at one another across the room and experience anew that union which had always been their precious, private, very personal bliss.

By Christmas 1945, she and Fred had comfortably established their new home in Boulder, Colorado. When she and Fred attended a student banquet at church, they brought home the red bows, some spruce, four wreaths, red candles and pine cones that had decorated the banquet tables. They were going to be thrown out. To Dorothy the abandoned treasure would fulfill her secret determination to make this the perfect Christmas.

"I need this reef, Mom!" Bobby pulled an evergreen wreath off the front door and held it to his chest. "Please, Mom! We just need this reef at school!"

With three more in reserve it was not at all hard to relent, and Bobby took the wreath to school. He was thrilled, because their classroom was the very first to have any Christmas decorations up. It seemed Bobby had his own plans for a perfect Christmas.

Dorothy was more than happy to share their Christmas bounty with his classroom, and loved her small son even more for his need to share with his new friends. And if anyone ushered in Christmas it was Carol whose hours at her dearly loved borrowed piano kept Christmas in the ear of the entire household.

Now there was the matter of finding a tree. The Boulder hardware store was the only place in town that had trees anywhere near a price range she could afford. So she ordered a four-foot tree.

"But please do make it a lovely, full four feet, if you can?"

The fellow on the other end of the line assured her he would select it for her personally. Then he asked for her name and immediately realized that he'd heard a bit about her family's war experience.

"It just has to be a nice tree, you know," she said, trying to hide her fear that he would send his most unworthy candidate. "It's the children's first Christmas since, since the—"

The prison camp? he'd asked.

"They're just seven and five years old, you see. And Bobby has never known Christmas outside the...outside—"

The prison camp, he said again.

"Yes."

You leave it to me, ma'am, he said. And after he'd scribbled down the address he hung up.

In Her Own Words
Dorothy's Postwar Memoir

> Saturday evening the tree was delivered. I had ordered a four foot one, and because I had to order by phone, and have had some bad luck with getting second rate goods palmed off at times, I capitalized on Santo Tomás and mentioned that it was the first tree the kiddies had had in five years, and that I did want a nice one.

> Well, they sent a lovely one, but it is **six feet tall** or more, and very well shaped. Charged what they had quoted for a four foot one. The kiddies were thrilled with it, and decorated it twice with the things we had before going to bed.

That evening they ate supper picnic-style beneath their beautiful tree that had been delivered by the store owner himself. Together they made plans for Christmas Eve, put the finishing touches on the decorations, and then washed up the dishes.

The very air was electric with anticipation of this first Christmas. The children had absorbed every bit of newness so easily that it nearly defied belief. How resilient they were. How preciously exuberant.

Fred stepped behind Dorothy and tugged off her apron as the last plate was dried.

"A most satisfactory meal, darling wife."

She leaned back into his familiar strength. The weight they'd already recovered made them once again a perfect fit.

"So good of you to say so, dearest husband," she smiled.

Life was far from settled, with Fred still discovering a path to get him back into the academic environment in which he thrived. But the threat was over. This new unknown was one they could easily face. Even happily face. They were safe in the arms of one another again. They had survived. There would be no limits to their rejoicing in the opportunity to face this new unknown together.

They turned to watch their beautiful children who were busy in the living room arranging the ornaments on the tree for the third time. Carol carried the red candles from the dining table to the mantel and Bobby straightened the tree skirt around the little crèche he'd moved from the window sill.

And then they stepped back, those children who had fulfilled her life's dream. Bobby sighed and shook his head slowly. He truly had never seen anything quite as glorious as their very first Christmas tree.

"Sweet Jesus, amen," he breathed.

Dorothy slipped her apron from Fred's hands and hung it on the inside hook of the pantry door. The lower hook. Her hand lingered on it for a moment as her eyes swept upward, across the pristine white coat she'd laundered, pressed, and hung out of the way. Behind the door. Where it would wait in case—just in case.

Fred switched off the living room lamp and paused a dramatic moment before plugging in the tree lights. Reds and golds and Christmas greens danced in the children's eyes, reflections of the lights on a tree that would forever define for them what Christmas was meant to be. They cast away three years of starvation and deprivation, three years of confinement by barbed wire and gunpoint. Three years of bombs and weevils and air raid shelters and dysentery and tropical ulcers.

Tucked away. Vanquished in the glow of that magnificent lighted spruce.

Dorothy handed Fred the angel to set atop the tree. And when it was seated, the children gasped. Its transparent wings and golden halo shimmered in the reflected light. Its open arms seemed to stretch and beckon.

Here. You're here. With nothing that can stand between you and tomorrow.

You're safe, the angel seemed to say. *You're home.*

"Oh, Carol," Bobby whispered. "It just gets gooder and gooder."

❧

DOROTHY IN 1923
FRESHMAN MEDICAL STUDENT

DOROTHY KINNEY CHAMBERS
IN 1996 AT AGE 95

Afterword

While Dorothy did not formally return to the practice of medicine, she came to the aid of countless patients over the remainder of her lifetime. She fulfilled her vision of providing daily care for the elderly by establishing the first elder-care program in Colorado called Elderhaus. She lost her dear Fred in 1985, and never abandoned their commitment to serving their fellow man, which she continued to exercise until her death in 2001 at the age of 100. Her legacy lives after her, reminding all who discover her story that in every aspect of her life, she was a valiant woman.

CAROL JOY CHAMBERS PARK, Dorothy's little songstress, grew into a wonderfully talented church organist. As a volunteer Chaplain for the Detroit Police Department and as Community Relations Director for the Northville Regional Psychiatric Hospital she exercised her unique insights into the human psyche. Her son Stephen and daughter Amy continue to reside in the Detroit area.

ROBERT BRUCE "BOB" CHAMBERS has rarely known a day in his life without a brush in his hand. His artistic gift has been exercised in countless ways including three decades as a professor of set design at the University of Texas and Southern Methodist University. For over thirty years his cartoons have been a much-anticipated feature in the monthly issues of KITPLANES magazine. A collection of his KITPLANES work has been published in *Out of the Basement*.

Bob's first experience at cartooning for the public took place in third grade. In his youth, Bob wrote a letter to General MacArthur and was honored to receive a note in return signed by the General. Bob served in the United States Air Force in 1962-67 honoring the family's debt to General MacArthur and the U.S. military forces who liberated the Philippines. Following in this line, his son Rick also served four years in the USAF. Rick's two children have each made their way through, and into, the United States Military Academy at West Point where MacArthur stands sentry over the Plain.

Bob's early career work appeared in Air Force Base newspapers around the world while he served in Vietnam and also could be seen in publications of the

Air Force News Service in 1966. His cartoons appeared in *Saturday Evening Post*, *Private Pilot*, *Air and Space*, *Pacific Stars and Stripes*, *Aero*, *Wings West*, and *Sport Flying* (England).

Bob has been married for over fifty years to his wife Mame, who he calls wondrous. Their son Rick and daughter Bobbi have gifted them with four grandchildren.

At the time of this publication, little "Wahboots Boos" was 78 years old. Bob was the catalyst for getting his family's story told. He and Mame live in Colorado. And yes, you will still find him most days with a brush in his hand.

BOBBI JOY CHAMBERS HAWK, inspired by Dorothy's tales of healing, attended medical school at Washington University in St. Louis followed by residency and fellowship to specialize in Perinatal-Neonatal Medicine, caring for high-risk newborns. Following her father and brother into the U.S. Air Force, she was stationed in Okinawa, Japan for three years serving the infants and families of those active duty men and women stationed in the Pacific. Upon their return to the U.S., her family settled in Lincoln, Nebraska. She currently lives and practices in Colorado.

September 5, 1991

Dear Grandma,

I apologize for not writing sooner, but school has enveloped me like a storm. I'm now most of the way through the third week of class, and I feel as if I'm in heaven! After waiting four years taking prerequisites, I am finally taking the classes I'm most interested in. I've come to feel that medical school is definitely the place for me. On several occasions I've had the feeling that I was in the right place at the right time.

The school is very research oriented...We have a few activities outside of classwork that are optional for those interested. One of these is the Perinatal Project which sends groups of first year and second year students out into the neighborhood clinics to educate young pregnant women about proper prenatal care.

I'm playing in the student/faculty jazz band called the Hot Docs...

I love you lots!

Bobbi

ABOUT THE AUTHOR

Granddaughter of a concert violinist, MARY POTTER SCHWANER began her musical career in elementary school with the family string quartet, but gave up the violin to study opera at the University of Nebraska-Lincoln. She devoted much time in her early career to performing, directing and promoting musical endeavors throughout Alabama, California and Nebraska. She was Founder/Artistic Director of the Young People's Pocket Opera in Alabama. A move to California resulted in four years as Founder/Artistic Director of the Lake Forest Showboaters, a community music theatre company.

In Mary's "other life" she was a computer tech support and graphic arts specialist and worked as Web Developer for the Nebraska Legislature, HDR Architecture and Engineering, for The National Arbor Day Foundation, and as Director of Web and Media Arts for St. Mark's United Methodist Church.

In her retirement she is a published author, writing novels of historical suspense under the name Bailey Bristol. *Courage in a White Coat* is her first biographical novel.

She lives in Nebraska with her husband of nearly five decades and joins him in doting on her grandchildren who, along with their parents—Ryan and Melissa and their spouses—are her dearest treasure.

Mary's enduring motto remains:

"May you have the vision and the voice to find new songs to sing."

DOROTHY AND FRED IN FRONT OF JOURNALIST ROY BENNETT'S
SHANTY. AT DOROTHY'S RIGHT ARE BENNETT'S TWO DAUGHTERS.

DOROTHY AND FRED REVISITED THE PHILIPPINES
IN 1962

SOURCES

BOOKS

Cogan, Frances B. *Captured: The Japanese Internment of American Civilians in the Philippines 1941-1945*. The University of Georgia Press. 2000.

Colquhoun, Robert. *A Free Frenchman Under the Japanese: The War Diary of Paul Esmérian, Manila, Philippines 1941-1945*. Robert Colquhoun translator and editor. Matador, Leicestershire, UK, 2015.

Hartendorp, A.V.H. *The Santo Tomás Story: With a foreword by Carlos P. Romulo*. McGraw-Hill Book Company, New York.

Holland, Robert B. *100 Miles to Freedom: the Epic Story of the Rescue of Santo Tomás and the Liberation of Manila, 1943-1945*. Turner Pub. Co., 2011.

Holland, Robert B. *The Rescue of Santo Tomás: Manila, WWII The Flying Column: 100 Miles to Freedom*. Turner Publishing Company, Paducah, Kentucky, 2003.

Lascher, Bill. *Eve of a Hundred Midnights: The Star-Crossed Love Story of Two WWII Correspondents and Their Epic Escape Across the Pacific*, William Morrow; Reprint edition (June 21, 2016), Harper Collins, 2016

Nash, Grace C. *That We Might Live: A Story of Human Triumph During World War II*. Shano Publishers, Scottsdale, Arizona, 1984.

Norman, Elizabeth M. *We Band of Angels: The Untold Story of the American Women Trapped on Bataan*, Random House, Reprint edition (June 29, 2011)

Prising, Robin. *Manila Goodbye: A Childhood Eden Destroyed by War...A Memoir Filled with Courage, Humour and Zest for Life.* Corgi Books, A Division of Transworld Publishers LTD, London, 1975.

Sams, Margaret. *Forbidden Family: A Wartime Memoir of the Philippines 1941-1945.* The University of Wisconsin Press, 1989.

Stevens, Frederic H. *Santo Tomás Internment Camp: With a foreword by Gen. Douglas MacArthur, 1942-1945.* Stratford House, Inc., 1946.

Utinsky, Margaret. *Miss U: Angel of the Underground*, Uncommon Valor Press, 2014.

Van Sickle, Emily. *The Iron Gates of Santo Tomás: The Firsthand Account of an American Couple Interned by the Japanese in Manila, 1942-1945.* Academy Chicago Publishers, Chicago, 1992.

Warne, Terry Wadsworth. *Terry: The Inspiring Story of a Little Girl's Survival as a POW During WWII*, Outskirts Press, 2012.

Wilkinson, Rupert. *Surviving a Japanese Internment Camp: Life and Liberation at Santo Tomás, Manila, in World War II.* McFarland & Company, Inc., Jefferson, North Carolina.

Wygle, Peter R. *Surviving a Japanese P.O.W. Camp: Father and son endure internment in Manila during World -War II.* Pathfinder Publishing of California, Ventura, 1991.

VIDEO

Victims of Circumstance. A Kawayan Production. Lou Gopal and
Michelle Bunn, producers. Edited by Lou Gopal. 2006

INTERNET

Radio Station KGEI Presents John Schneider's Voices Out of the Fog.
International Broadcast Station KGEI: 1939-1994. History courtesy of FEBC International
http://bayarearadio.org/schneider/kgei/kgei.shtml

Reports of General MacArthur - The Campaigns of MacArthur in
the Pacific, Volume 1. Prepared by his general staff. Library of
Congress Catalog Card Number: 66-60005
https://history.army.mil/books/wwii/MacArthur%20Reports/
MacArthur%20V1/index.htm

World War II Online Database, C. Peter Chen, founder and editor of
the database, The United States Library of Congress recognizes
WW2DB as a valuable online resource for its researchers.
WW2DB is filed under the control number 2011214255
http://ww2db.com World War II Database

LETTERS

Chambers, M.D., Dorothy Kinney. Five volumes of letters written by
Dorothy between 1928 and 1946 chronicling her work in India
and The Philippines.

Chambers, Fred. 80-page typewritten memoir and letters written to his
family.

SANTO TOMÁS LIBERATION SCENE

ADDENDUM

THESE WORDS WERE WRITTEN BY DOROTHY'S SISTER CAROLYN
UPON MEETING DOROTHY, CAROL AND BOBBY AT REPATRIATION

A great shout went up
The great room tensed with excitement—

Another hour—busses every fifteen minutes.

They are here!
    Dorothy and children,
    waiting for you.

        This thin ashen woman, My sister?
           We hugged and wept—our tears merged.

        The pounding of little fists on my body!
           Auntie, Auntie, we are here!
           We want to be loved too.

They had come home! These resurrected!

God's love held us together.
        Wiping out the years!
        The distance!
        The waiting!

           Carolyn Kinney Hoefflin

May 4, 1945

Dearest Families:

You can't imagine how good it seems to be able to write to you all from the shores of the good old U.S.A. and to be able to do so on a typewriter. This is the first time in some three and one half years that I have touched my hands to a machine and it feels good and at the same time funny.

We left Manila by boat on the 9th of April. It was a big boat, made good time, and for travel of that sort wasn't too bad. We stopped at Leyte and for a short time at the Eulithia Islands (?)—part of the Caroline group, and long enough at Pearl Harbor to pick up some F.B.I. men. We were in a big compartment with about three hundred bunks—only about two hundred women and children however, and there were others just like ours.

We slept on canvas bunks—the canvas laced onto a metal frame. The meals were good, altho the dining room was so hot and so NOISY that Carol used to beg not to have to go down to it, but inasmuch as it was against the rules to take food from the dining room to the compartments she just about had to.

There were complete blackouts, of course, from sunset to sunrise and no passengers were allowed on the decks during those hours. Life belts were supposed to be worn all the time.

About eight days after sailing I stooped over one morning to lay a blanket down on the deck for the kiddies to sit on and something slipped in my back with the result that I was in the ship's hospital for 14 days and was discharged the evening before we docked as the doctor was afraid the motion of the boat would throw things out again if I was up and about. The hospital was well equipped and very comfortable. Ruth Harris and Flora Ernst (the latter especially) came to the rescue and took beautiful care of the kiddies but it was a bit hard on them.

During that time we had a terrific storm at sea, and things more than rolled, tossed and tumbled, and "flew thru the air with the greatest of ease " (the compartments had the bunks in four tiers.) Bob woke up about 2:30 in the morning when things started in to sail, took in the situation, spied an M.P. and yelled, "Hey! Is this boat sinking?" Didn't seem to be worried about it, however. Some thought the noise was due to having been torpedoed, and the MP's had to put down a near panic in one compartment.

We tied up at the pier in San Pedro early Wednesday morning, but aside from the army and navy personnel who were returning on rotation no passengers were allowed to land until two. Then only those with in-hand baggage were allowed to land. Inasmuch as I had a box in the hold I had to wait until the hold was unloaded and all the baggage classified. I got off the boat about five or five-thirty. Got thru customs fairly quickly, and then took a bus for the Elks Club which they were using for receiving center.

Met Carol and Louis Jenson soon after arrival there and they looked out for the kiddies while I got "processed". I finally got a hotel reservation and ration books about nine-thirty. Carol then took the kiddies to the hotel while I stayed with Louis to see if I could pick up the baggage. It had not come in yet so about ten I decided to do without it for the night and went to the hotel. Flora Ernst had not yet registered so Louis went back to check on her and the next morning phoned to say that he had found her, that together they had finally found my bags, and that he had brought them to the hotel at 4 that morning.

Believe me, the whole group of red cross workers, and Louis in particular certainly didn't spare one bit of strength or helpfulness during the whole time. I gave the kiddies each a half of a sod. amytal tablet. Carol had had the fun of introducing them to the mysteries and delights of a bathtub and said she felt like a heel when she finally insisted that they get out. It was as good as a three ring circus for her.

Coming from the boat on the bus, one of the youngsters spied a herd of cows. She said "Oh, look at the goats". A number began to laugh, and Carol turned from the window and said, "Well, what are they then?"

The oil derricks, the traffic, the streetlights, the big buildings, the houses and flowers, were all so new to them. Carol said that when she took the kiddies to the hotel, Bob was just overcome at the idea of Aunt Carol having a car all to herself, and when they started down the streets and he saw all the neon lights he said "You know what? This looks just like a Christmas tree and the presents are the cars running up and down the streets."

They loved the hotel rooms—they were very attractive—and each had a three quarter bed to himself—and did Bob bounce up and down on it. They settled down and slept until about eight the next morning. We got up and went down to a breakfast place nearby and they sat on chairs up at the counter and had orange juice and pancakes and syrup and milk to drink.

Then we went shopping. I got a nice pair of Antioch oxfords and found a lovely pair of brown and white saddle oxfords (long her dream—from a Sears catalogue in camp) for Carol and nice pair of brown ones for Bob. They are the Tom Brown ones. Then we got some new socks for them, some new panties for Carol, and went to the Pig 'n Whistle for lunch. They had children's menus there and the kiddies loved it—had some jello and Carol had some buttermilk and loved it.

Came on back to the hotel, saw Louis Jenson again, and then started for Bakersfield and stopped for an hour with Uncle Ned and Aunt Gladys. I tried to get in touch with Jenny, but she is not listed in the directory and so I finally decided that rather than try to go way out there—sitting is not too comfortable yet, and I was so tired, decided to write her, and hope so see her in a week or so when I go to Los Angeles for some more shopping. Both youngsters loved the cousins—especially wee Ann, and had a grand time with Uncle Ned, who is looking fine. He is just the same old sweetheart that he always was.

We arrived back in Bakersfield after eight. I wanted to call Mother Chambers by phone on Wednesday night and when I couldn't then, thought I would get it in on Thursday, but by the time I had the kiddies fed, it was nine o'clock, and they said it would take three hours to put the call thru. Will try tonight, and get it in early. Asked Mother to wire Mother Chambers Wednesday night.

Last night after arriving when ready for bed, I ripped off the heavy adhesive strapping and had a good hot soak, and then took a Sod Amytal and went to bed. Feel much better this morning, but am going to get a good check up on Monday. This morning the children played with five year old Roger Clark for a while, gloried in picking some flowers, ate a bit of lunch and are both asleep. They have been asleep about an hour so far and I hope they sleep for another hour or so. When Aunt Carol comes home, they are going to open all the packages that are here—Carol is getting two more from the P.O. today. I feel that I could easily start a day goods store.

Aunt Gladys had a box full of lovely cotton materials that she and Mollie had been getting together, and with the pieces Carol has, the things you Denverites talk about and those that Mother Chambers mentions, I think that we are going to be more than well outfitted. The Red Cross gave Carol a cute little pleated beige wool jersey skirt and sweaters, and a darling Alice Blue coat (new), and gave Bob a cute little herring bone pattern coat in light blue and grey with tams, and gave me one of the Navy dress coats—has full zipped in lining, exquisitely tailored, lovely midnight blue, and said that I could keep it if I needed it. May do so. It would obviate buying a winter coat which I do not want to do if we are going back to the P.I.

It is such a joy to be in such utterly peaceful surroundings. Things were so noisy at the camp and on the boat that Bob, especially, was just shouting when he wanted to say something. This morning he said while at breakfast, "Gee, isn't it nice to have it so quiet". Am not pushing food on them just now, but did they enjoy the Naval oranges and some huge red apples, whole wheat toast and some cold cereal and milk this morning. Wanted about the same for lunch.

While we were docked, or rather anchored, near the Eulithia Islands, a boat came alongside to take off the band for a concert on a sister ship. Bob was leaning over the rail and watching the proceedings. One of the navigating officers was eating a lovely red apple. He offered another to another officer on the little boat and the officer replied "I don't want it". That was too much for Bob and he yelled down "I do". So the fellow looked up, spied Bob and threw it up to him and a woman standing next to him caught it for him. Was he thrilled. He divided it with Carol. They had tasted some quite tart apples there in Manila in the last few weeks. Bob had not liked them. He took a bite of this and said with a wry smile "I didn't like those apples in the camp, but oh, boys, this is good."

Bob is crazy to telephone Steve and can't see why if he just takes the receiver off the hook that Steve won't answer him.

My but we will be glad when Fred gets home. I feel awfully selfish to have the kiddies and realize that he is missing out on so much fun as they make all these new discoveries. Carol is going to visit school next week or around that time and I know will enjoy it.

Will try and get a lot more letters written tomorrow.

Loads and loads of love to one and all.

Dor

LETTER FROM FRED AFTER DOROTHY, CAROL AND BOB HAD LEFT FOR THE STATES

St. Tomas
April 10, 1945
Dear Mother:

Well, I'm a bachelor again. Dor and the kiddies left yesterday morning at 8 and did it leave a hollow feeling in me. However, I have survived these 24 hrs and it looks as if I would make it all right.

I immediately took Carol's bed apart and thus changed the appearance of the room but when I came across some of Bob's toys it was almost my Waterloo. But Dor was the thoughtful buddy as usual and left a letter for me to read after they had gone and it was so encouraging that it put new pep into me. We have gone thru much together these last few years and our ties have been considerably strengthened—they were quite strong from the start and grow stronger steadily. And as the kiddies grow older they become dearer than ever. They are so different: Carol, mystical and Bob practical.

Carol was a good sport about going to the States without Daddy but night before they left, at supper, she broke down and shed a few tears but Mother's eyes were moist too and that didn't help matters too much. We were singing our "Grace" before the meal and they asked to sing "Take the Name of Jesus With You". Guess it was a bit too suggestive. Anyhow, they were all brave scouts next A.M. and got off without a shower.

Bob was so thrilled about riding with the driver of the truck who took them to the ship that he didn't realize he was leaving his Daddy for a stretch. He has been so enthralled with military personnel and ordinance that he scarcely stopped long enough to eat his meals. I think you will find him interesting once you get thru his reserve.

Hope you can see the three of them soon but you may have to go to see them for we decided to stay put on this furlough and not waste energy and substance in running around. Plans call for a stop in Bakersfield with Carolyn and then over to get ready for establishing residence in Boulder just as soon as possible.

One slight hope is that Dor might be called to New York to discuss matters with (sorry pen went dry and no ink handy) the Board. In that case I hope she leaves the children with you to visit while she goes about her business and then stops on return to visit with you. You might suggest it in your first letters to her at 1818 3rd St. Bakersfield.

My plans here are still indefinite. I pulled every wire I knew to get to Iloilo and back in time to go home with the family but it was stymied at every turn. My last "trump" was Secy of Int. Mr. Confessor (he helped install me as Pres. of C.P.C.) who called Army officials and asked permission and transportation to our field. The response was "this month" but nothing definite in reply yet.

In the meantime I shall stay here and do what I can to be as useful as possible. The last two Sundays afforded opportunity to speak to soldier audiences: Sunrise Easter Service at Harris Memorial and regimental chapel near here last Sunday. It is inspiring and stimulating and I find an interest in genuine religion on the part of most soldiers. If I have to remain on our field for a protracted period I mean to do all I can along this line and in education (vocational counseling) to help the boys.

While I dislike being separated from the family and delaying my return to my country, I think of the many men in service who have not seen their family for years and I consider my case an easy one—especially since it was our privilege to be together in internment camp and to live as a family during the last year. There is much to be grateful for and we can never pay the debt for our release—truly we were bought with a price. I am glad to stay here and do all I can. The homecoming will be all the more thrilling. I am sure you appreciate my position. I shall write as often as possible.

Love to all,

Fred

Dorothy's Easter Sermon

Note: Dorothy begins by saying "Twelve years ago" because this sermon was given in about 1946. Twelve years prior to that she had just returned to India following her furlough, four years before she met Fred.

Twelve years ago, I arrived back in Gauhati Assam just at Easter time. The air was warm, almost hot, the sunshine brilliant, and the trees aflame with the blossoms--the poncianas or flame of the forest, the honori gos, and the acacias. Roses and flowers were in bloom. One of the younger missionaries had persuaded the church to use the baptistry for the baptismal services instead of going down to the river. It was rarely used because we were right on the bank of the Brahmaputra River and because of the fact that it required a full days' work for a water carrier to fill it. It was beautifully banked with ferns and flowers, and the service was lovely altho the church was small, very plain, and there was no choir. A number of young people were baptized during the service. There was no thought of Easter bonnets, new clothes, etc. Easter was a very special day, but in a different way from its observance here in the States.

The following year, the church voted not to use the baptistry as it was decided that it was more essential to make the service a witness for the Gospel. Early in the morning, around four, we were awakened by the nurses and school girls marching around the compound, thru the hospital, and around the bungalows singing the Easter carols--Christ the Lord is Risen today, Low in the Grave He Lay, and others. Why don't we do it in this country? I think it is even more beautiful than the singing of the Christmas carol at Christmas time. Following the opening of the service, the entire church wended its way down the lovely sloping lawns and across the River Road, down the embankment and out across the sands for some distance. People all along the road stopped, turned to watch, and many followed the church people down to the water's edge. A River Steamer anchored close by let out several blasts from its steam whistle, and dhobies--laundrymen, washing clothes on stones or boards, either stopped to watch, or kept on with their work oblivious to the service going on. The pastor waded out until he found a place where the water was sufficiently deep, and where the ground was fairly secure, and then one of the deacons waded out half way with a candidate, and waited for him, and then took the next one out. When the boys had been baptized, one of the deaconesses did the same for the girls, carrying with her a shawl-like wrap to throw around the girl as she came back up. Between each baptism, the members sang "Oh Happy Day". Following the close of the baptismal service, the church members returned to the church for the rest of the service. It takes a good deal of courage to become a Christian, and to muster thru baptism under such conditions.

The next Easter, 1937, was following my marriage and was spent in Jorhat. The baptistry there was in the church as they were a long ways from a river where such a service could be held. Many of those baptized were boys from the school there.

The following two Easters were spent in the U.S. It was a thrill to hear the choirs, the pipe organs, be one of the throngs that filled the churches, and yet there was a superficiality about it in some ways.

So many were there who perhaps would not again come until the next Easter. Just what did Easter mean to many of them--just a time to come out in a new outfit, or did they hold a sort of superstitious idea that if they came to church on Easter that somehow they had fulfilled their religious obligations for the year?

In 1941 Easter was spent in Iloilo. The chapel there on the College grounds, altho very unprepossessing on the outside, had a cloistered charm within. The students, robed in their blue choir robes, the benches filled with students and faculty, the small pipe organ, the lovely baptismal service, the fine sermon by the Filipino pastor, were lovely, and somehow it was real. One felt the upsurging of new life, the sacredness of life, and the glow of the renewal of faith in the Risen Lord.

In 1941 we were on our vacation in Baguio--the hill station in the Philippines. It is a beautiful spot, and it was a bower of flowers making us think of the hill stations in India. The church there was more like our western churches, and the service was conducted by the American pastor. There again one felt a bit of superficiality, and yet underneath was turmoil, the uncertainty, the fear of war. How could war and its shadows be part and parcel of the same picture of Easter--the Resurrection of the Lord of Lords--the Prince of Peace.

Rumors were flying, people were urging each other to leave the Philippines while there was time to get out. There was a need for the sense of security and peace of knowledge and belief in the Risen Lord, and one was conscious of that longing, spoken and unspoken, in the hearts of those in the service.

Easter Sunday of 1942 came just a few days before we were interned. In the morning the nurses, doctors, some of the people from the town of Calinog (to which the hospital had been evacuated in January), and people from neighboring barrios gather together in the improvised chapel under the part of the school house used for the operating room. The floor of the operating room was only about seven feet from the dirt floor, there were no walls except those made by shrubs and flowers, and ferns.

The pews were elementary school benches. The organ was a tiny portable one. The choir was made up of some of the nurses. The feeling of apprehension and fear was intensified over that of the previous year, and yet there was a sense of assurance that had been lacking before. That afternoon, we, Dr. and Mrs. Waters, Miss Ernst, Miss Buchner, and Miss Harris and ourselves, drove up to the little camp where the Covells, the Rounds, Miss Dowell, and Miss Erickson were staying, and later drove up to Dumalog where the Capiz hospital with Dr. and Mrs. Meyers and Miss Adams was situated. The subject of the conversation was the planning in the event that the Japanese invaded the island which seemed only a matter of days or weeks. Bataan had fallen. Each one had to decide what to do in his or her particular case. Each one had to decide where they could serve best. It had been requested that the hospitals remain open. At first the orders had been to disband them, but to disband a Christian, Mission, hospital under such conditions seemed like running away from opportunity and responsibility. Headquarters were consulted and the orders given to remove all military personnel from the areas around the hospitals--thus making them more or less neutral ground, and to keep the hospitals open, hoping that the policy of allowing missionaries to continue their work which seemingly was in effect in Manila would be a policy for the Islands. Those who had been in educational work, especially those connected with the college, felt that by going into the hills and trying to stay out of the hands of the Japanese, they could help the Filipinos and as we had been assured that it would be a matter of only a few months at the worst, they felt the chances of coming thru were better than if they allowed themselves to be taken. On the Friday following Easter, for no reason that we know of, U.S. forces gave the Dumalog hospital one and one half hours in which to leave the buildings and then burned them. Thus Dr. and Mrs. Meyers and Miss Adams felt that they should go into the hills. Easter Sunday of

1942 was the last time that we saw any of them. You know their story.

Down in Iloilo, in 1943, the protestants in the camp--only about twenty-five or thirty, longed for an Easter Communion service. It was decided to hold one early in the morning. One corner of our small grounds was a bit of a garden bordered with lovely oleanders in bloom, and with one or two trees, and into this area we brought some benches. Mr. Chambers conducted the service. Much had to be improvised. We had no communion wine or grape juice, and we made some from prune juice, a bit of lemon, and some coloring. There was no communion set, but one of them had managed to hang onto a small loving cup of silver. This was polished and used.

For the communion service, we knelt on the grass in the lovely early morning light, and I think that never have I experienced such a sensation of peace and absolute assurance as I had that morning. Everyone was hungry for the sense of peace and security, and I believe that service for many was the spiritual bread that they so sorely needed. The following year Easter services were spent in the Internment Camp in Manila. This was held in what was known as the Father's Garden--a place that had been specially set aside for the Catholic Priests connected with Santo Tomas University. This was used by the Internees for concerts, religious programs, and such. There was no communion service at that time, but the service was lovely. Tensions within the camp were mounting daily, restrictions were being increased almost daily, and I doubt that any service would have been allowed had the camp continued thru the next Easter.

In 1945, Feb. we were released from the Japanese when our own troops came into Manila. Easter came on April 8th, the day before I and the children left for the States. We had been allowed to attend the Palm Sunday services and the Easter services in the churches that remained in Manila.

We went to the Knox Memorial Methodist church. What a thrill it was to get into a church building, hear a real choir, and be a part of a real service. Many Army and military men were there and I think that I have never experienced such a sense of deep thankfulness and such a realization of exaltation--not in the victory from the standpoint of war, but in the fact that the Christian faith had triumphed--that there were people who had stood the test, who had suffered persecution, loss of loved ones, hardships that are not easily described, and yet who, because of their faith in Christ, in the ultimate triumph of his love, and the firm belief that he was real, living, and that because he lived, they too should have the life everlasting, had won thru. That these hardships had only brought about a deepening of their Christian faith, a widening of their sympathies, and that the seed which had been planted under difficulties had grown, that the plants were strong, able to branch out, and supply food and succor to those around them. Never have I seen collection plates so full--frequently the ushers had to stop and pack down the bills. Of course much of the offering came from troops in the service, and it was a thrill to realize that there was such deep devotion and longing to be found in our soldier boys. It was a revelation to many of the Filipinos and helped to counteract other things which they saw.

Last Easter I was in a cast but had the thrill of hearing the early morning services broadcasted from Arlington, Garden of the Gods, and Forest Lawn in Arlendale. The world was full of hope--a brave new world was to emerge, men would share in the good things of life, minorities would come into their own, nations were to become brothers.

BOBBY, CAROL JOY, AND DOROTHY
BOULDER, COLORADO 1946

C. U. PLACEMENT DIRECTOR HELD IN JAP PRISON

Boulder, Colo., April 6. — Colorado university's recently appointed placement bureau director, R. Fred Chambers, is back at the university where he received his master's degree in 1926, but he has seen a great deal of the world in the two decades which have elapsed between his duties on the campus.

Most vivid in his memory is the period when he and his family were imprisoned by the Japanese in the Philippines.

NEWSPAPER ARTICLE APRIL 6, 1946

BOB CHAMBERS AND HIS SISTER CAROL CHAMBERS PARK
STAND IN FRONT OF A SHERMAN TANK

Dorothy Chambers, Former Medical Missionary And Prisoner of War, is ABC Second Vice-President

MRS. Fred Chambers of Alton, Ill., second vice-president of the American Baptist Convention, was a missionary medical doctor in India and the Philippines for 20 years. Her first appointment was in 1928 when the Women's American Baptist Foreign Mission Society assigned her to the mission hospital in Assam, India. Her father, Bruce Kinney, is remembered for his 36 years of missionary work with American Indians.

Dorothy Chambers, with her grandson.

DOROTHY CHAMBERS

Dorothy Kinney and R. Fred Chambers met and married overseas. He was an American Baptist missionary at Jorhat Christian Bible School in Assam. They discovered that they had taken their degrees (hers in medicine, his in history) the same day from the University of Colorado in Boulder but had not met. She also has a degree in science from Denison University, Granville, Ohio.

helped establish the Jorhat Christian Hospital for women and children in 1937 and was the first doctor there. It was started with just a building and 15 iron beds, with board springs and straw mattresses. She was obstetrician, gynecologist, pediatrician and practitioner of tropical medicine. Additionally her staff included only two American nurses and five girls in nurses' training. Two years later, the hospital had 40 beds, running water, electric lights,

flush toilets, and considerably more staff.

Mrs. Chambers speaks also of the success of the Vellore (India) hospital which is a joint project of several mission boards which pooled their resources to make possible one large institution instead of several small ones. "Churches have lost a lot in the mission field by denominationalism," she said. "The people over there (in India) just don't understand why church people work separately."

In 1939, the Chambers were transferred from Jorhat to the Philippines where he became president of Central Philippine College. She was an associate physician at the Iloilo Mission Hospital.

 * * *

DURING WORLD WAR II they were interned for three years at Santo Tomas, which had been Santo Tomas College. Along with seven or eight other doctors, Mrs. Chambers served the 4,000 prisoners there. She was responsible for the children's ward which had 20 beds. Mrs. Chambers and their two children lived in the women's and children's section of the camp for two years, while her husband and all the men were assigned to another section. When the Japanese soldiers moved in, facilities were overcrowded and families were put together. Three or four families lived in a room 25 x 25 feet — one family in each corner.

After Manila was liberated, the Chambers came home. She weighed less than 100 pounds and the children weighed less

than they had when they returned to Boulder, Colo., and Mr. Chambers studied for another degree. They also served a church in Ft. Collins, Colo., before moving to Kansas City where he was a teacher at Central Baptist Theological Seminary. He was a Peace Corps volunteer in 1961 and served one year in Pakistan as a field liaison for Colorado State University.

 * * *

IN 1963 the family moved to Alton, Ill., where Fred Chambers became director of the Shurtleff Foundation on the campus of what is now Southern Illinois University. They live on the second floor of the attractive new foundation building.

Fred and Dorothy Chambers have a son who is an Air Force lieutenant in Viet Nam. His wife and baby boy are residents of Wichita, Kan. A daughter lives and works in Pittsburgh, Pa. The Chambers are members of the Upper Alton Baptist Church where she is active in the woman's society and has taught an adult church school class. She has served on the board of the American Baptist Women's Foreign Mission Society and as program chairman for the National Council of American Baptist Women.

Mrs. Chambers has expressed her full support of President Carl Tiller's four-point program for the American Baptist Convention this year. She believes that American Baptists should be full participants in the Consultation on Church Union.

IN DOROTHY'S OWN WORDS

In the Beginning...

I was always interested in missions and medicine. By age 12, I'd set my sights on becoming a physician. Yes, I was determined. I went to Denison University in Ohio and then to the University of Colorado Medical School, and got my M.D. in 1926. I'll brag a bit that I graduated 2nd in my class—MUCH to the chagrin of the male students. Becoming a WOMAN doctor was NOT easy in those days, let me tell you. And, medical schools would not accept me for a residency in obstetrics because this was NOT an "APPROPRIATE AREA OF PRACTICE FOR A WOMAN." So, I did my residency in psychiatry.

I always knew in my heart that God had a purpose for me in medicine. I felt that I wanted a life of service to the welfare of my neighbor, my neighbor being anyone anywhere in the world. That was initiated early on by an emergency experience of delivering a baby under a bridge in Denver and ministering to the mother who needed loving care.

A Call to Missions...

I grew up knowing ministry and missions in my home life, and the call came naturally. So, I applied to the Northern Baptist denomination (now ABC) and was appointed as an overseas medical missionary in 1927 by the WOMAN'S AMERICAN BAPTIST FOREIGN MISSION SOCIETY.

Here's what I wrote—

"I have no motive in entering missionary work other than to fulfill Christ's ideals and plan for the carrying out and bringing to pass of His Kingdom. I have always felt that the women of the Orient needed a physician as perhaps no other women ever did and that I would be privileged indeed if thru healing their bodies I could bring them into the knowledge of a friend who makes no distinction because of sex, race or color and who with His love would lift them out of their bondage and open new doors, and new opportunities to them and offer them new hope and peace thru his death and resurrection. I do not want to work for the women of the Orient, but with them."

I began my language studies and arrived on the field in Northeast India, in the state of ASSAM—in 1928—single, committed, and full of hope. I wrote home to say that it was the happiest time of my life. I wrote weekly letters regularly to my parents, and my mother kept all those letters!

At Gauhati...

I can tell you that what I found there was PRETTY CRUDE! It was a 45-bed hospital without running water or electricity, no ambulance, no sanitation services, and surgery was done on a rickety table by kerosene lamps or a flashlight. The needs of the people were overwhelming. But, I was young and eager—AND DARING—and began to make improvements, along with working very hard and being on call 24 hours a day.

I continued my study of the language, which I loved. I was able to translate a course in obstetrics for our Indian nurses. I designed bassinets for prenatal care, planned a hospital cookhouse, trained nurses, attended conferences. We were able to get half a dozen other well-trained women on staff.

Self-Taught Surgeon...

I taught myself surgery skills by correspondence study, and performed surgery under those primitive conditions. I allowed God to perform miracles through my surgeries. I often felt a divine power just beyond my fingertips as I performed some of the most difficult surgeries under many hardships. I also learned to do cataract surgery which was a big help to the people.

The first baby I delivered there was illegitimate and unaccepted by the family, so the staff and I gave the little girl loving care until I facilitated her adoption by one of the staff couples who wanted a child.

One day I was awakened at 2:00 A.M. when a woman in labor was brought in after a 4-hour oxcart ride. The native midwife had been unable to deliver the baby at home although she had followed her usual procedure of having the woman lie on the dirt floor—because a bed or anything else touched during childbirth would have to be burned. The hard mixture of mud and dung which coated the floor was filled with tetanus and other bacteria which often caused illness in both mother and baby. This woman's cervix, covered with mud and dung, was inflexible, and both mother and baby would have died without something being done immediately. So, I removed the cervix so the baby could be born. Six months later the mother came back to the hospital, healed and happy, to express her thanks!

Let me follow up with an interesting little story! Later when I returned home on furlough and wished to pursue some special obstetrics training (which was still NOT a profession for women), one of my medical school professors asked, in a very condescending tone, what kind of cases I'd had out there. I related that case to him. His reply was, "What a radical thing to do!" I calmly asked what he would have done in such a case; he had to admit he'd never had such a case!

I could honestly tell him that my cases had included every possible health problem, multiplied by cultural traditions, lack of sanitation, and the social situation.

Furlough after six years...

After six years in Assam, I spent my furlough in New York City and led a seminar on family planning and birth mortality at Johns Hopkins University.

When I got back to India, I met Dr. R. Fred Chambers. What a JOY! He was an educational missionary whose wife had died. He lived in another part of Assam—Jorhat. He was in charge of the Christian Boys School there. We married in 1936, and I moved there and became the first Physician-Surgeon at the Jorhat Mission Hospital for women and children; later became Director. The hospital was a building with 15 iron beds, two nurses, and five nurses in training. Within two years this hospital had 40 beds, running water, electric lights, flush toilets, and "considerably more staff."

Carol was born in India, by C-section. I was still weak when it was time for us to go to the U.S. on another furlough, quite a trip in those days by boat with a little baby!

But as always there was work to be done, and I performed eleven cataract surgeries the day before I left India! I did need to do those cataract surgeries.

Almost all our possessions we had packed for the trip were lost at sea, when the freighter they were on was sunk.

Prepared for the Philippines...

At the end of the furlough in September 1939, I was reassigned to the Philippines, where Fred began work as Dean of Theology of Central Philippine University, and in 1941 he became the President.

I intended to work with Fred at the University, but I soon found that the medical situation in the area needed my attention.

I felt God wanted me to continue serving as a doctor. So, I had to prepare for the Philippine Medical Examinations—a project made more difficult by my second pregnancy and also by not having my medical books which were on the ship from Assam. (Luckily, I got them back later, as they were rescued!) I passed the exams, but it cost me dearly: a long hospital stay and nearly the loss of my baby, due to dysentery which I picked up in Manila when I went there to take the medical exams. But, Robert Bruce Chambers was born by C-section, the Bruce being for my father.

I started my work at the mission hospital in Iloilo City by doing an appendectomy and did most of the care for women and children there, as well as teaching a nurses' class.

World War II came along...

War clouds were darkening over the Pacific all this time. As the war progressed, I along with the other medical staff stayed at our posts at the two mission hospitals because we felt we were where God wanted us to be. When the Japanese were invading Iloilo City, we moved the hospital to Calinog, and our family moved there, too.

It became obvious that the Japanese would take over Central Philippine University, so Fred hid the important university documents in a cave.

Shortly after learning that a Japanese invasion of the Philippines would definitely happen soon, all the missionaries in the region gathered with their families to discuss what to do. We discussed and decided on two options; each family could choose the best one for them to follow, and there would be no recrimination. (1.) To retreat to the rugged mountains to a place called Hopevale, where friendly Filipinos would bring food and supplies to those in hiding until the end of the invasion—estimated to be about 3 months (but turned out to be about 3 years) or, (2.) To remain serving at our mission posts facing almost certain capture and internment in a prison camp or worse.

19 members of missionary families chose to move into the mountains and hide.

We, among others, chose to stay at our posts and risk capture. We made this decision for two reasons: (1.) Didn't think two small children could make the long difficult climb into the hills, and (2.) Did not want to endanger the lives of the Filipino couriers who were at risk if caught aiding the enemies of the Japanese.

It was a difficult time, but I wrote this to my parents:

"Don't worry about us. Just pray that we here may do that which we find to do and do it well, and that we may not fall short of the challenge of this work out here. IT WILL TAKE A LONG TIME TO REPLACE ALL THE HATE IN THE WORLD WITH LOVE, but I have an idea that people are going to be more ready for it when this is over than they have ever been before. Surely this terrible war must bring to the mind and heart of every individual—especially Christians—the terrific need for the love of God in the heart of every individual."

Letter from Dr. Dorothy Chambers

(13 April 1942 - 1 week prior to internment)

ONE YEAR INTERNMENT AT ILOILO...

A few days after these words were written, the Japanese invaders took over our hospital, soon after Easter 1942. They took our family, along with about 50 others, into custody and transported us back to Iloilo. For the next 14 months we and about 100 Protestant and Catholic missionaries, American businessmen, teachers, and others were interned in an elementary school.

Conditions were crowded, food and fresh water were scarce, cooking was done over open fires, and all the work was done by the prisoners. We came with just what we could carry, so everyone's responsible positions, comforts, social status—all had to be left outside the gates. 90-100 were in the camp. Then in June 1943 we were transferred to Santo Tomas camp in Manila, and we were there for 20 months.

Two years in Santo Tomas...

It was a larger (4,000) internment camp, and had been a commuter college. The children and I were housed in the women's building with a 6'x4' space each. In our room there were 7 mothers and 12 small children.

Fred had to be in the gym balcony with the men's cots lined up a few inches apart. Fred could eat with us outside, and he often bathed the children by the only means available—just pouring cold water over them.

A treasure I cherish is the ONE photograph of the children which was allowed to be taken (by a Japanese photographer). We got to send two letters of 20 words each during that time and didn't get any mail for three years.

The camp was somewhat organized; we were allowed to have a camp committee, on which Fred served, to be a liaison with the Japanese; could request things for the camp. We could hold church services and organize some programs. A school and a general hospital were established through the camp committee's efforts. Of the 4,000 internees, one-third were children, one-third were over 65. There was SO much dysentery, typhoid, and other disease. We cooked over charcoal fires in big tin cans.

Fred was asked to teach, and he worked with the youth and counseled them to go to college when the war would be over. I was told to take over a children's hospital which was only a 20-cot shack; had a Japanese director and some American doctors and nurses. This work gave meaning to our life in the camp, and God's purpose in my life shone through as I saved the lives of many children; not a single child died during that time. I arranged with a lovely girl, Jean, to stay with Bob and Carol while I worked at the hospital; she did a great job, and later stayed with us in Boulder and we kept in touch with her for years.

After the bombing started, it was too dangerous for the children to gather at school. Only one shipment of Red Cross Comfort Kits was ever allowed to reach us.

Food grew scarcer and less nutritious with only 600 calories per day, and children received only half portions. The daily allowance was a serving of watery rice gruel with a few leaves of greens and six soy beans. How I worried about my children! I could get fresh heart, cut it up, braise it, and make a gravy. Delicious on rice and nutritious! Made dessert out of cornstarch and sugar. I cooked peanuts and made peanut butter. But, I almost ran out of the many ingenious ways I'd found to supplement their diet. Only 2 ½ oz. of water per child per day was allowed.

One good thing from having to work at the hospital, I did get meals, so I brought some of it home for the kids, which helped some.

But, we had so little to eat...and the kids stayed hungry...

Fred was very thin; both kids weighed less than they had 3 years earlier; I myself was down to 100 pounds, some of which was edema.

I recall our last Christmas before the war ended; Fred and I dug, scraped and boiled some canna roots, seasoned them with rock salt, and invited friends for our "feast" to celebrate the coming of Christ!

I could sew and I made clothes for the children out of any scrap I could find. And, I patched and darned Fred's and my clothes, and made something for us when I happened to get a bigger piece of cloth. I unraveled old sweaters and re-knitted them for sweaters for Carol and Bob.

A few internees (mostly the mixed American-Filipino persons who still had some connections) could hire people to build a shanty, so couples could be together. I remember one of the loveliest things done by one of the wealthy women, an American/Filipino citizen. She had a washing machine and washed menstrual cloths for the women—we just used rags.

Some people were good folks, others were greedy or selfish, or constant whiners.

And then, LIBERATION!

What a dramatic day February 3, 1945 was when an American plane flew low over the camp and the pilot dropped a goggles case with a note wrapped around it which read,

"Christmas will be here tomorrow or Monday."

That very evening American soldiers broke through at all costs to take the camp, setting the prisoners free the very week that the Japanese had set to liquidate the entire camp. Liberation! Freedom!

Sadly, all the missionaries who had gone to HOPEVALE were discovered by the Japanese and killed. At Green Lake there is a replica of Hopevale, a beautiful memorial.

I wouldn't want to go through those experiences again, but I am grateful for the deep lessons of life I learned and the friends all over the world that I have from those days.

I know how to live simply, to appreciate the things usually taken for granted (like home, food, privacy, cleanliness), how to laugh at myself and use sense of humor as good medicine, to value integrity in all situations. We saw human beings at their best and at their worst during the hardships of internment.

The children and I came home to the United States in 1945. Fred stayed on to recover the hidden University documents and to help many Filipino friends work to reopen the schools and college. Then he joined us back in America. We were not in good shape, but we gradually grew stronger and could go on with our lives. But, we were unable to return to the mission field due to our weakened health.

Nevertheless, we did stay active in the denomination. I served on the American Baptist Women's Foreign Mission Society Board, on the National Council of the American Baptist Women, and was a VP of American Baptist Churches in the late 1960's.

We kept up on all the work of the denomination, and also kept in touch with lots of missionary friends and had a keen interest in what was happening on mission fields.

Our interest in foreign students continued at universities and churches where Fred served. We organized Home Hospitality Programs at CU, CSU, and Southern Illinois University. We befriended many foreign students, taking them into our home and hearts—and keeping in touch with them over the years.

We came to the American Baptist Church in Fort Collins in 1954 and Fred served as the first full-time pastor. The church membership grew from 60 to 175, and we along with the congregation worked very hard building a new church building. Then Fred accepted an assignment as Professor of Missions at Central Baptist Theological Seminary in 1958.

In 1971 we returned to Fort Collins where Fred served once again as Interim Pastor for over a year. I started a sewing class for international women who were at CSU at the church. Many wives of foreign students were trying to learn

English and make ends meet financially, so were happy for an opportunity to socialize, practice English, and make garments inexpensively for their families. Students from at least 30 different nations benefited from these classes which were offered for years. A number of women from the church helped with the teaching and the child care. I always said these classes were about more than just sewing—they were BUILDING BRIDGES!

On a personal note, I have to admit I suffered from a deep desire to be stylish! I admit it, I wanted to look nice, even when we couldn't afford pretty clothes. We lived very simply and without much money, but I loved to sew nice clothing. Even if I do say so myself, I made some nice-looking things out of what I could find.

I loved, probably even coveted, beautiful fabric and would buy it whenever I could find some that didn't cost too much. I could design and make most anything—even made Fred's suits. I made my doctor's coats and dressed very simply, because that was best for doing my work, for keeping clean, and to be in keeping with the poor people around me. I always liked simple styles, which looked classic and high style. My sister even sent me a subscription to VOGUE, so I could keep up with the fashions while in the mission field! I liked to make dresses that draped a bit, simple but with a softened feminine look.

I was always active in the local church and in the community, and was honored as Church Women United's VALIANT WOMAN in 1982, an honor that humbles me to this moment.

Fred and I retired several times, but "for good" in Fort Collins. Our major mission in the last years was in the field of helping the elderly. We helped the Fort Collins church establish Elderhaus, the first day care for the elderly in the state. The Elderhaus ministry is now (at the time of this writing) in its 23rd year and has been a blessing to countless persons and families. I still had the opportunity to minister to people, and still wanted to "doctor" in emergencies even after moving into the nursing home.

Isn't it wonderful how God's mission continues from generation to generation?

I hope my life did have a strong Christian impact on at least some people.

Printed in Great Britain
by Amazon